a Apple

b Bull

at

d Dog

e Egg

f Fiſh

g Goat

h Hog

j Judg

k King

l Lion

m Mou

n Nag

o Owl

p Peacoc

q Queen

r Robin

ſ Squirr

1. *From a Toybook by Walter Crane,* THE BABY'S OWN ALPHABET *(1875)*

FROM PRIMER TO PLEASURE IN READING

An introduction to the history of children's books in England
from the invention of printing to 1914 with an outline of
some developments in other countries

by

MARY F. THWAITE

Second Edition

LONDON
THE LIBRARY ASSOCIATION
1972

Published by

The Library Association, 7 Ridgmount Street,

London WC1E 7AE

First edition, entitled 'From primer to pleasure', 1963

Reprinted with corrections and minor addenda, October 1966

Second edition, 1972

ISBN 0 85365 465 4

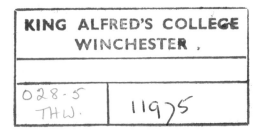
Printed in England by Dolphin Press Brighton   Williams Lea Group

Contents

Introduction

When this book was first planned over ten years ago, one of the main aims of the writer was to offer guidance to librarians studying the subject of children's literature for the Final Examination of the Library Association, and it was largely the outcome of experience gained in lecturing on the subject of the history of books for children at a series of full-time courses in Library Work with Young People held at the North-Western Polytechnic School of Librarianship in the 1950s. Another important object was to provide a general introduction to scholarly histories of the subject for the benefit of others interested in the link between children's books of today and those of the past.

Changes in the syllabus of the Library Association professional examinations have since tended to emphasise the bibliographical aspects of books for young people rather than literary history. The revised work now presented is less concerned with the needs of the student, but it attempts to provide librarians and others with a fuller general survey than the original edition. The point of view from which it is written, that of a librarian always much concerned with books for youth seeking to find enlightenment about their origin and background, is unchanged.

The original plan, setting out developments from the beginning of the nineteenth century onwards under the various types of books for children rather than in one chronological sequence, has not been altered. I feel that this enables the evolution of theme and form in children's books to be more easily followed, so this classified arrangement has been kept, although it has the disadvantage of dividing up some authors' works. A little more attention has been given to the influence of adult literature upon children's books, but this important subject remains very inadequately treated.

In the first edition the record ended at 1900. It is considered that the end of the century is an unsatisfactory termination for an epoch which did not change in essentials until the outbreak of the Great War of 1914–1918. Although the early twentieth century is not dealt with fully, as Marcus Crouch has covered it in his *Treasure seekers and borrowers*, the present history is continued into the Edwardian period and beyond when I felt this was fitting.

The text of the main part of the book (One to Four) has been revised and extended but in essentials it remains as before. The most important change is in part Five – Children's Books Abroad. This has been completely rewritten and considerably extended.

vii

I should like to thank many librarians and others concerned with children's books and their history for much helpful information. In particular I should mention the services of the Cheshire County Library, the Hertfordshire County Library, the Manchester City Library, the John Rylands Library, the Department of Printed Books of the British Museum, and the Library of the Victoria and Albert Museum. Many individuals have been most kind. I can only mention my special indebtedness to a few of them – Miss Joan Butler, Mrs. Christine Kloet, Mrs. Jill E. Grey, Miss Virginia Haviland, Mrs. Anne Renier, Mr. Sydney Roscoe, the late Dr. d'Alté A. Welch, and Miss Joyce I. Whalley.

I should also like to express my gratitude to the Swedish Institute for Cultural Relations with Foreign Countries for making it possible for me to make a short stay in Sweden in 1969, mainly to study at the Swedish Institute for Children's Books in Stockholm. I much appreciate the assistance given by the Head of the Institute, Mrs. Mary Ørvig, and also by other librarians and writers abroad who answered queries or sent me books and information.

List of Illustrations

Most of the illustrations are considerably reduced in size from the originals.

The design used for the endpapers is from an undated copy of *The Royal Battledore* (ca. 1780) in the Bodleian Library

1 Sources

1 PRINTING: ITS HERITAGE AND PROMISE

The sources of present-day books for young people go back far beyond the middle of the fifteenth century, when the invention of printing with movable types began to transform the dissemination of knowledge and ideas, and so help to shape the modern world. Children's books, perhaps more than their elder counterparts, still draw inspiration from the distant past, from traditional lore as old as the human race, and from treasured writings of ancient civilisations. Yet the art of printing is such an important milestone in the advance of book-making for young and old that its advent has been taken as the vantage point for the beginning of this survey. When the 'twenty-six soldiers of lead' could be enlisted to serve the needs of the people, then children's literature, as we now understand it, became a possibility.

Boys and girls in the dying world of feudalism, which the new art helped to hurry into its grave, had plenty of tales and wonders to feed their imagination – unwritten stories which had been their birthright since the beginning of mankind. They shared with grown unlettered folk these fabrications, for the storytellers, balladmakers, and 'old wives by the fireside' cared little about age groups, and spun their tales and verses for all the family. Oral literature belonged to the people and their children for centuries before the written or printed word.

Books specially designed for children were as yet as rare as swallows in a northern winter. The few made for youth in medieval days were strictly utilitarian and instructional, intended for budding grammarians, novitiates of the Church, or courtiers-to-be. Education was very much confined to the mastery of Latin and classical learning, and controlled by the Church. The warm light of Renaissance humanism might be melting the chill of arid Latinity with its discoveries of Greek and Roman literary treasures, but it only emphasised the classical bias in its illumination of new ends to serve. The idea of giving the child books to read for pleasure or entertainment was still unthinkable. 'A child is a man in a small letter' . . . wrote Bishop John Earle a little later . . . 'the older he grows he is a stair lower from God'.[1] Such a vision of the child as an innocent being only meant a more vital reason to discipline him on the road to learning and godliness.

It is understandable that children's books should have been rare in the days of the costly

---

[1] Earle, John. *Microcosmographie* (1628).

hand-produced book, and limited to books of learning. It is, perhaps, more surprising that printing did so little for many years to alter this situation. The printers naturally tended to multiply those books for which there already existed a demand, and for the young scholar this meant Latin grammars, texts, and colloquies, primers and catechisms, books to inculcate good manners and to promote virtue, and sometimes fables to teach morality. These were the books the printers found in existence for the young reader and these were the books they imprinted in large numbers to meet the requirements of parents, tutors and schoolmasters. It is true that works of more popular appeal, such as the popular fictions of the Middle Ages, were very soon produced by the early presses, but these were not intended for youth.

Not that children, then or ever after, were confined to books addressed to them. Even in those days, when every volume must be copied out by hand, a few privileged boys and girls had doubtless shared with their elders the delights to be found in the manuscripts which were the glory of an age without printing – bright pictures of lives of the saints, scenes from the Bible, or the fabulous creatures of the bestiaries. They might also have been lucky enough to pore over plainer texts recounting the magic of Merlin, the prowess of Lancelot, and battles with 'heathenesse' – maybe the tales told by Chaucer's pilgrims on their way to Canterbury from the 'Tabard' Inn, or the strange marvels of other lands as reported by that renowned if mythical traveller, Sir John Mandeville. But such secular material was not favoured for the reading of young people, and it was not likely to come their way very often. Boys and girls who learnt to read (and they may have been more numerous than has generally been supposed) would more probably, like Chaucer's *Hugh of Lincoln*, have their primer or ABC. But even lesson books were scarce before the days of printing, and much teaching was done orally.

About the beginning of the fifteenth century, children of the upper classes, however, were being given a new kind of book, for which the printers were to find a ready sale later on. These were little treatises, mostly in rhyme, of manners or courtesy, which had originated in France and Italy during the previous century. Their purpose was to teach the gently born youth some of the rules of behaviour or civility required by a society which had found new ideals mirrored in the literature of romance and chivalry. At first these books of manners were chiefly addressed to the 'bele babees', or noble youths, who were sent away at an early age to the court or to the house of a great lord to learn the arts of peace and war proper to their station, and the early manuals are as much concerned with etiquette and correct behaviour as with piety and morals. Later the style was adapted for compositions for the child of humbler rank, rather than for the young page at court. These books are an interesting innovation in the development of literature for children, for they were usually given to them in the vernacular not in Latin.

In *The Babees Book* (ca. 1475) the author begins with an invocation.

'May he who formed mankind in his image support me while I turn this treatise out of Latin into my common language, that through this little comment all of tender years may receive instruction in courtesy and virtue'.

The young reader is given advice on how to address his lord and how to behave, and guidance on many other day-to-day matters – 'That through your nurture and your governance you may advance yourselves to lasting bliss'.[1] In these little works maxims about moral conduct are frequent.

'Discover not your own good deed,
Neither for mirth, nor yet for meed.'[2]

Some of the courtesy books were in verse, some in prose. One of the best known was *Stans puer ad mensam*, ascribed to that prolific versifier, John Lydgate, and founded on the Latin *Carmen juvenile de moribus puerorum* of Sulpitius. Printed by Caxton in 1479 it remained a popular book until the end of the Tudor period.[3] Hugh Rhodes included a version of it in his *Boke of Nurture* (1545).[4] New manuals more fitted for the changing times were produced in the sixteenth century after the printers had circulated the old favourites. An early one which gave advice to the child with his living to earn was *The Young Children's Book* (ca. 1500). 'Be not idle', the child is exhorted, 'for Holy Scripture says to you of Christian faith that if you work, you must eat what you get with your hands. A man's arms are for working, as a bird's wings for flying . . . '[5]

A notable example was the *De civilitate morum puerilium* (1526), by Erasmus. This was translated into English by Robert Whittington, and printed by Wynken de Worde in 1532, as *A Lytell Booke of good Manners for Chyldren*.[6] In it English and Latin were set side by side, and it revealed that courtesy for the great humanist was not merely rules of behaviour: it lay in true consideration for others. There were other Tudor variants on the book of manners and good advice. One of the best known, written in rhyming couplets, was by Francis Seager, *The Schoole of Vertue and Booke of good Nourture for Chyldren to learn theyr Dutie by* (1557). It begins with a morning prayer and, like Erasmus, the author expresses the belief that true courtesy can only be achieved through piety, learning and virtue.

[1] *The Babees Book*. Rickert. (Bibl. 57).

[2] *Urbanitatis. Ibid.*

[3] *Short Title Catalogue* (STC) 17030 (Bibl. 49), also in Rickert (Bibl. 57).

[4] STC 20953.

[5] *The Babees Book etc.* Rickert (Bibl. 57).

[6] STC 10467.

'Experience doth teache and shewe thee playne
That many to honour by learning attayne,
That were of birth but simple and base –
Such is the goodness of God's special grace
For he that to honour by vertue doth ryse
Is double happy and counted most wyse.'[1]

It also marks the growing ascendancy of the manual of moral and religious instruction over the earlier guides to correct behaviour, reflecting the passing of old feudal ways and the rise of a new order. Practical manuals for youth on conduct and character persisted until Victorian times. One example in the writer's possession is by Mrs. Marshall of Manchester, *The Child's Guide to Good-breeding, founded on Christian principles* (1838). 'Good-breeding is but another name for the lesser duties of benevolence' she stated in her preface.

The book of manners or courtesy was, after all, only a kind of lesson-book. In later chapters school books will rarely be mentioned as they are outside the scope of this book, but in these early times they were the seeds from which were to grow the beginnings of a literature for boys and girls. The urge to instruct the rising generation was, as yet, all powerful, but there was a growing tendency to use devices in books to make instruction more inviting. Reading was regarded as the gateway to Latin and learning, or to piety and salvation, not as a pastime or a pleasure.

Edifying works for youth – and often for their elders, also – dominated the book market, therefore, for nearly three hundred years after Caxton set up his press in West-minster in 1476. There were more rudimentary productions than books of grammar, parental advice, and manners. About the middle of the fifteenth century, according to A. W. Tuer,[2] the hornbook, that once common but now vanished instrument of learning, came into being. This was not really a book at all. It consisted of a piece of board, usually of oak, about nine by five inches in size, with a handle at its base. On one side there was stuck a sheet of paper, setting out the alphabet, the nine digits, the Lord's prayer, and sometimes a syllabary. For protection the paper was covered with a sheet of horn, enclosed within a narrow rim of brass. On the other side might be engraved some splendid figure, such as St. George, or the reigning monarch, or even a mermaid. The hornbook was also called the 'Criss-Cross-Row'. So Charles Kingsley described it in *The Water Babies*, when Tom reached the cottage at the bottom of Hartover Fell, and found 'the nicest old woman' teaching 'twelve or fourteen neat rosy chubby little children'. The term was derived from the cross which usually preceded the alphabet, or perhaps it dates from the older nine letter alphabet strung on wire in the form of a cross, known before the

---

[1] STC 22135, Furnivall (Bibl. 55).

[2] Tuer, A. W. *The History of the Horn Book* (Bibl. 53).

4

hornbook. By Kingsley's day the hornbook was fast going out of fashion and would soon be only a memory. And so would its later variant, the more perishable though less clumsy 'battledore', introduced about the middle of the eighteenth century. This was a folded card bearing an illustrated alphabet, and sometimes a prayer, rhymes and proverbs. The earliest example seems to have been that issued by Benjamin Collins, the Salisbury printer and associate of John Newbery, in 1746. He backed his attractive little folding card with flowered Dutch paper, and records it in his account book as 'my own idea', although it was a joint venture with Newbery in publishing.[1]

The ABC was also given to children in the form of the primer, which was the medieval and Tudor child's reading book. The earliest to survive of many which must have been printed is *The BAC (sic) bothe in Latyn and in Englysshe*, printed without authority, by Thomas Petyt, about 1538.[2] Two years earlier John Gough had published a primer for children, *The Prymer of Salysbury Use, both in Englyshe and in Laten*,[3] and he was not alone in producing devotional works addressed to youth – among numerous examples for older folk – in early Tudor times. In the reign of Edward VI, Edward Whitchurch brought out entirely in English, *An ABC wyth a Catechisme* (1551).[4] This included the 'Letany', suffrages, and graces, and was intended as instruction before confirmation. Its clear, large, well-spaced type was more suitable for young eyes than most other early books.

The Petyt example, a much shorter and slighter work of eight pages, is the earliest of the genuine ABCs or child's reading books to survive. After the alphabet and syllabary, come the Lord's prayer, the 'Hail Mary' and the Creed. Then follow graces for various occasions, and the ten commandments put into halting rhyme for easy learning by heart.

> 'Lord grant me grace to honour The
> One God, and never to swear in vayne.
> The Holy Day to be kept by me
> My parents to obey and mainteyne.'

These ABCs and primers show clearly how much religion dominated instruction during the century after printing. Like the Prayer Book they required royal authority for their printing, and reflected the changing attitudes of authority as a new faith struggled for ascendancy against the old. Control over production and circulation of these profitable wares was obtained through licensing. Whitchurch could add *'cum privilegio ad imprimendum solum'* to his title-page, but Petyt's publication was unlicensed, and the control was far from complete.

[1] Welsh. *A Bookseller of the last century*, p. 172 (Bibl. 105).

[2] STC 19.

[3] STC 15992, Butterworth (Bibl. 50).

[4] Copy in John Rylands Library, Manchester.

The earliest primers and alphabet books were plain and unadorned. The first picture alphabet printed in England appears to be the little cuts illustrating the letters by objects in a reading book by John Hart, issued in 1570, *A Method or comfortable beginning for all unlearned, whereby they may be taught to read English, in a very short time with Pleasure . . .*[1] This pointed the way to the future, for in the coming century letters were to be set out in more attractive style, sometimes with riddles as well as tiny cuts to enhance the appeal of learning. Enticements of this nature were becoming prevalent in books for children by

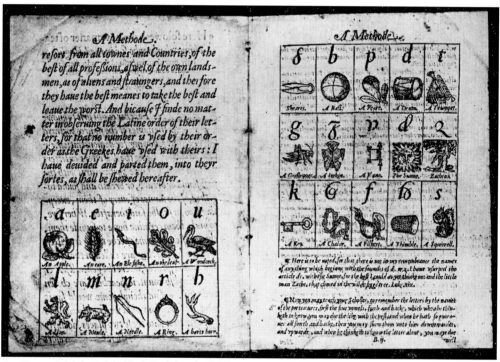

2. *Illustrated alphabet in John Hart's English reader (1570)*

the time a certain 'T.W.' made an alluring reading and spelling book of eight pages in the reign of Queen Anne, *A Little Book for little Children* (ca. 1702). In it there is a Lilliputian picture for each letter, interpreted in alphabet verses, and the famous nursery rhyme:

> 'A was an Archer and shot at a Frog.
> B was a blind Man and led by a Dog.'

Nonsense and jingles and similar cheerful devices were henceforth to be regularly enlisted to persuade the child into a knowledge of the twenty-six letters. In 1744, in John Newbery's first book of amusement for children, *A Little Pretty Pocket-Book*, appeared the light-hearted rhyme beginning:

[1]STC 12889 (Spelling of title modernised).

'Great A, B, and C,
    And tumble-down D,
The Cat's a blind Buff,
    And she cannot see'.

And in the nineteenth century the ABC was to take on a medley of shapes and moods and colours, in comic alphabets, animal alphabets, railway alphabets and a host of others. It was the theme of picture-books of high quality later in the century such as Kate Greenaway's *A Apple Pie* (1886) and some of Walter Crane's Toybooks. Since its first fashioning as hornbook and primer, the alphabet book has appeared in new guise in every generation. Today it is designed with infinite variety and often in rich colours for the young child's delight, very different in presentation from the simple beginnings in print four and more centuries ago.

In the early years, after printing ousted the hand-produced book, little thought was yet given to easing the path of learning or making books attractive to youth. Nevertheless, the value of stories to beguile young minds (and those not so young) had long been recognised. Stories, dangerous as they might be, could be moulded to press home moral and religious teaching. ' . . . Keepe them from reading of fayned fables, vayne fantasies, and wanton stories and songs of love, which bring much mischiefe to youth', advised Hugh Rhodes concerning the reading of children in his *Boke of Nurture* (1545).[1] But youth would have its fictions, and a wiser school of thought within the Church in the Middle Ages had made use of secular lore and allegories to preach the truths of religion. A popular collection of tales used by the monks for this purpose was the *Gesta Romanorum; or Tales of the Romans*, a Latin work popular on the continent and in England from the later thirteenth century[2]. This twisted the original tales and histories into strange forms. Everything has its symbolic interpretation, and superstition, sorcery and marvels abound. It was here that Shakespeare delved, and found the tale of the three caskets, and the history of Pericles. But usually the pagan originals are much overlaid with theological interpretation and parallels. In the application added to the story of Achilles, which tells how his mother tried to avert his foretold doom by disguising him as a woman, and of his death at the fall of Troy, Paris becomes the devil, Helen is the human soul, Ulysses is Christ, and the hero of the tale is the Holy Ghost. These stories were nothing like the genuine myths and tales of the ancient world which children were to have much later. They were selected and adapted from ancient sources with a deliberate purpose. The *Gesta Romanorum* is now forgotten, but it was a very popular book in its day, much used by writers and storytellers. There were numerous editions after Wynken de Worde

[1] From Furnivall's text (Bibl. 55).

[2] An English translation was printed by Wynken de Worde, ca. 1517. Bennett (Bibl. 47).

B

7

printed the first English version in the early unclouded years of the reign of Henry VIII, but its utility as a children's book lapsed by the end of the eighteenth century.

Very different was another example of the fabulist's art with roots in antiquity – perhaps the oldest book of all on the child's bookshelf today – *Aesop's Fables*. In every age this has had the distinction of being approved and adapted for youth. In style the Aesopian fable is akin to the folk-tale, but unlike most traditional lore, it had the good fortune in the ancient world to be moulded into an acceptable and enduring form. Often made into a school-book and burdened with additional moralities, it never lost those pristine characteristics which endeared it to young or unsophisticated minds. Brevity in telling, clarity of style, animal characters behaving like human beings, pithy lessons about conduct and shrewd dealing – these were features to give life to the fables in every genera-tion since their invention. There is little of high ethical purpose in the episodes. They are more like a fascinating looking-glass reflecting the follies of mankind. The long familiarity of the people with these old fables can be gauged by the number of sayings from them which are now a part of our common speech, such as 'sour grapes', 'a dog in the manger', 'a wolf in sheep's clothing', to quote a few of the best-known examples.

Whether Aesop, a Greek slave who lived about 550 B.C. on the island of Samos, first invented the fables is doubtful, but by the end of the fifth century B.C. they had become associated with his name. Later writers of the ancient world, notably the Greek Babrius and the Roman Phaedrus, made collections of the fables with their own additions, and the fables have been imitated, translated anew, or retold ever since.

The earliest printed version of *Aesop's Fables* in English was that translated by Caxton from a French edition, founded on Steinhöwel's German *Esop* (first printed ca. 1477). Caxton brought out his book in 1484. He put 167 of the old fables into English, not de-signing them for children, but 'for to shew all manner of folk what manner of thing they ought to ensue and follow'. The printer also copied the pictures, putting into his book nearly two hundred woodcuts derived from the foreign originals. The coarse-lined and bold cuts suit Caxton's plain text, and both pictures and stories would have much appeal for the ordinary citizen of the day and his young people. 'No-one has ever achieved a straightforward purpose in better English,' wrote Harvey Darton four and half centuries later. 'Caxton's *Aesop*, with infinitely little modernisation, is the best text for children today.'[1] It is certainly free from the long-winded moralisings of some later adaptations, but today his text is nearly forgotten.

Other printers followed Caxton's lead, but the early editions for children were mostly school-books. Over two hundred years after Caxton, Roger L'Estrange, renowned for his severities as Licenser of the Press after the Restoration, but less known for his interest in

---

[1] *Children's Books in England*, p.10 (Bibl. 5).

children's education, brought out a comprehensive collection of the fables in a large folio volume in 1692, *The Fables of Aesop and other eminent Mythologists*.

His folio without pictures was unlikely to attract the child reader, but it revealed that he had some real understanding of the predisposition of young minds for the 'hearing, learning and telling of little stories,' although he had the general reader very much in mind also. Morals and reflections were added expressive of the author's very individualistic viewpoint. These were not so tedious as they became in the hands of Samuel Croxall, whose popular selection of the fables for young readers came out thirty years later, *Fables of Aesop and others* (1722). Croxall inveighed against L'Estrange's 'pernicious principles' which served 'the Ends of Popery and arbitrary Power', and he also criticised the insufficiency of the book as a performance intended for children. Croxall's volume was dedicated to the five-year-old Baron Halifax, addressed with much flattery as 'the most lovely and engaging child that ever was born'. The divine's smaller book was successful in superseding its rival and was frequently reprinted. The oval cuts in rectangular frames, a style to be adopted by Thomas Bewick, were much to be imitated, but the long moral reflections are tedious. In the telling of the incidents, however, there are some pleasing touches, and it was to Croxall and a version made by Thomas James in 1848 that Boris Artzybasheff turned for his text when he made vigorous woodcuts for his *Aesop's Fables* (New York, 1933).

The Aesopian fable cries out to be illustrated as Caxton and his continental predecessors well knew. Since then many famous book illustrators have expressed the variety and wealth of its graphic opportunities, including John Tenniel, Walter Crane, and Arthur Rackham. Among more recent examples there are the realistic pictures by Maurice Wilson for the retelling of fifty-one of the fables by James Reeves (*Fables of Aesop*, 1961), who recasts them in the spirit of the original, 'adding nothing except an element of drama and the sense of immediacy'.

The Fables of Aesop, versified, retold, adapted, moralised or modernised in various ways have been a perennial part of children's literature, and this was especially the case after printing brought them easily within the child's reach. They are to be found in all kinds of medleys and miscellanies for youth, as well as in numerous separate editions. When John Newbery brought out his first book for children in 1744, he included four of them with new style moralities in the form of little letters from 'Jack-the-Giant-killer'. The infinite ways Aesop has been adapted for the child are truly astonishing.

Another beast fable of the later Middle Ages, popular among ordinary folk and young people, was *Reynard the Fox*, a history which satirised oppression and tyranny under the guise of a tale about animals. Caxton put the Flemish version by the elusive Willem into 'rude and simple englysshe', and printed it at Westminster in 1481 without any adornment except red or blue capital letters to mark the beginning of each short chapter. Again the printer had in mind the general reader rather than youth. Part folklore, part literary invention, Reynard is an account of the cunning fox and his trickery of the rest of the animals, including Isegrim the wolf, Sir Bruin the bear, Tibert the cat, and Chanticleer the cock, who complain of him at court to King Noble the lion. It was revived many times as a book for children, and Sir Henry Cole ('Felix Summerly') used Caxton's text as the basis for the version he published in his 'Home Treasury' series in 1843. It has been more highly regarded as a children's book on the continent than in England, but after being unavailable for some years, a new edition was published by Abelard-Schuman in 1969, a retelling by Roy Brown from the version made by Joseph Jacobs for children in 1895, directly founded on Caxton's text (Bibl. 60).

Other fables were written or adapted for children following the tradition of *Aesop* and *Reynard the Fox*. Among the most renowned are the verse fables by La Fontaine intended for a wide rather than a youthful public. The first six books of his *Fables Choisis* came out in Paris in 1668, and they are further considered with French children's books in Part V. Roger L'Estrange included a few of them in his volume of *Fables of Aesop* in the supplement he put at the end of his book, 'Fables of several authors'. A complete verse translation of the La Fontaine fables was made by Robert Thomson and published in 1806.

In eighteenth century England, La Fontaine, for all his influence, was not so well known as John Gay, whose original verse *Fables* have some similarity to the French classic examples in artistic unity, for both poets make the reflection or moral lesson a part of the verses. Gay popularised a style of verse fable which became very fashionable for the edification of youth in the days of the Georges. His *Fables* (1727) were invented for the amusement of the six-year-old Duke of Cumberland, according to the dedication to that young Prince. The elegant volume of fifty fables was evidently produced with young aristocrats in mind, for it was spaciously printed and each episode had its engraving. One tale, *The Hare and many friends*, became known as a separate publication for children, with the ending sometimes made more horrific.[1] Gay's fables are often met with in miscellanies for youth up to the Victorian era.

The fable, firmly rooted in tradition, and adorned in suitable style for each generation, was for long regarded as the most suitable form of fiction for young minds. Through its appeal it was hoped that boys and girls might be kept away from more dangerous fancies. But children were not to be restricted to what their elders thought fit for them – either in these early centuries of printing or afterwards. There were flowers to be picked of a wilder and more luxuriant growth than those carefully planted for them.

---

[1] *N.B.L. Catalogue*, pp. 567, 568. There is also an undated copy (ca. 1810) in the V. and A. Library (printed and sold by W. Belch.)

The early printers not only produced the books wanted by scholars and books of devotion and instruction. They were to bring entertainment in the vernacular to a widening circle of readers, who demanded more amusing fare. This was to be found, the printers well knew, in the still popular medieval romances, once the delight of an aristocratic society, and now to be disseminated to citizens who knew little of old feudal ways. Books of travel, chronicles, practical manuals to aid the work of getting a living and broadsheets about rebellions, campaigns and sensational happenings were also issued for the curious.

In these more credulous times, however, ordinary folk, grown and growing, were less dependent on the printed page for the stories and marvels they craved than they became in an era of universal education. Traditional lore existed everywhere in this green misty island, Chaucer's 'land, full of fairy folk', where Robin Goodfellow haunted the woods by Shakespeare's Avon, and atomies like Queen Mab vexed sleepers with strange dreams. Legends, superstitions, and old wives' tales, glimpsed in Shakespeare's plays, were only part of a vast unwritten store throughout the land, shared by young and old.

The time for such lore to be put into books for children was as yet far in the future, yet something of its substance in dressed-up literary form might be found in the old romances which the printers began to issue for a ready public. Frowned upon by serious and learned people, especially for their pernicious influence on youth, these fabrications contained amid all their prolixities and courtly *amours* sufficient of the rainbow hue of magic and adventure to beguile the young imagination. And they were to be as important in the long run in the shaping of a literature for boys and girls as all the primers and books of learning.

William Caxton (1421?–1491) began to print some of the most famous tales as soon as he took up the new art, very often translating them himself from French texts. His first book, the *Recuyell of the historyes of Troye*, taken from the French of Raoul Le Fèvre, was published at Bruges in 1475.[1] This was the first book to be printed in English, and it presented a much medievalised version of the ancient tale of Troy as it had been enjoyed by Burgundian society. Other favourites issued from his press when he set this up in England a year or two later included *Godfrey of Boloyne* (1481),[2] *Paris and Vienne* (1485),[3] approved of for children when safely rendered into Latin, by the Bishop Jean de Pins, and *The Four Sons of Aymon* (1489?).[4]

---

[1] STC 15375.

[2] De Ricci. *A Census of Caxtons*. 1909. No. 46.

[3] STC 19206. Blades, p.510 (Bibl. 54).

[4] STC 1007.

Wynken de Worde, who followed Caxton at Westminster after his death in 1491, also printed versions of the romances, including the very popular *Guy of Warwick* and *Bevis of Hampton*[1] about the turn of the century. Another printer who made it a prominent part of his trade was William Copland, who flourished about the middle of the sixteenth century. But the taste for this kind of literature was already on the wane in this brave new world of Elizabeth I. Very soon these once popular tales degenerated into much abridged chapbooks, shorn of their literary quality, and hacked into cheap and easy reading matter for the ignorant and uncritical.

Those few children able to seize upon the fictional productions of Caxton and his successors, however, would find in them something of the wonder and excitement their own books excluded. Here was a dream-like realm, sometimes melting into fairyland, a country of forests and castles, peopled by wandering knights, distressed damsels, hermits and enchanters, and infested by giants, paynims, or dragons. There were scenes of amazing adventures and combats, where right triumphed at last, and Christian faith defeated the powers of evil and sorcery. Improbabilities and long meanderings of plot and narrative did not detract from the power these inventions once had over the reader who wanted to escape into a fabulous world.

Guy of Warwick, an English tale associated with Warwick Castle, had all the attributes for popular success. Guy, the hero, is the son of the steward of the Earl of Warwick, and he loves Felice, the Earl's proud daughter. He becomes a great champion, wins his lady, goes on pilgrimage, slays the Danish giant Colbrond, outside the walls of Winchester, and dies in piety as a hermit. Equally celebrated was the story of the prowess of *Bevis of Hampton*, 'king and knight of great renown', who loved the 'fayre and bright Josian', a Saracen princess, and the tale tells of his faithful love and his prodigies of valour against the Paynims and other enemies. From France came the famous *Valentine and Orson*, another romance printed in England by De Worde about 1510. This recounts the history of twin princes born in a wood, one of whom is stolen and reared by a bear. Less well-known perhaps was the tale of *Melusine*, another French invention, written down by Jean d'Arras for the sister of the Duc de Berri in 1387. This fanciful composition tells of Raymondin's fairy bride of the fountain, and is a forerunner of *Undine* or Andersen's *Little Mermaid*. Sorcery and magic also play a part in the strange history of *The Knight of the Swanne*, and this has kinship with *Lohengrin* and the Celtic *Children of Lir*.[2] The theme is a familiar one, age-old in mythology and fairy lore, the metamorphosis of human beings

[1] STC 12541 and STC 1987.

[2] These three romances, and also *Guy of Warwick* and *Bevis*, were printed by De Worde. See Bennett's check-list (Bibl. 47).

Versions of all five romances are given by Ashton (Bibl. 65).

into animals or birds, and here Helyas, the seventh son of the king, at last breaks the enchantment which has turned his five brothers and his sister into swans. Magic and witchery also dominated the Carlovingian romance, *Huon of Bordeaux*, translated by Lord Berners from the French, and printed by De Worde in 1534.[1] Over half a century later, Huon's friend, the dwarf king of fairyland, Oberon, was to achieve greater fame as Puck's master in *A Midsummer Night's Dream*.

Such were a few of the 'feigned fables' which printing introduced to the steadily increasing reading public in the late fifteenth and early sixteenth centuries. Their influence on the development of literature for children, however, was not immediate, and it was another three centuries before these romances began to appear in anything much better for young readers than chapbooks. Notable retellings, apart from the King Arthur stories, and certain other legends, were not available until W. J. Thoms, Andrew Lang and F. C. Harvey Darton reshaped some of them for children in the nineteenth and early twentieth centuries.[2] Perhaps these survivals of medieval literature are more important in their influence, and as a treasure store from which writers for youth have drawn inspiration, than for their own sake. But there are some important exceptions. Chief among them is that much prized classic of children's literature – the legends of King Arthur and his knights of the Round Table.

It was Caxton's greatest if unwitting contribution to children's literature, this printing of the classic of Arthurian legend by Sir Thomas Malory in 1485, under the title of *Le Morte Darthur*.[3] Like other works of romance it was not intended for children, but it is important as the source and inspiration of most of the retellings of the King Arthur stories since these were first made. It is now known that the title of the book was not the author's but the printer's. Sir Thomas Malory, who founded his book on French and English material, wrote it while he was a 'knyghte prisoner' in Newgate, sometime between 1469 and 1470. An earlier manuscript than the text used by Caxton was discovered at Winchester College in 1934, but until then Caxton's Malory was the chief source used for the many adaptations and abridgements of the legends made during the last hundred years. Before the middle of the nineteenth century this magnificent cycle of stories was rarely put into the hands of youth.

[1] Listed by Bennett (Bibl. 47).

[2] For Thoms' edition see p. 100.

The Red Book of Romance (1905), by Andrew Lang, contains among others: 'Guy of Warwick', 'Bevis of Hampton', and 'Huon of Bordeaux'.

A Wonder Book of old Romance (1907), by F. C. Harvey Darton includes 'Guy of Warwick' and twelve other tales from romances. Darton also edited *The Seven Champions of Christendom* (1913), by Richard Johnson, first published in 1598. These were popular stories of knightly prowess.

[3] STC 801.

There was a voluminous store of Arthurian romance in existence when Malory selected from it and moulded it into a book of haunting prose, still echoing in the best Arthurian tales for children. He created a noble work of art of compelling and barbaric beauty from the mass of fiction medieval imagination had added to the traditional legends, and expressed in it, also, admiration of a heroic past in the history of his country. Writers for children who have retold the legends owe much to Malory, especially in those dramatic opening scenes, where the boy Arthur draws the sword from the stone, and the young king, guided by Merlin, takes *Excalibur* from the raised arm in the midst of the lake, or in the unfolding of the holy mysteries of the Quest for the Holy Grail. Above all perhaps, for power and drama there are the piteous and tragic scenes of the king's death, when, at last at the third bidding, Sir Bedivere casts the jewelled *Excalibur* back into the water, and the dying Arthur is borne away by the black-hooded Queens in the barge to Avalon, mysterious haven and Isle of the Blest.

Although Malory stands paramount as the source for the retelling of the Arthurian legends for young readers, authors have turned to other material for inspiration, especially this century. King Arthur was not always the ideal king and shadowy figure of French chivalry. The original Arthur was probably a historical character, a chieftain or leader of the British against the Saxon invaders early in the fifth century after the departure of the Roman legions. Tradition has it that he was the commander of the British at the great battle of Badon, when the Saxons were defeated. Geoffrey of Monmouth portrayed him as a warrior king in his fabulous *Histories of the Kings of Britain* written about 1148, and some Arthurian stories depict this more primitive and virile character of Arthur. It was Geoffrey who first told of the wizard Merlin, and very soon afterwards Wace, the Norman verse chronicler, introduced the Round Table in his *Roman de Brut*. The spirited histories of these early writers, these 'idle and pleasant tales of Britain', were soon to be taken over, however, by French writers of romance, who transformed the British leader and his warriors into the courtly and chivalrous figures later revealed in Malory's pages. Their adventures became a mirror reflecting the new ideals of knightly prowess mingled with courtesy and romantic love, where nobility, gentleness and Christian faith were interwoven with savagery, mortal combats, wars, and sorcery. At first in verse, then in prose, more and more tales were invented and added to the cycle.

One of the earliest and best French writers of romance was Chrétien de Troyes, whose writings of the late twelfth century are important material for Arthurian retellings. It was Chrétien who first introduced the character of Lancelot, and he also began one of the earliest Grail romances, in his *Perceval*, completed by other writers. Two well-known stories told by this French writer, omitted by Malory, are *Erec and Enide* and *Yvain*. Both these are also found in the Welsh *Mabinogion*, a collection of medieval bardic tales not available in a printed English translation until 1838–1849 (Bibl. 69) and may be better known under their Welsh titles of *Geraint and Enid* and *The Lady of the Fountain*.

Many other medieval sources of Arthurian romance have been explored by writers for children. A. M. Hadfield in her *King Arthur and the Round Table* (Dent's Illustrated Classics, 1953) derived some incidents from the ecclesiastical *Perlesvaus*, translated by Sebastian Evans as *The High History of the Holy Grail* (1898). Barbara Leonie Picard in *Stories of King Arthur and his Knights* (Oxford University Press, 1955) founds one story on an old ballad, *The Marriage of Gawain*. She also includes *Sir Gawain and the Green Knight*, that outstanding thirteenth century English addition to the Arthurian legends. Roger Lancelyn Green in *King Arthur and his Knights of the Round Table* (Puffin Books, 1953, later Faber) uses this and other Middle English sources, as well as Malory, and for the final adventures of Percivale he draws on that fine thirteenth century German work on the subject of the Grail, *Parzifal*, by Wolfram von Eschenbach, a poem with spiritual power and vision far transcending its medieval setting. These examples are quoted to give an idea of the wealth of material that lies behind the children's versions of one set of popular legends – the Arthurian cycle of tales.

In the early years of printing and for long afterwards, Malory's book was without a rival in the field. Few other Arthurian romances were yet printed, and unlike many other medieval tales, they were not popular with chapbook printers, perhaps because of their length and complexity. Those few children who read about the knights of the Round Table were most likely to have done so in the text that Caxton gave to the world. The printer directed his book to 'noble princes, lords and ladies, gentlemen or gentlewomen', not to youth, but nevertheless he was uneasy about its moral standards. In his preface he refers to his intent in setting the 'noble historyes' in print that readers of whatever estate or degree should 'take the good and honest actes in their remembraunce . . . for herein may be seen noble chivalrye, courtesy, humanity, frendlinesse, hardynesse, love, friendship, cowardise, murder, hate, vertue, and sin. Do after the good and leave the evil . . . '

Nearly a century later Roger Ascham was to condemn Malory with other books of chivalry for their 'open mans slaughter and bold bawdry'.[1] Like other 'ungracious' books, frowned upon by humanist scholars and divines, *Le Morte D'Arthur* was certainly not approved of for youth.

The length and unfamiliar style of Malory, however, were barriers for the less able reader, and probably few children knew the fascination of the great book before 1862, when Sir James Knowles (1831–1908) gave them an excellent simplified version, *The Story of King Arthur and his Knights of the Round Table*. Tennyson's first *Idylls of the King* had just begun to create new interest in an Arthur idealised as 'the blameless king', and the

[1] Ascham, Roger, *The Scholemaster* (Bibl. 77).

Idylls had a powerful influence on Knowles and others who retold the legends after him. Knowles, a great admirer of the poet, dedicated his book to him, but he did not soften or over-romanticise it. He tells a straightforward story, avoiding adult complexities, and this version, with a slightly amended title, has endured to the present time as one of the best presentations founded on Malory and little else. Another nineteenth century version, even closer to Malory's text, is *The Boy's King Arthur* (1880), by the American Sidney Lanier. He re-arranged Caxton's twenty-one books into six, and did little more than abridge them and replace archaisms.

BALLADRY AND ROBIN HOOD

The romances circulated by the early printers and used by Malory as his raw material were literary compositions already written down for the amusement of a leisured and cultivated class. There were other legacies from the Middle Ages slower to find their way into print or written form of any kind – among them the ancient ballads of England and Scotland. These were of unknown or common authorship, flourishing where a written literature had little impact on the people. Originally created, probably, for singing and dancing, with refrains and repetitions, they were kept alive and altered in form through oral tradition. The live ballad belongs essentially to the two centuries before printing. Afterwards it became debased and imitated, descending to the trash of the broadsheet, the invention of the printer's hack of the kind carried by Autolycus in his pack.

The ploughman's child would be far more likely to hear one of the few ballads associated with the exploits of King Arthur and his knights than to learn anything from Malory's book. Certain ballads were made from the romances, and some romances were based on traditional stories, which also found their way into ballad literature, but usually subject matter and style are distinct.

The ballad is simple and direct, little concerned with comment or feeling, rarely digresses, and is vigorous and unadorned. Most popular ballads told a story, and children, with their elders, no doubt enjoyed any which came their way — such as the stirring tale of action, *Chevy Chace*, or the spell-binding magic of that ballad of elfland, *Thomas the Rhymer*, and many others. Historical events, battles by land or sea, ghosts, witches, adventures, tragic love, mirth and sorrow — balladry covered every kind of theme.

Most popular of all with young and old, at least this side of the Border, were the ballads of Robin Hood. In children's literature Robin Hood is the supreme ballad hero, who has never lost his appeal, finding his way today not only into books, but into films, radio and television.

The earliest rhymes about Robin Hood were printed about 1500, but very few of the Robin Hood ballads now extant are genuine folk ballads of the later Middle Ages. Most of them are sixteenth and seventeenth century inventions, by which time characters such as Maid Marian had been added, and the adventures of the outlaw and his men were made into prose tales as well as into 'garlands' of verse. Unlike his rival in popular favour, King Arthur, Robin Hood is a hero of the people, not of the court, although he may be said to resemble his royal compatriot in that he also has a claim to historical existence, beneath all the accretion of legends associated with his name.

The ballads of Robin Hood are first mentioned in *Piers Plowman* (ca. 1360–70), and over two centuries later Michael Drayton records in his *Polyolbion* (1612–22):

'In this our spacious isle, I think, there is not one
But he hath heard some tales of him and Little John.'

One of the oldest surviving ballads to be written down is *Robin Hood and the Monk*, which begins:

'In somer, when the shawes be sheyne
    And leves be large and long,
Hit is full mery in feyre foreste
    To here the foulys song.
To se the dere draw to the dale,
    And leve the hillès hee,
And shadow hem in the leves grene
    Under the grene-wode tre.'[1]

So the reader (or listener) is plunged straight into the open-air forest life to which these ballads belong, as a prelude to the story of the false monk and how Robin Hood was rescued from prison. This is a world where an outlaw is trusty and brave, true to his fellows, kind to ordinary folk, and generous to the poor and the oppressed. Robin and his men are loyal also to God and the King, but at war with the powers of tyranny and the rich lords of the Church. The outlaw is drawn as a valiant leader, merry of heart yet sometimes touched with melancholy, pious and charitable, yet a ready fighter against his enemies.

Other genuine ancient ballads among the forty or so Robin Hood ballads which exist are *Robin Hood and Guy of Gisborne*, *Robin Hood and the Potter*, and the fragment *Robin Hood's Death*. More important than any of them is that fifteenth century rustic folk epic, *The Lytell Geste of Robyn Hode*, founded on older material and still the main source for modern stories for children about the hero of Sherwood Forest.

This narrative in verse was first printed by Wynken de Worde about 1500, but its composition may be a century earlier. In eight 'fyttes' consisting of 256 verses, each of four lines, it tells of Robin Hood's aid to a poor knight, Sir Richard at the Lee, the deliverance of the Sheriff of Nottingham into Robin's power by Little John, the outlaws'

---

[1] *The Oxford Book of Ballads*, 117 (Bibl. 72).

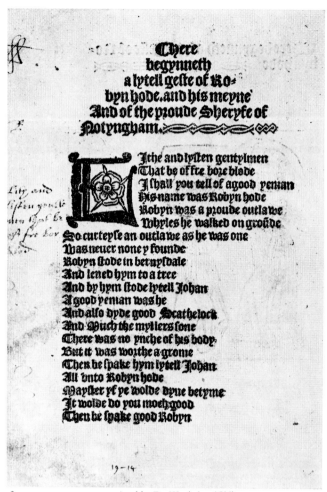

Here begynneth a lytell geste of Robyn hode, and his meyne And of the proude Sheryfe of Notyngham.

Lythe and lysten gentylmen
That be of fre bore blode
I shall you tell of a good yeman
His name was Robyn hode
Robyn was a proude outlawe
Whyles he walked on grounde
So curteyse an outlawe as he was one
Was neuer none y founde
Robyn stode in bernysdale
And leved hym to a tree
And by hym stode lytell Johan
A good yeman was he
And also dyde good Scathelock
And Much the myllers sone
There was no ynche of his body
But it was worthe a grome
Then be spake hym lytell Johan
All vnto Robyn hode
Mayster yf ye wolde dyne betyme
It wolde do you moch good
Then be spake good Robyn

3. THE LYTELL GESTE, *as printed by De Worde (ca. 1500)*

shooting at an archery tourney and the Sheriff's treachery, and at last the coming of the king to the greenwood (King Edward here and not King Richard) to find Robin, whom he invites to court. There the outlaw dwells 'but twelve months and three', and then he pines for his old life of freedom in the forest.

> 'Alas! then said good Robin Hood,
>   Alas and well a way!
> If I dwell longer with the king,
>   Sorrow will me slay.'[1]

So he goes back and lives again the old life, and the poem ends with a brief account of his death by treachery at Kirklees Priory, where

[1] *Oxford Book of Ballads.* 115 (Bibl. 72).

> 'Sir Roger (and the prioress
>   A springe for him did) lay
> And there they betray'd good Robin Hood
>   Through their false play.
>
> Christ have mercy on his soul,
>   That died upon the rood!
> For he was a good outlaw
>   And did poor men much good.'

The present-day story about Robin Hood for children must still be judged by its fidelity to the sturdy spirit of these ancient rhymes, so close to the life of the people. By Elizabethan times Robin Hood had become the favourite subject for May Day plays and games, and very soon his adventures were to be set forth in cruder style and purveyed by the chapbook sellers. It was not until Joseph Ritson published the first comprehensive collection of the ballads in 1795 that an important source became available for reputable writers, who then began to introduce the outlaw into literature. Sir Walter Scott made him the robust Saxon leader, Locksley, in *Ivanhoe* (1819). Three years later there appeared *Maid Marian*, by Thomas Love Peacock, a boisterous, mock-heroic novel, where Robin's love story, of which the old ballads say nothing, plays a great part, and the outlaw is no plain yeoman but the rightful Earl of Huntingdon. Martin Parker had claimed this noble lineage for the outlaw in *A True Tale of Robin Hood* in the seventeenth century.

The first versions for children came out in the nineteenth century. One of the earliest was *Robin Hood and his merry Foresters*, written by 'Stephen Percy' (i.e. Joseph Cundall), an attractive little volume with hand-coloured lithographs by John Gilbert, published by Tilt and Bogue in 1841.[1] But this and other adaptations for youth did not survive, and it was not until Howard Pyle, the American writer and artist, brought out his splendid volume, *The Merry Adventures of Robin Hood* (1883), that children had a book of real quality on the theme. The vigorous line-drawings and old-world narrative vividly recreate medieval Sherwood and closely follow the outline of the old ballads. Richly embroidered as it is with picturesque detail, it perhaps lacks the directness and simplicity the child of today expects, and its popularity has now waned.

But from the time Pyle gave such a book of distinction to youth on these old green-wood ballads, there were to be Robin Hood stories for boys and girls nearly every year. In 1912 Henry Gilbert created a spirited tale of adventure from the material in his *Robin Hood*, putting in new incidents and characters, but preserving the familiar figures much as the old balladmongers knew them. Carola Oman is a modern writer who has contributed an outstanding if unusual version in her *Robin Hood, Prince of Outlaws* (1939), setting the tale in the days of Edward II, and bringing in certain lesser known ballads such as *Rose the*

---

[1] Maclean, R., *Victorian Book Design*, p.40 (Bibl. 156)

Red and White Lily, not usually assigned to the Robin Hood cycle. For a more recent re-telling among many others, *The Adventures of Robin Hood*, specially written for Puffin Books (1956), Roger Lancelyn Green has drawn on a wide range of material, from *The Lytell Geste* to the romantic play by Alfred Noyes (1926). In the 1960s there have been the ambitious and rousing verse retellings directly founded on individual ballads, by Ian Serraillier — *Robin in the Greenwood* (1967) and *Robin and his merry Men* (1969). In the second work, the author reshapes the old rhymes of *The Lytell Geste* into modern English verses, preserving the pattern and rhythm of the original, and faithfully following the narrative, except for his omission of Robin Hood's death at the end.

These few examples indicate something of the wide variety of treatment possible in re-creating the old tales for the entertainment of succeeding generations, and testify to their enduring vitality in children's literature.

Ballads, including those about Robin Hood, which printing now began to bring to the people in the pedlar's pack, were not looked upon with any more favour by those in authority than were the romances. Certainly many ballads and songs of the early centuries after printing were vulgar or feeble travesties of their prototypes, the genuine folk ballads of the Middle Ages. But some endured as popular favourites especially in nursery literature. One of the best known is that tragic tale, *The Children in the Wood; or the Norfolk Gentleman's last Will and Testament*, first printed in 1595, and better known eventually as *The Babes in the Wood*.[1]

Few traditional ballads were written down or printed, however, at this time. It was not until 1765, when Bishop Percy published part of the now famous seventeenth century folio manuscript collection in his *Reliques of ancient English Poetry*, that the folk ballad became well-known and influential in printed literature. And it was nearly another century before such ballads began to find their way regularly into anthologies of verse for young people.[2] One of the best nineteenth century collections of genuine old ballads suitable for young readers was William Allingham's *Ballad Book* (1865). This included *The Lytell Geste of Robyn Hode*.

---

[1] Entered in the Register of the Stationers' Company, 15th October 1595.

[2] A selected edition of Thomas Percy's *Ancient Ballads*, 'for the use and entertainment of young persons', by 'A Lady', was published by Vernor, Hood and Sharpe, J. Harris, etc. in 1807. (*Toronto Catalogue*, p.75, Bibl. 46).

DEVELOPMENTS IN THE SIXTEENTH AND SEVENTEENTH CENTURIES

It is a truism that the attitude to children and their books in any period cannot be understood without some knowledge of its thought and culture – especially as these are expressed in writings for their elders. This is particularly so in the sixteenth and seventeenth centuries when books for children began to appear in some quantity, although this may seem minute by modern standards. H. S. Bennett quotes a total of 1040 publications issued by the printers between 1550 and 1559. Thirty years later the output was nearly doubled.[1] But very few of these works were addressed to children. And the books intended for them very much revealed an educational purpose with an emphasis on the promotion of religion and virtue.

Sir Philip Sidney, defending the art of the poet against Puritan criticism, stressed the power of imaginative writing to 'delight and teach' – and so to move men to goodness. 'Poetry ever sets out virtue in her best colours' – again he sees the poet wielding enchantment for a noble end. 'With a tale forsooth he cometh unto you, with a tale which holdeth children from play, and old men from the chimney-corner. And pretending no more, doth intend the winning of the mind from wickedness to virtue . . .'[2] Sidney, a spokesman for the new learning which enriched Tudor England with treasures from Italy, Greece, and Rome, might extol the reading of Homer and *Chevy Chace*, but in his homage to virtue he was expressing the generally accepted view.

'Truth of religion, honesty in living, right order in learning' were the three ways in which the young scholar was to be guided to walk, according to one of Sidney's contemporaries, more concerned with tuition, Roger Ascham.[3] As the brightness of the Elizabethan age faded with the onset of the stormier seventeenth century, the Puritan trend grew stronger, and the pre-eminence given to religion (rather than to Sidney's Plato-inspired virtue) became more marked.

> 'Forasmuch as Piety is to be preferred before all earthly Things, the School Master shall do his best in the Compass of his Calling to sowe the Seeds of Godliness in the Myndes of his Schollers both by Precept and Example . . .'

runs one of the Orders of Richard Hale in his foundation of Hertford Grammar School in 1616. 'The end then of learning is to repair the ruins of our first parents by regaining to know God aright, and out of that knowledge to love him, to imitate him, to be like him,

---

[1] Bennett, H. S., *English Books and readers, 1475–1557* p. 194; (Bibl. 47). *Ibid* 1558–1603 p. 271.

[2] *Apologie for Poetrie* (1591). (Bibl. 82).

[3] Preface to *The Scholemaster* (Bibl. 77).

as we may the nearest by possessing our souls of true virtue, which being united to the heavenly grace of faith, makes up the highest perfection,' wrote Milton in his tract on *Education*, published in 1644. Whatever else the young scholar might learn, the ultimate aim was the welfare of his soul.

Reading was now to achieve a new importance as the scriptures became the newly won privilege of the people in the countries of the reformed faith. The Bible was no longer to be a text interpreted by the priesthood, but the right of every man to read for himself in his own tongue. The English version by Miles Coverdale, printed abroad in 1535, was issued at Southwark, by James Nycolson, in 1537, as 'set forth with the kynges most gracious license.'

The power and majesty of the Bible in English literature and religious life reached its zenith with the publication of the Authorised version of 1611. But the Bible had long been familiar to children and ordinary folk, although its circulation in English waited so long. The Church had made its stories and episodes a part of its teaching from earliest days. In the early days of printing Caxton had set before the reader some of the best known Old Testament stories, as well as lives of the saints, in 1483, in his translation of *The Golden Legend* of Jacobus de Voragine. But those ignorant of Latin knew little of some parts of the scriptures until an English Bible became available to all. And the increasing tendency as it became established in the life of the nation was to lead children towards reading it as a whole and indivisible book. They were often expected to go to it immediately after they had mastered their alphabet and syllable exercises. 'I shall forbear to add more', wrote John Bunyan, after setting out the alphabet and brief reading lesson as a prelude to his verses in *A Book for Boys and Girls* (1686), 'being persuaded this is enough for little children to prepare themselves for Psalter or Bible'.

After 1611 it was the felicitous and splendid phraseology of 'King James's Bible' which became the possession of the people, both on church lectern and in their homes, and this text is still used for some finely illustrated Bible books for children today. In the sixteenth and seventeenth centuries the reading of the scriptures increasingly dominated the education of youth. Paraphrases, epitomes and rhymed versions of the Bible, long enjoyed at least orally since the days of Caedmon and especially in the form of mystery plays, continued to appear but in rather different style. But no attempt seems to have been made to present Bible stories in a suitable form for children until the eighteenth century.

Benjamin Harris brought out his *Holy Bible* 'done into verse for the benefit of weak memories' in 1698, and Nathaniel Crouch used Bible themes as warning sermons in his *Youth's Divine Pastime* (1691) – 'forty remarkable scripture stories, turned into common English verse . . . very delightful for the virtuous imploying the vacant hours of young persons . . .' Earlier rhymed adaptations, among them Clapham's *A Briefe of the Bible*, *drawn first into English Poesy* (1596), and tiny epitomes such as the 'Thumb' Bible, *Verbum sempiternum* (1614),[1] by the water poet, John Taylor, were not addressed to children.

The unusual hieroglyphic Bible, invented to intrigue the curious mind of youth, dates from the seventeenth century. One of the earliest must have been that by Elisha Coles, *Youth's visible Bible*, included with twenty-four copper-plates in his *Nolens Volens*, a Latin lesson-book of 1675.[2] A little later drawings were used to replace certain nouns in the text instead of words as in the *Hieroglyphic Bible* issued by T. Hodgson in 1783.

John Newbery brought out a *New Testament adapted to the Capacities of Children* in 1755, and also an abridged Bible advertised the next year. Miniature Bibles were brought out by later Newberys, including *The Pocket Bible for little Masters and Misses* issued by Francis Newbery in 1772.[3] The first successful presentation of Bible stories for children must surely be assigned to Mrs. Trimmer. In 1782–1784 she produced, chiefly for Sunday Schools, six formidable volumes of *Sacred History*, consisting of selections from the scriptures with annotations and reflections, and followed this with something much simpler, a series of prints accompanied by easy lessons, in 1786 and 1790.[4] These lessons set out Bible incidents in a simple style, blending the words of the original with a connecting link to explain the events described. But the forerunner of the modern Bible story for children, which does not seek to drive home any theological meaning, but lets the narrative speak for itself, is to be found in the little volumes *Bible Events*, issued to inaugurate the 'Home Treasury' series by Sir Henry Cole in 1843.

These few examples illustrating the development of the Bible story for children can only suggest the wealth of material to be explored, which has culminated in our own day in the fine literary achievements of such writers as Walter de la Mare and Margherita Fanchiotti.

Another religious book which came to rival the Bible as recommended reading for the young, soon after its publication in English in 1563, was the famous *Actes and Monuments* of John Foxe, better known as Foxe's *Book of Martyrs*. In recording the suffering and witness of Protestants to their faith under persecution, Foxe was giving the Church in England its own 'lives of the saints', and also foreshadowing and inspiring the pious little histories

---

[1] Sloane, p.48 (Bibl. 74). Clapham's *Briefe* is STC. 5332.

[2] *N.B.L.* 228 (Bibl. 41).

[3] Roscoe, 27, 28, 30, 35 (Bibl. 104).

[4] *A Series of Prints of Scripture History designed as Ornaments for those Apartments in which Children receive the first Rudiments of their Education.*

A Description of a Set of Prints of Scripture History . . . contained in a set of easy Lessons.

John Marshall. 1786.

There were 32 Old Testament stories in this set. In 1790 a similar set for the New Testament by Mrs. Trimmer was published.

which Puritans and other divines were soon to write with much fervour for boys and girls. Not least in the effect and influence of this famous book were the bold cuts depicting executions and tortures – although the unconcerned expressions on the faces of the victims may have mitigated the horrific impact on young minds.

Before little works implanting religion in this fervent style began to be produced in some quantity for children in the seventeenth century, there was a notable exception to the ordinary style of publication for them – very different from their lesson-books, books of manners or parental advice. This was a work by Thomas Newbery 'very preaty for children to rede', published in 1563 under the title *A Book in Englysh Metre, of the great Marchaunt Man called Dives Pragmaticus*. Its aim was to teach young citizens to 'read and write wares and implements in this world contained', for it is a rhyming catalogue, a list of merchandise of every kind, set out gaily if without much literary art. 'What lack ye, my masters? Come hither to me,' the author invites over and over again. Here can be found a medley of things bought and sold in the marts of Elizabethan England – books and ballads, candlesticks, lutes, cross-bows, tooth-picks and much else. At the end comes the needful moral advice, with a tiny picture of Death, the skeleton, leading a woman by the arm.

> 'Honest mirth in measure is a pleasant thyng.
> To wryte and rede well, be gyfts of learning.
> Remember this well, all you that be young,
> Exercise virtue, and rule well your toung.'

On the title-page of this fourteen page booklet is another pigmy cut – a man leading a child. It is all very matter-of-fact, but significant as a forerunner of the secular literature for youth which emerges in the eighteenth century.

The name of Newbery, too, might be hailed as a happy augury. It was a descendant of these printer Newberys of Shakespeare's London who was to win greater renown in the making of books for boys and girls in nearly two hundred years' time. But under the Stuarts, the scene became more sombre for the young reader. Publications for the child were to be over much preoccupied with his spiritual welfare until a glint of sunlight broke with the accession of Queen Anne.

William Sloane, in his detailed and scholarly study of children's books of this period, lists 261 items published for children between 1557 and 1710, excluding educational works (Bibl. 74). Nearly all these books are directed towards moral improvement or religious teaching. Some are books of parental advice or instruction, others are homilies or warnings against wickedness, and rarely are religious doctrines or moral exhortations allowed to make way for lighter fare. Gloomy as they may appear to the twentieth century reader, there are signs of a growing tendency to present the necessary advice in a more palatable or interesting fashion. Titles sometimes promise enjoyment, not always fulfilled by the text.

For example *The Child's Delight* (1671), by Thomas Lye, proves to be chiefly a primer with tiny pictures to aid pronunciation. But the need to entice the child to reading and improvement through reading is beginning to win adherents.

Among them was William Jole, Vicar of Sarratt in Hertfordshire. He penned one of the more cheerful books of the period in *The Father's Blessing* (1674). This promises on its title-page 'Verses, Riddles, Fables, Jests, Stories, Proverbs, Rules of Behaviour, and other

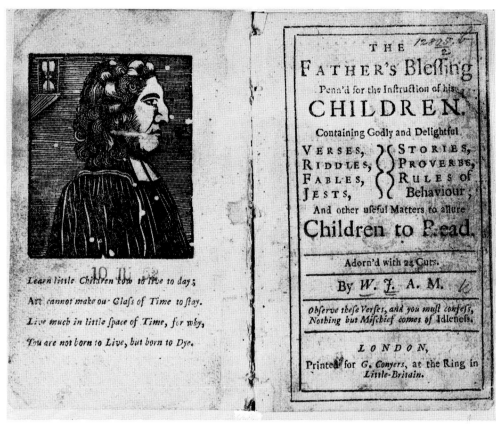

4. *A typical seventeenth century book for children*

useful Matters to allure Children to read . . .' as well as twenty-four cuts. Although the imminence of death (never far away in those days of heavy child mortality) and the need to prepare for the life hereafter are never absent from Jole's thoughts, he writes in a happy as well as admonitory vein.

'Dear Children', his preface begins, 'a little House must not have a large Porch, nor a little Book, a great Preface . . .' He discerns that what is most likely to affect the reader is what 'did affect the Writer', and then breaks into the rhymed couplets in which most of his book is written.

> 'If you delight to read what I have writ,
> God grant you Grace, that you may practise it.
> Those little Children that are wise
> Do fear the Lord and tell no Lyes:
> And if their Minds to good they bend
> A Blessing will on them attend.
> The Lord will keep them in his Ways,
> And make them happy all their Days'.

The little cuts are of animals and familiar objects and illustrate the rhyming riddles at the end of the volume. 'What it is with which you play with Maids for Tansies on a leisure Day? – a Ball.'

Not all seventeenth century books for children were so mild and gentle in tone. Others were more fearsome. One of the most popular was the well-known little book by another divine, James Janeway (1636?–1674), one of the clergy ejected for refusing to conform in 1662. This was *A Token for Children* (1671–72). Its expressive sub-title reveals its theme – 'being an exact Account of the Conversion, holy and exemplary Lives and joyful Deaths of several young Children'. Janeway, as aware as Jole that death was an ever present threat to young life, wrote with a passionate sincerity, obsessed by the dangers besetting young souls. In his first preface he addresses himself to parents and teachers, and he exhorts them 'to be faithful in instructing and catechising your young ones'. 'Are you willing that they should be Brands of Hell?' he asks. 'Are you indifferent whether they be damned or saved?'

He also writes a preface in not very different strain for his little readers, his 'dear Lambs'. 'How do you know but that you may be the next Child that may die?' he asks them. It was not a rhetorical question in those days when children often saw brothers or sisters or little companions being carried away to the churchyard. In such a world was it not wise to look beyond? 'Where are you then if you be not God's Child?' Janeway asks. He assures them that they may be safe if they will. He intends only their welfare. 'You may hear now, my dear Lambs, what other good Children have done, and remember how they wept and prayed by themselves, how earnestly they cried out for an Interest in the Lord Jesus Christ: you may read how dutiful they were to their Parents: how diligent at their Book: how ready to learn the Scriptures and their Catechisms . . . how joyfully they died'. He tells them of hell, 'a terrible Place, worse than a thousand Whippings', and finally begs them, 'If you love me, if you love your Parents, if you love your Souls, if you would escape Hellfire, and if you would go to Heaven when you die, do you go and do as these good Children. And that you may be your Parents' Joy, your Country's Honour, and live in God's Fear and die in his Love, is the Prayer of your dear Friend, James Janeway'.

A Token for Children was published in two parts, both being available in 1672. The children he describes are drawn from life, and some are of tender years, not four or five years of age. His second exemplar, not three years old, 'when he could not speak plain would be crying after God'. These prodigies set an example to their families by their piety and their excesses of weeping and praying after holiness. Sabbath-keeping, reading the scriptures, and listening to sermons are their delight. When they find themselves stricken with illness they are glad 'they are marked out for the Lord'. They do not want pity for their sufferings or for their approaching death, and those who stand and watch are awed by the rapture of these young souls on their way to everlasting bliss.

Such doctrines as Janeway and other writers of his persuasion expounded for youth strike modern readers as morbid. But in the seventeenth century they had a wide appeal, and Janeway's book found much favour. It was reissued many times, and an American edition was printed in 1700. It was still popular on both sides of the Atlantic in the first half of the nineteenth century. Perhaps its fascination lay in its overdrawn religious emotion heightened by fear of hell. Certainly Janeway and others made something of a melodrama of this struggle to outwit death and the devil. His book was more successful than other books of the period we should now consider more suitable as saner spiritual fare for young minds, such as Jole's little volume or Bunyan's book of rhymes.

Another writer belonging to the more fanatical school of faith was Thomas White. His warnings of the fate awaiting wicked children were even more alarming than those of Janeway. In *A Little Book for Little Children*, ascribed by Sloane to the year 1674, White begins indulgently – 'My dear pretty children, let me show you how dear you are to God'. But this mood soon changes to warnings and exhortation, especially about fearing 'the Devil at thy elbow' and the fire and brimstone of his kingdom. After much advice in this vein, there follow histories of Christian martyrs in the style of Foxe, with grisly details of tortures inflicted on the victims, who are often young children. Reading in itself may be just another snare of the devil. 'When thou canst read, read no ballads and foolish books', White bids his young readers, 'but the *Bible* and the *Plain-man's Pathway to Heaven*: Mr. Baxter's *Call to the unconverted*: read the Histories of the Martyrs that died for Christ, and in the *Book of Martyrs*'. No copies of this chastening work appear to have survived until the twelfth edition of 1702, a tribute in itself to its appeal to the taste of the age.

None of these writers are remembered today nor do their books for youth survive, much as they influenced and apparently gratified their own generation and after. But the Puritan spirit which engendered them had far-reaching effects on the national character and on the development of books for children, enduring in new forms through the centuries as firm rocks of spiritual faith and moral integrity amid many changing winds and waves of contemporary fashion.

Puritanism in the seventeenth century gave children something more than outmoded theology in their books. It produced for them one of the great books of the world, a classic for the young as well as for the men and women for whom it was written. *The Pilgrim's Progress* (1678) was not intended for boys and girls by its author, John Bunyan (1628–88). But they found in this wonderful allegory something far more absorbing than the edifying manuals specially written for them. After nearly three centuries it still keeps its place on the child's bookshelf, although it is much less read today than in the years when it had few rivals. Like all great stories of popular appeal, it has inspired artists in every period to give it a fitting contemporary dress. Two outstanding examples since the war are editions illustrated by Clarke Hutton and Edward Ardizzone, both issued in 1947.

Its author was a plain man of not much education, who followed his father's trade of tinker in Bedfordshire. After coming home from serving in the Parliamentary forces, Bunyan thought more and more about religion, and began to repent the wild unthinking ways of his youth, when he used to read merry books, ballads and newsbooks – 'George on horseback, and Bevis of Southampton' – in preference to scripture, and he played games on Elstow Green on Sundays. He became a dissenter from established doctrines and was stirred to preach. Soon after the Restoration he was imprisoned for doing so without a licence, for these were the days of intolerance when groups of people stole out into the woods at night or met secretly behind locked doors to hear forbidden preachers. Bunyan lay in Bedford gaol for twelve years. And there, in a last term of imprisonment before his final release, he wrote in the similitude of a dream the immortal tale of Christian's pilgrimage.

It was no wonder that the book attracted young minds, for it possessed the excitement of a quest, and the narrative could be enjoyed without lingering over the theological interpolations and inner meanings. Giants, desperate encounters with foul fiends like Apollyon, snares and pitfalls such as the Slough of Despond and Vanity Fair, faithful friends and dangerous enemies, strange visions, rewards for bravery and endurance – all these had a strong appeal, and in the sunnier, less militant second part, which came out in 1684, telling of the pilgrimage of Christiana, Christian's wife, with her four boys, and Mercy, her friend, there was a noble champion in Mr. Greatheart to fulfil the role of hero and win young admiration.

More typical of its period than Bunyan's masterpiece is the little book he wrote for children in 1686, when he was fifty-eight – *A Book for Boys and Girls; or, Country Rhimes for Children*. His love for his own children, especially for his 'poor blind Mary', was perhaps its chief inspiration, but its literary form owes much to the emblem writers, Francis Quarles and George Wither. Emblem books, which used devices or objects from the everyday world to illustrate divine truths or moral ideas, were not as yet written for children, and the mode was beginning to decline when Bunyan adapted it for his rhymes.

Two years before Bunyan's book was published, Nathaniel Crouch attempted to encourage a wider interest in the emblem book by adapting it to the taste of the less discriminating reader. His *Delights for the Ingenious* includes fifty illustrated emblems derived from Wither. There are also riddles in verse and a new invention intended to captivate the curious – a cardboard index dial to be used as part of 'a moral game'.[1]

Pictures of the objects selected were an important feature of emblem books, but Bunyan's volume was not issued with illustrations until 1707, by which date his original work had become abridged and amended. In the ninth edition of 1724 the title was changed to *Divine Emblems; or, temporal things spiritualized*. In the original edition of 1686 there are seventy-four subjects selected for his meditations, formed into unequal, rough little rhymes which bring to life the pleasant Bedfordshire countryside the author knew so well, and the simple things of daily living among its cottages and fields. Most of the verses are very different from the harsh and urgent sermonising of Janeway and White, but every theme has its religious lesson and application. We breathe, however, more often the soft air of the Interpreter's house and the Delectable Mountains rather than the dark atmosphere of the valleys of fiends and hobgoblins. The note of guilt and sin and hell-fire is not absent but there is also at times a lyric sweetness, and a true understanding of the things which interest a child. Such is the child's invitation to the bird in the bush to come and live with him (No. 31) and the brief lines on the swallow (No. 8).

> 'This pretty Bird, oh! how she flies and sings!
> But could she do so, if she had not Wings?
> Her Wings bespeak my Faith, her Songs, my Peace.
> When I believe and sing, my Doubtings cease.'

Nothing is too small or unimportant to yield its lesson of spiritual enlightenment. There are verses on 'The Frog', 'The Snail', 'A Penny Loaf', 'The Fly and the Candle', 'The Cackling of a Hen', 'A Lanthorn', and also thoughts on deeper matters – 'Death', 'Time and Eternity', 'Beauty'.

Bunyan, like most other writers for children at this time, set out at the beginning of his book an alphabet and brief spelling lesson. And in his preface he indicates he is not only writing for those not yet grown, but for larger folk, the 'Boys and Girls' who 'do play with all the frantic Fopperies of this Age'. He will entice them by their playthings,

> 'To show them how each Fingle-fangle
> On which they doting are, their Souls entangle.'

Little things, he believes, may lead children and very often their elders to the Divine. That is his purpose. But although Bunyan tried to fit his verses to the child's understanding, they were not to hold the child's attention. His book in its amended form had still something of a vogue in the eighteenth century, but afterwards it was forgotten. Arthur Mee,

---

[1] Sloane, p. 142 (Bibl. 74).

in his *Children's Bunyan* (1929), included a few of the verses, usually shorn of their religious 'application', but they are rarely met with nowadays in anthologies.

Bunyan was no poet, and his genius lay elsewhere. But nothing in his book of verses for children comes up to the level of the song of the shepherd boy in *The Pilgrim's Progress*, where Mr. Greatheart guides Christiana and her companions through the valley of humiliation.

> 'He that is down needs fear no fall;
>   He that is low, no pride;
> He that is humble, ever shall
>   Have God to be his guide.'

Many other seventeenth century books for children might be described, many of them bearing a family likeness to those by Janeway and White. Anticipating the proseletysing zeal of these writers were two Baptists, Henry Jessey and Abraham Chear, whose writings for youth were gathered together by H. Punchard, and issued as *A Looking-glass for Children* in 1672. This includes two histories of pious and suffering children by Jessey, who died in 1663, and various verses by Chear, who died five years later after a long period in Exeter gaol. Chear is best remembered for the verses he wrote in 1663, now printed in this collection beginning:

> 'When by Spectators I am told
>   what Beauty doth adorn me:
> Or in a Glass, when I behold,
>   how sweetly God did form me.
> Hath God such comeliness display'd
>   and on me made to dwell?
> Tis pitty, such a pretty Maid,
>   as I, should go to Hell.'

By the end of the century a more tolerant and less vehement religious spirit began to permeate some little books of instruction and edification for boys and girls. With the reign of Queen Anne came William Ronksley's *Child's Weeks-work* (1702?), much less formidable than some of its predecessors. Ronksley believed that the 'gay and airy temper' of little ones needed some gratification, and he planned his aid to reading as a series of simple rhymes, beginning with a verse alphabet, and graded to make a four weeks' course of reading. To please his readers is as much his intention as to lead them to piety and goodness – so his Invitation makes clear.

> 'Come, take this Book
> . Dear Child, and look
>   On it a while, and try
> What you can find
> To please your Mind;
>   The Rest you may pass by.'

Robert Russell also practised a style of impressive simplicity in addressing his young readers in *A Little Book for Children* . . . which came out in two parts in 1693 and 1696, but he used it to wage the old uncompromising war with childish iniquity – 'describing who they are that are good children, and also who they are that are wicked children,' with precise and dramatic effect.

Of all seventeenth century publications for youth, however, probably the most famous was an importation from the continent. This was the first picture-book for children, designed for their interest as much as for their instruction, by the renowned Bohemian divine, educationalist and idealist, John Amos Comenius (Komensky) (1592–1670). His *Orbis Sensualium Pictus* (*Visible World*) was more than a picture encyclopaedia to teach boys and girls Latin side by side with the vernacular in a new direct method. It expressed his dream for social reconstruction, and his ideas about God's universe. But it had a very practical aim. 'A little book, as you see, of no great bulk,' he wrote in his preface, 'yet a brief of the whole world'. Set out in its pages, with an illustration detailing each item, were the names and descriptions of a great range of objects, activities, and phenomena. In words and pictures children possessed for the first time 'a little encyclopaedia of things subject to the sense', as well as a pleasant system of learning Latin.

Comenius believed that children could best be taught through their powers of sensual observation, and so he appealed to their delight in pictures. He was a great innovator, not so much in acknowledging the importance of illustrations as in using them effectively. First published in 1658 in Nuremberg, in Latin and German, *Orbis Pictus* was translated into English the next year by the schoolmaster, Charles Hoole. There were twelve English editions by 1777, but it was even more popular in Europe. It was certainly a landmark in the history of books for children being their first compendium of everyday things, and the forerunner of the modern picture encyclopaedia – and of all books where illustrations play a leading role.

Comenius was a pioneer whose ideas were slow to make an impression on more conventional minds, although his book had much influence. Few books in the seventeenth century made use of pictures, and if they did, these were much subsidiary to the text. For pictures to take a prominent place was indeed a revolutionary step.

Little cuts, it will have been observed, had already appeared in a few children's books to lighten the task of learning to read, or to emphasise moral instruction. Towards the end of the Stuart period Nathaniel Crouch, an enterprising publisher bent on exploiting the reading needs of a widening public, began to make a regular use of cuts to enhance the appeal of his publications. He used them to emphasise warnings against misbehaviour in both his *Youth's Divine Pastime* (1691) and *Young Man's Calling* (1678), this last being founded on an earlier work, the *Young Man's Monitor* (1664) by Samuel Crossman. Crouch, who issued his various works under the sobriquet, 'R. B.' or 'Richard Burton', was in the book trade to make a living, and although he brought out godly histories to satisfy a still widespread demand for them, he was no religious intent on saving souls. He looked around for other wares to attract customers. He had utilised emblems, with the addition of a gimmick, in *Delights for the Ingenious*, where copper-plates and illustrated riddles were important features.

Material to fascinate young and old he also found in history and biography. 'His Talent lies at Collection', wrote John Dunton, a contemporary bookseller in his memoirs in 1705. 'He has melted down the best of our English Histories into Twelve-penny Books, which are filled with rarities and curiosities; for you must know his Title-pages are a little swelling . . .' [1]

---

[1] *Life and Errors*, 1818. vol. 1, p. 206. vol. 2, p. 435.

2 Foundations

I   REASON VERSUS FAIRY LORE

Throughout the seventeenth century zealous propaganda for religion, or exhortations and aids to godly living and salvation, had been characteristics of most literature produced for both younger and older readers. Gradually the need to present these subjects in more easy or entertaining fashion had been recognised in books designed for youth, and stories, riddles, cuts and other harmless attractions had begun to lighten the path to reading. So when religious strife began to abate before the advance of a calmer gospel of reason and toleration after the Revolution of 1688, the purpose of amusement, already admitted, was soon harnessed for the making of books suited to the more genial and secular spirit of the new century.

Religion, important as it was, and as it continued to be for many generations to come, was now to lose something of its partisan virulence and its dominance in literature. It was at least to be presented in a new and more indirect way. Newton's discoveries had revealed a mechanical universe of order and light, where the discerning might perceive that an omnipotent Supreme Being, governing his creation by immutable laws, had displaced the vengeful and anthropomorphic God of Calvinism and the Old Testament. The growing belief that religion should foster serenity and rational conduct required something different for boys and girls than harrowing tales of martyrs and holy dying. Certainly children must still be taught to be good, but now the emphasis was to be more concerned with character and conduct in the life of here-and-now rather than with preparation for the life hereafter. Virtue and industry brought their own rewards, and Christian principles, confirmed by the clear judgment of reason, were regarded as a necessary foundation to success and happiness both in living and in earning a living. Amid these changing ideas, the real beginnings of a secular literature for children were to emerge.

'The two great Ornaments of Virtue, which show her in the most advantageous Views, and make her altogether lovely, are Chearfulness and Good-nature', wrote Addison in 1711 in *The Spectator* (No. 243). These qualities, promulgated by Addison, Steele, and other essayists, in the new diurnal sheets, where vice and ignorance were ridiculed rather than reviled, were soon to find their way into books for the young, with other borrowings from the elder branch of literature.

Such sentiments were a reflection of the cooler and more prosaic temper of the new epoch, moulded and mirrored in the philosophy of John Locke. Locke's writings had as powerful an effect on the making of books for children as they had on education and other aspects of thought. Speculation and imagination had proved to be dangerous. Let man, therefore, confine himself to using his powers of observation and experience in examining the world around him. In education Locke was not quite a pioneer in pleading for a more humane and sympathetic approach in training the young, but his voice became audible when such rational ideas were more acceptable. He put forward not altogether novel schemes centred on the awakening of interest and methods of play. Harsh punishments he believed were harmful, and he advocated milder disciplines, with rewards as incentives. 'Thus children may be cozened into a knowledge of their letters . . . and play themselves into what others are whipped for'.[1] He also affirmed that virtue and character were more important than knowledge. These two principles, play and the formation of right habits of morality and conduct, pervaded much eighteenth century literature published for boys and girls.

Locke also recommended, when gentle and persuasive methods had succeeded in teaching the child to read, 'some easy pleasant book, suited to his capacity . . . wherein the entertainment that he finds might draw him on and reward his pains in reading, and yet not such as should fill his head with perfectly useless trumpery, or lay the principles of vice and folly'.[2] Fairies and fairy lore, 'goblins and spirits', with other superstitions, he regarded as belonging to the useless trumpery. Imagination and enthusiasm were to be avoided – as were unintelligible ideas about God, the Supreme Being whom children should be taught to love and reverence. The sober light of reason and common-sense was to illumine the child's life.

Locke regretted the scarcity of suitable books to further his purpose. In addition to the Scriptures, there seemed to be only *Aesop's Fables* and *Reynard the Fox*, of which he could approve. Like Comenius, whose work may have influenced him, he believed in the usefulness and attraction of pictures, and when he produced for the young scholar a Latin and English version of Aesop in 1703, he added four pages of 'sculptures', each with sixteen tiny engravings of animals, to make it 'more taking'.

The encouragement of rational judgment and a distrust of the imagination were to mark out the path of children's literature both in England and in Europe for many years. Such a climate was too chilly for the fairies, who vanished underground into chapbook literature, or found for a while a more congenial air across the Channel. In France there was an interim before the rule of reason took command. The flowering of the fairy tale

---

[1] *Some thoughts concerning education* (1693), ¶ 149 (Bibl. 83, 84).

[2] *Ibid.* ¶ 156

there at the end of the seventeenth century therefore introduces a welcome and significant interlude in this story of children's literature.

The cult of the *conte de fée* was chiefly for the salon not the nursery. The glitter and splendour of the Sun King's court were fading under the restrictions fallen upon it since the ascendancy of Madame de Maintenon, and perhaps it was to recapture something of former glory, or to escape the restraints of an increasingly vigorous censorship, that writers turned to the fairy tale. So an idealised version of the court was created, a 'Fairy Versailles', in tales of romance and enchantment created for the amusement of fine ladies and gentlemen. The stories very often have little true kinship with the genuine folk-tale, although traditional themes were used, as well as incidents from medieval romance. They are chiefly literary creations, mostly frivolous, but sometimes improving, about royalty in a magic world. Many reflect the society of the French court of the late seventeenth and early eighteenth century, but everything is transformed into a realm outside reality, where fairies and ogres foster or menace the course of true love between prince and princess, and where enchantments wreak strange metamorphoses. Jewels grow on trees instead of blossoms, palaces are made of diamonds or lapis lazuli. And when royalty masquerades in peasant guise, rural life is an idyllic wonderland, where shepherds wear rose tafferty and garland their flocks.

Amidst all this glittering artifice there was published one work as fresh and natural as a spring meadow – a little masterpiece, which has endured through the centuries to become that dearly loved classic, *Perrault's Fairy Tales*. 'Then and for the first time, French children, and later all the children in the world, had a book after their own heart . . .',[1] wrote Paul Hazard. This little volume of eight stories was first published in 1697 as *Histoires ou Contes du Temps passé, avec des Moralitezs*. It was understood to be the work of M. Charles Perrault (1628–1703), who had already written three verse tales founded on old themes. Perrault was a notable Academician, and Comptroller of the Royal Buildings, but these new fairy tales bore not his name but that of his son, Pierre D'Armancour, in whose name the dedication was made to 'Mademoiselle' (Elisabeth Charlotte d'Orleans, the King's niece). Scholars disagree as to whether Perrault *père* or *fils* (or both) was the real author, but what is undisputed is the charm that these tales have held for every generation since they first appeared. Six of them are the best loved stories children have in their earliest years – *The Sleeping Beauty* (*La Belle au Bois dormant*), *Little Red Riding Hood* (*Le Petit Chaperon rouge*), *Bluebeard* (*La Barbe bleue*), *Puss-in-Boots* (*Le Maistre Chat, ou le Chat botté*), *Cinderella* (*Cendrillon*), *Hop o' my Thumb* (*Le petit Poucet*). The other two tales, *The Fairies or Diamonds and Toads* (*Les Fées*), and *Riquet with the Tuft* (*Riquet à la Houppe*) are less well known.

[1] *Books, Children and Men*, p. 8 (Bibl. 12).

Founded on traditional themes, some of which had already appeared in two Italian collections, *Le Piacevoli Notti* (1550–53), of Straparola, and *Il Pentamerone* (1634–36), of Basile, these stories have become familiar in other guise. Cinderella, for example, is the English *Catskin* and the German *Aschenputtel*, but it was Perrault who invented the fairy godmother and the famous glass slipper. Rarely have the tales been surpassed in the telling, for the author blends Gallic wit with literary grace and the aptness of peasant speech. Unlike many of his contemporaries who wrote fairy tales, Perrault was writing for children. It is plain in the frontispiece which depicts an old nurse or peasant woman sitting with a distaff, spinning her tales to three listening children. Above runs the inscription 'Contes de ma Mère L'Oye' – it is Mother Goose's first appearance as a nursery character.

Short verse moralities were added at the end of each story, probably to give the correct impression of serious purpose, then so necessary everywhere in books intended for the young. But they have a hint of cynicism. For example (appended to *Cinderella*), to succeed you need not only good qualities, such as wit, courage and good sense, but god-fathers and godmothers also. Today these verse moralities are usually omitted, and the endings of the tales of *Little Red Riding Hood* and *The Sleeping Beauty* are sometimes softened. The woodman saves the little girl from the wolf just in time and the episode of the Queen Mother attempting to kill and eat the children of the Sleeping Beauty is left out. But at least one English edition has appeared since the war presenting the Perrault stories exactly as the tales were written (Bibl. 88, 89).

When these famous fairy tales first became available in an English translation is still uncertain. It now seems likely that the earliest was that translated by Robert Samber, advertised in the *Monthly Chronicle* for 31st March 1729. A copy of this edition survives in the United States, and is available in facsimile (Bibl. 87). It included, in addition to the eight prose tales of Perrault, a more sophisticated and less attractive story about a clever and virtuous princess, who outwitted a wicked prince, *L'Adroite Princesse* (*The Discreet Princess*), now known to have been written by his niece, Jeanne l'Heritier. Very soon separate tales were taken over by the chapbook makers, and it is probable that they first became known to children in this country in this form, although there were twelve editions of the collected stories by 1802 (Bibl. 90).

Nothing else of the quality of the Perrault tales was forthcoming for young readers from the fairy tale mode in France. This went on until about the middle of the eighteenth century, when it declined on the growth of rationalism as propounded by Locke and Voltaire. Later fairy tales, including an example by Rousseau, were increasingly to be a vehicle for parable or moral instruction. The voluminous writings of the period were collected into a vast *Cabinet des Fées* in forty-one volumes (1785–89).

Some of the stories still survive in children's books, notably certain tales by the Comtesse

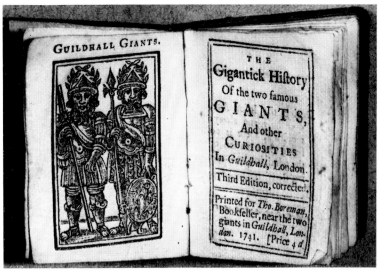

5. *Frontispiece of the first French edition of Perrault's Fairy Tales (1697)*
6. *One of the tiny series by a predecessor of John Newbery (p. 45)*
7. *The earliest English periodical for children (p. 44)*

7   37

d'Aulnoy (1649–1705), whose *Contes de Fées* first appeared in 1697 and 1698. She delighted in telling of strange transmutations of princes and princesses into beasts, birds, insects, and even plants, and among the prettiest of such stories are *The White Cat*, *The Blue Bird* and *The Hind in the Forest*. She liked to indulge in daydreams of luxury. If gold is wanted, then there are fifty towers or five hundred cart loads full of it, and she scatters precious stones like pebbles. Romantic love plays a prominent part in her tales, and she has a high regard for nobility of birth. Any peasant hero or heroine is generally found sooner or later to have been stolen from some royal palace as an infant. The best of her stories, however, still hold much appeal for children and are often found in modern collections of fairy tales. Many of them, and others by her contemporaries, were included by Andrew Lang in his 'Colour' Fairy Books at the end of the nineteenth century.

A perennial favourite is the well-known *Beauty and the Beast*. It was adapted from an ancient folklore theme by Madame de Villeneuve, and included in the *Cabinet des Fées*. But it was another French writer, Madame Le Prince de Beaumont, who gave it the form which has endeared it to the nursery ever since she included it in her *Magasin des Enfans* (1756).

French fairy tales, except in a moralised form, were rarely looked upon as suitable reading for children in the eighteenth century, although older folk, including Jonathan Swift, might find them diverting. 'I borrowed one or two books of *Contes de Fées*, and have been reading them these two days', he wrote to Stella in January 1712. By that date a full English edition of the Tales of Madame d'Aulnoy was available, and some of them had been issued here as early as 1699. Mrs. M. Cooper, an enterprising publisher, who rivalled Newbery in some of her innovations, intended *The Court of Queen Mab* (1752), an edition of nine of the stories, 'for the innocent amusement of children', but also had in mind 'those of more advanced age and riper judgment'. To the d'Aulnoy stories she added a fairy tale in verse by Thomas Parnell and 'Queen Mab's Song'. It has been claimed that John Newbery issued an edition of Perrault as *Mother Goose's Tales* before his death in 1767, but there is no direct evidence to support this. On the whole, the fairy tale was discouraged as children's reading, unless it could be amended to point a lesson.

The popularity of the fairy tale in France was soon to be rivalled by the Oriental tale, with its even more bizarre and exotic attractions for jaded literary tastes. In 1704, M. Antoine Galland, returned from Constantinople, enraptured the literary world of Paris with the first volume of his translation of the Arabian tales, the *Mille et une Nuits*, folk-tales from various Eastern sources, ostensibly told by Scheherazade to entrance a royal husband and save her life, and known by English-speaking children today as *The Arabian Nights' Entertainments*. Galland's work, which ran into twelve volumes, was very soon translated into English, and made a great impression. But here again, these fabulous histories of sorcery and wild fantasy were rarely given to children except in moralised form, although like the fairy tales, they became material for the chapbook printers.

The *Arabian Nights'* was to be a potent influence on the writers of the Romantic revival, and so eventually on children's literature, but in the eighteenth century it was taken over by the moralists. A typical eighteenth century version for youth, showing the tendency to use the eastern tale to inculcate right conduct, was written by Richard Johnson, a hack writer who wrote some of his more improving works under the pseudonym, 'the Rev. Mr. Cooper'.[1] His *Oriental Moralist*, a selection of the tales, 'with suitable reflections adapted to each story', was published by E. Newbery in 1791. He affirms in his preface his intention to cull from the original 'a nosegay for his youthful friends', having 'expunged everything which could give the least offence to the most delicate reader'. 'I have, in many instances,' he goes on, not satisfied with mere deletion, 'altered the fables, and have given them a turn which appeared to me the most likely to promote the love of virtue . . . ' Under these limitations it is surprising that the stories are so readable and retain so much of the attraction of the original. His *Story of the Wonderful Lamp* is very little hampered by his purpose, although he attempts to show at the end how the history of Aladdin and the evil African magician has its moral relating to the right use of wealth.

Some editing and selection are essential before presenting these ancient tales of 'fabulous wealth and candid bawdry'[2] to children. But a wider interpretation of what was suitable mental fare for them prevailed in the nineteenth century when other translations became available. Many children's versions were inspired by the carefully expurgated translation of E. W. Lane, published in 1839–41. Yet in 1898 when Andrew Lang produced his selection for young readers, he went back to Galland's text, and this edition by Lang still endures as one of the best for them today.

CHAPBOOKS

The publishers of books for enlightened eighteenth century circles knew that parents and guardians and tutors wanted sober facts not fantasies for the growing mind. Less reputable publishers, then as now, were less concerned with polite theories about education. They knew what ordinary folk, both young and old, wanted, and they intended to purvey cheap books sure to sell. The unsophisticated masses, encouraged by authority to read, so that they might know their Bible, were as ready to imbibe all kinds of

---

[1] Weedon, M. J. P. *Richard Johnson and the successors to John Newbery* (Bibl. 100).

[2] Dawood, H. J., *trans. The Thousand and one Nights* (Bibl. 95).

lurid improbabilities in print as they were to enjoy old wives' tales, gossip, and superstitions. It was these conditions which gave rise to the rapid growth of chapbook literature in the eighteenth century. The lapse of licensing for the printing trade in 1695, and the growing interest in secular literature, were other potent contributory causes.

Chapbooks were the flimsy little productions sold by the 'Running Stationers' (also described as 'Walking' and 'Flying Stationers'), and were usually hawked around the countryside at cottage doors, village fairs, and other places where likely customers might be found. The salesmen were itinerant pedlars or chapmen, who usually sold other wares besides penny and halfpenny books. Among the better chapbooks were versions of the old romances already described. Now they had degenerated into a travestied and shortened form to make appealing tales for a new public. Some of the most popular romances turned into chapbooks were *Guy of Warwick*, *Fortunatus*, *Valentine and Orson*, *The Seven Champions*, *St. George and the Dragon*, and *Bevis of Southampton*. Other popular items were native tales of humbler origin, still nursery favourites, including *Dick Whittington*, *Jack and the Giants*, and *The Children in the Wood*. Later in the eighteenth century came single tales taken from Perrault, d'Aulnoy, and the *Arabian Nights'*.

Chapbooks showed much variety in their subject matter, and were by no means confined to stories which have survived to form part of children's literature. As well as medieval fictions and traditional tales, there were all kinds of superstitions, morbid and sensational matters, quite unsuitable for children, and aimed at a credulous and uncritical public. Such were the accounts of ghosts, witches, crimes, monstrosities, and religious warnings, these last often featuring the devil with cloven hoof and pronged fork. Fortune-telling, prognostications, and the interpretation of dreams were also very popular, and so were coarse jests, as in *The Mad Pranks of Tom Tram*.

History and scripture were often much debased to provide the necessary sensation, although some sober and serious little works of piety might also be found among the chapbooks. Samuel Pepys bought 'penny godlinesses' as well as 'penny merriments', and the Bible in abridged form was adapted for the profitable trade. One example, apparently based on Benjamin Harris's original verses of 1698 (p. 22), and also intended 'for the benefit of weak memories', was issued by John White, an early chapbook-maker of Newcastle upon Tyne. *The Holy Bible* is here presented in about a thousand lines covering both Old and New Testaments and the Apocrypha.[1] Even more popular than Bible summaries were the *Divine Songs* (or *Hymns*) of Isaac Watts, which were frequently purloined as chapbook material after their publication in 1715.

In style and appearance chapbooks were of inferior quality, though designed always to attract the customer. An important feature was their illustration, consisting of rough and

---

[1] *N.B.L. Catalogue*, 377 (Bibl. 42).

badly carved woodcuts, often inept for the text, the same blocks being overworked to serve a variety of incidents. The pages were usually neither cut nor stitched, merely folded. But notwithstanding their crudities and imperfections, chapbooks have a distinct importance in the evolution of literature for children. They were not only read by young people in their day, forming a kind of 'underground' or 'comic' literature of the period. They had some influence on the format and contents of children's books when these began to cater for the entertainment of the reader and become a regular part of the publishing trade. And in an age of rationalism they kept alive, although in rudimentary fashion, some traditional and imaginative stories which boys and girls were unlikely to meet with as yet in any better form. Some famous classics, notably the *Robin Hood* legends, *Robinson Crusoe* and *Gulliver's Travels* must have reached a much wider and younger public through the pedlars' travestied copies than in their original state.

8. *A popular eighteenth century chapbook*

Early in the eighteenth century when chapbook literature began to multiply considerably, the main London house for its manufacture was that of William and Cluer Dicey, a father and son partnership. Boswell records a visit to the Dicey printing house in Bow Churchyard in July 1763. 'There are ushered into the world of literature *Jack and the Giants*, *The Seven Wise Men of Gotham*, and other story-books which in my dawning years amused me as much as *Rasselas* does now . . .' He could not resist the appeal of his 'old darlings', so he purchased two dozen and 'had them bound up with the title *Curious Productions . . .*'

William Dicey had come to London from Northampton about 1730, when he set up his chapbook printing house in Aldermary Church-yard, later removing to Bow Church-yard. Towards the end of the century John Marshall also issued chapbooks from Aldermary Church-yard, and there were many other London chapbook makers active in this heyday of their manufacture. Soon they circulated also from many provincial towns. John White of Newcastle upon Tyne had started in the business by 1711, and he was followed later in the century by Thomas Saint, another Newcastle printer, who was to employ the famous wood-engraver, Thomas Bewick. The chapbook began to change in style about the turn of the century, and the nineteenth century chapbooks, especially those issued by J. Kendrew of York (about 1803–1840) and J. G. Rusher of Banbury (from about 1808 onwards), were mainly produced with the young reader in mind.

A list printed in one of Kendrew's chapbooks about 1820 includes several Perrault tales besides *Cinderilla* (sic), a Newbery invention, *The History of Giles Gingerbread*, a brief *Robinson Crusoe*, and nursery rhymes, for example *The Death and Burial of Cock Robin*, *The House that Jack Built*, and *The Adventures of old Mother Hubbard and her Dog*. These publications of the early nineteenth century were smaller than those which preceded them in the seventeenth and eighteenth centuries. They have the familiar feature of a picture – sometimes on a paper cover – to introduce their title, and often little cuts inside as well. The older chapbooks were eight or sixteen pages, often merely folded, but these prettier trifles for the young usually spread their contents over twenty-four or thirty-two of tinier dimensions, and presented a more finished appearance. Much of the former vulgarity has disappeared in the subjects chosen. The improvement is probably due to the influence of Sunday School literature, and the emphasis on an appeal to youth.

One of the firms to survive longest was the Catnach Press, responsible for many cheap and gaudy little books, ballads and broadsides, not only intended for the younger generation, from about the second decade of the nineteenth century until mid-Victorian times. By then the era of the chapbook was over, although the inheritors of Catnach's business were still active until the 1880s. Jemmy Catnach, the founder of the firm at Seven Dials, came to London after the end of the Napoleonic wars, and began to produce 'catchpenny' street literature on a wide scale for a gullible elder public in the form of murders, scandals, criminal confessions, and other contemporary sensations. But he also brought out less alarming productions as farthing, halfpenny and penny books for children. The pages might be coarsely printed, but the contents were usually innocuous and well-adapted to the needs of little readers. Catnach intended to entice their interest, but he could add a little moral advice at times in the old-fashioned way, claiming that

> 'Instruction unto youth when given
> Points the path from earth to heaven.'

Alphabets, nursery rhymes, plentiful if bad pictures, scripture sheets, riddles, fun, verses, old tales retold, these were some of the attractions he offered to the young.

It was the last flare before the fire died out – this success of the Catnach Press. When Victoria came to the throne, the chapbook vogue was already beginning to decline. Its era was giving way to the rise of periodical literature and other cheap publications for youth. So these long popular wares, which had provided easily accessible (if unrecommended) reading matter for the people and their children from the days of Bunyan's youth, gradually disappeared from the market, to be supplanted by the 'Penny Dreadfuls', 'Bloods', and 'Strip Cartoons' of a more literate epoch.

II JOHN NEWBERY AND THE BEGINNING OF THE PUBLISHING TRADE FOR BOYS AND GIRLS

At the end of 1743 a young bookseller-publisher arrived in London from the country town of Reading to seek fresh scope for his industry and abilities. Already he had published a number of books at his premises, 'The Bible and Crown', in the Market Place there, where he also dealt in patent medicines and haberdashery. A farmer's son, educated chiefly through his own reading, he had married his employer's widow and risen to be the owner of a profitable business, which included a local newspaper, *The Reading Mercury*. As yet he had published no books for the entertainment of young readers, the activity to bring him fame, although in 1742 he had reprinted John Merrick's *Festival Hymns for Charity Schools* – a third edition. Within the next twenty-four years, however, from the setting-up of his publishing house and bookshop in London until his death in 1767, he was to make the irregular and tentative business of publishing for children into an important and profitable trade. In brief, this was the achievement of John Newbery (1713–1767).

He was not entirely the pioneer in the field he was to conquer as was once claimed for him. There were other publishers active in the production of little works for the rising generation which should possess sober good sense and inculcate right conduct, carefully avoiding the religious excesses of the previous age, and so fill the dearth of suitable books pointed out by Mr. Locke. Mr. Newbery with his alert mind would be well aware of this. He would also know the approved and established books for the young, the religious works, the lesson-books, the manuals of good advice, and *Aesop's Fables*, of course. Another edition had appeared in 1740, selected and amended from L'Estrange, by the novelist, Samuel Richardson. And it was more than likely that he knew those influential and good-humoured works – *The Tatler* and *The Spectator* – for there is a reflection of their temper and spirit in many of the books he issued. Certainly he would also have read two other outstanding successes of the early eighteenth century, now classics for readers of all ages, with long and far-reaching influence on children's books – *Robinson Crusoe* and *Gulliver's Travels*.

Defoe's masterpiece was published in 1719, and it is further considered later with the development of the adventure story. It was not merely a first-rate narrative about a castaway on a desert island, but also the history of a soul's discovery of its creator, and a lesson in self-reliance and ingenuity. So much so that it soon commended itself to imitators as a suitable model to be used to convey instruction to youth, especially after Rousseau had praised it in *Emile* in 1762.

Gulliver's Travels, by Jonathan Swift (1667–1745), appeared seven years later in 1726. Here, too, the aim was to enlighten humanity, this time through satire in no kindly spirit.

As with Crusoe, shipwreck and voyages to strange places befall Gulliver, but there is little resemblance between their experiences. Unlike Defoe's hero, Gulliver finds himself in no unpeopled wilderness. He comes upon communities of strange beings, manipulated by their inventor to reveal the follies and vices of the human race. The appeal to children in this powerful satire lay in its setting – a world of fantasy and topsy-turvydom, where boys and girls not six inches high play at hide-and-seek in Gulliver's hair, and the hero, shrunk to a tiny mannikin in a land of giants, nearly drowns in a Brobdingnagian bowl of cream. Swift perhaps had latent in mind his native Irish legends as well as the tales of Madame d'Aulnoy and the *Arabian Nights'* when he penned Gulliver's adventures. He would doubtless have been astonished to know that the book has endured chiefly as a classic for children, who ignore the satire they cannot understand, but who revel in incidents about atomies and giants.

Newbery made use of the idea of Lilliputia, the land of Gulliver's first exploration, but without the contrasts in stature so fascinating in the original. Voyages to imaginary countries, including Lilliput, form the theme of several improving little histories in his publications, notably in *The Lilliputian Magazine*, a venture which was apparently first launched in monthly parts in 1751, but survives only in a collected volume published in 1752 or 1753. Newbery's Lilliputians, however, are also the little people for whom his magazine was designed, and in its pages a 'Lilliputian Society' for his small customers is set forward, founded on the principles of 'the Usefulness of Learning and the Benefit of being good'. A list of young subscribers is also included.

The contents were intended to be diverting as well as improving. Accounts of travels to imaginary lands – such as Master Jemmy Gadabout's Voyages to Angelica, and Master Ramble's account of 'The Rise and Progress of Learning in Lilliput' – were interspersed with riddles (with answers in a later number), songs and verses (hinting at Christopher Smart's authorship), pictures and other delights. There was also the story about Tommy Trip and his dog Jouler, and their encounter with the Giant Woglog – a tale that New-bery included also in *A Pretty Book of Pictures* very soon afterwards.

A greater influence on Newbery's early publications for children than either Defoe or Swift was undoubtedly John Locke and his ideas about education already mentioned. It was probably due largely to Locke's suggestions, that the task of reading should be made interesting to children by letting them play their way to learning, that a new kind of book had already appeared on the market when Newbery arrived in the metropolis.

There had already been foreshadowings of things to come. In the reign of Queen Anne the breakaway from didacticism has already been noted in the form of a little reading and spelling book of twelve pages – *A Little Book for Little Children*, by 'T. W.' (ca. 1702). Very different from the Puritan volume with the same title, by the minister, Thomas White, this is a light-hearted composition, proffering alphabet, spelling lesson, rhymes and riddles in happy style. The beginning of the alphabet rhyme 'A was an Archer and shot at a Frog' has already been quoted from it, and this makes its first appearance here in a children's book. Another attraction was that puzzle of mispunctuation

> 'I saw a Peacock with a fiery Tail
> I saw a blazing Star that dropt down Hail'

Tiny cuts added their allurement. It seemed that enjoyment as a general aim in books for boys and girls could not be far away.

Whether Newbery came across this impressive trifle is uncertain. It is much more likely that he knew the work of Thomas Boreman, established 'near the Two Giants' in Guild-hall, where he launched a number of tiny books for boys and girls, between 1740 and 1743, humorously dubbing them 'Gigantick Histories'. These were even smaller than the little books to come from the house of Newbery, being only two inches high. Bound in covers of Dutch flowered paper, another Newbery feature, they are addressed to 'Little Masters and Misses'.

'During the infant age, ever busy and always inquiring', writes Boreman in one of his prefaces, 'there is no fixing the attention of the mind but by amusing it'. The style is engaging. He goes on to promise his little readers, if each of them buy one of his books

> 'Then very soon
>   I'll print another
> Which for its size
>   Will be its brother.
> Such pretty thoughts
>   It will contain
> You'll read it o'er
>   And o'er again.'

Boreman's small volumes are mainly concerned with London and its history and description, with the fabulous represented by the story of Gogmagog and Corineus in *The Gigantick History of the Two Famous Giants* (1740). A list of young subscribers, a feature already observed in Newbery's later *Lilliputian Magazine*, and midget chapters are set out in good clear print. There is more than a hint in these 'Histories' that Boreman's illustrious successor found ideas there. Yet Newbery's *Historical Descriptions of London*, published in 1753 in three volumes, are very different from these simple works by Boreman, for they were designed as solid stuff for elder readers. It is in presentation rather than in subject matter that there is a family likeness.

About the same date another publisher was showing similar ingenuity in providing attractive forerunners of Newbery. This was T. Cooper at 'The Globe' in Paternoster Row. In 1742 he advertised *The Child's New Play-thing*, a little work 'to make learning to read a *Diversion* instead of a *Task*', dedicating it to the infant Prince George, whose picture formed the frontispiece.[1] Included were scripture-histories, fables, songs, pro-verbs, moral precepts, and most notable, stories – shortened versions of the long estab-lished favourites, *St. George*, *Fortunatus*, *Guy of Warwick*, and *Reynard the Fox*. By the next year, 1743, Cooper was evidently succeeded in business by his widow, who then issued a second edition, the earliest to survive.

Some of the phrases in these pages have a familiar ring. They were soon to echo in the admonitory letters which Jack-the-Giant-killer was to address to Master Tommy and Miss Polly in Newbery's first book for them. Like Newbery, the Coopers aimed to please their child readers, but there is also a resemblance in the never relaxed intention 'to ground them in the principles of knowledge and virtue'.

St. George and his companions might give this *Play-thing* a flourish, but after all it was mainly a lesson-book. There was more originality in another little work which Mrs. Cooper advertised in the *London Evening Post* for 22nd–24th March 1744, only three months before Newbery was to set a new standard in beguiling advertisements with his notice for *A Little Pretty Pocket-Book*. Mrs. Cooper's announcement ran –

> 'This Day is published. Price 6d. bound. *Tommy Thumb's Song Book for all little Masters and Misses* . . . by Nurse Lovechild.'

It heralded the first nursery rhyme book for children, and so marked a red letter day indeed in the history of their literature. The illustrations in the tiny volume (it measures about three by one and a half inches) are exactly suited to the mood of the verses, which are chiefly the familiar favourites of infancy – 'Hickory, Dickory, Dock', 'Little Tommy Tucker', 'Baa, Baa, Black Sheep' and similar ditties.

Some not so pleasant and now forgotten rhymes are included, but on the whole this is a gay collection presented for the young child's sheer entertainment. Some musical terms run in random style at the base of the pages, printed facing in black and red alternatively – 'Pronto', 'Timoroso', 'Recitatio', etc. Intended to be sung to the very young 'by their nurses until they can sing themselves', these comments have to serve instead of any musical score. The sole surviving copy in the British Museum is marked 'Voll. II'. This may explain the absence of the usual introduction in the style of the day setting out the purpose of the book. Did the American publisher, Isaiah Thomas, copy exactly its prefatory letter which the advertisement promised when he brought out an edition in 1788 (Bibl. 107)? It was on 'nursing' or the bringing up of young children, addressed to Nurse Lovechild, who is advised not to sing the songs too loud or to frighten her charges by any mention of 'a Bull Beggar, Tom Poker, Raw Head and Bloody Bones'. Nor should nurses swing infants with their heels backwards 'lest they dislocate their backs . . . ' This letter does not appear in the English copy. Yet there is some mystery about this matter of two volumes,

---

[1] Alston, R. C., 551 (Bibl. 33).

46

for no mention is made of them in the press notice, and in the same year (1744) a sequel to *Tommy Thumb* was advertised in the *Daily Advertiser* (23rd May) as *Nancy Cock's Song Book . . . a Companion to Tommy Thumb's and the Second Volume of that great and learned Work . . .'*

These nursery rhymes and jingles have many and diverse origins, as Peter and Iona Opie have shown in that mine of information on the subject, *The Oxford Dictionary of Nursery Rhymes* (Bibl. 106). They had long been sung or chanted to babies, as Nurse Lovechild intended, before they found their way into print. From this time onwards, after Tommy Thumb's debut, they became a regular feature of publishing for children. Other collections of rhymes soon followed. Unharnessed to serious purpose and allied to pure nonsense, these collections of jingles and songs for the very young were the first works of true entertainment printed for children, enduring through every generation. Today they form some of the gayest and richly adorned picture-books for the under-fives.

There is much doubt as to whether John Newbery published the book of nursery rhymes associated with his name – *Mother Goose's Melody* – although nursery rhymes appeared in many of his volumes for boys and girls. It has many Newbery features with verses set down with mock-serious or playful captions or comments. These have suggested Goldsmith's authorship. The second part of the book consists of the songs of Shakespeare, a notable innovation, for rarely for some time to come were such pearls to be strung for young readers.

Whether this delightful compilation was Newbery's or Goldsmith's work or by a later hand is not known. An advertisement in the *London Chronicle*, 30th December 1780– 2nd January 1781, makes it plain that it was 'Now first published from the papers of that very great writer of very little books, the late Mr. John Newbery . . .' There is no evidence for any earlier copy being printed.[1]

The idea of amusement, even for its own sake, was gaining ground steadily during Newbery's lifetime. But it must not be forgotten that weightier stuff was still the general rule. Amusement was regarded as tarts or gingerbread – a reward for the consumption of plainer fare. Moral advice or useful lessons, however lightly handled, dominated most books for youth during the eighteenth century, and for at least two decades afterwards.

It is perhaps significant that, as these new elements of amusement were finding their way into books for boys and girls, the domestic novel for their elders was being launched upon the world. *Pamela*, by Samuel Richardson (1689–1761), first appeared in 1740, and its title-page indicated that here also serious purpose was to be linked with a new kind of entertainment for the reading public. Richardson had perhaps teenagers in mind in writing this tale of 'Virtue rewarded', for his avowed aim was 'to inculcate the Principles

[1] Weedon, M. J. P., *Mother Goose's Melody* (Bibl. 108).

47

of Virtue and Religion in the Youth of both Sexes'. Older children might read these letters narrating the trials and triumph of the heroine, but for those who found the prolixity of the volumes too formidable, there were soon to be abridgements. In 1756 a much shortened version for youth of the three novels by Richardson was brought out by R. Baldwin as *The Paths of Virtue delineated*. This presented the long-winded histories of *Pamela, Clarissa* (1747) and *Sir Charles Grandison* (1753) in one volume. Francis Newbery, John Newbery's nephew, also issued abridged editions of each of the three novels in 1769, but it does not appear that his uncle preceded him in the venture, although he may have been associated with Baldwin in the 1756 publication.[1]

John Newbery certainly followed the trends of the time and drew ideas for his publishing from many sources. None the less his achievement is not to be underrated. He imprinted a style of his own upon the books he made for children, organised their production and marketing with fertile ingenuity and much industry, and firmly established juvenile publishing as a regular and important part of the book trade. And so the publication of his first book for children's entertainment, whatever it may owe to its predecessors, can still rightly be regarded as a historic milestone in the development of literature for youth.

First advertised in the late spring of 1744 (an announcement setting a new style in diverting advertisements may be seen in the *Penny London Morning Advertiser* for 18–20th June of that year), *A Little Pretty Pocket-Book, intended for the Instruction and Amusement of Little Master Tommy and pretty Miss Polly* . . . was issued from Newbery's premises near Devereux Court, just outside Temple Bar, where he had established his business under his old Reading sign, 'The Bible and Crown'. Newbery promised among other attractions, letters from Jack-the-Giant-killer, and a Ball and Pin-cushion, 'the Use of which will infallibly make Tommy a good Boy and Polly a good Girl'. More serious was the advice to their elders, set down in the preface, with its Lockean principles for making children 'strong, hardy, healthy, virtuous, wise and happy'.

According to Newbery's biographer, Charles Welsh, the publisher had another establishment, as well as the Devereux Court premises, when he set up in London at the end of 1743, near the Royal Exchange at 'The Golden Ball', but no confirmatory evidence has been found for this City address. In 1745, before he was securely established, there came the Jacobite Rising, and this evidently brought upon him financial difficulties. By September of that year he had removed to that long popular centre of the book trade – St. Paul's Church-yard, and here at the corner of Canon Alley (recently swept away in new development), opposite the North Door of the Cathedral, he centred all his efforts at one house, changing his sign to 'The Bible and Sun'. Here he built up a flourishing business as publisher and bookseller for both adults and children. Nostrums and remedies, which by

---

[1] Welsh. *A Bookseller of last Century* p. 300, (Bibl. 105). Roscoe 315–317 (Bibl. 104).

1746 included the famous Dr. James' Fever Powder, were not the least profitable part of his trade.

This first little book for the amusement of children, which the unknown publisher brought out within a few months of coming to London, was evidently a success. In 1747, when Newbery seems to have been for a time closely associated with two other book-sellers, R. Baldwin and W. Owen, a second edition was published, and it continued to appear regularly on Newbery's list, reaching a twelfth edition by 1767. Published at sixpence (with ball and pincushion eightpence), it contained (judging from the earliest surviving complete copy dated 1767) alphabets, moral maxims, verses, proverbs, and four Aesopian fables, as well as letters from Jack-the-Giant-killer, which had little to do with fairy-lore, conveying nothing more exciting than advice about behaviour. It had two features, however, which set it apart: a familiar and friendly style, and descriptions in verse of the games of every kind which children enjoy. Rough little cuts illustrate each game, and there are maxims appended, these often being much less apt than the pictures. There is nothing of notable literary quality about the book, but it has a pervasive spirit of play and open-air enjoyment never overshadowed by the frequent moralities. The alphabet rhyme already quoted from it illustrates its cheerful tenor.

Newbery followed *A Little Pretty Pocket-Book* with a regular output of publications for boys and girls, producing in his lifetime more than forty little works which mingled instruction with amusement, and nearly always successfully avoiding dullness. Most of them were very small (about four by two and a half inches) and gay in covers of flowered and gilt paper. According to Francis Newbery, the publisher's son, they sold in their thousands.[1] Most of them were frequently reissued. So well read and much handled were they that the more popular items have rarely survived in early editions, and some are only available in later versions printed by Newbery's immediate successors. It is a tribute to their attractiveness and contemporary appeal. Those that have endured best are naturally the more educational in their purpose – the spelling books, dictionaries, histories, Scripture abridgments, and that compendium of knowledge for the young scholar, *The Circle of the Sciences*, further described in a later chapter.

Between 1744 and his death in 1767, John Newbery established the young reader's right to have books published regularly – books which are the ancestors of the story books of everyday life enjoyed today. He showed that books for young people must be properly designed and marketed, and that they could be a steady source of profit. He looked for worldly success but he was more than an opportunist, for his books reveal a genuine affection for boys and girls and a real understanding of what appeals to childish fancy, as far as this might be indulged in a rational age. To his little readers he inscribed

---

[1] Welsh, pp. 22–23 (Bibl. 105).

himself 'Your Friend' or 'Your old Friend' as he exhorted them to be good. The pages of his books are full of playful and humorous touches and he well knew the fascination that animals and quaint names have for the young mind. There is the giant, Woglog, Tommy Trip who rides upon his dog, Jouler, old Zig Zag, who understands the speech of birds and beasts, Tom Telescope, the young master who investigates the Newtonian universe, Nurse Truelove, Giles Gingerbread, the boy who literally lived upon learning by eating his gingerbread letters as he learnt them, Margery Meanwell, better known as Goody Two-shoes, and others. Animals take a leading part in some stories, especially in Goody Two shoes' famous history, where Jumper the dog, Ralph the raven, Tippy the lark, Willy the lamb and Tom Pidgeon help Mrs. Margery when she attains the dignity of village schoolmistress. The necessary admonition is also there, but it is administered with a light hand, making good conduct into something of a game.

Newbery's enterprise in launching the first periodical for children – *The Lilliputian Magazine* – has been referred to above. This has been ascribed, with other Newbery books for children, to Oliver Goldsmith (1728–1774), but its date (1751) precludes the possibility. It is probably largely the work of the poet, Christopher Smart, soon afterwards to be Newbery's son-in-law. Goldsmith was not to meet Newbery for another eight years, and he was as yet in Ireland. It was early in 1759 that Goldsmith began to contribute to various Newbery publications and become involved with the publisher in the financial intricacies described in the Newbery biography by Charles Welsh. He very likely wrote several of the later Newbery books for children, as well as those few traced to him. It has been claimed that Goldsmith penned the greatest of them – the once-famous but now forgotten *History of Little Goody Two-shoes* (1765). But it has also been attributed to Griffith or Giles Jones and to Newbery himself. It was the novelist who testified to Newbery's prowess in his *Vicar of Wakefield* (1766), where Newbery appears as 'the philanthropic bookseller of St. Paul's Churchyard, who has written so many little books for children . . .'

Although the authorship of *Goody Two-shoes* remains a mystery, there is no doubt about its quality and importance in the evolution of a literature for children. F. J. Harvey Darton has given the best assessment and description of it in his chapter on John Newbery in his *Children's Books in England* (Bibl. 5). 'It was almost the first piece of English fiction deliberately written to amuse children only', he states. A claim might be made for Sarah Fielding's connected story of incidents among girls at school, *The Governess* (1749), but very little else could rival it. There had been homilies, fragments, fables, short tales, and medleys, but nothing, not even *The Governess*, had the charm or continuity of this long complete tale about Margery Meanwell and her rise from obscurity to grandeur.

The book was announced to the world in the *London Chronicle* at the end of December 1764 as being in the press and speedily to be published, and there is some evidence from later editions that it was not issued until April 1765. A unique copy of the first edition (bearing the date 1765) has not long ago come to light and been acquired by the British Museum (Bibl. 103). By 1766 it was in a third edition, and although like other Newbery books, *Goody Two-shoes* bears the marks of its period, its charm of style, humour and feeling ensured it a longer life than its companions on Newbery's shelves. Its appeal to the discriminating is witnessed by Charles Lamb, who praised it in a letter to Coleridge in 1802, when he lamented that it was almost out of print, banished with other classics of the nursery by 'Mrs. Barbauld's stuff'.[1]

The narrative is as much concerned with social matters as with individuals, and its gifted author, whoever he may have been, brings to life rural England in the eighteenth century, revealing his sympathy with a virtuous and hard-working peasantry, dispossessed under inclosure by harsh landlords. Villainy is personified in the landowner, Sir Timothy Gripe, and in Farmer Graspall, and innocent poverty and goodness in the orphan heroine, little Margery (better known as Goody Two-shoes), her brother Tommy, and the good clergyman and his wife who befriend them while they can. The felicities of style and the sentiments call to mind *The Deserted Village*, by Goldsmith, which was to be published in five years' time, and fix its rank as a minor classic. There are plenty of features in this tale to endear it to the young reader, and the woodcuts, crude as they are, really play a part in the story. When little Tommy is made a sailor, there he can be seen in uniform and tricorn hat. 'Pray look at him', bids the text. Another affecting little scene shows how Tommy wiped away Margery's tears – 'thus' – with the end of his jacket when he leaves her to go away to sea.

The story tells how poor orphan Margery, whose father had died of a violent fever 'in a place where Dr. James' Fever Powder was not to be had', gets her two shoes instead of half-a-pair, learns to read, becomes 'a trotting tutoress' and teaches children, not merely their letters but lessons for the conduct of life, with wise sayings such as –

> 'He that will thrive
> Must rise by five'.

Ghosts and superstitions are a target for the author's ridicule, particularly in the chapter where Margery is shut in the church after Lady Ducklington's funeral. The 'thing' she hears in the dark turns out to be Snip the dog, so they both go to sleep in the pulpit, until Margery alarms the village by ringing the bell. Little Goody is sure there are no ghosts to frighten good children and eighteenth century common sense is firmly in control. Later on the heroine is accused of witchcraft, but this comes about because ignorant folk do not know that her 'charm' to tell the weather is not sorcery but a barometer. She has now

---

[1] *Letters of Charles Lamb*, vol. 1, p. 326. (Bibl. 148).

become the head of an Academy where the animals she has rescued from cruel boys help her to run the school. At last she wins the reward of all her industry and virtue by marrying the Lord of the Manor. As Lady Jones she is left a widow, and can show the true use of riches by doing much good. Tommy the little sailor has returned, and (in the third edition) tells the story of how he made his fortune. Villainy comes to a bad end, for Sir Timothy falls on hard times and Graspall has to seek the help of the parish. Margery, displaying true Christian forbearance, has no wish for revenge on them for their unkind treatment of her, and desires that the farmer's children 'might be treated with care and tenderness'. This brief outline of the plot can give little idea of the charm of the *History of Little Goody Two-shoes* set forth according to its title-page –

'for the Benefit of those
Who from a State of Rags and Care,
And having Shoes but half a Pair;
Their Fortune and their Fame would fix,
    And gallop in a Coach and Six'.

'See the Original Manuscript in the Vatican at Rome' – it goes on – 'and the Cuts by Michael Angelo'. Such absurdities very often embellished Mr. Newbery's press notices and publications for youth.

'Trade and Plumb Cake for ever. Huzza!' runs the slogan on the frontispiece of the *Twelfth Day Gift* (1767). It sums up the famous publisher's attitude to this matter of books for boys and girls. Selling his wares was just as important as their making. A favourite device was to draw attention to other publications on his list in the unfolding of some little history, as in the *Valentine's Gift* (1765). Here Mr. Worthy relates how, as a little boy who hated school, he was taken into a closet where 'all Mr. Newbery's books lay in the window'. He became very interested in them and in the various Newbery characters, and before dinner he had read *Nurse Truelove's Christmas Box* with such avidity that he could not spare time to drink a dish of chocolate. Trade was a vital business, but Newbery did not forget the attraction of 'plumb cake' where his little readers were concerned.

It must be remembered that John Newbery's books were designed to meet the needs of his time, and that they were limited in their appeal to the growing middle-class, who required for their offspring books in keeping with their own aims and ethics; so that his books, like most children's books of every generation ever since, have vanished with the society for which they were fitted. What he began, however, in the production of attractive books for the young 'Masters and Misses' of his day became a permanent part of the book trade. So he was responsible for the real beginning of children's publishing.

It is fitting therefore that the name of John Newbery should be honoured and preserved among those now concerned with books for youth. This has been done in the United States by the institution of a 'John Newbery' Medal, awarded since 1921 for the most distinguished book to be published each year in that country. The New England printer, Isaiah Thomas, of Worcester, Massachusetts, had introduced many of the Newbery books to American children in the latter part of the eighteenth century, and more will be given about his activities in the chapter on North America. Today the seal 'Newbery Medal Award' on English editions or imported copies of some outstanding American publications for children is a welcome reminder over here of the name of the enterprising publisher who issued and sold so many gay little books at his bookshop under the shadow of St. Paul's over two hundred years ago.

III   THE CHRISTIAN TRADITION – FROM ISAAC WATTS TO THE SUNDAY SCHOOLS

The beginning of a truly secular literature for children in the eighteenth century did not mean that religious teaching was no longer regarded as important. It was to be a very strong influence on the making of books for the young for another century and more, although, as time elapsed, religion tended to become more and more what it is today – a separate class among many types of publications for children, not an integral part of their books. But the fervour of belief was fading under the Georges – religious enthusiasm was out of fashion. Nevertheless, Christianity and its teaching were deemed essential for the unsophisticated, although very often in a milder and gentler form than the hell-fire doctrines of the previous age. Locke, the apostle of toleration, was a supporter of these more liberal views of the faith, but he firmly advocated a Christian education and the reading of the scriptures. In the new Charity Schools, established under Queen Anne, children were given Testament or Bible, and that popular treatise on holy living – *The Whole Duty of Man*, first published in 1658, and frequently reprinted for later generations.

Boys and girls in more affluent circles than the Charity Schools were intended for – the fortunate possessors, perhaps, of some of the Newbery books, or similar new-style productions – would usually find there many reminders about the need for piety and Christian observances. 'All good Boys and Girls say their Prayers at Night and in the Morning, which makes God Almighty love and bless them' runs the text on a page of of *A Little Pretty Pocket-Book*. Shorn of fiercer implications, the teaching of religious faith was still very much a characteristic of books for boys and girls in the Newbery era.

Former Puritan traditions and more orthodox beliefs, however, still remained a vital force, to be revived by the Evangelical movement at the end of the century. Sectarian controversies and uncompromising theology, if less prominent, were still very much alive, as can be witnessed by the continued popularity of such books as Janeway's *Token*

53

for Children, and the ready sale of sensational chapbooks telling of saintly prodigies and the awful fate of sinners, such as *The Children's Example*, (ca. 1700) where Mrs. Johnson's pretty innocent child eludes the snares of Satan, is warned by an angel of her approaching death, and by her dying words encourages other children to escape damnation.

Early in the eighteenth century these Puritan elements in literature for the young were shaped into a new and appealing form by the great hymn-writer and non-conformist divine, Dr. Isaac Watts (1674–1748). In *Divine Songs, attempted in easy language for the Use of Children* (1715) he succeeded in presenting to childish understanding, easy-to-learn, rhythmical verses, in simple language, setting down religious lessons in a new way. They were much to be learnt by heart in nurseries and schoolrooms for nearly two hundred years. Although these verses have been much imposed upon young folk by their elders, for the first time they had religious rhymes they could grasp and enjoy. Sometimes the sentiments recall the old theology of fear, not the more rational and gentler gospel of love. There are harsh warnings against sin, for example –

> 'The Lord delights in them that speak
>   The words of truth; but every liar
> Must have his portion in the lake
>   That burns with brimstone and with fire.
>
> Then let me always watch my lips
>   Lest I be struck to death and hell
> Since God a book of reckoning keeps
>   For every lie that children tell.'

Watts dedicated his collection of verses to the three young daughters of Sir Thomas and Lady Abney, whose guest he was at Theobalds, their country-seat in Hertfordshire, for many years until his death. To scare them and 'all the children that shall read these *Songs* to furnish their memories and beautify their souls like yours . . . ' was not his intention. He believed in a God of retribution, but also in a God of love, an omnipotent being who had created the wonders of the earth and sky, who 'will not disdain to hear an infant sing'. There is charity and joy, as well as threats of punishment for wrongdoing, in these rhymes, but the modern reader may well find them complacent, even arrogant.

> 'Lord, I ascribe it to thy Grace
>   And not to chance as others do
> That I was born of Christian race,
>   And not a heathen or a Jew.'

Marred as they are now by such outmoded theological conceptions, at their best these *Songs* by Watts put into words suitable for a child something of the wonder and humility of the young soul before the majesty and mystery of God's creation.

Watts expressed his aim in the preface addressed to all concerned in the education of

Song XXIII.

OBEDIENCE TO PARENTS.

LET children that would fear the Lord
Hear what their teachers say ;
With reverence meet their parents' word,
And with delight obey.

73   K

9. *From a Victorian edition of* DIVINE SONGS *(1866)*

children. He wanted the songs to be a diversion, and hoped that one would be learned every week. To the hymns he appended several moral songs, adding to them after the first edition, and intending them to deliver children 'from the temptation of learning idle, wanton or profane songs'. These moral songs endured longer than the hymns. Two of them, 'Tis the voice of the sluggard', and 'How doth the little busy bee' have been immortalised by Lewis Carroll in his parodies of them in *Alice's Adventures in Wonderland*. By that time, a hundred and fifty years after they were written, Watts' verses were made into some very prettily illustrated volumes for Victorian nurseries. Alice and her young friends would know them very well.

Some of Watt's lines may still be remembered, as from frequent repetition they have almost become sayings of the language, such as –

> 'Birds in their little nests agree
>   And 'tis a shameful sight
> When children of one family
>   Fall out and chide and fight'.

Most charming of all his verses is the cradle hymn beginning

> 'Hush! my dear, lie still and slumber
>   Holy angels guard thy bed!
> Heav'nly blessings without number
>   Gently falling on thy head.'

Watts' *Songs* deserved their immediate and lasting popularity, and they had a wide influence on the making of verse for children, inspiring many imitators. Almost forgotten today, they mark the beginning of versemaking with a genuine feeling for the mind of the child.

None of the versifiers for youth who followed Watts was able to capture his pleasing and easy style until the Taylor sisters set a new standard in the field nearly a century afterwards. The volumes of religious verses which appeared during the century were mostly quickly forgotten. John Wright's *Spiritual Songs for Children* (1728) was closer in spirit to Bunyan and the seventeenth century than to Watts. Another non-conformist divine, Philip Doddridge, attempted *The Principles of the Christian Religion* in 'plain and easy verse' for the young. Published in 1751, this was soon forgotten. The same year another little volume of verses made a wider appeal, reaching a seventh edition by 1767. This was *Visions in Verse for the Enlightenment of younger Minds*, by the St. Albans physician who cared for William Cowper in his madness – Dr. Nathaniel Cotton. Published anonymously, these nine 'visions' outline moral qualities in the typical style of the day, praising temperance, simplicity and virtue, and presenting a hazy rose-tinted religion, more to the prevailing taste than the fire and brimstone threats of Janeway and Watts. More inspired and far-seeing than all this minor religious verse, however, is the little book of poems, written not long before his death, by Christopher Smart – *Hymns for the Amusement of Children*, published by his brother-in-law, Thomas Carnan, at the end of 1770.

John Newbery and his family had for some years become estranged from the poet, who had married the publisher's step-daughter, Anna Maria Carnan, in 1752. Separated from his wife and fallen on evil times, after bouts of religious mania and madness, Smart was befriended by Carnan and asked to prepare something for publication. These *Hymns* (most of them written in a debtors' prison, where he died the next year) were the outcome. Smart put something of his lifelong religious musings and experience into these simple verses, expressing a spirit of charity and a childlike faith in God's love. Foreshadowing Blake, these verses have little of the admonitory tone of Watts and the orthodox school. 'O give us Grace to love' is his cry, and unlike Watts he would embrace heathen and Jew and all men in his plea for mercy and blessing. These poems are naïve at times, but expressive of deep and sincere religious feelings. They range beyond childish comprehension, but the language is direct and much of the matter appealing, as in the stanzas on 'Mirth', which end –

> 'With white and crimson laughs the sky
>   With birds the hedgerows ring.
> To give the praise to God most high
> And all the sulky fiends defy,
>   Is a most joyful thing.'

Half-visionary, half madman, Smart was a true poet. There are gleams reminiscent of his famous *Song to David* in these Hymns. And in his sense of the union of God with nature, he anticipates the romantic and imaginative approach to life and literature of the coming century.

As the eighteenth century advanced, this growing sensibility to the beauty of nature increasingly affected writings for children. Smart was not alone in presenting to children divinity and love revealed in the natural world. Mrs. Barbauld, born Anna Laetitia Aikin (1743–1825), was a Unitarian writer who became much involved in her younger days with the education of small children, teaching little boys at her husband's school in Suffolk soon after her marriage. She became a pioneer in the making of suitable books for the very young, and she is also important as a writer for children who attempted to awaken their thoughts of God in an imaginative way. 'A child, to feel the full force of the idea of God, ought never to remember when he had no such idea', she wrote in her preface to her *Hymns in Prose* (1781). Such a feeling must come early to the child, she avowed, associated with 'all that a child sees, all that he hears, all that affects his mind with wonder and delight'. Wonder and delight: these words kindle expectations, like a beacon. And although rationalist views prevented her giving them full expression, they show something of her sympathy with the needs of infancy.

She paid her tribute to Watts, but chose to present her hymns in a rhythmical prose, as she considered poetry should be 'elevated in thought and style'. Her phrases may sound a little pompous, but she set before the child a religion of solace and serenity, eschewing doctrinal matters and warnings of damnation. God is presented as omniscient and loving, greater than all the lovely and powerful beings on earth. He takes care of all creatures in sleep, he lives in the stars. Death is a despoiler, but the child must not weep, for Jesus has conquered death.

These rapt musings about God and nature were much to popular taste, and Mrs. Barbauld's *Hymns* reached a twenty-fourth edition by 1824, and was still reprinted for Victorian children. 'Nothing, o child of reason, is without God – let God therefore be in all thy thoughts' is a central theme of these little studies, which express an idyllic faith and a sincere appreciation of the beauty of the natural world. 'Her feeling for the poetry of nature', wrote Florence V. Barry of Mrs. Barbauld, 'was the nearest approach to a Renaissance of Wonder in children's books'.[1]

Influenced by Rousseau, and akin to Wordsworth in her approach to religion and nature, Mrs. Barbauld's ideas have more in common with the 'moral school' of writers described in the next chapter than with orthodox Christian writers for youth.

Important influences for the promulgation of older authoritative Christian tenets were emerging as the eighteenth century elapsed. A new fervour was arising in religion, manifested in the preaching of John Wesley and the rise of Methodism, and also in the Evangelical movement which followed in the Church of England. This revival of faith was allied to increasing philanthropic activity and service in promoting education, evoked by the social evils caused by the Industrial Revolution and other circumstances which led to distress among the poorer classes. Among the efforts for their amelioration, with important consequences for children and their reading, was the establishment of Sunday Schools.

Sunday Schools were not an innovation when Robert Raikes, the Gloucester printer and newspaper proprietor, started his scheme there in 1780, but it was Raikes' publicity and encouragement which resulted in a general movement for their institution all over the country. The printer confessed that his enterprise was accidental rather than planned. 'Some business leading me one morning into the suburbs of the city, where the lowest of the people (who are principally employed in the pin-manufactory), chiefly reside, I was struck with concern at seeing a group of children at play in the street. I asked an inhabitant whether those children belonged to that part of the town, and lamented their misery and idleness – 'Ah, Sir!' said the woman to whom I was speaking, 'Could you take a view of this part of the town on a Sunday, you would be shocked indeed; for then the street is

[1] *A Century of Children's Books*, p. 149 (Bibl. 3).

filled with multitudes of these wretches, who released on that day from employment, spend their time in noise and riot, playing at chuck, and cursing and swearing in a manner so horrid, as to convey to any serious mind an idea of hell, rather than any other place'.[1]

It was to check 'this deplorable profanation of the Sabbath' that Raikes formulated his plan. This was to employ women who could teach reading to accept children on a Sunday, on payment of a shilling for their services. The co-operation of the local clergy was sought, and very soon Sunday Schools spread rapidly. Mrs. Trimmer established her schools at Brentford in 1782, and Hannah More, a well-known writer associated with the 'Clapham Sect' of Evangelicanism, began her schools in the Mendips soon after she had settled at Cowslip Green late in the 1780s. A Sunday School Society was in being in 1785, and by 1797 there were 1086 schools attended by 69 000 pupils. Raikes' estimate of a quarter of a million children at 'these little seminaries' in 1787 is now considered to be much exaggerated.[2] In 1803 the Sunday School Union was founded to co-ordinate and support much pioneer and local effort, and the number of pupils was then approaching 850 000.[3]

The early Sunday Schools did not confine their activities to children or to religious instruction, although the payment of teachers soon gave way to the voluntary principle. These schools were often the only means the working classes, young and old, had for learning to read, and although, like the earlier Charity Schools, Christian teaching was their prime purpose, the Sunday Schools served secular needs by providing the elements of instruction. Especially was this so before the movement for voluntary day schools was well established in the first half of the nineteenth century.

One of the earliest and most notable writers of children's books to be inspired by the needs of the new Sunday Schools, was Mrs. Trimmer. Sarah Trimmer, born Kirby (1741–1810), began her writings with *An Easy Introduction to the Knowledge of Nature* (1780), prompted by Mrs. Barbauld's *Lessons for Children* (1778–9), and the needs of her own children. In it she had outlined a slight sketch of Scripture history, and she developed this further in her *Sacred History selected from the Scriptures* . . . published in six volumes, 1782–6. Its aim was to interpret the Bible to youth and 'immature minds'. Later she was responsible for the issue of a series of prints on both sacred and profane history (with lessons to accompany them) for display in nurseries and schoolrooms.

Her publications for Christian education and Sunday Schools were soon to be taken up by the *Society for Promoting Christian Knowledge*, an Anglican institution founded in 1699 to promote the Charity Schools, and now to be revivified to help Sunday Schools and

---

[1] *Gentleman's Magazine*, June. 1784, pp. 410–411.

[2] Jones, M. G., *The Charity School movement*, p. 153 (Bibl. 110).

[3] Ellis, Alec. *A History of Children's reading and literature*, p. 2 (Bibl. 9).

other evangelical causes. On their approved list of publications published at the end of *Some Account of the Life and Writings of Mrs. Trimmer* (1814) (Bibl. 122) were included the author's manual of Sunday School organisation and management, *The Oeconomy of Charity* (1786), various aids to teachers, scripture abridgements, prints, lessons, spelling books and other works helpful to the Sunday School teacher or scholar. The S.P.C.K. were also to step up their own publishing, later rivalling the Religious Tract Society in the issue of cheap little works of piety and self-improvement.

Mrs. Trimmer was one of the earliest writers to supply the schools before the prolific issue of tracts and similar material. She never flagged in her energies. Her devotion to the cause she had at heart, and her achievements in a period when the betterment of the poor and unlettered was left almost entirely to voluntary effort, win admiration and respect. Her opposition to fairy tales, vividly described by Darton, may prejudice many readers against her, but, as he admits, 'The importance of Sarah Trimmer is that she *was* important'.[1]

A firm supporter of the Church of England, she was a stalwart opponent of Rousseauist ideas, and she became increasingly alarmed about the rising number of 'unsound books' being published for children about the turn of the century. It was to counteract this mischief that she founded her second periodical, *The Guardian of Education* (1802–6). From 1788–9 she had edited *The Family Magazine*, designed 'for the use of the servant's hall or kitchen', and in it she had begun her guidance in reading. Now in *The Guardian of Education* she firmly set before her public orthodox judgments on contemporary books intended for children and young people. With unfailing zeal she showed herself to be a biased but enthusiastic pioneer in the systematic reviewing of juvenile literature, and this will be referred to again later.

Mrs. Trimmer is best remembered, however, not for her work for Sunday Schools, her manuals of instruction, or her reviewing, but for the story *Fabulous Histories* (1786), later known and prized in Victorian nurseries as *The History of the Robins*. It was designed for her own large family, who had expressed a wish that animals could talk. Love of nature and kindness to 'the brute creation' were part of her creed, and she had pointed out to the lower orders their duty to be kind to animals in *The Two Farmers*, published the same year as her story about the robins. This more famous and enduring tale, dedicated to the Princess Sophia, preached the same lesson to young gentlemen and ladies of more elevated circles, and it will be described further with the development of the animal story.

The spread of cheap literature of an irreligious or subversive nature was looked upon as a real danger to the welfare of society at the end of the eighteenth century. The ferment of revolutionary ideas which had brought about the Revolution in France was regarded as a

---

[1] *Children's Books in England*, pp. 96, 160 (Bibl. 12).

threat to established order everywhere, especially after violence and terror had succeeded to hopes of liberty and enlightenment. To counteract these influences harmful to morality, religion, and the established order, it was apparent that something more was needed for the guidance of the masses than Sunday Schools and charitable works. The answer was the circulation of religious literature to rival the less wholesome wares of the chapmen.

'Vulgar and indecent penny books were always common', wrote Hannah More to Zachary Macaulay in 1796, 'but speculative infidelity, brought down to the pockets and capacities of the poor, forms a new era in our history'.[1] Hannah More (1743–1833), an influential member of the 'Clapham Sect' and a well-known writer of her day, was not alone in her alarm at the effects of unsuitable publications on the poorer classes now learning to read and in the belief that all the work of the Sunday Schools would be ineffective without 'safe books' being provided, but she had the energy and ability to turn her theories into action. She saw that instructional and devotional works were not enough – fiction and interesting stories and ballads were needed to oust the vulgar, trashy or anti-religious pamphlets which appealed to the public, and it was chiefly due to her that the series of 'Cheap Repository Tracts' was launched. These productions imitated the chapbooks in appearance and price (necessary features if they were to rival them on the market), and they presented the benefits of religion, sobriety and honest industry in tales of vigorous action, well-constructed in plot, and narrated in simple and direct style. The project, launched in March 1795, was amazingly successful, 300 000 copies of the tracts being sold within the first six weeks, and two million within a year. First marketed through Hazard of Bath, and by John Marshall in London, over a hundred were published by 1798, when the series came to an end. But the venture had paved the way for the formation of the Religious Tract Society in 1799, and henceforth a steady supply of suitable and cheap little books to help the work of the Sunday Schools and to promote the Christian education of young and old was assured.

The 'Cheap Repository Tracts', especially the more popular titles, were reprinted many times in the nineteenth century. They were not addressed to children, but to the poorer classes generally, to whom they brought a message of faith and hope to enable them to bear their hardships and improve their situation by industry and pious living. There was no suggestion that anything might be done to alter the social order. This complacency may now strike a repellent note, but Hannah More (who wrote many of the tracts herself under the pseudonym 'Z') and her collaborators did something to expose to the world the misery of the labouring classes, and by portraying their humanity and their virtues, as well as their weaknesses, showed the wealthy their duty and responsibilities. One of the earliest and most famous of the tracts, *The Shepherd of Salisbury Plain* (1795),

[1] Spinney, C. H., *Cheap Repository Tracts* (Bibl. 119).

THE
HISTORY
OF
TOM WHITE,
THE
POSTILION.

Sold by S. HAZARD,
(PRINTER to the CHEAP REPOSITORY for Religious and Moral
Tracts,) at BATH;
By J. MARSHALL,
At the CHEAP REPOSITORIES, No. 17, Queen-street Cheapside,
and No. 4, Aldermary Church Yard; and R. WHITE, Piccadilly,
LONDON; and by all Booksellers, Newsmen, and Hawkers, in
Town and Country.
☞ Great allowance to Shopkeepers and Hawkers.
Price 1d. or 4s. 6d. per 100. 2s. 6d. for 50. 1s. 6d. for 25.
[Entered at Stationers Hall.]

10. *An original 'Cheap Repository Tract' (1795)*

depicts the efforts of an honest labourer to maintain his family on a wage of ten shillings a week. *The History of Hester Wilmot* (1797), also written by Hannah More, describes the good influence of Sunday School and religion on the eldest child of ungodly parents, and the transformation her new way of life makes in their lives. Hard work, temperance, humility, and unselfishness are virtues to bring contentment – so these little tales demonstrate. Some were treated as serials, and Watts' *Divine Songs* was issued early in the series.

There was no intention of educating poor people or their children beyond their station. Hannah More's aim was similar to that of Mrs. Trimmer and other philanthropists – 'to infuse principles of Christianity' among the lower orders. And whatever other books might be provided, a sound knowledge of scripture was the basis of their system. Tracts and Sunday School publications were now to be in constant demand, and other publishers soon entered the field. The S.P.C.K. began to increase its output, and there were provincial firms, such as Houlston of Wellington (Salop), which specialised in the trade. Houlston had a London house by 1828, and published many penny books for Sunday Schools by Mrs. Sherwood and her sister, Mrs. Cameron.

The work of Mrs. Sherwood (born Martha Mary Butt, 1775–1851) properly belongs to the nineteenth century, but as a writer for children she is so much concerned with Christian teaching and the aims of the Sunday School movement that her books can perhaps be best considered here. More austere and Calvinistic in her theology than either Sarah Trimmer or Hannah More, she shares with them the gift of writing correct and clear English prose. A daughter of the rectory, she recalls in her journal her early delight in her beloved Teme valley, bounded by the distant Malvern hills. Strict discipline was combined with parental kindness in her upbringing, and she remembered her childhood as a time of happiness. From her earliest days she made up stories.

As a young girl Mrs. Sherwood confessed she liked finery and pleasure. But by 1801 when the family had moved to Bridgnorth, and she was twenty-six, she wrote in her journal – 'Lucy (her sister) and I had begun to suspect that a life of worldly pleasure was not agreeable to God'.[1] She and her sister eagerly accepted an invitation to take charge of the local Sunday School, and it was for her pupils there that she designed her first book, *The History of Susan Grey*, published by Hazard of Bath in 1802. Its author later realised its imperfections – she thought it showed inexperience and that it touched on things she would rather choose to avoid. It is a tale in the tradition of the pious histories of the seventeenth century (a style which was to inspire much Sunday School literature), telling of youthful piety and early death. Susan, an example to all the village girls, is only in her twentieth year, when after many trials and victories over temptation, she is laid beside her parents in the churchyard. Didactic as it is, it has a vitality and simplicity of style which were to be characteristic of all Mrs. Sherwood's writings for youth.

In 1803, Miss Butt married her cousin, Henry Sherwood, an army officer, and two years later she sailed for India. Already she was firmly set upon her life's work as teacher and writer. On the journey she read *The Arabian Nights'* – and although she later realised that the tales were not 'correct' for young people, she confesses 'I was so little aware of it, that I never withheld the books from my own children'.

She had begun her second story, *The History of Lucy Clare*, first published in 1815, a story of piety and filial affection, set in the Teme valley, like *Susan Grey*. Very soon she became deeply concerned with the instruction of the children of the soldiers. She had her own children to care for and educate also, and she lost her second child, Henry, as an infant. But neither family duties, nor sorrows, nor the climate of India prevented her from carrying out her self-imposed tasks. She became more and more convinced of the depravity of human nature. Original sin was very real and terrible, and she was much influenced in these beliefs by Henry Martyn, the great missionary, when he came to Cawnpore. It was he who inspired her to write *The Indian Pilgrim* (an imitation of Bunyan for Hindus), written in 1810, and first published in 1817. The conversion of the heathen became a prime duty and this was the theme of one of Mrs. Sherwood's most famous stories, *Little Henry and his Bearer* (1814), the first missionary tale for children. This narrative describes the life and death of a pious little English boy, and the conversion of his Indian bearer to the Christian faith, but it does more than show the author's concern for the Christian religion as the only way to salvation. It recreates the Indian scene and tells a story in vivid phrases.

On her return to England in 1816, Mrs. Sherwood found her writings much in demand, and within the next thirty years, tracts, penny stories, and longer tales flowed from her copious pen. She was also much occupied in training her own family, her system mixing

---

[1] *The Life and Times of Mrs. Sherwood, 1775–1851: from the diaries of Captain and Mrs. Sherwood.* (Bibl. 120).

fun and charades with a strict upbringing of Bible reading and prayers. For some years she kept a school.

Though constantly preoccupied with Christian doctrine and the need to stamp out evil passions and original sin, Mrs. Sherwood exhibited true quality as a writer for youth. She could draw child characters in a convincing way, and tell a story felicitously. Her most popular and enduring book, *The History of the Fairchild Family*, may well be hailed as one of the first real family stories for children. Children are depicted there as real persons, not as puppets created for a purpose. She had begun the work in India, and the first part of the story came out in 1818, to be followed by two further parts much later, in 1842 and 1847, the last being completed by her daughter. The author makes plain her intention on the title-page, where the book is described as 'a child's manual, being a collection of stories calculated to show the importance and effects of a religious education'. As in many other stories designed for little readers of the middle classes in this period, leisured parents, amply provided with servants, devote much of their time to the upbringing of their family. And for Mrs. Sherwood parental discipline was absolute. Wickedness – such as disobedience, lying, stealing food – is severely punished, but the frightfulness does not end there. These minor misdemeanours not only bring retribution here and now. They lead to eternal damnation.

It is in this atmosphere that the three Fairchild children, Lucy, Emily and little Henry, are reared. Yet they are not cowed and unhappy – or rarely for long. Punishment does not prevent them getting into mischief again and again, and their resilience under the system makes for credibility. The parents are careful to explain why the child is being punished, 'I did not punish you, my child, because I do not love you', says Mrs. Fairchild to her little boy, after she has shut him up without food or drink until dark, for stealing two apples, and lying about the theft, 'but because I wished to save your soul from hell'. There are interpolated tales to underline the awful warnings against sinfulness, and prayers and texts and hymns are inserted to emphasise the religious lessons. Part one ends on a very gloomy note with the episode of 'The Happy Death' – but to the writer it was not at all depressing, for death is not to be feared but welcomed by the child who has found the way to salvation.

One of the most terrible experiences the children are made to undergo is the fearsome visit to the gibbet on Blackwood. To show them the evil effects which can result from giving way to their passions, Mr. Fairchild takes the children, a servant carrying little Henry, to see the corpse of a murderer hanging in chains. This gruesome episode is quoted by Darton in full.[1] But such awful scenes, and threats of retribution in this world and the next, never quite overcome the children's spirit. There is an impression through-

---

[1] *Children's Books in England*, p. 176 (Bibl. 12).

out that basically they feel secure and happy. How can this be? Is it the sense that all the punishments and warnings are manifestations of a deeply felt parental love and intense faith? And that harsh discipline imposed on them is done for their sake? Whatever the reason, the little Fairchilds are a lively and irrepressible trio, and their adventures, later purged of much of the theology and frightfulness, continued to be very popular throughout the nineteenth century. A new edition, suitably edited by Mary E. Palgrave and charmingly illustrated by Florence M. Redland, was issued by Wells Gardner in 1902, and reached an eighth edition by 1931. It is a tribute to Mrs. Sherwood's ability as a writer for children that this book endured so long.

Mrs. Sherwood's attitude to youth and religion are now completely out-of-date, but her didacticism did not prevent her writing many tales, which are little masterpieces of their kind. One of the most appealing is *The Little Woodman and his Dog Caesar* (1818), suggested by the Bible story of Joseph and his brothers. The incident where the abandoned William, left in the forest by his wicked brothers, is saved from the wolf by his faithful dog has the force and suspense of a modern adventure story. But, as usual, the writer must press home the moral, and insert her biblical texts. 'And now, my dear children', she finishes this history of William who repaid evil by good, 'I would have you learn from this story to make God your friend: *for such as be blessed of Him shall inherit the earth: while they that be cursed of Him shall be cut off* (Psa. xxxvii, 22)'.

Mrs. Lucy Cameron (1781–1858), the sister of Mrs. Sherwood, also wrote many tracts and pious little stories and, with Hannah More, these three women writers were the most gifted practitioners in the art of creating something novel in literature for youth – simple, improving and attractive tales designed to interest poorer boys and girls. Their work marks the beginning of a universal cheap literature produced for a new rapidly growing class of readers, the children who were learning to read in the Sunday Schools, and a little later in the voluntary day schools. It is a foreshadowing of the coming era of State Schools, compulsory education, and the great changes of the Victorian age.

IV ROUSSEAU AND THE MORAL SCHOOL

'Reading is the curse of childhood, yet it is almost the only occupation you can find for children. Emile at twelve years old will hardly know what a book is'.[1] If Jean-Jacques Rousseau (1712–1778) intended to startle readers who held conventional views in his epoch-making treatise on education, *Émile* (1762), he certainly succeeded. 'The child who reads ceases to think, he only reads', he inveighs again. 'He is acquiring words, not

---

[1] *Émile*, Bk. II, p. 80 (Bibl. 125).

knowledge'.[1] When Emile is ready for books, he is to be given one book only. No, not the *Bible*, nor *Aesop's Fables*, nor any other approved text for youth. The book chosen is *Robinson Crusoe*. It was plain to the revolutionary thinker that Crusoe, in a harder school than his own imaginary pupil, had learnt realities in a not dissimilar way, by finding self-reliance and lessons for living in his solitary struggle against the forces of nature. It is the kind of book which Emile, brought up amidst natural surroundings to find out things for himself, will be able to appreciate.

In describing Emile's education, which takes place under the guidance of an enlightened tutor (an imperfect substitute, it must be understood, for a parent, and here, Jean-Jacques himself), the author championed the child's right to happiness and freedom. Education should be a joyful experience. The pupil, through exercise of mind and body, close to Nature, the great teacher, may find out all he needs to know – the duties of man. But the tutor must always be close at hand to see that the right experience comes at the right moment.

Notwithstanding its many exaggerations, the influence of Rousseau's treatise on educational theory and practice and on children's books was tremendous. In his outlook Rousseau owed a good deal to Locke, and like the English thinker, he was firmly against fairy tales and fantasy. 'Men may be taught by fables: children require the naked truth'.[2] Aesop and La Fontaine were too difficult for children to understand. He disagreed with Locke in this and other matters, and he broke with the rationalist outlook of the *philosophes*. Imagination was dangerous, he agreed so far with them, but he did not place all his confidence in reason. Feeling, sensibility, the language of the heart, these were things the child could understand, and true guides to living. Under their sway the divine voice of conscience, rather than the intellect, would point the way to virtue and happiness. Control of the passions was the key to felicity: vice and misery followed their indulgence.

Rousseau also saw mankind and childhood corrupted by the artificialities of society, and fashionable life he condemned especially. He would remove the child from the corrupt influences of urban life and bring him up in rural seclusion. Manual work was not to be despised, not even by the wealthy and well-born. Making and doing were to be the bases of the child's progress towards health and virtue. 'He (Emile) must work like a peasant, and think like a philosopher, if he is not to be as idle as a savage'.[3] Such ideas were repellent to both the rationalist and the orthodox, both Catholic and Protestant. The book was burnt by the *Parlement* of Paris, and its author fled to Switzerland.

Rousseau's strictures against society and the contemporary system of education were

---

[1] *Émile*, Bk. III, p. 131. (Bibl. 125).

[2] *Ibid.*, Bk. II, p. 77

[3] *Ibid.*, Bk. III, p. 165

probably less heinous in the eyes of authority than his theistic views, where he discarded dogma and formalism, seeing divine omniscience in everything in creation. He set down his beliefs in *Émile* as 'The Creed of a Savoyard Priest'. God speaks to the heart of man, and man, a free creature, best finds his way to truth by faith in conscience or the inner voice of feeling. Revelation or abstract reason are not necessary to find religious reality. Such unorthodox and liberal ideas, based on the ethics of Christianity, but leaving out most of its dogma, and allied to a reliance on sensibility as a guide to right conduct, pervade many of the moral tales for youth which *Émile* inspired. Not all the philosopher's theories were adopted. Writers modified them to suit their own taste. In particular they ignored his warning against early reading, judging by the number of books soon to be published with the aim of inculcating a Rousseauist love of virtue in young minds.

In France two famous practitioners of education were especially impressed with many of Rousseau's ideas – Arnaud Berquin and Madame de Genlis. Both of them wrote children's books which reveal their indebtedness to the philosopher and which deeply influenced the writing of the moral tale.

Arnaud Berquin (1749–1791), a man of feeling with a tendency towards self-dramatisation, had devoted his life to the cause of youth, and in January 1782 he produced the first number of a periodical work entitled *L'Ami des Enfans*, inspired by German ventures of the same kind, especially *Der Kinderfreund* launched in 1775 by C. F. Weisse. In twenty-four monthly numbers Berquin gave boys and girls in France, and very soon elsewhere, a series of little moral tales, dramas, letters and dialogues, much charged with sensibility. Fairies and wonders are carefully avoided, but tears and exhibitionism abound. Most of the episodes are simply presented, however, with narrative skill, and many concern the relationship of children with ever-watchful parents. To achieve a violent contrast between good and evil ways, everything is much magnified. And the habit of papas and mammas of weeping tears of joy when they find out their child is truthful, benevolent or unselfish is a little embarrassing. Yet these compositions had their merits and they won great esteem in their own day. There are pleasant features to offset the author's unnatural paragons of virtue or fearful examples of wrong-doing and the overheated emotional atmosphere. Berquin had an instinct for the dramatic and a sincere love of nature, and sometimes he paints a charming scene of virtue and truth amid rural simplicity. But he was careful not to attack the social system and his writings very much belong to the pre-Revolutionary era.

L'Ami des Enfans was translated into English and published in London from 1783–1786. Other English versions followed including one by the Rev. Mark Anthony Meilan in 1786. Perhaps the most popular was a selection and adaptation entitled *The Looking Glass for the Mind*, compiled by Richard Johnson, writing under his imposing sobriquet, 'The Rev. W. D. Cooper'. This was published in 1787 by E. Newbery, and re-issued

11. John Bewick's engraving for Flora and her lamb (1792)

with cuts by John Bewick in 1792. Johnson freely adapted and anglicised his originals, and followed this first Berquin selection with another volume on the same pattern, but more of his own invention – *The Blossoms of Morality* (1789), again much enlivened with attractive Bewick cuts seven years afterwards. Johnson preserves Berquin's exaggerated sentiments and situations without his happier style. But true feeling and tenderness light up the drab fabric at times, as in the tale of Flora and her lamb, where a little girl revives an apparently dead lamb, and cares for it. But Baba becomes more than a 'pet. 'In the space of a few years Flora had a very capital flock' – so virtue in this kind of writing is not only to be prized as 'the Fountain of Happiness' but the way to material reward.

Madame La Comtesse de Genlis (1746–1830), Berquin's contemporary, was another well-known personality of her day who turned her attention to pedagogy and the creation of improving literature for youth. She moved in more exalted circles than Berquin, and was so successful with her experiments at Belle-Chasse that her friend, the Duc de Chartres (later the revolutionary Philippe Egalité), made her tutor of his three sons in 1782, when the eldest, the Duc de Valois, was nine years old. The Comtesse believed intensely in practical education, in theatricals, tableaux, wall pictures, and such aids to learning, and in 1779–1780 she brought out a series of moral plays, the *Théâtre d'Education*. She owed as much to Fénelon, the saintly Archbishop of Cambrai, for her ideas about training the young as to Rousseau. Religion she placed as the foundation of her scheme, and constant occupation and surveillance were its main pillars.

Fénelon, whom Rousseau too had venerated, had acted as tutor to a prince nearly a hundred years before Madame de Genlis, his pupil being the grandson and heir of Louis XIV. For the boy he had written a series of fables as well as the more famous *Aventures de Télémaque*. In the fables, first published in 1718, he had been bold enough to use magical and mythical figures to present lessons in morality. Fairies and nymphs use their powers to guide the destiny of mortals, and there are animal fables also, on the Aesopian model. These fables became known in English, and they were also included in the *Cabinets de Fées* in 1785. But *Télémaque* became more influential and more admired. It was much commended for young people for at least a century after its first publication in 1699. Louis XIV saw in it a criticism of his regime and government, and stopped the

Paris printing before it was completed. Fénelon, who was apparently in ignorance that his manuscript had been sent to the press, was in disgrace. The king's action, however, had little effect on its circulation, for complete editions were printed in Brussels and The Hague the same year, and very soon it was translated into English.

This book, originally written for the king's grandson, was an elaboration of the Homeric adventures of the son of Ulysses in quest of his father, and it certainly criticised tyrannical systems of government and self-indulgent luxury in living. Poetic and noble in conception, it is marred by the many pronouncements on conduct by Mentor (the young Telemachus' guide, and the goddess Minerva in disguise). Yet the background of fable and mythology might well be alluring to young readers in a rational age when such lore was rarely put within their reach.

Fénelon had also written a manual on the education of girls (*L'Éducation des Filles*, 1787), which included some perceptive ideas about children's reading, as well as advice on the upbringing of daughters. Madame de Genlis found a good deal to her taste in Fénelon's system of piety, simplicity, and gentle discipline. But her writings show that she also had theories of her own – soon to be famous, not only in France. She put her recommendations in a series of letters addressed to a mother who wanted guidance about her children's education, published as *Adèle et Théodore* (1782). Her most famous work 'proper for infancy' is probably *Les Veillées du Château* (1784), a series of moral stories told by the author in the person of Madame de Clémire, who supplements the teaching of her children at her *château* in the country by evening readings. The children are naturally foolish enough to want fairy tales. Well, they shall be given something more wonderful, for her stories will be true. They will be about marvels, but all will be founded on facts. So Madame de Clémire narrates her wonders – a tree which rains down poison, a palace built of ice, a ball of fire in the sky, a mountain of flame – adding references to their origin in the works of eye witnesses. But the listeners are not entirely satisfied, especially Pulchérie. She interrupts an account of a vision of castles under the sea with a cry of delight. So they are to have a *conte de fée* after all! 'Not at all', replies the unruffled mother, 'this last phenomenon in the same way as all the others is caused by Nature'. 'But the Fairy Morgana. There is such a being?' questions the child hopefully. The answer is firmly in the negative. Only ignorant peasants believe in the fabulous creatures. Fairies are the illusions of poor uneducated people.

The works of Madame de Genlis were very soon available in English and, like Berquin, she had many admirers in this country.

One of the most ardent Rousseauists in England was Thomas Day (1748–1789). He might be termed the English Berquin, for there was much affinity and mutual esteem between the two writers. Day, however, exhibits a more robust and less sentimental strain than Berquin in his writings for youth. He is now chiefly remembered for that once famous moral tale, *The History of Sandford and Merton* (1783–1789).

'Every page is big with truth', he affirmed of *Émile*, and he showed not only by his writing how much he revered the teachings of Jean-Jacques, for he followed the unusual plan of trying to put his philosophical beliefs into everyday living. His personality was a strange mixture of benevolence, sincerity and eccentricity. One of his less successful schemes of practical education was his attempt to rear two orphan girls on the Rousseauist model (the ideal partner for Emile and her training are described at the end of Rousseau's treatise). Day's aim was to mould a suitable wife for himself, but the experimenter was disillusioned at the result, and eventually married an heiress. But he never abandoned his principles, holding to them with a praiseworthy – or obstinate? – tenacity. Eventually they caused his death, when he tried to break a dangerous horse by gentle methods.

Like other disciples, Day could vary the master's tenets to suit his own views. The philosopher had considered that reasoning was beyond a child's capacity, but many of the English moral school of writers, including Day, disregarded this part of his teaching, and leaned more upon the earlier ideas of Locke, who believed that a child could be trained to exercise his judgment from an early age. It was only necessary to show the child the consequences of his actions, then he would quickly discover Rousseau's golden maxim – that goodness brings happiness and wickedness leads to misery. True as this may be in general terms, it was demonstrated with amazing rigidity in fiction for young readers at this period. Cause and effect in behaviour were shown to work with a clockwork precision and inevitability.

The influence of *Émile* is visible throughout *Sandford and Merton*. But Day had another model to inspire him – *The Fool of Quality* (1766–1770), a moral tale about the upbringing and perfecting of the younger son of an earl, by Henry Brooke, another Rousseauist. Day's fictional presentation of education on Rousseau's plan uses the device of contrast – a favourite contrivance of the moral school of writers. It describes the effect of education on two boys, at the outset different in everything but their age. Tommy Merton is the spoilt child of a rich merchant from the West Indies; Harry Sandford, the son of a local farmer, personifies all the Emilean virtues including self-reliance, good-nature, benevolence and courage. Mr. Merton is impressed by Harry's quick action in saving Tommy from a snake, and decides to send his son to be educated with him, in the care of a model tutor, Mr. Barlow, a clergyman.

The story unfolds the transformation of Tommy from a foolish, weak and selfish young gentleman, soft from rich living, into a hardy and virtuous little boy on the Sandford model, who prizes industry, practical knowledge, and benevolent actions instead of finery and wealth. Tommy and Harry tend to be puppets rather than real boys, though Tommy's misfortunes on the road to learning have some liveliness and the pursuits of the boys have some interest. But the narrative is broken up by many interpolations and often tedious digressions, in the form of 'readings', intended to emphasise the moral purpose of the writer. Some episodes, for example 'Androcles and the Lion' and the Highlander's account of his life in the army and encounters with North American Indians, are more entertaining than others. One of the most inept and unsuitable is surely that headed 'History of a surprising cure of the gout'.

Notwithstanding its defects and its over-purposeful nature, *Sandford and Merton* was a great success, and had sufficient vitality to survive throughout the nineteenth century.

Day was particularly in sympathy with Rousseau's attacks on the artificiality of society, and in another tale, *The History of Little Jack* (first published in Stockdale's *Children's Miscellany* in 1787), he chose a more elemental theme – the history of a foundling brought up in the wilds by a pious old man, and suckled by a goat. The virtuous ways the boy learns far from the haunts of men stand him in good stead when the old man dies, and after various adventures as a marine in India, and elsewhere, he comes back to England, goes into business, and makes a fortune. Jack has learnt to look upon idleness and self-indulgence as the great enemies of contentment and success. In later years he often related the story of his life 'in order to prove it is of very little consequence how a man comes into the world, provided he behaves well, and discharges his duty when he is in it'.

The 1780s brought a spate of moral tales and improving histories for boys and girls, besides the works of Berquin, Genlis and Thomas Day. Mrs. Elizabeth Newbery, who continued the publishing business of her husband, Francis Newbery (the nephew of John Newbery), was very active in the last two decades of the century, at her premises at the top of Ludgate Hill (not far from the address in St. Paul's Churchyard where Thomas Carnan still carried on his stepfather's more famous trade). She and her manager employed Richard Johnson to write or adapt many volumes as well as his versions of Berquin, and *The Arabian Nights'*. When Carnan died in 1788, the old firm passed to Newbery's grandson, Francis Power, for several years, but whether it was then taken over by Elizabeth Newbery is now uncertain. Certainly the Newbery name was kept very much alive by the many new volumes she issued for the entertainment and improvement of boys and girls until about 1800, when the business came into the possession of her manager, John Harris.

Another active publisher of moral tales was John Marshall, of Aldermary Churchyard, who issued most of the works of Lady Eleanor Fenn and Dorothy and Mary Kilner, all popular authors of their time even though their identity might be unknown. Few books for children at this period acknowledged their authorship, most disguising their origin under pseudonyms or appearing without any name at all. Lady Fenn, who specialised in simple works to lighten the path to reading, wrote as 'Mrs. Teachwell', 'Mrs. Lovechild' or 'Solomon Lovechild'. She invented many of her little aids for her nieces and nephews.

One of the most well-known was a two-volume composition with the inviting title – *Cobwebs to catch Flies* (1783). A system of graded reading 'in short sentences adapted to children from three to eight years', it offers advice about behaviour as it progresses. This advice is sometimes put into the mouths of the young characters, as in the episode of the two brothers allowed to attend the fair, on condition they do not ride in the merry-go-round. James dissuades his younger brother from disobeying their mother's command. 'How happy I am to have an elder brother who is so prudent', says Ned, but his correct behaviour does not prevent his heart dancing to the notes of the ditty sung by the children being 'tossed'.

The moralising of fairy tales (when they were admitted by the creators of juvenile literature at this period) was recognised as a cunning method of utilising for good the youthful predilection for the fabulous. Lady Fenn, like most of her contemporaries, considered that the only safe fairies to introduce to children were moral guardians, preferably in dreams, when the facts of real life might justifiably be suspended. In *The Fairy Spectator; or, The Invisible Monitor* (1789), Mrs. Teachwell tries to console her pupil, Miss Sprightly, who has dreamed of a lovely gauzy being metamorphosed from a dragon-fly, by inventing something more rational. 'I will write you a dialogue where the fairy shall converse, and I will give you a moral for your dream . . . ' is her promise. And she carries it out, turning the lustre of the dream into very sober daylight. Even a magic rose proves only to be an aid to good conduct, pricking the recipient whenever anything is done amiss – and thoughts as well as actions affect it.

Pseudonyms were a favourite device in these days when the authorship of children's books was regarded as a very inferior branch of writing. The sisters-in-law, Dorothy and Mary Kilner, wrote as 'M.P.' or 'M. Pelham', and 'S.S.' respectively. Like Lady Fenn they were much concerned with guiding the child towards usefulness and good behaviour (and so to happiness), but they were less engaged in teaching the child to read. Both the Kilners wrote with a sedate charm of style, and revealed a perception, ahead of their time, of the things which appeal to children, although sometimes pranks described have an eighteenth century crudity. Fantasy might be taboo, but a young person's attention might be caught by the artifice of letting a mouse tell its own story, or by a peg-top or a pin-cushion having adventures. Their aim was felt to justify such indulgence of childish fancy, and it is expressed very well in the Preface which Dorothy Kilner (1755–1836) wrote for her *Life and Perambulation of a Mouse* (1783). It was 'no less to instruct and improve, than . . . to amuse and divert you. It is earnestly hoped that as you read it, you will observe all the good advice therein delivered, and endeavour to profit by it: whilst at the same time, you resolve to shun every action which renders those who practice them, not only despicable, but really wicked . . . ' Wickedness to the Kilners was a terrible thing and must not be allowed to take root.

72

This popular history of a mouse's adventures is one of the best moral tales of the period, and it is further described with the animal story in a later chapter. Another of Dorothy's books, *The Village School*, is considered with the development of the tale of school life. Both the Kilners wrote some works of rather more serious religious purpose for youth, as well as stories designed to please the reader in the process of his improvement. Mary Kilner (born Maze, 1753–1831)[1] was perhaps a little kinder towards childish inclinations than her sister-in-law. Her *Adventures of a Pincushion* (intended for 'young ladies') and *Memoirs of a Peg-top* were both published early in the 1780s, but perhaps her most pleasing tale is her account of the experiences of a country clergyman's little daughter – *Jemima Placid* (ca. 1785). The heroine, six-year-old Jemima, is a tender-hearted little girl, personifying 'cheerful obligingness', and the sub-title of the tale – 'the Advantages of Good Nature' – indicates the purpose of the writer in telling her experiences. Her estimable character is contrasted with the vanity and ill-manners of her two London cousins, to whom she goes on a long visit when her mother is ill. Mild and unexciting as Jemima's adventures are, there are some sympathetic touches in their presentation, cramped as they are within the moral formula. Jemima may be insufferably good, but she also has childish feelings and weaknesses, and the reader can share them – especially in minor matters, when she says goodbye to her brother's rabbit, chooses presents for her family or receives a new doll.

Less perceptive of childish interests and more uncompromising in her reverence for reason was a more gifted writer – Mary Wollstonecraft (1759–1797), the first wife of William Godwin and the famous champion of women's rights. In *Original Stories from Real Life* (1788), she wrote for the publisher, Joseph Johnson, a moral tale based more firmly on Rousseauist ideas than those written by the Kilners. In Mrs. Mason, who takes charge of the education of Mary and Caroline, she presented the female counterpart of Mr. Barlow, the perfect tutor. The unfailing superiority and stony lack of sympathy with the propensities of youth of this ideal preceptress evoked from E. V. Lucas the epithet 'Gorgon'.[2] The virtues the lady seeks to foster may be excellent, her standards praise-worthy, but in seeking to apply them she lacks the human touch. Mrs. Mason – like many other grown-ups then concerned with the upbringing of children – regarded them as a lower form of life. 'Children must be governed and directed', she declares, 'until their reason gains strength to walk by itself'. Even the Blake engravings added to the 1791 edition, emphasising the tender and more idyllic features of the text, could not humanise the infallible Mrs. Mason. Like Thomas Day, Mary Wollstonecraft introduced various episodes and histories to illustrate different moral qualities for the enlightenment of

[1] Mary Kilner's second name was Ann not Jane. See Jill E. Grey's note, *Book Collector*, Winter 1969, p. 519.
[2] Preface to a reproduction of *Original Stories* (Bibl. 134).

Mrs. Mason's pupils. Two years after its publication she translated from the German a rather more natural story of moral education – *Das Moralische Elementarbuch* (1785), by C. G. Salzmann – giving it an English setting as *Elements of Morality* (1790).

Joseph Johnson, the publisher, whose circle included William Blake, William Godwin, Mary Wollstonecraft, and other rebels against the conventional pattern of society, was soon to introduce a writer for children of rather different quality – Maria Edgeworth (1767–1849). She was later to win fame as a novelist, but now she showed how the moral tale could be transformed by the art of a born storyteller. In an age more favourable to the expression of her natural gifts of humour and imagination, she might have proved a great writer for children. But hampered by the conventions of her time, and much controlled by her revered and overbearing father, she disciplined her effervescent spirit sufficiently to conform to prevailing taste and to satisfy her critical if appreciative parent. Richard Lovell Edgeworth was a powerful personality, benevolent, confident, much interested in mechanical inventions and in education. He was four times married, so that Maria, left motherless at six years old, had a large family of brothers and sisters as audience for her storytelling. Edgeworth also found plenty of opportunity in his family to try out his educational theories with his eldest daughter's assistance. At first he was much dominated by Rousseau, and in his early years he was a close friend of Thomas Day, but later he modified some of his more advanced opinions. In 1798 he produced, in co-operation with Maria, a useful and sensible scheme of training the young – *Practical Education*. 'The general principles that we should associate pleasure with whatever we wish our pupils should pursue, and pain with whatever we wish they should avoid, forms . . . the basis of our plan of education', he wrote in the preface. The ideas behind this system were expressed in the series of tales which Maria produced, first for her family, and then for a wide circle of young readers.

When Maria was fifteen years old she left England with her father and the family to take up residence at the estate he had inherited at Edgeworthstown in Ireland. From the testimony of her letters it was a very happy household. Tears were rare. The Irish countryside and its people were to inspire her finest writings, *Castle Rackrent* (1800) and other novels of Irish life, but most of her writings for boys and girls have an English background.

Her first volumes of 'wee, wee stories', *The Parent's Assistant*, were apparently issued by Johnson in 1795, but no copy of any edition before 1796 has survived. Further tales were added in later editions, and the work contains her best stories for children. Purposeful as they are, with the culmination of rewards for honesty, industry and cheerful good nature, they are written with captivating skill. Her child characters are real beings – not dummies manipulated to point a moral, so often a characteristic of the moral tale by her contemporaries. Miss Edgeworth's good children are seldom prigs, and surprisingly likeable – a rare achievement. Especially attractive is the impulsive Rosamond (said to be founded on the author herself), who so often fails to apply the rational powers her mother is so anxious to cultivate in her. 'Use your judgment, Rosamond', is frequently the only guidance the child is given. So it happens that she chooses the pretty purple jar in the chemist's window instead of a much-needed pair of shoes. The jar turns out to be plain glass, filled with a useless liquid. But Mamma insists that Rosamond must abide by her own choice. It is Rosamond who wins the young reader's sympathy in her struggles and errors in a world where adult common sense is law.

Unpleasant characters in the stories are no less credible, so that the contrast between simple goodness and villainy or selfishness often becomes piquant and exciting. Anne Thackeray Ritchie, in her introduction to the Macmillan edition of 1897 of *The Parent's Assistant*, has expressed the essence of the art of Maria Edgeworth. The stories 'open like fairy tales, recounting in simple diction the histories of widows living in flowery cottages, with assiduous devoted little sons, who work in the garden and earn money to make up the rent. There are also village children busily employed and good little orphans whose parents generally die in the opening pages. Fairies were not much in Miss Edgeworth's line, but philanthropic manufacturers, liberal noblemen, and benevolent ladies in travelling carriages do as well, and appear in the nick of time to distribute rewards or to point a moral . . .'

The quality and readability of the best tales have preserved them for the twentieth century, although the author's long popularity is now only a memory. The last edition of her tales for children was in 1948, when seven stories (all from *The Parent's Assistant*) were issued in the Watergate Classics series, as *Lazy Lawrence and other stories*, the others being *The Orphans*, *The False Key*, *Simple Susan*, *The White Pigeon*, *The Birthday Present* (a Rosamond story), and *Forgive and Forget*. Two of the stories, *The Orphans* and *The White Pigeon* are set in Ireland.

Maria Edgeworth's stories were unequal in merit, and many were so much concerned with education or moral instruction that they have not lasted as long as *The Parent's Assistant*. She wrote a large number to illustrate the theories of education advocated by her father, and this was the purpose of the series, *Early Lessons*. This was published in ten parts in 1801, comprising *Harry and Lucy* (begun by Edgeworth, and finished by his daughter), *Rosamond*, and *Frank*, with a few miscellaneous tales taken from the earliest editions of *The Parent's Assistant*, including the first item in *Rosamond*, the story about the purple jar. Sequels describing the progress and experiences of the same characters when a little older, followed from 1821–1825. *Rosamond* is by far the most lively of the series. *Frank*, designed for young children, is less appealing, although Ruskin praised it in his memories of his childhood reading. The hero is too much the little paragon, naïvely seeking permission for the simplest actions. *Harry and Lucy* is more concerned with the dissemination of practical information and is described in a later chapter.

In 1801 Maria Edgeworth published some stories for older children as *Moral Tales*, and three years later came another series for young people in their teens, *Popular Tales*. Both these collections are more didactic and overdrawn than her stories for younger readers, and her efforts seem to have suffered from more direction from her father, who gave his blessing to both works in the prefaces, indicating the intention 'to display examples of virtue'. Interesting and readable as some of them prove, ranging over a variety of situations and settings, they do not express the humour and charm of this gifted storyteller at her best.

In the new century the writings of Maria Edgeworth eclipsed in demand the works of the pioneer she much admired – Mrs. Barbauld. It was the latter's *Lessons for Children* which had helped to inspire the Edgeworth's series for rather older children – *Early Lessons*. Maria also much valued the long popular *Evenings at Home* (1792–1796) – 'the best book for children of seven to ten that has appeared', according to the preface of *Practical Education*. It was described in the *Monthly Review* (November 1793) as 'a collection of very pretty tales to awaken the growing mind to enquiry and the use of its reasoning powers, and to inspire it with sentiments of humanity, virtue and piety'. The work was chiefly that of Dr. John Aikin, Mrs. Barbauld's brother, but it included a moral fairy tale and thirteen other pieces by his more famous sister. This 'juvenile budget' in six volumes offered entertaining instruction and was constantly reprinted during the nineteenth century.

Mrs. Barbauld's ideas about presenting religion to children at the earliest opportunity did not appeal to the Edgeworths. They preferred to omit the subject entirely in writing for children, not because they opposed religion, but because they felt it was fraught with too much contention and sectarian prejudice – like politics. Maria Edgeworth does not introduce the Deity into her tales – not even 'the Supreme Being' met with in many other moral tales of the period. Thomas Day, in the person of Mr. Barlow, explains to Mr. Merton how unconventional ideas about education can be reconciled with Christian faith. Mary Wollstonecraft uses Mrs. Mason to point out to her young charges that 'the greatest pleasure life affords (is) that of resembling God by doing good'. An undogmatical belief in a wise, all-powerful, beneficent Creator, consistent with a firm reliance on reason rather than revelation, marks the divergence between the Rousseauist school and the orthodox, such as Mrs. Trimmer and Mrs. Sherwood, who wrote for the Sunday Schools. Yet the moral qualities each group sought to foster were very similar.

Maria Edgeworth influenced many writers who followed her, chiefly women. But already when she began authorship many earnest ladies, dedicated to the cause of education and the promotion of virtue, were filling the bookshops with volumes designed 'for the amusement and instruction of young persons'. They usually disguised their identity under pseudonyms, or by such vague descriptions as 'A Mother' or 'A Lady'.

Sometimes they achieved a pleasing clarity of style, or introduced a few natural features to relieve the artificiality of form and plot, but most of their works conform to a very mediocre pattern of humourless and insipid reading. The creator of *Rosamond* and *Simple Susan* may have quickened enthusiasm and inspired imitators, but Miss Edgeworth's daemon, which even the strait-jacket of didacticism could not vanquish, was a will-o'-the-wisp beyond the reach of her contemporaries.

One admirer, who acknowledged her debt, was Mrs. Mary Hughes (formerly Robson). She invented stories for real children, like her exemplar, writing for her nephews and nieces as 'Aunt Mary'. One of her earliest publications was *Aunt Mary's Tales, for the Entertainment and Improvement of Little Girls* (1811). Its engraved frontispiece is typical of the style of the day both in design and subject. Charity to the poor – an essential incident in every moral tale – is here illustrated by the self-denying heroine presenting her untasted dinner to a poor woman with an infant on her lap, and another at her side. Mary Hughes's little puppets have a semblance of life in their progress under the ever watchful eyes of mother or governess – another very familiar feature, this continual supervision by elder folk. So was the author's practice of insinuating bits of information about botany or birds or other subjects in the narrative.

Other influences were still potent. Another contemporary of Maria Edgeworth, Mrs. Mary Pilkington (born Hopkins, 1766–1839), made an abridgement for youth of Marmontel's *Contes Moraux*, and imitated Madame de Genlis with her *Tales of the Cottage* (1798). Among her many writings perhaps the most interesting is a pseudo-Eastern tale, *The Asiatic Princess* (1800), in which a little Siamese princess discovers the west and receives an education 'befitting a future ruler'. Dedicated to the Princess Charlotte, it outlines the experiences of Princess Merjee on her travels through Europe under the guidance of an English lady and her husband, and introduces as her companion a negro girl rescued from slavery. Virtues and vices are painted in very heightened colours by this writer, so much so as to draw adverse comment from such a champion of morality as Mrs. Trimmer.

Mrs. Pilkington wrote many of her tales for a new firm, Vernor and Hood, who published some works in association with the better known house of E. Newbery. In the 1790s E. Newbery issued many moral tales including a popular story by Mrs. Pinchard of Taunton, *The Blind Child; or, Anecdotes of the Wyndham Family* (1791). The writer preferred to be known on the title-page as 'A Lady'. Her aim was to repress the excessive softness which brings evils upon its possessor, and to reveal the nature of true sensibility.

A little later a productive writer of didactic fiction for young people began her career – Mrs. Barbara Hofland (born Wreaks, 1770–1844) who began to write early in the nineteenth century. She ranged over many periods and places, including Asia Minor, Egypt and India, for the scenes of tales presenting the triumph of virtue and industry over difficulties and temptations. Her most famous book, *The Son of a Genius* (1812), is said to have been inspired by the improvident nature of her husband, a landscape painter. It won international fame and was dedicated to her son, then thirteen years old. Its message to the young is to put no trust in genius, but to rely on industry and their Heavenly Father.

One of the most prolific of the moral school of writers was Mary Belson, later Mrs. Elliott. From about 1812 a stream of her artless and edifying tales and verses swelled the lists of publications for youth, especially of the Quaker firm of Darton, although there is no evidence that Mrs. Elliott belonged to the Society of Friends.[1] Mrs. Elliott, like others, realised that moral lessons could be conveyed as effectively in verse as in prose, and she had the Taylor sisters, whose poetry for children is considered in a later chapter, as a shining example to follow. But she captured little of their skill. One of her best known prose tales is *The Orphan Boy or, A Journey to Bath* (1812). This is probably one of the two little gilt books brought back by John from the fair for the Fairchild children, and Mrs. Sherwood describes how little Henry found much to please him in this tale of how an orphan made good.

Another author on the Darton list, known to be of Quaker persuasion, was Priscilla Wakefield (born Bell, 1751–1832). She specialised in works which conveyed useful knowledge, although the need for moral guidance was never forgotten. She used letters or fiction very often to make instruction less obvious, thus following the example of many of her colleagues, and descriptions of nature and countries were her main subjects. But in one of her early works, *Juvenile Anecdotes, founded on facts* (1795), she was more concerned with advice on right conduct and the eradication of unsound principles. Reading had many dangers. Few books written for children were consistent 'with that simplicity which is the chief ornament of an unperverted mind'. She commends the action of a cautious mother who, before allowing any new purchase into the hands of her offspring, cuts out 'as many leaves as contained passages likely to give them false ideas, or to corrupt their innocence'. The children being dutiful and well-trained show no interest in what has been deleted.

'I am a very comical old woman', declared 'Arabella Argus' in her preface – 'not a serious preface' – to her 'liberal young public', in *The Juvenile Spectator* (1810). Like the renowned Mr. Spectator of a hundred years ago, she intends to comment on the foibles of mankind – this time the most delightful part of it, those who are growing not grown. There is a real personality behind 'Goody Argus' who comments on, and advises, and corresponds with the young people she observes unseen. Letters are included from the young characters (and others), with her replies, and although she sermonises and criticises, and never diverges from her firm precepts that religion and duty are of the first import-

---

[1] Jordan, Philip D., *The Juvenilia of Mary Belson Elliott* (Bibl. 132).

ance, she has sympathy with her readers' fondness for the marvellous rather than the moral (although she will not indulge it). The lively style and humour of the book break through her serious admonitions. 'Don't be in a hurry: give breath to your old friend', she ends her preface to the second part of her *Spectator* in 1812. She can apologise for tedious matters and make fun of herself – such good-humoured understanding between writer and reader recalls something of the old Newbery spirit. Yet the matters Mrs. Argus disseminates differ little from the usual teaching – it is her style which gives them vivacity and interest. Later she was to allure boys and girls to goodness through the medium of a donkey telling his life history. The ever popular attraction of animals for children was well understood by the moralist writers, and something more about the unidentified 'Mrs. Argus' and her tale about a donkey will be given later, with some details about other animal moralities.

The impression must not be left that the moral tale was always lofty and high-principled in intention. Some efforts, not the least interesting, are concerned with mundane matters and prudent conduct in everyday life. There are many examples of 'awful warning' tales about the nemesis sure to follow upon heedless or foolish actions, such as playing with fire, throwing away a pin or a piece of cord. In verse the Taylors were to create some engaging little lessons about such unwise or thoughtless habits. In prose, perhaps the most outstanding tale of this kind is *Waste not, want not*, by Maria Edgeworth, included in *The Parent's Assistant*. This relates a sequence of events following the opening of two parcels. Harry cuts the cord of his, and throws it aside, but the wise Ben unties the cord of his parcel, and puts it into his pocket. And then follows a chain of inter-related happenings, which bring misfortune to the thoughtless Hal, all due to his first careless action, while things go very successfully for the prudent Ben. A good storyteller like Maria Edgeworth could handle the theme in an amusing and convincing way, but in less able hands the 'awful warning' tale, both in prose and in rhyme, became the stuff of parody.

A typical book of practical advice is *Dangerous Sports* (1803), by James Parkinson, a well-known surgeon. This is 'a tale addressed to children warning them against wanton, careless or mischievous exposure to situations from which alarming injuries so often proceed', and describes some very horrid incidents of what can happen by leaving a penknife open, jumping from a high place, or not thinking before tasting or swallowing. Another specimen is the anonymous *Tales uniting Instruction with Amusement: consisting of The Dangers of the Streets; and Throwing Squibs*,[1] published by J. Harris about 1810. One episode concerns the history of two brothers, Edward and George. Edward at nine years

---

[1] This example and *Dangerous Sports* are taken from Tuer *Stories from Old-fashioned Children's Books* (Bibl. 28).

of age is commendably sensible and prudent, 'as cautious in walking the streets of London as a man of forty', while the thoughtless George, a year younger, after many narrow escapes from injury, falls under a loaded wagon, and later hobbles about with a wooden leg, repenting his giddy behaviour and saying to himself, 'Ah, how cautious children ought to be in walking the streets!'

These few examples can only indicate some of the most important achievements and trends of the moralistic writing for children, which dominated the later Georgian period. It was highly esteemed and supported by the middle and upper class society for which it was chiefly fashioned, and the 'fair authoresses' who produced most of it had much in common with the ladies writing novels with a similar moral flavour (though spiced with more sensibility and melodrama) for the subscription libraries. Even Mrs. Radcliffe and the Gothic school of novelists, who disseminated horror, heightened sentiment and suspense to fascinate the Catherine Morlands of the time, realised the need to serve the cause of virtue. At the end of *The Mysteries of Udolpho* (1794), Mrs. Radcliffe hopes that her tale has done more than please her readers. 'O! useful may it be to have shown, that, though the vicious can sometimes pour affliction upon the good, their power is transient and their punishment certain . . .'

The dead weight of didacticism fell more heavily on books intended for children, however, for these excluded sensationalism and matters likely to inflame the young imagination. But although now lost in oblivion (except perhaps for a few of the best tales by Maria Edgeworth and a handful of poems by the Taylors), they once had a great vogue. And they should not be judged entirely from the standpoint of our present amoral and unconfined superiority. Sometimes the reader of these faded pages may be surprised by an unexpected charm – not of mere quaintness – generated by the writers' 'fairy-tale' vision of a simple and certain happiness, attainable for life not by magic, riches, rank, or cleverness, but by right conduct.

The moral tale, with all its limitations, certainly contributed something of value in the evolution of children's books. Standards of style and construction were established, the author's name began to matter (at least in the later stages), and new devices for presenting instruction and advice in more amusing fashion led to a widening demand for real entertainment in print for boys and girls. So these rather dull and unexciting little histories of young Henrys and Carolines learning how to find the path to virtue and happiness prepared the way for books of wider scope and true literary merit.

3 The Dawn of Imagination

FROM *SONGS OF INNOCENCE* TO *GRIMM'S FAIRY TALES*

Before the end of the eighteenth century the reaction against the rule of reason had begun, but in books for children it came later than in literature for their elders. The voice of prophecy and revolt was most clearly raised by that isolated genius, William Blake (1757–1827), whose book of lyric poems, *Songs of Innocence* (1789), was the bright if unheeded sunrise of a new era.

Blake was poet, artist and visionary. For him the mechanistic universe of Newton and Locke was dead and meaningless. The perception of truth and reality lay behind the corporeal world in the creative power of the imagination, 'the Divine Body in Every Man . . . ' It was this revolutionary idea of the transcending importance of the imagination which was to produce the Romantic movement and to change fundamentally the whole conception of the nature and needs of the child during the coming century, with a consequent deep influence on the writing of children's books. The idea of the child as a being with a vision of his own, not as an ungrown man or woman to be quickly moulded to fit into an adult world, found vivid expression in these *Songs*, 'Every child may joy to hear', wherein Blake expressed his vision of youth unsullied by society.

Wordsworth, no less than Blake, but closer to the realities of nature and visible things, saw childhood as a time of magical 'other-worldliness', and knew the vital power of imagination over the heart and mind of youth. In his autobiographical poem, *The Prelude*, completed in 1805, he records his early delight in the *Arabian Tales*, and praises similar lore for youth in preference to the prevailing system of training the child 'to worship seemliness' which drives him 'within the pinfold of his own conceit'. Better far than all the facts and skills the model child has been able to master are:

> 'the wishing cap
> Of Fortunatus, and the invisible coat
> Of Jack the Giant-killer, Robin Hood,
> And Sabra in the forest with St. George!
> The child whose love is here, at least, doth reap
> One precious gain, that he forgets himself.'[1]

Coleridge also had fed his young mind on the wild tales and wonders that children continued to read, surreptitiously if not openly, in an age of enlightenment which

---

[1] *The Prelude*, V, 460, 298, 336, 341–6.

condemned them. They found them, as the poet did, in village shops, or among the wares sold by travelling chapmen. Referring to his childhood reading in a letter to Thomas Poole in October 1797, Coleridge wrote: 'My father's sister kept an *everything* shop at Crediton, and there I read through all the gilt-cover little books that could be had at that time, and likewise all the uncovered tales of Tom Hickathrift, Jack-the-Giant-killer, etc., etc. . . . ' In a further letter a week later he testifies to the value of this kind of reading in childhood. 'Should children be permitted to read romances and relations of giants and magicians and genii? I know all that has been said against it; but I have formed my faith in the affirmative. I know no other way of giving the mind a love of the Great and the Whole . . . '[1]

Another critic of the typical books for children of his day was Charles Lamb. A letter to Coleridge in October 1802, where he lamented that ' . . . Mrs. Barbauld's stuff has banished all the old classics of the nursery' has already been quoted. He goes on to dismiss the knowledge conveyed in most children's books of the time as 'insignificant and vapid', claiming that it gave the reader 'conceit of his own powers' instead of 'that beautiful interest in wild tales, which made the child a man, while all the time he suspected himself to be no bigger than a child. Science has succeeded to poetry no less in the little walks of children than with men. Is there no possibility of averting this sore evil? Think what you would have been now, if instead of being fed with Tales and old wives' fables in childhood, you had been crammed with geography and natural history . . . '[2]

To all the Romantic writers, in various ways, the imagination was of the first importance. But it was Wordsworth, above all, who put into matchless verse his vision of the child trailing clouds of glory from the eternal, seeing a light which would gradually fade, as he grew up, into the light of common day. Heaven was soon to lie about infancy, and the Little Nells and Paul Dombeys of Victorian fiction were in sight. The child, no longer regarded as an ineffectual and incomplete adult-to-be, was often in the century ahead to be idolised as a little demi-angel, living closer than his elders to the 'immortal sea'. The change of viewpoint did not come quickly, but eventually it dominated the attitude to youth, bringing much sentimentalism into books for all ages, but also inspiring some of the greatest books for children ever to be written. Not least, it was a driving force in the movement for much needed progress in children's welfare and education.

The child, at last, was put at the centre, and his need to wonder and laugh and dream and to live in a world of his own making was recognised. It was even given exaggerated importance in later Victorian times, when it could lead to over-fanciful and too preciously whimsical creations by less disciplined writers for the young. Nevertheless, the great

[1] *Collected Letters of Samuel Taylor Coleridge*, edited by Earl Leslie Griggs, 1956. I. 208, 210.
[2] *Letters of Charles Lamb*, I, p. 326, (Bibl. 148).

advance in admitting the need to train the child's imagination and allow it freedom to grow, brought far more benefits than disadvantages. Reason and discipline were no longer to be the ruling powers in shaping a literature for boys and girls. All kinds of fabulous lore, long subterranean in the life of the people, were now to be moulded anew to give children fresh vistas of truth and delight. This did not mean, as sometimes is believed, that principles of morality and religion were to be excluded from books for children. It only pointed to a wider and more sympathetic understanding of the child's needs, and so the enlistment of new allies in fostering his true welfare in reading. There are subtler and more powerful ways of presenting moral ideals in children's books than by precepts or artificial stories shackled down with purpose. The Victorians knew this well.

The advance of imagination in children's literature was at first hesitant, but there are signs of its awakening in the first decade of the nineteenth century – and even before this date. Instruction harnessed to amusement in matter of fact style did not entirely dominate publications for young readers. There were certain other features, and a few new developments, significant for the future, as the new century opened. The fairy tale had never been quite banished, although moralised almost out of existence in polite literature for the young. The activities of the chapbook-makers have been described in a former chapter, and their garbled versions of the old romances, the Arabian Tales, the Perrault stories, and other favourites, circulated in increasing numbers. More reputable publishers, too, occasionally produced genuine fairy tales for youth. Two editions of the Perrault or Mother Goose Tales were issued in the second half of the eighteenth century by B. Collins of Salisbury in collaboration with the firm of F. Newbery, and a twelfth edition came out in 1802 (Bibl. 90). Mrs. Cooper brought out some of the d'Aulnoy stories as *The Court of Queen Mab* in 1752, addressed to children as well as older readers. But compared to the chapbooks and the approved persuasive and instructional literature for the young, this kind of publication was scarce. Nursery rhymes and jingles for young children were growing more plentiful, but there was a general ban on the tale of wonder or fantasy, except by the purveyors of 'sub-literature', always ready to exploit the market. So that good editions for children of the old fairy tales were rare as rubies in the period of the moral tale.

The demand for books for children was steadily growing, and certain publishers at the turn of the century seemed to feel that spring was in the air. In a lesser degree than poets and visionaries they perceived that the buyer of children's books (to say nothing of the child reader) needed something different from the stereotyped tales 'for the improvement and amusement of youth' crowding the bookshops. Just as in the 1930s, within the writer's own memory, when a few enlightened publishers began a movement for the improvement of quality in books for children, and broke away from conventional patterns, so in the first decade of the nineteenth century, a similar little Renaissance began.

The trend was as much concerned with the appearance and illustration of books as with their content. The extreme crudity of woodcuts in books for children was arrested by the accomplished craftsmanship of Thomas Bewick (1753–1828), the great wood-engraver, whose earliest work for children's books was done before he finished his apprenticeship with Beilby in Newcastle upon Tyne in 1774. *A New Invented Hornbook* is ascribed to the year 1770. Better known is *The New Lottery Book of Birds and Beasts* published the next year. In 1779 Bewick illustrated an old favourite from John Newbery's list, *The Pretty Book of Pictures for Little Masters and Misses: or, Little Tommy Trip's History of Beasts and Birds*, and in the years that followed he and his less-gifted and short-lived brother John (1760–1795) produced many woodcuts for children's publications. Probably many young readers, in common with ten-year-old Jane Eyre, would find Thomas Bewick's *History of British Birds* (1797–1804) as fascinating as anything the artist specially designed for them. Seated behind the curtain in Mrs. Reed's parlour, Jane found the vignettes especially interesting and mysterious. Doubtless there was equal, if more direct, appeal for young eyes in the engraver's fine *Quadrupeds* (1790). Thomas Bewick also illustrated, with his brother, for the Newcastle publisher, T. Saint, (who issued many of the early Bewick books), a new edition of *Select Fables* (1784), and the Ritson collection of Robin Hood ballads (1795), printed for the London publishers, T. Egerton and J. Johnson. Thomas Bewick later began publishing his own works, including *Fables of Aesop and others* (1818), which he dedicated to 'the Youth of the British Isles'.

The production of well-illustrated books for children was still very much in the future, but after the Bewicks had set a new standard, there are signs of improvement, although the general standard continued poor. Very early in the nineteenth century colour was introduced to make publications more attractive – hand-colouring in these days before colour printing, usually offered at a higher price than the alternative 'plain' copies.

The Lilliputian format of the eighteenth century for little readers persisted for some time. Two miniature sets of books issued early in the new century, with attractive pictures, were *The Infant's Library* (1800–1801), published by John Marshall, and *A Miniature Historic Library*, issued perhaps ten years later, by Darton, Harvey and Darton. These tiny picture-books of instruction were about two inches square, and boxed in little wooden cases. Such minuteness was unusual. Most books for children were now duodecimo in size, considerably smaller than their modern or Victorian counterparts.

William Blake might be hailed as the first great author-artist in children's literature if his *Songs of Innocence* (1789) (further described later), made in his own style of illuminated printing, had been intended as a publication for boys and girls. His book and its sequel, *Songs of Experience* (1794), were little known in his lifetime. It can now be seen how remote these masterpieces were from the ordinary aspirations of the book-makers of the period. But without any claim to the artistic excellence or originality of Blake, cheerful little copper-plate engravings, lending themselves more suitably to hand-colouring than woodcuts, became an engaging feature in an increasing number of books for youth. In more and more instances pictures were being designed to suit childish understanding and appreciation. But there were many exceptions, stiff and formal as their accompanying text.

One of the most enterprising publishers to make innovations in publications for children at the beginning of the nineteenth century was John Harris. Harris had been manager to Elizabeth Newbery, the widow of Francis Newbery (nephew of John Newbery), and about 1801 he came into possession of the firm. In November of that year he published a moral animal tale, *The Dog of Knowledge; or, Memoirs of Bob the Spotted Terrier*. This was very much a commentary on life and morality, but the next year Harris showed his intention to widen the scope of his productions by issuing a volume of *Mother Bunch's Fairy Tales* (N.B.L. No. 431, Bibl. 42).

Two years later in 1804 he brought out, with suitable little cuts, *Dame Partlet's Farm*, a grave and gay piece in prose and verse, evidently inspired by *Goody Two-shoes*. Grief for the good old lady's sudden death is to be lightened by her bequest of 'a cheesecake and a pie' to each little girl and boy who get by heart the hymn she has written for them. In a rhymed preface Harris advertised his shop at the top of Ludgate Hill, quoting a 'little master' who had bought a book there for a penny.

> 'With covers neat, and cuts so pretty,
> There's not its like in all the city.'

New publications were coming out apace to meet demands, but this same year of 1804, Mrs. Trimmer noted with disapproval the publisher's practice to revive old popular tales, the example being *Valentine and Orson* (*Guardian of Education*, IV, 75).

Harris intended to give the children's book world a variety to suit all tastes. In 1805 he produced for the nursery the famous set of verses, *Old Mother Hubbard and her dog*, written and illustrated by Sarah Catherine Martin. There is some evidence that the gist of it was known as a traditional rhyme before Miss Martin embellished it, as Mrs. Trimmer, reviewing it in the *Guardian of Education* (IV, 413) recollected it as familiar in the days of her youth.[1] This comical work was a great success, and there was no doubt that the publisher was well able to exploit the wide if as yet inarticulate demand for the more fanciful and less didactic. He seized a further opportunity at the end of 1806, when some appealing verses appeared in the November issue of *The Gentleman's Magazine*. Harris published this rhyme, *The Butterfly's Ball and the Grasshopper's Feast*, on 1st January 1807, with minor alterations, and engravings of illustrations by William Mulready, 'a shilling

---

[1] See also *Opie*. pp. 319–321 (Bibl. 106).

plain or one and sixpence coloured'. The author, William Roscoe, was a Member of Parliament and a Liverpool banker, who went in for serious authorship. He had written this trifle for his own son, and it soon won outstanding and enduring popularity.

It describes the festivities of the insects in the woods, where their table is a mushroom, and their table-cloth a water-dock leaf, in couplets a little mannered but full of airy fancies and free from maxims about conduct. Such was its impact that imitations very quickly followed. A sequel, *The Peacock at Home* by 'A Lady' (Mrs. Catherine Anne Dorset), was commissioned and published by Harris the same year (1807). This followed the same pattern of happy if trivial invention, with touches of humour and fancy to help along the metre. The Spoon-bill obligingly ladled the soup, and the Taylor bird made new clothes, including a doublet of red for the robin. In another companion volume issued by Harris, *The Elephant's Ball and Grand Fête Champêtre* (1807), by 'W.B.', there is a very patriotic finale to the animals' revels when the lion sings 'Rule Britannia' and a loyal toast is drunk. In these numerous rhymed fantasies contemporary manners are mingled with ingenious fabrications about birds, beasts and other creatures. Few outlived their generation, and none surpassed the novel charm of Roscoe's invention, still to be found occasionally in present day anthologies.

Harris was astute enough to continue the issue of didactic works for youth in the accepted style of the day as well as innovations like *The Butterfly's Ball* – always paying attention to the attractions of format and illustration. He followed the fashion for midget books of instruction with his *Cabinet of Lilliput* (1802),[1] a set of twelve volumes of informative stories, not three inches square. He was lavish with coloured engravings, and he added gaiety to learning in such works as *The Paths of Learning strewed with Flowers* (1820), a pictorial grammar, and *Marmaduke Multiply's merry Method of making minor Mathematicians; or, The Multiplication Table illustrated* (1816).[2] He continued with his practice of issuing volumes of fairy tales and traditional material, and in 1823, with a special flourish, he brought out *The Court of Oberon; or, The Temple of the Fairies*, a collection of tales from Perrault, d'Aulnoy, *The Arabian Nights'* etc., under the headings, 'Tales of Mother Goose', 'Tales of Mother Bunch', and 'Popular Tales'.[3] The illustrated title-page shows the fairy king in a frame of dainty winged beings holding a garland of stars, as if rejoicing at their long-delayed welcome.

There were many other publishers as well as the prolific Harris active in the children's book trade in these years of the Napoleonic wars. The pioneer, John Marshall, of Aldermary Churchyard, who had published the works of Lady Fenn, and the Kilners, in the

[1] *Gumuchian*, 998 (Bibl. 37).

[2] *Children's Books of Yesterday*, p. 47 (Bibl. 13). *N.B.L. Catalogue* 108 (Bibl. 42).

[3] *Tuer*, pp. 407–8 (Bibl. 27).

1780s, had now other branches in the City. William Darton, a Quaker (later in partnership with Harvey) who had set up business about 1785 in Gracechurch Street, published the poems of the Taylor sisters, and many improving, simple, and well-illustrated little books of a sober rather than a fanciful nature, and his son was to follow a similar style of publishing early in the new century at Holborn Hill.

John Stockdale in Piccadilly had published the stories of Thomas Day and *The Children's Miscellany*. Joseph Johnson of St. Paul's Churchyard followed his success with Mrs. Barbauld's works with those of Maria Edgeworth. There was Tabart and Co.'s Juvenile Library in New Bond Street, responsible for the publication of some of the old fairy tales as 'Tabart's Popular Stories'. Everywhere there were signs of the steady development of juvenile publishing.

One of the most important and new-fashioned among these publishers of books for youth was William Godwin (1756–1836), the author of an outstanding revolutionary treatise, *An Enquiry into Political Justice* (1793). This brought upon the author the condemnation of society, and, much later, the admiration of the young Shelley. The poet was to marry Godwin's daughter Mary, the child of his first wife, Mary Wollstonecraft, who died in 1797. It was Godwin's second wife, Mary Jane Clermont, who evidently formed the plan to start a bookshop and publishing business for children in 1805. It was necessary to conceal Godwin's part in the venture, because of his reputation as atheist and revolutionary, so the firm was at first put under the name of the manager, Thomas Hodgkins, and a year or two later, under that of Mrs. Godwin. In 1807 the business was removed from the neighbourhood of Oxford Street to Skinner Street, near Holborn Viaduct. Notwithstanding Godwin's lack of business ability, the Juvenile Library seems to have been well patronised, although financial difficulties brought it to an end by 1825.

Godwin himself wrote for the firm anonymously, chiefly under the pseudonyms 'Edward Baldwin' and 'Theophilus Marcliffe'. He attempted little of his own invention, and wrote histories, lives, and a book of fables – *Fables, ancient and modern* (1805). Serious simplicity is the keynote of his writings for youth, and in these fables for younger children he retells some familiar examples from Aesop and other fabulists, striving to make the endings 'happy and forgiving'. He invents a few fables as well as adapting his borrowings. In his effort to make everything innocuous and pleasing to the child he sometimes destroys the original meaning of the fable, as in 'The Dog in the Manger'. He adds to it an incident of a child taking a plate of meat to the dog when it is hungry, and saying to it 'I should give you nothing to eat, as you prevented Papa's horse from eating'. This was the first item issued by the new firm. There were two editions: one in two volumes with seventy copper-plates after Mulready, probably engraved by William Blake, and a one volume edition with fewer pictures. There was also an edition in French, translated by the

'Editor of Tabart's Popular Stories'. From the advertisement in another Godwin publication, *Dramas for Children* (1808), it seems that the translator may have been Mrs. Godwin, not Godwin himself. This same person wrote the *Dramas*, founding them on L. F. Jauffret's *Théâtre de Famille* (1800). Easy books in French became a speciality of Godwin's Juvenile Library.

There was also an attempt to cater for the demand for fun and absurdity. Philip James in *Children's Books of Yesterday* (Bibl. 13) reproduces the title-pages of two Godwin items both issued in 1806 which express more mirth than morality – *A Continuation of the Moving Adventures of Old Dame Trot and her comical Cat* (evidently a sequel to *Old Dame Trot and her comical Cat*, published by T. Evans in 1803), and *Gaffer Gray; or, the Misfortunes of Poverty: a Christmas Ditty very fit to be chanted at Midsummer*. These followed what is now a more famous rhyme or nursery tale penned by the future Elia. And it was in giving to the public the books for children written by this great writer, Charles Lamb (1775–1834), and by his sister, Mary Lamb (1764–1847), that the publishing house of Godwin may now be best remembered.

Lamb, in a letter to Wordsworth on 1st February 1806, referred to the little work which Godwin under the name of Thomas Hodgkins had published the previous November.[1] This was *The King and Queen of Hearts*. It was a slight affair on the old nursery theme, illustrated with copper-plate engravings of pictures by the young artist, William Mulready, whose life Godwin, under the pen-name Theophilus Marcliffe, had described in another of his publications, *The Looking-glass*, the same year (1805). Whatever may have stimulated the writing of this amusing little piece, the initiative for a second and more famous work evidently lay with the publisher, probably Mrs. Godwin. Perhaps a French work – *Contes Moraux amusans et instructifs à l'usage de la Jeunesse, tirés de Tragédies de Shakespeare* published in London in 1783 – may have suggested the idea. By May 1806 twenty of Shakespeare's plays were being made into tales for children. Mary Lamb had by then completed six of the comedies and Charles was at work on the six tragedies to be included in the book.

When *Tales from Shakespear* (sic) came out in two volumes in 1807, after some of the stories had been issued separately, the credit for the whole work was given on the title-page to Charles Lamb, not with his intention. He was dissatisfied with the illustrations, said to be engraved by Blake after Mulready, but whatever the imperfections of this first edition, it marks a milestone in the history of children's literature. After the aridities of the moral tale, it has the charm of a wild and woodland garden. The theme was new, the source brimful of poetry and romance, and the reshaping for 'little people' was done with taste and skill, so that the result is neither paraphrase nor abridgement, but stories with an

---

[1] *Letters of Charles Lamb*, I, p. 420 (Bibl. 148).

artistic quality of their own. Through their love of the great original, the Lambs captured something of the greatness of the plays, cleverly taking up Shakespeare's own phrases at times when they might be woven into the story. Problems for adult understanding are avoided, and there is little writing down or moralising. Mary, however, felt she must go further than Puck at the end of *A Midsummer Night's Dream* in asking her readers 'only to think that they have been asleep or dreaming' if they are offended 'with this story of fairies and their pranks'. 'I hope', she concludes apologetically, 'none of my readers will be so unreasonable to be offended with a pretty harmless Midsummer Night's Dream'.

This consciousness of expected opposition to wonders and the supernatural rarely appears, however. The Lambs knew that in Shakespeare there was far greater treasure for young readers than in most of the books of their day, and so *Tales from Shakespear* has endured as one of the best retellings for youth from great literature ever undertaken. It also still stands as a book to be enjoyed for its own literary charm.

Perhaps more startling, though less successful, was the next venture in writing for children by Charles Lamb – *The Adventures of Ulysses* (1808). This was a version of Homer, designed as an introduction to the much esteemed *Adventures of Telemachus*, by Fénelon. Lamb founded it on Chapman's translation of the Odyssey, first published in 1616. The author had some difficulty with Godwin about 'horrors' in his manuscript, which the nervous publisher wished him to modify. One alteration, the giant's vomit in the Cyclops episode, was made by Lamb, but the rest he refused to change. 'If you want a book, which is not occasionally to *shock*, you should not have thought of a tale which was so full of anthropophagi and wonders', he wrote in a letter to Godwin in 1808.[1] Homer diluted to conform to the squeamish taste of the day did not appeal to the admirer of Chapman's Homer. He knew the appeal of primitive lore and wild tales for youth – and so the book came out as the author had written it.

The Lambs were never to invent very much in the way of fiction. They used second-hand sources or personal recollections as the chief material for their children's books. *Mrs. Leicester's School*, published anonymously in 1808, is chiefly the work of Mary Lamb, and she recalls in the histories of the young ladies some of her vivid childhood memories. Three of the ten tales are by her brother Charles. Although the book has a delicate charm, it lacks action, and so has failed to keep its place as a book for children as long as its literary excellence might deserve. It is further considered with the history of the school story in a later chapter. *Poetry for Children*, published in two volumes in 1809, is also described later. This was the last joint work of brother and sister. It bears more marks of the conventions of the day than their other books for children, and was the least successful.

The last composition which can definitely be attributed to either of the Lambs is the

---

[1] *Letters of Charles Lamb*, II, p. 53 (Bibl. 148).

verse story by Charles, founded on the old fairy tale, 'Prince Désir' (included by Madame Le Prince de Beaumont in her *Magasin des Enfans*, 1756), and published in 1811 as *Prince Dorus; or, Flattery put out of Countenance*. It is a pleasing little work, merry in mood, illustrated 'with fifteen elegant engravings' by Mulready. *Beauty and the Beast* (also in *Magasin des Enfans*), a similar trifle, was published by Godwin the same year. This has been attributed to Lamb but there is no real evidence for his authorship.

Freedom for fairy lore in books for children was really in sight in 1823. This year saw the publication of the first volume of the English edition of what we now know as *Grimm's Fairy Tales*. This famous classic was issued here as *German Popular Stories* in two volumes (1823–1826), and consisted of selections of thirty-one and twenty-four stories, nearly all of them taken from the *Kinder- und Hausmärchen* of J. L. K. Grimm (1785–1863) and W. K. Grimm (1786–1859). The German brother folklorists and philologists had collected the tales from oral tradition, and begun their publication in Germany in 1812. The translator, Edgar Taylor, also used one or two other sources in framing his versions of the tales. He selected only stories less familiar to the English reader, which would also satisfy 'the scrupulous fastidiousness of modern taste, especially in works likely to attract the attention of youth'.

In his preface Taylor makes a plea for popular fictions and traditions, and there are echoes of Lamb's strictures on the children's books of the day in his complaint that ' . . . philosophy is made the companion of the nursery; we have lisping chemists and leading-string mathematicians: this is the age of reason, not of imagination . . .' He continues boldly. 'Our imagination is surely as susceptible of improvement by exercise as our judgment or our memory'. His claim is that as long as 'there is no interference with the important department of moral education', the result of the reading of works of fancy and traditional tales can only be beneficial to children.

The two volumes were illustrated by George Cruikshank, whose vigorous etchings expressed the spirit of the tales in all their eeriness and elemental humour. What a rage the ugly Rumpelstiltskin shows! His foot fairly splinters the floor. How the wind blows at the young man whistling through the air on the fox's tail in 'The Golden Bird'! The first appearance of the Grimm stories in English is to be hailed not only as a landmark in fairy lore for children, but as a production for them where illustration and text achieve real harmony.

With the publication of *German Popular Stories*, the voice of the people and the phrases of their storytellers, long enjoyed by the unlettered, enter children's literature. It reveals no ethereal or romanticised world, although magic and marvels abound. There are kings and princesses, but ordinary folk too: soldiers, woodcutters, tailors, shoemakers, or young apprentices in search of their fortune. The old crones and goblin creatures who weave their spells here have little kinship with the gauzy-winged creatures of Titania's train.

12. A Victorian reprint of the first English edition of Grimm's Fairy Tales

Birds and beasts join in human adventures, avenging unkindness or aiding the good-natured. There are pure beast fables like 'Chanticleer and Partlet', and some familiar stories in a new guise, such as 'The Sleeping Beauty' (Dornröschen) and 'Cinderella' (Aschenputtel). Folklorists were to find variants of many of the stories all over the world, and advance the theories that they enshrined a debased mythology or expressed the deep unconscious wishes of the people. Their hidden meanings or sources, however, are less important in the history of books for children than their value as material to satisfy the young imagination and their influence on the writing of children's books. *Grimm's Fairy Tales* heralds a new era. From now on the ever-widening exploration of the lore and legend of the past was to be a major element in the making of books for boys and girls, and so new springs of inspiration were created for authors to invent original tales of wonder and fantasy.

For young readers who had outgrown the age for fairy tales, other trends of the new century were to bring enrichment. The interest in folklore, balladry, and traditional tales was only part of the quest for the past by the romantic imagination. The curtain of the present was soon to be rolled back by that great Romantic, Sir Walter Scott, to reveal wide panoramas, full of vivid colour and action, of life in other lands and past times. His Waverley novels were to inspire a new kind of fiction for young and old. No longer would the here-and-now, within narrow and rather featureless confines, and its perfectability, be the main concern of books for older any more than for younger children. Far places, forests and prairies peopled by redskins, the magic of islands, the lure and terrors of the seas, and the white man's push into the unknown – these, as well as tales of chivalry and battles long ago, were to be the stuff of fiction for youth in the days ahead. The heady waters of imagination were breaking through the firm ramparts of reason slowly but surely, and on their tide a new kind of literature was to be born in Victoria's reign. In essence it was to be the same, except for contemporary style and idiom, as the books on the shelves of the children's library today.

4 Flood Tide: The Victorian Age and Edwardian aftermath

I DEVELOPMENTS IN THE NINETEENTH CENTURY

In the last chapter it was claimed that the ascendancy of the imagination was the most important and far-reaching influence in children's literature during the nineteenth century. With imagination came freedom, originality, and above all, ever-widening horizons. Yet, as always, there was no sudden or complete break with the past. The boundless realms of fantasy and romance were new territories added to familiar country, rather than an abandonment of former traditions and practice. Many well established works of the previous age, such as *Evenings at Home, Sandford and Merton* and the Edgeworth stories, were still great favourites in the Victorian nursery, and the rising power of utilitarianism was very much on the side of the useful and practical in reading matter for old and young.

The didactic tale was certainly not banished. It was reshaped to suit the temper of the times. Much less formal and artificial in conception and plot than that of the earlier 'moral school', it took on a more human aspect, emphasising the importance of character-building rather than rational conduct. Often it presented youth making a successful way in the world from very modest beginnings, and achieving a good life through self-reliance, honesty and perseverance. It is exemplified in the many works by 'Peter Parley', pseudonym of the prolific American writer, Samuel G. Goodrich, and his several English imitators. Matter-of-factness and usefulness were its watchwords, and the makers of this kind of literature for youth set their face firmly against the swelling current of fairy lore and sensationalism. Christian principles, sometimes proselytising and enthusiastic, sometimes of a calm and undogmatic nature, were usually featured in this new type of purposeful story, and it was now more often addressed to children of humbler station (now beginning to read in increasing numbers) than was the earlier moral tale. Among the writers who produced this kind of fiction in the middle years of the nineteenth century were William and Mary Howitt. They brought to their writing a sincere and unaffected quality of their own, and Mary Howitt especially produced many pleasing if unexciting tales suited to the readers of their own day – but soon afterwards forgotten, the fate of most publications for children, then and now.

More popular and enduring than the stories presenting useful lessons for living and right principles (often using the old device of contrasted personalities), were the works highly charged with emotional and uncompromising religious tenets in the style of *The Fairchild*

93

Family, where threats of hell and the rewards of paradise for behaviour perhaps provided a substitute for the excitements of secular melodrama. The tale of piety and pathos, often featuring a tearful sentimentalism Mrs. Sherwood would have despised, became a frequent best-seller in the Victorian period. Little manuals of more direct religious purpose found almost equal favour. Such was the successful *Peep of Day* (1833), by Mrs. Favel Lee Mortimer, which reached a sale of a quarter of a million copies by 1867.

But, as the century elapsed, stories which presented religion more indirectly proved to be more effective and durable. A long-popular and world famous favourite was *Jessica's First Prayer* (1867), the best-known of many similar stories by 'Hesba Stretton' (Sarah Smith, 1832–1911), and a pathetic and deeply affecting narrative about a ragged waif who finds religion and salvation. Less realistic, but exuding similar naïve Christian propaganda, were the works of Mrs. O. F. Walton. *Christie's Old Organ* (1875) describes a poor old man's progress to his 'Home, sweet Home' in Heaven, and his influence on an orphan boy who befriends him. *A Peep behind the Scenes* (1877), by the same writer, was even more affecting and enduring, and both this and *Jessica's First Prayer* were still being requested by children in a poor industrial area in the early 1930s. They are perhaps the best-known of a mass of such works issued in the mid-Victorian period.

OLD TREFFY PLAYS A TUNE.

13. *From the 1888 edition of* CHRISTIE'S OLD ORGAN

The attraction of these tales lay in their sentimentality and the sympathetic identification of the reader with the poor lonely orphan child, who finds, after many trials, happiness and security through religion. These tales were the heirs and companions of the Sunday School literature and the tracts, to be produced in ever-increasing numbers by the Religious Tract Society and other publishers as the century advanced.

The religious life of the nation, stirred to new activity by the Evangelicals, and a little later by the Tractarians and the High Church movement, was intensely strong in Victoria's reign, notwithstanding growing doubt, and it deeply affected children's books and bookmaking. *Peep of Day* was followed by other religious books for youth, often intended

94

for 'Sunday reading'. One of the most successful, reaching a thirty-seventh edition in 1874, was by the Bishop of Winchester, Samuel Wilberforce (1805–1875), *Agathos and other Sunday Stories* (1840). But the best of the older publications kept their place. especially the frequently repeated *Hymns* of Isaac Watts, and that rival of the Bible for Sunday reading, *The Pilgrim's Progress*. The March sisters, like other young people of their day both in fiction and real life, found in Bunyan's great story a source of inspiration to help them in their daily lives.

So it was that, extensive and sweeping as the innovations were to be in children's books in this great century of change, publications designed for the religious and moral education of youth sold in larger numbers than ever before. But gradually they were to be rivalled by other kinds of literature as the juvenile book trade expanded to meet the demands of an increasing population and the spread of education. Much of this recreational literature was still firmly founded on the principles reflected in the Sunday School books and the tracts. So that, although the circle of secular books and their scope was rapidly widening, few books for children left out religion altogether until the later Victorian age.

There were other circumstances and ideas affecting books for children, as well as religion, in this age of national advancement. Most marked was the widespread belief in individualism and voluntary effort, a natural accompaniment of the *laissez-faire* doctrine advocated for industry and government. This spirit is vividly reflected in the writings of Samuel Smiles, especially in the famous *Self-help* published in 1859. 'The solid foundations of liberty must rest in individual character' was one of his main beliefs. Through self-discipline and cheerful application to work and study, success and happiness were to be found, and the human race, not only the self, would be benefited. This concern with self-improvement and service to others is a prominent feature of Victorian children's books.

The industrialisation and urbanisation of the nation, following the technical advances of the Industrial Revolution, were creating profound social changes and much misery and unrest among the masses, especially in the first fifty years of the century. Amelioration of the conditions of the poor and the workers was very much left to voluntary effort, and various humanitarian and philanthropic movements undertook much valuable service, the prelude to later state intervention and assistance for the welfare and education of the people. There was a growing demand among artisans for knowledge, and this led to the formation of the Society for the Diffusion of Useful Knowledge in 1826. The Society began to issue its cheap series, the Library of Useful Knowledge, the next year, under the direction of that pioneer of publishing for the masses, Charles Knight. The emphasis was very much on the factual, and this applied to the publications for youth begun in 1833. About the same time came the establishment of Mechanics' Institutes and their libraries, which often made some limited provision for children.

But the pallid children of the factories were little served by these institutions, which tended to help the lower middle classes rather than the poor. The work of the Sunday Schools was for them all important. Books and periodicals were distributed to their scholars in increasing volume, although library provision was generally very meagre. Not so very long ago the writer came across the remnants of such a library belonging to a Dissenting chapel in 1840. The collection was by no means confined to works of religious teaching, but included tales and histories. One of them, an anonymous undated little work called *The Struggles of a Village Lad* (published by William Tweedie), is a typical production of its time – a minute social document describing its author's rise to become rector of his village, and his memories of his early schooling and reading.

Although attendance was much hampered in the early decades of the century by so many possible scholars working long hours in field or factory, week-day schools were being provided increasingly for children of the poorer classes. Since the beginning of the 1800s many schools had been organised on the rival monitorial systems introduced by Andrew Bell, a Church of England clergyman, and Joseph Lancaster, a Quaker. These institutions, although they led to quarrelling between religious factions, had done much to bring elementary education of a simple kind within reach of many children of the people. Statistics can be misleading, for many children attended school for short periods only, but those collected by Henry Brougham in 1820 indicate that one in fourteen or fifteen of the population were then receiving some kind of education. Before 1803 the number of children at school was one in twenty-three of the population.[1] In 1833 the Government made the first state grant for education by voting a sum of £20 000 in aid of private subscriptions for the erection of school houses. The grants were administered through the two School Societies which had been formed to promote the Bell and Lancaster systems (virtually the same in their methods of rote-learning and use of older pupils as teachers but different in religious belief) – *The National Society for Promoting the Education of the Poor in the Principles of the Established Church throughout England and Wales* (1811), and the unsectarian *Royal Lancastrian Association* (1810), soon to be renamed *The British and Foreign Schools Society*. State aid had begun, but it proceeded slowly, always assisting rather than supplanting the voluntary efforts of the various religious denominations. In 1870 the State at last took legislative action to make good deficiencies by setting up School Boards to provide schools where they were needed, to be paid for from the rates, and also powers were introduced which might be used to enforce school attendance of scholars between five and ten years of age. Compulsory attendance was not generally achieved for another decade, however, under further legislation. After the 1870 Act the spread of education was much accelerated, and school attendance rose from one and a

[1] Barnard, H. C., *A Short History of English Education* (Bibl. 153).

quarter millions that year to four and a half millions in 1890.[1] This growth in the number of young scholars had far-reaching effects on publications for youth, especially in the production of cheap literature.

Keeping pace with the advances in education, and even preceding them, was the public library movement, initiated in 1850. Limited and unequal as the service was throughout the nineteenth century under rate limitation, it forged ahead steadily, especially in the larger towns, and many an urban child, at least, had free access to books towards the end of the century. After various pioneer services for children in Manchester and other towns from the 1860s onwards, the first separate library for children was opened in 1882 in Nottingham, and three years later it was reported that the young members had a choice of nearly 3000 books.[2] It marked the beginning of important children's library developments which have made good literature available everywhere for boys and girls in our own day.

The development of schools and libraries was a potent force in the expansion of juvenile publishing – as was the growth of the population and the decline in the death rate. And the same technical advances which helped to create a demand for education and reading matter were assisting publishers to speed up and cheapen publications to satisfy the growing reading public – old and young. The mechanical manufacture of paper was introduced into this country in 1803, and the use of wood-pulp for its making became general fifty years later. The steam-powered press and cloth-binding were important innovations in the 1820s. Illustration processes were also much affected by technical developments. Lithography was invented at the turn of the century, and the first successful colour printing was introduced in the 1830s. In the second half of the century, the application of photography began to revolutionise methods of printing and illustrative processes, at first without any gain in quality. But the cause of cheapness and the wide dissemination of printed matter gained immeasurably from all these aids.

The expansion in the market for children's books was accompanied by a discovery that children were not all of one pattern, as it seemed to the publishers of the previous era, but that age, sex, and interests might vary. Towards the middle of the century there is a branching out on a wide scale into different types of books – aimed at different types of readers, including books for older boys, books for girls, and books for younger children. Some of these trends are traced in detail in the chapters that follow. This broadening of interest and more individual appeal among publications at first led to some original works

[1] In state-aided schools only. Quoted by G. M. Trevelyan. *English Social History*, 1944, p. 581 (Bibl. 158). See also Altick, Richard D., *The English Common Reader*, p. 171, (Bibl. 152).

[2] J. Potter Briscoe, at the L.A. Conference, 1885, quoted by W. A. Munford, in *Penny Rate*, 1951, p. 109. For information about early children's services by the public library, and the development of school libraries see Ellis, Alec, *A History of children's reading and literature* (Bibl. 9).

of merit, but afterwards to much slavish imitation and repetition and setting up stock patterns – one of the worst features of the commercialisation of the children's book trade before the death of Queen Victoria. Quantity and cheapness were essential if demand were to be satisfied, but the multiplication of the second-rate and tawdry, characteristic of the later Victorian period, was fortunately accompanied by a continuing progress towards quality in every type of book for children. Books of merit were much outnumbered by their inferiors, however – a tendency prevalent ever since.

Another distinctive feature of the Victorian age was the rise of periodical literature, both the cheap and sensational and of high quality. In the second half of the century some magazines for youth reached a high standard from which they have steadily declined. On the other hand, the cheap and lurid productions, the penny and halfpenny 'dreadfuls', made vast strides since Brett established his *Boys of England* in 1866, and paved the way for the mass circulation of sensational, easy-to-read comics devoured by the generations of the present century.

The achievements of the era, however, proceeded by fits and starts, rather than by orderly progression. After the bright promise of the first decade in the shape of liberated fancy and dawning imagination in books for boys and girls, and the landmark of *German Popular Stories* in the 1820s, there was a disappointing halt. In the 1820s and 1830s the religious or moral tale was still the prevailing reading material available for children, and a steady output along established lines continued. Lessons of conduct and useful instruction were still much favoured by those concerned with children's reading, and flights of fancy were suspect. These sentiments were soon to be gratified by the innumerable works of 'Peter Parley'.

The author of the original tales of Peter Parley was Samuel G. Goodrich (1793–1860), a New Englander. In his youth he had found the old fairy tales, especially the incident of the wolf in Little Red Riding Hood, frightening and shocking and – what was worse – untrue. At ten years old he discovered Hannah More's *Shepherd of Salisbury Plain* exactly suited to his taste. Twenty years later in 1823, already 'an instructor of youth', he visited this country and met the famous writer and philanthropist, whose tracts he so much admired. He became confirmed in his belief that children do not need fiction but truth. 'Could not history, natural history, geography and biography become the elements of juvenile works in place of fairies and giants and mere monsters of the imagination?'[1]

Inspired by the example of Hannah More in writing and publishing her tracts, he set up his own publishing business in Boston in 1826, beginning his long series of popular little books with *Tales of Peter Parley about America* in 1827. The next year there followed *Tales of Peter Parley about Europe*, and such was their success, and others which came after,

[1] Goodrich, S. G., *Recollections of a lifetime*, 1856, vol. 1, Letter XIII, vol. 2, p. 168 (Bibl. 160).

that they were soon brought to England. The publisher of some of the earliest tales to appear here, at first by agreement with Goodrich, was Thomas Tegg (1776–1845). Later Tegg, like other publishers, used the name Peter Parley for other works, much to Goodrich's disgust. The American's style and pseudonym were copied by many English imitators, and spurious 'Peter Parleys' became more common than the genuine article. Among the English Peter Parleys were William Martin (1801–1867), George Mogridge (1787–1854), who hid his identity as 'Old Humphrey', 'Ephraim Holding' and other sobriquets, and Samuel Clark (1810–1875), an editor of some of the original Goodrich books for English readers. Clark was a partner in the firm of Darton and Clark, and he used a variety of pennames, in addition to Peter Parley, notably 'Reuben Ramble' and 'The Rev. T. Wilson'. Authentic editions of genuine Peter Parleys, often edited by Clark, were usually published by this firm, afterwards Darton and Co., but Goodrich protested at their issue of 'counterfeit Peter Parley books', which he labelled 'nauseous in style, matter and purpose'. The coronation of the young Queen inspired another publisher, Charles Tilt, to use the name in his *Peter Parley's Visit to London during the Coronation of Queen Victoria* (1838).

The Peter Parley books had certain features in common, although the kindly simplicity and good sense and enthusiasm for knowledge shown by their originator gave pre-eminence to Goodrich's own works. Like the earlier moralists, the authors excluded the marvellous and magical, and depicted the everyday world, usually with directness and natural feeling, often marred by a fatherly condescension. The success of these publications, genuine and imitative, was amazing. Goodrich disclosed in his *Recollections* that he was 'the author and editor of about 170 volumes, and of these seven millions have been sold'. He was, of course, referring to his own works – not including any counterfeits. The enormous popularity of the series is also evidence of the rapid growth of the children's book trade, both here and in America, in the middle of the century.

The dominance of the useful and purposeful in children's books in the 1830s was not unchallenged. At the end of this decade it is refreshing to meet natural and naughty children in Catherine Sinclair's *Holiday House* (1839), cited as the real breakaway from the old type of moral tale, and described in a later chapter. Liveliness and naturalism were much needed in tales of everyday life, and this showed that they were surely on the way. And early in the 1840s there came welcome signs of a revulsion from 'Peter Parleyism', and a long-delayed surge forward in the 'Renascence of Wonder' in children's books.

Anti-Peter Parleyism was the avowed aim of the 'Home Treasury' series of 'Felix Summerly' (Sir Henry Cole, 1808–1882). Cole was a well-known friend of the arts and one of the organisers of the Great Exhibition of 1851. He produced this series from 1843 onwards, inspired by the needs of his own children, intending to give young readers some of the best of their nursery tales and traditional stories in artistic form. The publisher was Joseph Cundall (later it was Chapman and Hall), and the printer was Charles Whittingham.

The illustrations included pictures from old masters and work by some of the best artists of the day. Cole lists twenty items in the series, four of them concerned with painting or artistic pastimes.[1] Although there is nothing of outstanding quality to remark in these small books, they are pleasing, clearly printed, and easy to read. The covers of the first items, bound books, were red or green, attractively gilt. Later volumes were issued both in paper and in stiff covers. All had coloured illustrations at a higher price than plain copies – 3s 6d or 4s 6d for the early issues compared with 2s or 2s 6d uncoloured. Later items were a shilling or 2s 6d, according to style.

Cundall later published a similar cheaper series of traditional books for boys and girls, 'Gammer Gurton's Story Books,' retold by W. J. Thoms (1803–1885), under the pseudonym Amb Mer (Ambrose Merton), and these were also available in a collected edition, *The Old Story Books of England* (1845).[2]

The 1840s were remarkable for much more than the re-issue of old traditional tales in a worthy form for children. These years saw the beginning of a golden age of imaginative writing for the young, which may be said to date from 1846 with the publication of the first Hans Andersen tales in English and the first book of Lear nonsense. The adventure story was well on the way with the books Captain Marryat wrote for children in this decade. With the 1850s the tide is flowing fast. Kingsley and Ballantyne launch the true

[1] Cole, Sir Henry. *Fifty years of public work* (Bibl. 159).

[2] For the Home Treasury series see Maclean, R., *Victorian Book Design*, pp. 38–42 (Bibl. 156).

The following list of titles in the series published in 1843 and 1844 is chiefly taken from copies in the British Museum or Victoria and Albert Museum Libraries.

1843   *Bible Events*. First series (illus. after Holbein)
          Traditional Nursery Songs Pts. 1 & 2
          Sir Hornbook (by T. L. Peacock)
          Beauty and the Beast
          Little Red Riding Hood
          The Ballad of Chevy Chase

1844   *Puck's Reports to Oberon* (four new fairy tales) 2 vols.
         1   *Grumble and Cheery: The Eagle's Verdict*
         2   *The Sisters: Golden Locks*
          Jack and the Beanstalk
          Bible Events, Second series (illus. after Raffaelle)
          Bible Events, Third series. *The Life of our Lord Jesus Christ* (illus. after Dürer)

Reynard the Fox, No. 15 on Cole's list, was first issued as an expensive production in the series in 1843, with forty coloured plates by Everdingen.

Other items followed including *Cinderella* (1844?), *Jack-the-Giant-killer* (1845), *Tales from Spenser's Faery Queen* (1846), and *Dick Whittington* (1847).

The Old Story Books of England contained: *Sir Guy of Warwick*; *Sir Bevis of Hampton*; *Tom Hickathrift*; *Friar Bacon*; *A True Tale of Robin Hood*; *The King and the Cobbler*; *Patient Grissel*; *The Princess Rosetta*; *Robin Goodfellow*; *The Blind Beggar's Daughter of Bethnal Green*; *The Babes in the Wood*; *Fair Rosamond*.

adventure tale for boys and every kind of story is taking shape. Fantasy's fine flowering is in the 1860s, reaching its peak with the first of the *Alice* stories, unforgotten and unsurpassed, in 1865. In the 1870s the creation of the artistic coloured picture-book by the engraver and colour printer, Edmund Evans, working closely with three gifted artists, Walter Crane, Kate Greenaway, and Randolph Caldecott, is perhaps the most outstanding achievement among many others. The next decade brings glory to the tale of adventure with that superb creation concerning skullduggery and pirate gold – *Treasure Island* (1883) – by a master craftsman of letters, Robert Louis Stevenson. And there are signs at last of emancipation among books for girls. Towards the close of the century a new brilliant star has risen, the young Kipling, whose *Jungle Book* (1894) and *Second Jungle Book* (1895) thrilled young and old by their forceful originality. Fairy lore, steadily gaining ground through the years, was further enriched in the last decade by the work of scholars like Andrew Lang, Joseph Jacobs and others.

This was indeed an age of gold in children's literature. Works of distinction in every field of writing for children were produced and the various branches of their literature were established as we know them today. But as has already been observed, books of quality were much in a minority. The rapid expansion of the juvenile book trade to meet the needs of a mass of new literate or semi-literate young people led to the exploitation of cheapness, quantity and standardised forms of writing for them – a situation not much improved in our own times.

The tendency for children's books to be streamlined into series or 'libraries' was already apparent in the days of John Harris, who brought out his 'Cabinet of Amusement and Instruction', with *The Butterfly's Ball* as the first issue in 1807. Later he produced a 'Little Library' of books of information. By the 1840s such serried ranks of productions for children were very popular with publishers. The excellent 'Home Treasury' series has been described above. Among many others, of varying quality, were Tegg's 'Tales for the People and their Children' (to which the Howitts contributed), W. S. Orr's 'Young England's Little Library' and Darton's 'Holiday Library'. Chambers' rather sedate 'Library for Young People', including improving tales and books of information, began in 1848. T. Nelson and Sons in the early 1850s were advertising many 'Sabbath School Rewards' and gift books. Their series of 'Sabbath Stories for Little Readers' ranged in price from a farthing to sixpence, but they also had a 'Royal Juvenile Library' at two shillings and sixpence.

Cheap series of picture-books were also becoming plentiful, some of the earliest being produced by Thomas Dean (Dean and Munday, later Dean and Son) in the third decade. Publishers of books for boys and girls multiply as the century proceeds, and their lists grow longer. The trend towards series arranged under prices becomes engrained. By the last quarter of the century such well-known publishers of children's books as Blackie and

Son, Thomas Nelson and Sons, George Routledge and Sons, Ward, Lock and Co., Frederick Warne and Co. were large concerns, and their lists and sales of books were beyond anything that John Newbery or John Harris might visualise.

One of the most enterprising publishers in the second half of the nineteenth century was George Routledge, whose important role in the publishing of picture-books will be given in detail later. The Routledge catalogue of Juvenile Books in circulation about 1881 is an interesting and revealing example – a comprehensive and reputable list of its time. Items follow the usual practice of division under series and 'rewards', and here are arranged in descending order of price, from five shillings to two shillings, under various categories. Other publishers had much cheaper wares, but nothing below two shillings is in this list. There is a good deal of second-rate material of contemporary appeal, but much also of excellent quality. About 470 separate editions are listed, possibly a quarter of these being duplicated in more than one series. The different sections are headed 'Boys' Books', 'Girls' Books', 'Coloured Reward Books', 'Books of Adventure', 'Historical and Biographical Prize Books', 'Picture Books', 'The Young Ladies' Library', 'Album series', etc. Many classics are here, including *Robinson Crusoe, Gulliver's Travels*, the Andersen and Grimm Fairy Tales, and there are long-established favourites like *Sandford and Merton*, Watts' *Songs, Evenings at Home*, and Maria Edgeworth's Tales. This catalogue epitomises the great changes that had taken place from the beginning of Victoria's reign, for now there is set out a wide range of books to suit differing tastes and ages, including picture-books for young children. There are plenty of adventure stories for boys, many by Mayne Reid, W. H. G. Kingston and Jules Verne. There are stories of school life, mainly for boys, and stories of family interest for girls, including *Little Women*. There are historical tales, notably Marryat's *Children of the New Forest*, books of information, natural history, science, history, biography and travel, Fouqué's Tales, *Uncle Tom's Cabin*, the fairy stories of Lord Brabourne (E. H. Knatchbull-Hugessen). Among much else of importance or ephemeral appeal is listed, under books for girls, that sad, long-popular island idyll, *Paul and Virginia*, by Bernardin de St. Pierre, first published in 1788 in France.

The development of the periodical press led to sporadic but increased reviewing of children's books. This is a vital function in literature for children, if it is to be regarded as a serious art. From their foundation in the second half of the eighteenth century, the monthly reviews devoted to literature and culture had included some brief notices of publications for children, increasingly so from about 1800 onwards.

The *Critical Review* for May 1807 gave a eulogistic account of *Tales from Shakespear*, placing it above all the books of the day for children, referred to as sordid trash. Both the *Monthly Review* and the *British Critic* reviewed *The Butterfly's Ball* with its successor, *The Peacock at Home*, at the end of the same year (1807), and both rated the sequel higher than the original. Many other examples could be found, but the whole subject awaits much serious and methodical research before any true judgment is possible.

Since the first edition of this book was issued in 1963, there has been a major contribution to the subject in the United States. Dr. Richard L. Darling in *The Rise of Children's Book Reviewing in America, 1865–1881* (Bibl. 168) analyses reviews in the main American literary journals in the rich period following the Civil War until the publication in 1882 of *Books for the Young*, by Caroline M. Hewins, and her subsequent compilation of an annual anthology of reviews of children's books for *The Library Journal*. The author analyses and evaluates with much perception the reviewing of many children's books, both of American origin and importations from abroad, and sets the material in its background. He briefly touches on children's book reviews for the same period in two leading English journals, *The Athenaeum* and *The Saturday Review*. He has shown that serious and enlightened attention was often given to children's books in literary periodicals in America, and perhaps further investigation might show a similar situation here. The field is practically unexplored.

One of the earliest attempts at the systematic reviewing of children's books in England was that by Mrs. Trimmer in her periodical, *The Guardian of Education*. In its pages, during its publication for the five years 1802–1806, she surveyed all the books for children and young people which came to her notice. Her reviews were well-considered, often very comprehensive, but always biased by her strong convictions in favour of the established Church and its principles. This painstaking effort to cover all publications issued for youth deserves high praise, even though her views were prejudiced. To a new edition of *Robinson Crusoe*, for example, she gave cautious approval, but felt that it should not be given to '*all boys* without discrimination, as it might lead to an early taste for a rambling life and a desire for adventure'.

Another landmark is the critical survey of children's books in the *Quarterly Review* for June 1844 by Elizabeth Rigby. This lengthy article laid down some enlightened standards, attacking in particular 'the interdict laid on the imagination' and 'the mania for explanation'. The mediocrity of the books of the day was criticised, and the author pleaded for the 'sphere of fictitious and allegorical life', needed by children in their reading, instead of the factual trivialities thought to be identical with truth. It enumerated many works approved, and praised especially *Robinson Crusoe*, Scott's *Tales of a Grandfather*, 'Felix Summerly's' series, Grimm ('an exquisite book for children'), Mrs. Trimmer's *Robins*, Croker's *Fairy Legends*, and Marryat's *Masterman Ready*. Some educational works and books by the moral school are included but only one by 'Peter Parley'. 'We should be happy', writes the author with enthusiasm, 'if, by calling attention to the real excellence and beauty of a genuine child's book, we could assist in raising the standard of the *art* itself – the only effectual way, it seems to us, of checking the torrent of dressed-up trumpery, which is now poured out upon the public.'

This seems to be the first full critical assessment of children's books at a particular date. Over forty years later Charlotte Yonge surveyed the scene in *What Books to Lend and What to Give* (1887), but she had in mind books specially suitable for 'Church school and parish work'. She listed nearly a thousand items with comments, but the result was scarcely an independent assessment of the best children's books of her day, as she had a definite circle of readers in mind.

The inclusion of children's book reviews in their own periodicals is another subject deserving of full investigation. Notices about children's books appeared in an early and short-lived monthly, *The Young Gentleman's and Young Lady's Magazine* (1799–1800), and other journals for the young might be found which followed the practice. Mrs. Gatty, who founded a first-rate magazine for young people – *Aunt Judy's Magazine* – in 1866, showed discernment in making interesting book reviews a regular feature of its pages. In June 1866 there appeared enthusiastic notices about two new publications, *What the Moon Saw*, by Hans Andersen, an established author, and *Alice's Adventures in Wonderland*, by a newcomer.

Another sign of maturity in the junior branch of literature was the publication of at least three full-scale works on the subject before the century was ended. The first was a survey of children's books of the day, *Juvenile Literature as it is*, by Edward Salmon published in 1888, and based on articles contributed by the author to the *Fortnightly Review*, the *Nineteenth Century*, and other journals. His object was 'to give all charged with the mental and moral welfare of the rising generation an idea of the books written for girls and boys', and he believed it was the first effort of its kind – at least in book form. It is interesting as a contemporary account and as a reflection of the critical standards of the period. Moreover, it contains what must be one of the earliest enquiries into children's tastes in reading, founded on the replies of about two thousand young people between the ages of eleven and nineteen.

Interest in the development of children's books in the past was already manifested in the latter half of the century. Charlotte M. Yonge had contributed a series of three articles to *Macmillan's Magazine* on 'Children's Literature of the Last Century' in 1869. In 1891 came the first full-length history of children's literature by Mrs. E. M. Field – *The Child and his Book*. This work is still most readable and a useful source of information about the medieval period. The third publication was to emphasise the growing importance of the artist in children's book-making – Gleeson White's *Children's Books and their Illustrators*, issued as a special number of *The Studio* in the winter of 1897–8. It revealed that pictures and design had achieved a new status, and that the role of the artist now rivalled that of the author in the production of books for children. This end-of-century account also indicates how much childhood had become idealised as a precious and uncorrupted state, to be looked upon with nostalgia and yearning, a time of innocence that should be prolonged as far as it could be and sheltered from the harshness of an adult's world. Freud's unveiling of the unconscious, and Frazer's revelations of the primitive mind were to make their impact only gradually in the coming century. In the 1890s decadence and cynicism might be attacking the stronghold of morality and religion, but the rose-coloured realm of childhood was yet intact. In this *Studio* publication, the frontispiece is typical of prevailing taste. Here is 'King Baby' enthroned and beribboned, and Watts-Dunton is quoted later to introduce the child as the 'new Hero', for whom 'painters and designers are vying with poets and with each other in accommodating their work to his well-known matter-of-fact tastes and simple directness . . . '

The work of Charles Welsh (who had collected the information for Salmon's reading enquiry above) and of Andrew Tuer, in the investigation of old children's books and their publication in facsimile, is another sign of growing interest in the whole field of literature for boys and girls in the closing years of the nineteenth century.

Yet 1901, the year the old Queen died, does not really mark the end of an era, either in the life of the nation, or in the literature published for her young citizens. The 'flash Edwardian epilogue' has more in common with its preceding decade than with the years of the Great War of 1914–1918 and after, when so many accepted values and traditions were shattered. 1914 rather than 1900 is perhaps the natural watershed for the close of this survey and the real beginning of the new century's emancipation from Victorianism. Until the outbreak of war many old ideals and conditions persisted. There was still the weight and wealth of Empire guiding British policy, the same brilliant if waning power of upper-class society leading opinion and fashion, the same educational practices in being, with the young folk of the well-to-do segregated from the scholars in the public elementary schools. Progress on the old lines rather than innovation is characteristic of the early years of the twentieth century, although changes are already foreshadowed by the beginning of experiment in educational methods and wider opportunities opening in secondary education with the passing of the Balfour Education Act in 1902.

In books for the young, many end-of-century tendencies continued in the Edwardian era. The supply of cheap and trivial reading matter for the junior mass reading public (now everywhere receiving the rudiments of learning) grew steadily. But the increasing trend towards quality that had begun in the 1840s also showed renewed vigour. Indeed, the first decade of the new century, following the pattern of a hundred years ago, has a claim of its own to special distinction in the chronicle of children's literature. The stories of Rudyard Kipling and of E. Nesbit, the first *Johnny Crow* books of Leslie Brooke, the work of such illustrators as Arthur Rackham and the Robinson brothers, the little nursery gems of Beatrix Potter, the matchless *Wind in the Willows* (1908), the early poems of

Walter de la Mare and the compelling magic of his *Three Mulla-Mulgars* (1910), the whimsical and endearing *Peter Pan* – these form a constellation of shining lustre. Popular 'self-educators' had for many years been a feature of publishing, but children were now to have knowledge and information brought to them in a new imaginative form – when Arthur Mee, a young and enthusiastic employee of Harmsworth, produced the first number of *The Children's Encyclopaedia* on 17th March 1908.

Looking backwards from the present moment in time, in this bustling age of speed and mechanism and space travel, these years before the first World War seem dim and far away. The children's books once read by little boys in knickerbockers or little girls in frilly pinafores wear a quaint and *passé* look. But an observer then might remark that greater changes had taken place in book-making for children during the hundred years since John Harris produced and sold his grave and gay little volumes at the top of Ludgate Hill. By the dawn of the twentieth century vast developments had occurred, and true literary and artistic standards had been created, despite the menacing waves of cheapness and quantity. Fashions in style are mutable. Technical inventions control the physical make-up of books. But the art of imaginative writing cannot be fettered by contemporary forces. Creativity blossomed in lavish exuberance in this epoch of Lear, Carroll, Stevenson and Kipling, producing some enduring classics to delight readers then and now. So the art of writing for children was founded and a beginning made possible in the formation of values.

The chapters that follow attempt to trace something of the history of this abundant period under the various kinds of literature which came into existence, up to the close of the Edwardian era (where fitting) rather than coming to an abrupt halt at the end of the reign of Victoria. Much was achieved, much once important is now deservedly forgotten. But there is little doubt about the most precious legacy of this epoch for the future. It lay not in diversity, greatly increased output, or homage to childhood, but in a few imperishable books of timeless appeal. These would be stars to steer by in the exciting teeming world of children's books to come.

II   FAIRY LORE AND FANTASY

The medieval heritage of romance, balladry and similar literature and its long-delayed admittance into books for children has been described in foregoing pages. Also its survival, mainly in travestied chapbook form, in the age of reason. But the collection of oral traditional tales and their editing for children's reading is largely the achievement of the nineteenth century. It begins for English-speaking boys and girls with the publication of *German Popular Stories*, by the brothers Grimm, in 1823–1826, and it steadily developed from this time onwards, alongside with the rediscovery for youth of the written literature of the Middle Ages. So traditional tales, gathered from all over the world, permeated increasingly into children's books in this prolific Victorian epoch. No less important, the publication of such material encouraged writers to invent original tales of wonder and magic, as well as to recast ancient lore into a suitable form for young readers. And with the original story of fantasy or make-believe, created in the middle and later years of the nineteenth century, children's literature reaches the highest attainments, measured against any standard, past or present.

The Grimm stories were first in the field of oral fairy lore for children, but they were not the only gift from Germany to influence their books. The German Romantic movement of the late eighteenth and early nineteenth centuries used the *Märchen* for writings of more sophisticated appeal and wider scope. Some of the tales of De La Motte Fouqué and other writers of the German Romantic school encouraged a taste for the wilder landscape of romance and the supernatural – explored also by the castle-dungeon-spectre school of Mrs. Radcliffe and her contemporaries. But German influences are particularly potent in children's bookmaking throughout this century of great development. Fouqué's shorter tales especially were much in vogue. One of his most popular was *Undine* (1811, English translation 1818), a charming story about a water nymph who married a knight and so gained a human soul. Fouqué created his own gilded image of medieval Christendom and knight-errantry in fabrications of compelling if superficial quality. In *Sintram and his Companions* (1814, English translation by Julius Hare 1820), the author took as his theme Dürer's engraving, *The Knight, Death and the Devil*, and mingled religious allegory, heroic deeds, sorcery, and romance, in a tale about a young knight who wrestled with the powers of good and evil. Many of these tales, like the Gothic novels enjoyed by young Catherine Morland, were perhaps more appealing to young people in their teens than to the readers of fairy tales.

The search for traditional lore in these islands had already begun with the collection of ballad literature before the eighteenth century was ended. In the new century, deeply under the spell of old balladry and stimulated by the German Romantic writers, Sir Walter Scott carried it further by the publication of his *Minstrelsy of the Scottish Border* in 1802–1803. Others, such as Allan Cunningham, were inspired to collect northern traditional tales, forerunners of J. F. Campbell, whose comprehensive and influential excursion into Gaelic folk-lore – *Popular Tales of the Western Highlands* – came out in 1860–1862.

In 1825, before the second volume of the Grimm stories appeared in this country, T. Crofton Croker produced the first volume of his *Fairy Legends and Traditions of the South of Ireland*. Although not specially addressed to children, these tales remembered by the folk of Ireland, and told in their idiom, would have a strong appeal for the young mind. They recount the pranks of the numerous and varied fairy beings of the emerald isle, the 'good people' who dance in their fairy grounds in the moonlight, the 'Cluricane' or 'Leprechaun' who disappears in a twinkling if the human eye is taken off him, the 'Fir Darrig' all in crimson (the Irish Robin Goodfellow) and other creatures. There are legends about giants and mermaids, enchanted lakes and mountains, and about fairy gold, which turns into yellow furze blossoms or stones above ground. A second volume of this fascinating fairy lore followed in 1828. The work was praised by Sir Walter Scott, and translated into German by the brothers Grimm. Celtic folk-lore is perhaps the richest store of all, and the publication of these Irish tales and anecdotes marks a milestone in its exploration.

It was neither Germany nor Celtic Britain, however, but Denmark, which was to give the world the first great writer of fantasy for children. Hans Christian Andersen (1805–1875) was born at Odense, the son of a poor cobbler, and nurtured in his early youth on the traditional tales of the Danish countryside, the more exotic *Arabian Nights'* and other romantic literature. He put something of the happiness of these early years of childhood,

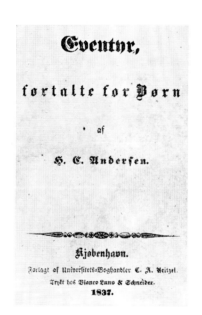

14. *How Andersen's first fairy stories appeared in Denmark*

before his 'storyteller' father died, into one of his tales for boys and girls, *Ole Luckoje* (Wee Willie Winkie). His youthful struggles for advancement, his frustrations, and eventual success are symbolised in another famous story, *The Ugly Duckling*. Writing for children was no part of his life's ambition, however. His intention was to become a famous poet, playwright, or novelist, and at first he looked upon his children's tales as mere bagatelles, unaware that here lay his lasting fame. It was a momentous year, 1835, when waiting for his first novel, *The Improvisatore*, to be published, he brought out a little volume of four fairy tales. Published in Copenhagen, *Eventyr, fortalte for Børn* consisted of four stories chiefly on folk-tale themes – *The Tinderbox; Little Claus and Big Claus; The Princess and the Pea;*

Little Ida's Flowers. Later the same year a second volume followed containing *Thumbelisa; The Naughty Boy; The Travelling Companions*. In 1837 came two of his most famous tales – *The Little Mermaid* and *The Emperor's New Clothes*. A new series of stories in 1845–1846 established his growing fame, and gave to the world that beautiful tale *The Snow Queen* and other favourites. More fairy tales followed, and various collected volumes until 1872, when the last of his tales was issued.

It was not until 1846 that the first English translation of some of the Andersen stories appeared. Mary Howitt was already an admirer of the Danish writer, and she translated the first of his tales to be published in English as *Wonderful Stories for Children*. This was published by Chapman and Hall, with colour plates by Vizetelly, and presented ten stories – *Ole Luckoje*; *The Daisy*; *The Naughty Boy*; *Tommelise*; *The Rose-elf*; *The Garden of Paradise*; *A Night in the Kitchen*; *Little Ida's Flowers*; *The Constant Tin Soldier*; *The Storks*. Two other selections of tales followed during the year 1846, *A Danish Story Book*, translated by Charles Boner and published by Joseph Cundall, and *Danish Fairy Tales and Legends*, translated by Caroline Peachey, and published by Pickering. Both these volumes contained *The Ugly Duckling* and *The Little Mermaid*, as well as a few already included by Mary Howitt, and some newcomers.

Andersen's stories have suffered a good deal from mistranslation, sometimes being put into English from German versions. The tendency in Victorian times was to soften, embellish, vulgarise, even to alter. Much of the writer's crisp style, colloquial directness and humour, therefore, was lost for English readers, but the spell of Andersen could not be quenched by such treatment. Mary Howitt, it seems, in spite of blunders, caught something of his true spirit, and the stories soon won great popularity. Andersen used old folk-tales and also drew on his own memories and experiences for his inventions, but it was his genius for personifying and vivifying everything with wonderful imaginative power, as a child will do, yet with a vision and art beyond a child's capacity, that made him a master storyteller. His birdlike fancy soars and darts everywhere, among the winds, oceans and stars, and also among the little familiar things of kitchen and roadside. He can make a tale about a darning needle, an old bottle, or a street lamp just as felicitously as one about a mermaid below the sea, or a prince in quest of the Garden of Paradise. Some of his later stories have a more moralising tone than his earlier writings, but he usually threads any lesson cunningly into the fabric. The power of love to overcome evil is a recurring theme, vividly expressed in the sacrifice of the little mermaid who chooses to walk on sharp swords and lose her beautiful voice for the sake of the Prince, and in the courage of the child Gerda who braves the icy wastes to rescue her little playmate Kay from his enchantment by the Snow Queen. The art of Hans Andersen is as fresh and spontaneous as the genuine folk-tale, but the sentiment and tender feeling, the gleams of old-fashioned piety and poetic beauty, the flashes of humour, are entirely his own. His name remains one of the greatest in children's literature. The institution of an international award in children's literature in 1953, the 'Hans Christian Andersen' award, presented every two years to a living writer, is a natural and conclusive tribute to his enduring fame.

With the arrival of the fairy tales of Hans Andersen in England in 1846, the literary future of the tale of fantasy was assured. The old traditional stories were being put into a fitting contemporary dress in the 'Home Treasury' series, but Andersen was an inspiration to writers to follow in his footsteps and invent new fairy tales. Another pointer to the growing popularity of the fairy tale, notwithstanding opposition from the Peter Parley school, is the admittance of more fun and fancy into books with moral purpose. In 1839, Catherine Sinclair included in her book, *Holiday House*, 'Uncle David's Nonsensical Story about Giants and Fairies', where the lesson of Master No-book, and his experiences with the contrasted fairies, Do-nothing and Teach-all, are conveyed with much fooling and fancy.

In 1844 another 'improving' fairy tale exhibited the same trend towards levity and freedom. Francis Edward Paget (1806–1882), writing under the pen-name, 'William Churne of Staffordshire', presented to youth *The Hope of the Katzekopfs; or, the Sorrows of Selfishness*, and wondered if the present generation of young people 'could learn wisdom from a Tale of Enchantment'. It was written in the style of the courtly fairy tale of French lineage, and it has been described by Roger Lancelyn Green as 'the first real fairy story of its kind, written in English . . . '[1] Amusing and full of magic incidents as it is, the moral purpose is never forgotten, and the author's aim is to show how selfwill and selfishness lead to disaster and unhappiness.

The Grimm stories were a continuing source of inspiration. A warm admirer was John Ruskin (1819–1900), whose declared opinion in their favour in his introduction to a new edition in 1868 carried much weight with many matter-of-fact minds still doubtful of the wisdom of letting children read fairy tales. By that date Ruskin had become a national oracle of taste and was listened to with respect. Earlier, before he became famous as a great teacher of art and life, he had essayed the art of the fairy tale, in 1841, at the request of twelve-year-old Euphemia Gray, later to become his wife. The result was a tale steeped in his love of mountains and running streams and the old Teutonic legends – *The King of the Golden River* – still enjoyed by children. It was not published until 1851, when it came out with spirited drawings by Richard Doyle. Ruskin later stated his belief that 'children have no need of moral fairy tales', but in this legend of Stiria and the quest of the three brothers to find the river of gold, he shows that kindness and self-denial bring true success, and such teaching is an integral part of his lively and charming story.

---

[1] *Tellers of Tales*, p. 24 (Bibl. 11).

The Rev. F. L. Paget, Rector of Elford, edited a series called 'The Juvenile Englishman's Library', published by J. Masters, 1844–1849. It was designed to promote Church of England principles. *The Hope of the Katzekopfs* was No. 2.

15. *Richard Doyle's illustrated title-page for Ruskin's fairy tale*

The widening range explored by writers in fairy literature in the 1840s is illustrated by the publication of Montalba's *Fairy Tales of all Nations* in 1849. He includes about thirty tales never before translated into English, including some tales from Eastern Europe, as well as stories from more familiar sources.

The invention of fairy tales to amuse their own or their friends' children was to become a popular activity among writers as the century advanced. Nonsense, being a Victorian speciality, frequently invaded such compositions. William Makepeace Thackeray (1811–1863) created his 'extravaganza' or 'fireside pantomime', *The Rose and the Ring* (1855), from a set of Twelfth Night cards he had drawn for his two daughters and their friends. There may be a feeling of pasteboard about this story of the Royal Courts of Paflagonia and Crim Tartary, but it carries the reader along at a great pace, and it is full of exciting and comical happenings. At the end true love conquers, Prince Giglio recovers his kingdom, and marries the long-lost Princess Rosalba. The astonishing and mischievous Fairy

Blackstick then 'sailed away on her cane, and was never more heard in Paflagonia'. Before she left she undid her spell on Gruffanuff, the porter at the palace, whom she had turned into a brass door knocker for attempting to shut her out, in one of the funniest scenes in the story. *The Rose and the Ring* set a standard in light-hearted make-believe. It was illustrated by the author, who disguised his identity on the title-page as 'Mr. M. A. Titmarsh', and it has proved of enduring appeal.

Writers of children's books were also looking into the remote past for their material. Charles Lamb had already produced a fine version for youth of Homer's *Odyssey* in his *Adventures of Ulysses* (1808). This was a welcome contrast to the carefully prepared little question-and-answer manuals of mythology, the approved method of setting Greek and Roman myths before the young reader in the early years of the century. By the middle decades more imaginative ideas had gained ground. In New England, Nathaniel Hawthorne (1804–1864) began his retellings of Greek myths for children in 1851 with the publication of *A Wonder Book*, containing six stories, among them Perseus and the Gorgon's Head, Midas and the Golden Touch, and the Three Golden Apples of the Hesperides. It was followed by a second volume in 1853 – *Tanglewood Tales* – with The Golden Fleece, Theseus and the Minotaur, and four more ancient Greek tales. Hawthorne aimed at substituting 'for the classic coldness, which is as repellent as marble' a tone 'in some degree Gothic and romantic'. He also attempted 'to purify the heathen wickedness' of his sources. Both *A Wonder Book* and its successor, therefore, are transformed into something rather different from their literary originals, although they have some new attractive features. Hawthorne was accused of 'gothicising' the stories, and Charles Kingsley (1819–1875) found them vulgarised.

Kingsley was by then well-known as a novelist, and in 1855, fired by Hawthorne's example and dissatisfied with his rendering, he wrote a volume of old Greek fairy tales for his three children as *The Heroes* (dated 1856, but like many other Victorian books for children, coming out in time for Christmas the previous year). 'I love these old Hellens heartily', he wrote in his preface, and his romantic temperament, poetical gifts and admiration for the heroic fitted him well for the task. Three of the oldest Greek legends – *Perseus*, *The Argonauts*, and *Theseus* – are retold more fully by Kingsley than Hawthorne's dozen examples, and he uses a rhythmic prose to enhance their remote, dramatic, and saga-like quality. 'My dear, good, admirable old ladies' is the style of the address of Hawthorne's Perseus to the three Gray Sisters by the icy sea. 'Venerable mothers' is Kingsley's phrase. Kingsley's treatment all through is more in keeping with the elemental world of the legends. Hawthorne tends to prettify them in a romantic if appealing fashion. Yet both versions have their claims to excellence and both have become classics.

Nothing comparable with the work of Lamb, Hawthorne and Kingsley in interpreting the stories of ancient Greece for young people was published until later in the century, when the teacher and classical scholar, Alfred J. Church (1829–1912) brought out his *Stories from Homer* in October 1876, with illustrations from designs by Flaxman. This is a straightforward rendering of selections from both the *Iliad* and the *Odyssey*, presenting the events in the order in which they occurred rather than as they appear in the originals. Church retold many other stories from classical and medieval sources, but he reported in his autobiography that it was his Homer which 'has been the happiest venture of my books'.[1] It was published in two separate volumes as *The Story of the Odyssey* and *The Story of the Iliad* in 1892, and early in the twentieth century Church reframed his material in a more simple form as *The Children's Odyssey* (1906) and *The Children's Iliad* (1907). About the same time Andrew Lang was to give to children a more haunting and imaginative version of Homer, and the stories of *Perseus, Theseus* and *The Golden Fleece* in his *Tales of Troy and Greece* (1907).

The myths of the Norse peoples were first presented in suitable story form for children in *Heroes of Asgard, and the Giants of Jotunheim; or, the Week and its Story* (1857), by Annie Keary (1825–1879), aided by her sister Eliza. Sources used were Mallet's *Northern Antiquities* (1770) and *Northern Mythology* (1851–1853), by Benjamin Thorpe. The first edition had for frontispiece a steel engraving depicting the Scandinavian cosmology, with its great ash tree, the serpent coiled at its roots, and the abode of darkness below. The stories are set in a framework for their telling – a Victorian family in the Christmas holidays, with a storyteller uncle, and the young people following each episode with questions and conversations about what it all means. Modern editions omit the framework, but show that these stories, which paint a slightly idealistic picture of this world of the old Norse gods, have a lasting appeal. From now onwards boys and girls were to have the chance of reading fascinating tales about Odin and the other gods, their fight with the giants, their coming to their palace in the sky, and other marvellous happenings concerning these pagan deities, such as the story of Balder the Bright, and the wonderful apples of Iduna. The authors end their book with Odin's dream of the Twilight of the Gods and a vision of the light to come, the light of the Christian revelation.

Norse folk-tales, said to contain like others, something of a debased mythology, were collected by P. C. Asbjørnsen and J. I. Moe, and published in Norway in 1841–1844. From this collection Sir George Webbe Dasent (1817–1896) translated his *Popular Tales from the Norse* (1859). Among the sixty tales in his book, there are *East of the Sun and West of the Moon* (already included by Montalba in his 1849 volume), *The Princess on the Glass Hill*, and other now well-known favourites. As in the Grimm collection, there are beast fables and tales of rough humour, as well as more romantic fabrications, many being variants of

---

[1] *Memories of Men and Books*, 1908. Ch. xvii. Church states his *Stories from Homer* came out in October 1876. The earliest copy in the B.M. Catalogue is dated 1878.

stories already known. Dasent did not intend his work especially for children, but brought out for them a volume of *Selections* in 1862. The larger work still remains a most important source for the retelling of Norse fairy tales, and it was followed in 1874 by a further selection from Asbjørnsen and Moe, *Tales from the Fjeld*. Sir George Dasent also translated some of the Icelandic sagas, notably *The Story of Burnt Njal* (1861).

Another addition to fairy literature in the 1850s deserving mention is the still popular *Granny's Wonderful Chair and its Tales of Fairy Times* (1856), by Frances Browne (1816–1879). The author, who was blind, centred seven stories of fairyland, full of charm and old-world morality, upon the device of a magic chair which responds to the child's request for a story.

In the next decade the tale of fantasy for children reached its zenith with the publication of the matchless *Alice's Adventures in Wonderland* in 1865. Two years, however, before this burst upon the world, a very different kind of fairy tale had won acclamation – *The Water Babies* – by Charles Kingsley. It was published in 1863 after being serialised in *Macmillan's Magazine* from August 1862 to March 1863. It had not the timeless genius of the two *Alice* stories of Lewis Carroll, but it possessed its own elements of greatness. In writing his earlier book for children, *The Heroes*, Kingsley was inspired by his love of ancient Greece and its literature. In this new story, written for the latest arrival in the family, five-year-old Grenville, other facets of his personality and pursuits are revealed. Kingsley was a Church of England parson, an idealist, a man of enthusiasms and prejudices, with a passion for natural history and much sympathy for the poor and oppressed. Into *The Water Babies* he poured his knowledge of the rivers and seas, his sense of wonder and reverence for life, his anger against cruelty and social injustice, especially concerning the plight of the chimney sweeps' climbing boys, and he added many comments and castigations. It is a strange medley of a book, with gold shining out everywhere, especially in the opening chapters, where Tom, the little sweep boy, meets Ellie in the great house, finds out how dirty he is, and escapes from his persecutors down Lewthwaite crag to find a new life as a water baby in the river. These scenes reflect the beautiful wild green landscape of Littondale in Yorkshire (the Vendale of the book) and its sparkling river Skirfare.

Digressions and little homilies date *The Water Babies*, but they are only excrescences on the real story, which is ageless as fairyland, intensely real, full of magic and tenderness, and overflowing with vitality. With Tom, the child reader explores the marvels of the deep, visits the Shiny Wall and the Whales, and gets to Mother Carey's Haven and the Other-end-of-nowhere. It may be all 'fun and pretence', as the author confesses at the end, but children still enjoy the wonderful vistas and excitements of Tom's world, where there is also a gleam of eternal truth.

This was an excursion into fairyland seen through the eyes of a lover of nature. More original, and entirely lacking sermonising asides, was the story very soon to rival its popularity in the nursery. The first Alice story, *Alice's Adventures in Wonderland*, was already in being when Kingsley's fairy tale 'for a land baby' was published in 1863, although it was not to be printed for another two years. Charles Lutwidge Dodgson (1832–1898), better known to generations of children and their elders as Lewis Carroll, was a Fellow and Lecturer in Mathematics at Christ Church, Oxford. In the later years of the 1850s he became acquainted with three little girls, the daughters of Dean Liddell, and soon he was in the habit of making up stories for them. He had always been clever at writing, inventing games and puzzles, making up nonsense, and had produced a family magazine when at home with his brothers and sisters. Words and logic – and logic upside down – were as fascinating to him as numbers and calculation. On 4th July 1862, Dodgson with his three little companions, Alice, Lorina, and Edith Liddell, and another friend, Canon Duckworth, set off from Folly Bridge in a rowing boat up river for a picnic. Years later Dodgson described his memory of that afternoon, and how, under the cloudless blue sky, the boat drifted on its watery mirror, and the stern demand came for a story from the three children 'hungry for news of fairyland'. 'I distinctly remember . . . ' he wrote, 'how in a desperate attempt to strike out some new line of fairy-lore, I had sent my heroine straight down a rabbit-hole, to begin with, without the least idea of what was to happen afterwards'.[1] However, the story was continued, and might have been forgotten, like many others he had invented, if Alice had not asked him to write it down for her. Dodgson did so carefully, illustrated it, and presented it to her some time in 1863 as *Alice's Adventures Underground*.[2]

The suggestion was made by Henry Kingsley (the brother of Charles Kingsley) that the story should be published, and George Macdonald supported the idea, trying the book out on his own family with success. Dodgson now rewrote the story and added to it. His own drawings were not good enough for publication, so John Tenniel was asked to illustrate the book, with many hints and instructions from its creator. It was at last issued by Macmillan (the publisher of Kingsley's books for children) in 1865, as *Alice's Adventures in Wonderland*, by Lewis Carroll, but the whole edition was almost immediately withdrawn, as author and artist were dissatisfied with the printing. A new edition by another printer was issued by Macmillan the same year, and its success was immediate and never flagging. Within two years French and German translations were in hand. Six years after its first appearance, Lewis Carroll, who liked to keep his identity a secret, produced a second volume of Alice's adventures, *Through the Looking-Glass and what Alice found*

---

[1] *The Diaries of Lewis Carroll* (Bibl. 178). Roger Lancelyn Green quotes from Dodgson writing about 'Alice on the Stage' in *The Theatre*, 1887 (vol. 1, p. 182).

[2] The original MS. is now in the British Museum (Bibl. 176).

there, dated 1872, in time for Christmas 1871. It was equal to, though perhaps a little different from, its brilliant predecessor.

With these twin masterpieces, the work of fantasy for children reached a pinnacle never surpassed. They exhibit an astonishing rightness in every word and situation. Adults delight in the cleverness, the hidden logic, the wise nonsense, the quotable phrases, yet to a child their fascination has little to do with such refinements. For him the appeal lies in the story, where strange and amusing things happen, and all kinds of funny and fascinating creatures behave with the most convincing oddity. Wonderland becomes a real place – as vivid as dreamland. What gives the tales such perfect balance and certainty is the character of Alice herself, who never changes in her nature however large or small she may grow, or however queerly the verses she knows by heart are changed in the speaking. Sensible, good-natured, charmingly gentle and lovable, she personifies the best traits of Victorian childhood.

> 'It's *very* provoking', Humpty Dumpty said, after a long silence, looking away from Alice as he spoke, 'to be called an egg – *very*!' 'I said you *looked* like an egg, Sir', Alice gently explained. 'And some eggs are very pretty, you know', she added, hoping to turn her remark into a sort of compliment.'[1]

Alice always tries to pacify or put into a good temper, and her steadiness only intensifies the effect of the absurdity and magic all around her. Both tales have their own inner pattern of construction, for which children probably care little, *Alice's Adventures* being based on a game of cards, and its sequel on a game of chess. Both books were illustrated by Tenniel, and although other artists have since interpreted the stories, Tenniel's pictures remain firm favourites as the truest delineation of Alice and her Wonderland.

Charles Dodgson was a man of deep religious principles, reserved with adults, but adept at making friends with children, especially little girls. In these stories about Alice he gave them no lessons of conduct, only such as were synonymous with laughter and delight. Most absurd and hilarious of all were the verses considered with nonsense rhymes in the next chapter. His later stories, *Sylvie and Bruno* (1889) and *Sylvie and Bruno concluded* (1893) are different and lack the unity of the *Alice* books. They show the author in the more serious mood expressed in *An Easter Greeting to every Child who loves Alice*, published in 1876. The origin of the Sylvie and Bruno books goes back to a fairy tale which Dodgson wrote in 1867 for *Aunt Judy's Magazine*, at the request of Mrs. Gatty, and the episodes 'Fairy Sylvie' and 'Bruno's Revenge' were based on this. Gradually over many years Dodgson shaped from 'an unwieldy mass of literature' a continuous story which was published as the *Sylvie and Bruno* volumes. Although they do not equal the artistic quality of the *Alice* stories, their mixture of fairy tale, novel and dream has a distinct charm,

[1] *Through the Looking-Glass*, Ch. vi

and the creator of Wonderland breaks out into his old delicious fun at times, as in the episode 'Bruno's Picnic'.

The continued success of *Alice's Adventures in Wonderland* and *Through the Looking-Glass* inspired many imitators, possessed of little of Dodgson's originality, discipline of thought and literary craftsmanship. The whimsical and wildly fantastical, the comic degenerating into silliness, became the worser features of this imitative school. Greater writers realised that the work of Lewis Carroll was unique, and struck out for themselves into fresh regions of fantasy.

One of the finest writers to do this was George Macdonald (1824–1905), a contemporary and friend of Dodgson. In 1858 he had published *Phantastes*, a romantic and dream-like novel, not addressed to children, although its blend of allegory and medievalism might well appeal to readers in their teens who enjoyed the Fouqué tales. George Macdonald's religion invaded every part of his life and thought, and his vivid imagination recreated the unseen world of spirit and magic in stories of rare power and charm. A volume of his tales of fantasy for children appeared in 1867 as *Dealings with the Fairies*. This contained a frolicsome story about a princess deprived of 'gravitation', 'The Light Princess', and four more tales of rather deeper meaning, 'The Giant's Heart', 'The Shadows', 'Cross Purposes', and 'The Golden Key'. The stories were illustrated by Arthur Hughes, whose drawings so well expressed the tender feeling and other-worldliness of Macdonald's writings for the young.

One of the best books Macdonald wrote is *At the Back of the North Wind* (1871), again illustrated by Hughes. It tells of Little Diamond, the coachman's son, and big Diamond, the coach horse, and the child's marvellous experiences with the mysterious lady, the North Wind, who takes him to a country which might be fairyland or dreamland or paradise. The sad and sentimental ending of the book spoils it today for some readers, and it has some typically Victorian touches, but the opening chapters are among the greatest in children's literature. Other fine stories, which have survived to delight children today, are the two Princess books, *The Princess and the Goblin* (1872) and *The Princess and Curdie* (1883). These tales mingle the symbolic fight of good against evil with exciting action and descriptive writing. What ugliness the author delineates in the shape of wicked goblins and other monsters! As a contrast there is idyllic beauty personified in the Princess Irene's fairy great-great-grandmother. A noble ideal of devotion and service animates the miner's brave son, Curdie, in his quest to save the Princess, and although Macdonald teaches lessons by the way, his storytelling has compelling power.

Some of the novels of Charles Dickens (1812–1870) are increasingly enjoyed by young readers, but the great novelist wrote very little for them. His *Christmas Books* (1843–1848) are all partly fantastical, and intended for family reading rather than for small folk. The first and best-known, *A Christmas Carol*, has long been their possession, however, and is now probably better known by children than their elders. Much less famous is Dickens' little work in four parts for young readers, *A Holiday Romance*, first printed in an American magazine *Our Young Folks* and also in *All the Year Round* in 1868. This is pseudo-childish authorship reflecting children's ideas, and perhaps as amusing to adults as to the young readers for whom it was written. Four children between the ages of six to nine years each make up a story for the improvement of grown-ups, finding much of their inspiration in their reading. The stories comprise *The Trial of William Tinkling*, *The Magic Fishbone*, *Captain Boldheart and the Latin Grammar Master*, and *Miss Orange*. Best remembered of these clever, archly funny inventions is *The Magic Fishbone*.

Jean Ingelow (1820–1897) is perhaps better known for her poetry than for her stories for children, but in *Mopsa the Fairy* (1869) she produced a fantasy of distinct charm if rambling construction. Jack discovers a nest of fairies in an old thorn tree, and begins a series of marvellous adventures by flying to fairyland on the back of an albatross. Mrs. Craik (Dinah Maria Mulock, 1818–1887) was most famous in her day as the author of *John Halifax, Gentleman* (1856), but she also wrote children's stories of real quality. Her now forgotten *Alice Learmont* (1852) is a little gem of a story, Scottish in flavour, and inspired by the Border legend about Thomas the Rhymer. She edited a collection of 'best popular fairy tales' in *The Fairy Book* (1863), and in 1872 published a tale for young children, *The Adventures of a Brownie*. Her most famous story for boys and girls, better remembered in the United States than over here, is *The Little Lame Prince and his travelling Cloak* (1875), a fantasy described by the author as 'a parable for young and old', a sad, charming story, with its own inner moral meaning.

Less famous, but no less gifted, a writer was Mary de Morgan (1850–1907), the sister of the artist and novelist William de Morgan. Her best-known book of fairy tales, *The Necklace of Princess Fiorimonde, and other stories* (1880), illustrated by Walter Crane, was republished in 1963, with two other volumes of her stories, *On a Pincushion* (1877) and *The Windfairies* (1900), also with their original illustrations. Mysterious, romantic, evocative of Hans Andersen in their blend of feeling and fancy, sometimes recalling ancient legends, these are well-written tales that deserve to endure.

Juliana Horatia Ewing, born Gatty (1841–1885), wrote many delightful fairy tales with grace and more than common artistry, most of them firmly rooted in the world of every-day life, often revealing gentle lessons for living. One of her earliest and best is *The Brownies*, which came out in the *Monthly Packet* in 1865. It is a tale within a tale, a device the writer was fond of, and tells of two motherless little boys, whose tailor father finds they are a burden to him and to their grandmother, because they are lazy and useless, and the housework does not get done. So they go to look for a Brownie to come at night to do all the work. In clever and fanciful fashion Mrs. Ewing tells how they find out that *they* and no one else are the Brownies, and how they secretly get up early and do the work. The theme conveys little of Mrs. Ewing's dexterity of treatment which makes it captivating. It was apparently from this story of children who turned themselves into Brownies that the name of the junior branch of the Girl Guide movement was taken. Two other tales in similar vein, and included with *The Brownies and other Tales* when this was published in book form in 1870, are *Timothy's Shoes*, in which a pair of magic shoes, given to Timothy, pinch him if he does not do the right thing, or they go off on their own, giving his secrets away, and *Amelia and the Dwarfs*, in which a naughty child is taken away by these fairy creatures, and must rectify her misdeeds and find a four-leaf clover before she can escape their power and return home. Other tales in the collection are *The Three Christmas Trees*, *The Land of Lost Toys*, and *The Idyll in the Wood*, and the illustrator was George Cruikshank. Mrs. Ewing's *Old-Fashioned Fairy Tales* (1882) first appeared between 1869 and 1876 in *Aunt Judy's Magazine*, the medium for most of her writings after it began in 1866. These fairy tales reveal a wide variety of mood and inspiration, close in spirit to the 'old originals', but softened in tone, and sometimes distilling serious thoughts. Nearly all Mrs. Ewing's books have a hint of fantasy in them, but her work will be further considered with the story of home and school.

Less subtle in their creation, but of more popular appeal than the fairy stories of Mrs. Ewing, are the many tales by Mrs. Molesworth (Mary Louisa Stewart, 1839–1921). She began to write novels in the 1860s under the pseudonym of 'Ennis Graham', but from 1875 she turned to works for children, beginning with *Tell me a Story*, illustrated by Walter Crane, and published that year. She also dropped the pseudonym. Her first book of tales includes one partly founded on her own childhood memories of Manchester days, when she invented fairy characters from the contents of her mother's workbox – *The Reel Fairies*. After the success of *Carrots*, described later, she published in 1877 perhaps her most successful and enduring fairy tale, *The Cuckoo Clock*. The clock is a magic clock with a fairy Cuckoo who befriends the lonely Griselda, not very happy living with two maiden aunts. It is a humorous, sometimes perverse fairy being, this Cuckoo, the first of a race of crochety, unprepossessing fairies, like the Psammead and the Mouldiwarp, later to appear in the stories by E. Nesbit. Mrs. Molesworth relates magical happenings to everyday life, and Griselda, after her adventures in Butterfly Land and at the other side of the moon, safely comes home all the wiser for her fairy friend's giudance and advice.

The Tapestry Room (1879) is another of this author's fine stories of fantasy to survive. The tale is set in France, which Mrs. Molesworth knew well, and here the fairy is a rough-spoken old raven. Through its help the children, Jeanne and Hugh, are able to get into the castle on the tapestry, and they have some exciting magical journeys, until at last the raven tells them a history about their ancestors and bids them farewell. Mrs. Molesworth wrote fewer tales of magic than of family life, but three other notable examples are *Christmas Tree Land* (1884), a mysterious tale of the visit of two children to a castle in an enchanted pine forest, where real life and make-believe merge indistinctly, the dream-like *Four Winds Farm* (1887) and *The Ruby Ring* (1904). Although more sentimental, Mrs. Molesworth recalls in her more visionary moments in these tales something of the power of George Macdonald.

A well-known contemporary of Mrs. Molesworth, famous in his day as a writer of fairy tales, was E. H. Knatchbull-Hugessen (1829–1893), later Lord Brabourne. Inspired to write stories for his own family, he produced his first volume in 1869 as *Stories for my Children*, and followed this with other pleasant and fanciful volumes, sometimes reminiscent of Hans Andersen, sometimes over-wordy and striving too much after comic effect. His literary capabilities did not include the story-telling powers of a Mrs. Molesworth, however, so that his works are now forgotten.

The great personality in the literature of fairy lore towards the end of the nineteenth century is undoubtedly Andrew Lang (1844–1912), a native of the Scottish Border country, and classical scholar, poet, and folklorist. When he brought out the first of his 'Colour' Fairy Books in 1889, it was felt that the interest in fairy tales was declining, and the emphasis was on stories of real life. Lang did a great deal to bring in attractive guise to children fairy stories of every kind, traditional or invented, known and unknown. In the first volume in the series, *The Blue Fairy Book* (1889), he began by giving them some favourite tales from Grimm, Perrault, and d'Aulnoy, with a few from the *Arabian Nights'*, Asbjørnsen and Moe, and English tales such as *Dick Whittington* and *Jack-the-Giant-killer*, taken from chapbooks. He also included two Scottish tales, the original of Lamb's *Prince Dorus* (*Prince Désir*, by Madame Le Prince de Beaumont), and a much abridged version of *Gulliver's Travels* as *A Voyage to Lilliput*. In later volumes, which followed regularly until the last, *The Lilac Fairy Book*, came out in 1910, he went further afield, and fairy lore from all over the world found its way into these volumes, 'We see that black, white, and yellow people are fond of the same kind of adventures', he wrote in his introduction to *The Pink Fairy Book* (1897). 'Courage, youth, beauty, kindness have many trials, but they always win the battle; while witches, giants, unfriendly cruel people, are on the losing side. So it ought to be, and so, on the whole it is and will be; and that is the moral of all fairy tales...'

Andrew Lang accomplished a great deal of serious research into fairy tales. He edited with scholarly notes a reprint of the first French edition of Perrault (Bibl. 91), and wrote a lengthy introduction on the origin of fairy tales for the complete edition of Grimm in 1884 (Bibl. 144). Most of the stories in the Fairy Books were retold by Mrs. Lang or by other helpers, but Andrew Lang's wide knowledge and editorship were the foundation of the venture. The 'Colour' Fairy Books have won lasting popularity, and are being re-issued in a new format, with a few omissions, by Longmans, the original publishers.

Lang also wrote fairy tales of his own invention. The first, *Princess Nobody* (1884), is a slight tale written to fit some illustrations by Richard Doyle, previously published in 1870 as *In Fairyland: a Series of Pictures by Richard Doyle, with a poem by William Allingham* (p. 134). Lang's story is in the amusing Fairy Court style, but his next story was different. This was filled with the faery spirit of the north, and based on traditional legends of the Border and his memories of boyhood haunts. He called it *The Gold of Fairnilee* (1888), and he tells the story of a boy, Randal Ker, whose father was killed at Flodden. Randal is taken away to fairyland, rescued through the efforts of his little English friend, Jean, and finally the two children discover an ancient treasure with the help of fairy magic. *Prince Prigio* (1889), and its sequel, *Prince Ricardo* (1893), are again in the gay and artificial style of *The Rose and the Ring*. The final book about Pantouflia and its Royal Court, the setting for *Prince Prigio* and *Prince Ricardo*, is his *Tales of a Fairy Court* (1907), but the two earlier stories were also included as *Chronicles of Pantouflia*, with *The Gold of Fairnilee*, in the collected edition, *My Own Fairy Book* (1895). Excellent as his original stories are, Andrew Lang's great contribution to children's literature does not lie there, but in his work as scholar and editor.

Another scholar and folklorist, who invented little of his own, but who brought many folk-tales to children in suitable form was Joseph Jacobs (1854–1916). In *English Fairy Tales* (1890–1894, 2 volumes), he set down in a vernacular style which preserved the flavour of the originals, some eighty-seven traditional tales of this kingdom. 'My ambition,' he states in his introduction, 'was to write as a good old nurse will speak when she tells fairy tales'. He wrote his tales for children, and added notes for those interested in sources and variations, finding his material in chapbooks, ballads, and existing collections, such as those made by James Orchard Halliwell, whose second volume of nursery literature, *Popular Rhymes and Nursery Tales* (1849), contained many prose tales (his earlier book, *The Nursery Rhymes of England* (1842) being almost entirely devoted to rhyming folk-lore). The notes by Jacobs have usually been omitted in editions of the tales for children, but there has been a recent reprint of the whole work in the Bodley Head series of important classics of this kind being put into splendid modern dress.

Tom Tit Tot is a Suffolk variant of the German *Rumpelstiltskin*, and such famous tales as *Childe Rowlande*, *The History of Tom Thumb*, *Whittington and his Cat*, *The Children in the Wood*, and *Tom Hickathrift* are interspersed with newcomers, including some stories from Scottish and Celtic sources. The storyteller can still find much treasure here.

In 1892 Jacobs published a collection of *Celtic Fairy Tales*, following it with a second volume in 1894. The stories are taken from a wide variety of sources, Irish, Gaelic and Welsh, and begin with 'the earliest fairy-tale of modern Europe', *Connla and the Fairy Maiden*, taken from the twelfth-century *Book of the Dun Cow*, but dating back perhaps to the days before St. Patrick. Many different types of story are included, ranging from the sorrowful and romantic *Children of Lir* and *Deirdre* to humorous peasant narratives.

The same year, 1892, there also appeared Jacobs' *Indian Fairy Tales*, chiefly founded, like the Celtic volumes on existing material in print. Mary Frere (1845–1911) had begun the collection and publication of traditional tales of India with those told to her by her native *ayah*, in *Old Deccan Days; or Hindoo Fairy Legends current in Southern India* (1868), and Flora Annie Steel (1847–1929) had also written some folk-tales for children called *Wide Awake Stories*, published in India in 1884, and ten years later issued in England as *Tales of the Punjab as told by the People*. Both Miss Frere's and Mrs. Steel's Indian stories were used by Jacobs, as well as other sources, both old and new. He drew upon the *Bidpai Fables* and the *Jataka Tales*, realising that many of these ancient Eastern tales had long been known in the west. Early Indian folk-tales were collected, he pointed out, more than two thousand years before Grimm.

Other countries were by now making their contribution with folk stories for boys and girls. From the Southern States of America there came the tales told by the negroes, set down by Joel Chandler Harris (1848–1908), as *Uncle Remus, his Songs and Sayings* (1880), published in England in 1881 as *Uncle Remus and his Legends of the old Plantation*. These were talking beast fables, often showing an African or Indian origin. Jacobs considered that he had traced the Indian source of the Tar Baby episode in a Jataka tale. The hero of the Uncle Remus tales is Brer Rabbit, a lovable trickster who overcomes by guile his enemy the wolf and the other animals. Kipling, aged sixteen, and still at the United Services College in Devon, found the stories fascinating. His *Jungle Books*, referred to later with the development of the animal story, were all his own in their style and originality, but they have a basic relationship with these negro tales and other animal fables.

Another scholar, R. Nisbet Bain (1854–1909), worked chiefly in the Slavonic field. He brought out his *Russian Fairy Tales* in 1893, founding them on the *Popular Russian Märchen* of Peter N. Polevoi, published in St. Petersburg in 1874. This was a selection from the great collection issued by Afanasiev from 1855 to 1864. Bain followed his Russian tales with *Cossack Fairy and Folk Tales* in 1894.

The tales collected in Denmark by Svend Grundtvig were published as *Danske Folkeeventyr* between 1876 and 1883, and English versions for children were in being by the end of the century. Jane Milley translated eighteen of the stories as *Fairy Tales from afar* (1900), and J. Christian Bay made a collection of popular stories and fairy tales from several sources, including Grundtvig, in *Danish Fairy and Folk Tales*, published by Harper in New York in 1899. These examples indicate how folklore of every kind was invading children's books by the end of the nineteenth century, a development which was to be steadily continued in the years ahead.

In the last decade of Victoria's reign writers of fairy tales began to explore the more exotic regions of romance, and children's books inclined away from nature and realism. Studied craftsmanship and a poet's feeling for words characterise the fairy stories of both

Oscar Wilde (1856–1900) and Laurence Housman (1863–1959). For Wilde the visions of art were more convincing than the world of existence, and his tales for children are polished prose poems aglow with imagery, and perhaps more to be appreciated by older readers than the usual readers of fairy tales. Nine tales are comprised in the two books, *The Happy Prince and other Tales* (1888) and *A House of Pomegranates* (1891). Some of them have a sad or cynical note, some enshrine a moral allegory as, for example two favourites in the first volume, *The Happy Prince* and *The Selfish Giant*.

Laurence Housman wrote fairy tales full of enchantment and romance, more naturalistic in style than the highly artificial Wilde stories. Like some other contemporary writers, anticipating Tolkien in our own times, he did not believe that fairy tales were intended only for children. 'The value of fairy tales is . . . not to be found by considering children in particular', Tolkien was to write in his brilliant essay 'On Fairy Stories' in 1947 (Bibl. 172). And in these *fin de siècle* years, when the tenets of aestheticism were found to be unsatisfying, some romantic spirits began to feel that fairyland might be worth recapturing and not be left entirely for the delight of the young. Housman's four volumes of tales were produced in a style not designed for young readers. Finely printed with his own illustrations engraved by Clemence Housman, they consisted of *A Farm in Fairyland* (1894), *The House of Joy* (1895), *The Field of Clover* (1898), and *The Blue Moon* (1904). Selections for children were not made from them until 1922.

Kenneth Grahame (1859–1932) had included an amusing rather than a romantic fairy tale in his *Dream Days* (1898), entitled *The Reluctant Dragon*. It is about a dragon who is lazy and wants a quiet life rather than a combat with St. George, and it is set in the country of the Berkshire Downs. But neither *Dream Days*, nor its predecessor, *The Golden Age* (1895), were books for children, although they have much significance in the development of children's literature. Never before had anyone set down so vividly and faithfully, with such charm of style, the imaginative realities of the life of childhood as recalled in later years. The five children – one of them the author – are shown to have an important life of their own, superior to that of the 'Olympians', the adults who are too blind to see the marvels of the elf-haunted life around them.

A few years afterwards Grahame had a son of his own, 'Mouse', for whom he invented a bedtime story that later became *The Wind in the Willows* (1908). This fantasy about Mr. Toad, the Mole, Ratty and other animals of the countryside, mingles deep feeling and joy in nature with fun and excitement, magic and wonder. It will doubtless long remain as one of the best-loved and best-known of twentieth century classics for children.

Whether Edith Nesbit (1858–1924) was inspired to write about dragons through her admiration of the work of Kenneth Grahame, and his dragon tale in *Dream Days*, is uncertain. But soon afterwards, in the March issue of the *Strand Magazine*, 1899, there appeared the first of her series of dragon stories. 'The Book of Beasts' narrated the adventures of a small boy whose ancestors were wizards as well as kings, and who finds that he has the power to make the beasts depicted in a book come alive as he turns the pages – hence the menace of a great red dragon. H. R. Millar, inimitable interpreter of Nesbit scenes and characters, illustrated the episodes. They varied in type, but most of them exhibited a characteristic the writer was to make particularly her own – magic and wizardry centred around quite ordinary children. Published as *The Book of Dragons* in 1900, they were followed by some other tales of fantasy, *Nine Unlikely Tales for Children*, the next year, again after magazine publication. All these, however, were only a prelude to something more notable. In 1901 some stories of more connected plan appeared in the *Strand* under the title of *The Psammead*. They came out in book form the following year, again with delightful drawings by Millar, as *Five Children and It*. E. Nesbit now demonstrated that she was a master of the craft of writing fantasy for children in a new way, a writer who could present lively happenings concerning real children, with humour and insight, yet combine with this ordinary life marvels and strange happenings from the supernatural world. She was no romantic, although she was fascinated by the past, and her fairy beings, like the sand-fairy in this first complete tale of fantasy, are earthy, cross-grained creatures. And the children do not find magical happenings bring the millenium. Here the five children are excited to find that their discovery, the Psammead, can grant them wishes, but the results are fraught with unforeseen consequences, sometimes calamitous.

Recreating the past in stories through magical devices was well established in the first decade of the twentieth century. E. Nesbit followed *Five Children and It* with other tales of magic, and took her child characters back in history quite often, though never further than ancient Egypt, introduced in *The Story of the Amulet* (1906).

The hobgoblin of English folk-lore, Puck, was the tutelary spirit chosen by Rudyard Kipling to introduce Dan and Una to scenes and people of bygone Britain in his *Puck of Pook's Hill* (1906) and *Rewards and Fairies* (1910). These stories belong to history perhaps rather than fantasy, but there is at least one bit of real folk-lore in the first book, 'Dymchurch Flit', where Tom Shoesmith (or is it Puck?) tells an old Sussex legend about the departure of the fairies across the Channel. Past and present merge in these tales about 'Merlin's Isle of Gramarye', but it is Puck, 'the oldest, old Thing in England', with his spell of oak, ash and thorn, who puts a girdle of fantasy about these brilliant recreations of the past.

J. M. Barrie put a potent spell of his own upon children's literature in Edwardian days, but his *Peter Pan*, both story and play, are considered in the next chapter. Much whimsy and winsomeness flooded into children's books in his wake, unworthy of his brilliant fancy, but the fine and lasting contributions of Grahame, Nesbit and Kipling were matched by another writer of distinction who made his debut in this golden decade – Walter de la Mare (1873–1956). In 1910 there appeared a story about a strange quest by three monkey princes to find an ideal country – very different from Barrie's Never-Never-Land – the flowery, long-sought valleys of Tishnar. It was an imaginative saga of dreamlike enchantment and high adventure, perhaps not always easy to understand, but possessing a powerful and poetic beauty for the perceptive reader. De la Mare, a poet of rising renown, with a feeling for the world invisible, the ghoulish, and the joys of childhood, wrote the tale for his own children. Entitled *The Three Mulla-Mulgars*, and not very attractively produced, it became little known until it was re-issued in 1935 as *The Three Royal Monkeys*.

Since it broke into the open in the 1840s, the shining stream of fairy lore and make-believe for children had become a wide river by the end of the Edwardian era. Amidst the plenitude was much tinsel and frippery, but also much of true quality. The best achievements of these early twentieth century years maintained the high standard set in the Victorian age by Andersen, Carroll and Macdonald. Together they gave to the future a brilliant and lasting heritage.

III   NONSENSE, VERSE AND DRAMA

Fun and hilarity in children's books are by no means confined to those to be noticed in this chapter, but an attempt will be made to trace some of the chief works which have had laughter as a main object. Riddles and jests, often in harness, go back far into the past in popular literature, and both children and older folk appreciated the absurdities, and sometimes the coarser humours, of the chapbooks, where much old material survived. Nursery rhymes and nonsense can hardly be separated, and something about their entry into children's books has been described in foregoing pages. John Newbery introduced humour very successfully into many of his books for boys and girls, but a volume specially devoted to it is one of his least attractive publications. This was *Be Merry and Wise; or, The Cream of the Jests and Marrow of Maxims for the Conduct of Life, published for the Use of all Little Good Boys and Girls, by Tommy Trapwit, Esq.*, (1753). It is too adult in tone and too typical of its day to deserve much attention. Other Newbery books introduced lighter and more pleasing humour, including one already mentioned as a possible compilation by the publisher, but not issued until some years after his death – *Mother Goose's Melody* (pp. 47).

Levity was breaking through during the reign of the moral school of writers, not only in volumes of traditional nursery ditties. The Taylor sisters came near to absurdity, at least on the surface, with *Signor Topsy-Turvy's wonderful Magic Lantern; or, The World turned upside down* (1810). The pictures by their brother, Isaac Taylor, are really more comical than the verses, for these rather satirical rhymes about the horse turned driver, the hare roasting the cook, and other inversions of the common order, have lessons for humanity.

John Harris, the enterprising publisher at the top of Ludgate Hill, made several excursions into nonsense in the first quarter of the nineteenth century, as well as publishing nursery songs such as *Original Ditties for the Nursery* (1805). The earliest book of limericks was issued in his 'Cabinet of Amusement and Instruction' as *The History of Sixteen Wonderful Old Women* (1820). Humorous tales in verse that Harris published ranged from the popular *Comic Adventures of Old Mother Hubbard and her Dog* (1805) to animal absurdities like *The Monkey's Frolic* (1825). The firm of Godwin also ventured into the realm of humour, and amusing and nonsensical verses were becoming the fashion in the early nineteenth century. A well-known example was *Dame Wiggins of Lee and her Seven Wonderful Cats*, published by Dean and Munday in 1823. The verses are ascribed to R. S. Sharpe and Mrs. Pearson (the old lady herself), and the illustrations were by R. Stennett. It was revived in 1885, with additional verses by John Ruskin, and additional drawings by Kate Greenaway.

In Victorian days nonsense for youth descends at times to the crudely farcical or laboriously comic. But it also found exponents of genius. In 1846, a little book of limericks accompanied by the funniest sketches, appeared with nothing to denote its authorship but these verses on the cover:

> 'There was an old Derry-down-Derry
> Who liked to see little folks merry,
> So he wrote them a book
> And with laughter they shook
> At the fun of that Derry-down-Derry.'

The verses and illustrations had already caused shrieks of laughter among the young people at Knowsley, Lord Derby's great house in Lancashire. There Edward Lear (1812–1888), a young artist employed to illustrate the owner's fine collection of animals and birds, would sometimes visit and entertain the nurseries 'where children and mirth abounded'. He confessed later that the source of his inspiration for the use of the limerick was a verse from *Anecdotes and Adventures of Fifteen Gentlemen*, published by John Marshall about 1822.

> 'There was an old Man of Tobago
> Lived long on rice, gruel, and sago,
> But at last, to his bliss,
> The physician said this:
> To a roast leg of mutton you may go.'

126

Lear's book was nonsense 'pure and absolute', and the sharp, childlike drawings portraying the various characters, the old persons, old men, young ladies from Sparta, Calcutta, Dorking and other parts of the globe, enhanced the absurdity. Further verses and pictures were added later, and on the issue of the third edition in 1861, Lear, who was known as a serious landscape artist, acknowledged his authorship. In 1871, came *Nonsense Songs, Stories, Botany and Alphabets*, containing two peerless pieces, 'The Owl and the Pussey Cat' and 'The Jumblies'. *More Nonsense* appeared the next year (for Christmas 1871), and in 1877 *Laughable Lyrics*, which included some of the best manifestations of Lear's rhythmic gifts and his flair for the invention of words – 'The Yonghy-Bonghy Bo', 'The Pobble', and 'The Quangle-Wangle'. Lear's ear for verbal music and his sensitivity of feeling make his nonsense something more than mere frivolity.

> 'The Owl and the Pussey-Cat went to sea
>   In a beautiful peagreen boat.
> They took some honey, and plenty of money,
>   Wrapped up in a Fivepound note.'

In this and much of Lear's matter for laughter there is a contact with reality, an expression of self-caricature sometimes disguising an inward loneliness, which gives life to it, and makes its appeal as fresh now as when it was created.

Very soon the 'Derry-down-Derry' had a successor who also knew the secret of awakening children's laughter. The two *Alice* stories of Lewis Carroll are just as full of nonsense as of magic and fantastical adventure – a perfect blend of make-believe. Nowhere is nonsense more gloriously in control than at the Mad Hatter's Tea-Party, or in the trial scene, or where the Cheshire cat vanishes slowly 'ending with a grin, which remained sometime after the rest of it had gone'. But it is particularly the verses which should receive attention here. In *Alice's Adventures in Wonderland* these are chiefly parodies, inserted most aptly and adding greatly to the fun. Dodgson took as his originals verses he knew the three Liddell sisters would have learnt by heart. Two of the songs of Isaac Watts, 'How doth the little busy bee' and ''Tis the voice of the sluggard' are transformed into 'How doth the little crocodile' and ''Tis the voice of the lobster'. Jane Taylor's famous poem, 'Twinkle, twinkle, little star', is recited by the Hatter as 'Twinkle, Twinkle, little bat! How I wonder what you're at!' And so on. In *Through the Looking-Glass* there are verses of even more originality and brilliance. Like Lear, Dodgson enjoyed inventing words. 'Jabberwocky', which Alice finds as a 'Looking-glass book' *sounds* just like sense.

> 'Twas brillig, and the slithy toves
>   Did gyre and gimble in the wabe;
> All mimsy were the borogoves
>   And the mome raths outgrabe.'

Alice is naturally puzzled, but Humpty-Dumpty later explains it to her. 'The Walrus and the Carpenter' is a more straightforward, mock-sorrowful ballad, not considered at all amusing by the tender-hearted Alice, for she thought both characters very unpleasant.

In 1876, still hiding his identity as Lewis Carroll, Dodgson published *The Hunting of the Snark: an Agony in eight Fits*, perhaps a book for adults as much as for boys and girls. It was illustrated by Henry Holiday, and although people looked for hidden meanings, the author avowed it to be merely nonsense, and that he himself did not know what a 'Snark' was!

The first book of rhymes by William Brighty Rands (1823–1882) came out anonymously in 1864 as *Lilliput Levee*, and contained some pieces very close to nonsense, if not in the Lear or Carroll undiluted strain. 'Topsyturvey-world' is a little rhyme on the old theme of the natural order of things inverted. 'Frodgedobbulum's Fancy', a long poem, is a story in rhymed couplets about a giant 'with teeth like the prongs of a garden rake', who goes to Banbury in search of a wife, takes away the fair and lissom nine-year-old Marjorie, but comes to grief by forgetting the rule about his magic boots, putting the wrong leg in the one Marjorie has left behind, so blowing up his castle, and is carried away to the North Pole. More absurd, if not so versatile, was *Nursery Nonsense; or, Rhymes without Reason*, also published in 1864, by the scholar D'Arcy Wentworth Thompson (1829–1902), and illustrated by C. H. Bennett, a notable comic artist of the period. The verses are close in style to the nursery jingles of traditional pattern. For example there is 'Crazy Arithmetic'.

'4 in 2 goes twice as fast
    If 2 and 4 change places.
But how can 2 and 3 make four,
    If 3 and 2 make faces.'

The comic invention of the nineteenth century never flagged, and Hilaire Belloc (1870–1955) carried on the art with *The Bad Child's Book of Beasts* (1896), *More Beasts for Worse Children* (1897), and *Cautionary Tales: designed for the Admonition of Children between the ages of eight and fourteen years* (1907). The pictures were by B.T.B. (Lord Basil Blackwood), accentuating the delight of these drolleries, which parodied the moral verses of a century earlier in an individual and mock-serious fashion. The introduction to the first book makes plain what is intended.

'I call you bad, my little child
    Upon the title-page,
Because a manner rude and wild
    Is common at your age.

The moral of this priceless work,
    (If rightly understood)
Will make you – from a little Turk –
    Unnaturally good.'

There was also nonsense in prose to amuse young readers – not so common as the more favoured verse. A book of extravagant absurdities in prose very popular throughout the nineteenth century was *The Adventures of Baron Munchausen*, first published in 1785. The author was Rudolph Erich Raspe (1737–1794), a German who fled to England, and wrote this book of amazing adventures in English. The Baron was a real person. The author merely borrowed his name for these extravagant 'tall stories' supposedly related by the Baron over his wine. The episodes describe the crocodile which swallowed the head of a lion as it jumped over the teller's head, the horse tethered to a steeple in a great snowstorm, and similar incredulities.

Verse of a more serious kind than nonsense rhymes and nursery ditties had been in favour for children long before this lighter fare. Fables in verse and homilies teaching religion in rhyme were among the earliest books designed for youth, as early chapters in this history have tried to show. John Newbery included serious and secular rhymes as well as more light-hearted verses in his little books in the middle of the eighteenth century.

One or two of the most pleasing, probably by Christopher Smart, can be found in *The Lilliputian Magazine* (1752). Newbery also gave 'children three foot high' *A Collection of Pretty Poems* in 1756, but 'Thomas Tagg's' volume was too high-flown in sentiment and rhetorical in style to be of much value.

After Newbery religious verse was increasingly rivalled by the productions of the moral school of writers who often turned to rhyme to convey lessons about conduct and prudent advice, believing with Watts, yet without his poetic gift, that verse would make a deeper imprint on the child's memory. Not until the early nineteenth century are there genuine signs of poetry specially addressed to children for their delight rather than their edification. Rhymed fantasies, beginning with *The Butterfly's Ball* in 1807, have already been noted as a feature of this period, and more impressive and influential work, mingling pleasure in simple things with old-fashioned didacticism expressed in a happy and appealing way, is to be found in the writings of Ann and Jane Taylor.

But before they came on the scene or the eighteenth century was ended, a poet of genius was to take poetry for children into the realm of pure literature. The work of William Blake (1757–1827) was outside the main stream of children's literature, and his lyric poems, *Songs of Innocence* (1789), like much of the best poetry for the young, was not specially addressed to them. They were little known until about the middle of the nineteenth century. Then these verses, now so highly valued, began to find their way into anthologies for young people – especially 'The Piper', 'The Lamb', 'The Little Black Boy' and 'Night'. Children's editions of 'These songs of happy chear' have now been interpreted by other artists, but in 1789 Blake put his poems into a book of his own making, etching it on copper by his own method, and encircling the verses, so full of light and laughter and tenderness, with leafy tendrils and curling flame, merging into marginal pictures of pastoral beauty. *Songs of Experience* came out five years afterwards

16. *From an original print by Blake in 1789*

in 1794. Here the imaginative vision of innocence has been darkened and transformed by life and suffering. But, from this later volume, children's poetry gained at least one great lyric – 'Tyger, Tyger, burning bright'.

Blake was a rebel against the conventional theology of his day, and his unorthodox, profoundly-felt views, which moulded his life and art, shine out especially in 'The Divine Image' in his *Songs of Innocence*. He reveals God as Mercy, Pity, Peace and Love, with these qualities universal in man also.

> 'And all must love the human form
> In heathen, turk or jew;
> Where Mercy, Love and Pity dwell
> There God is dwelling too.'

There is a great gulf between these sentiments and the theology of Watts. And it was to the writer of orthodox hymns and songs, and not to Blake, that makers of verse for children still looked for their inspiration. But there are indications of a new spirit arising in verse for the young – not merely in the fanciful little rhymes about insects, birds, and other denizens of the natural world in the style of *The Butterfly's Ball*. Faint gleams of it are visible in *Poetry for Children* (1801), selected by Lucy Aikin (1781–1864), and containing a few of her own poems as well as some favourite extracts and examples of verse she thought suitable and 'within the comprehension of the well-educated child as soon as he should at all be able to feel the beauties of real poetry'. She confined her selection chiefly to simple themes, although the style is often rhetorical and formal. There are a few extracts from Pope's Homer, and Miss Aikin also included several items by the famous Mrs. Barbauld, her aunt. What is striking, however, is the simplicity of language of the few poems by Lucy Aikin herself. Nothing is here of much quality, but the subjects are pleasing – a robin set free, an Italian and his marmot, a little traveller from Lapland, and the famous, pathetic history of Prince Lee Boo.

Miss Aikin was a pioneer feeling her way, without the skill or the lasting charm of style of her contemporaries, Ann Taylor, later Mrs. Gilbert (1782–1866), and her sister, Jane Taylor (1783–1824). Among the makers of rhyme who addressed themselves to boys and girls, they were the first who really entered into the child's world, and interpreted it in easy, entertaining fashion. Admonition and encouragement to good and sensible behaviour were never far away, but they were put forward in a playful never frightening way.

Watts' *Hymns*, in spite of imitators, were still unrivalled as serious verses for children at the beginning of the nineteenth century, when the Taylors began a new era of verse-making for the young with *Original Poems for Infant Minds* (2 volumes, 1804–5). It was published by the Quaker firm of Darton and Harvey, and contained pieces by Adelaide O'Keefe and one or two other contributions. But the largest share of it was the work of the Taylor sisters. The publishers were already familiar with the writing abilities of the Taylor family, and both Ann and Jane had contributed to Darton's *Minor's Pocket Book* since 1799. The firm commissioned them to provide something more ambitious – 'specimens of easy poetry for children . . . moral songs or short tales in verse'. The sisters set to work and the result was something novel and lightsome in the realm of literature for children. The verses had an immediate success, and were followed by a second work, *Rhymes for the Nursery*, in 1806.

The Taylors were engravers, but all the family wrote also, and it was a happy, pious, and industrious non-conformist household. The secret of the appeal of Ann and Jane Taylor's verse lay in its humour and simplicity, and their understanding of childish interests. Sad disasters certainly follow naughtiness – witness the revealing titles, 'Meddlesome Matty', 'Careless Matilda', 'Greedy Richard' – but the tone and style were fresh and natural. Serious thoughts there are in plenty in the Taylors' rhymes, but there is also revealed true delight in childish experiences among familiar things at home and out-of-doors.

Jane especially explored the world of nature, and both the sisters wrote of such things as birds and flowers, animals, the farm, the seasons, night and day, earth and sky.

'What millions of beautiful things there must be
In this mighty world ! – who could reckon them all?
The tossing, the foaming, the wide, flowing sea,
And thousands of rivers that into it fall.'

So begins Ann Taylor's 'Beautiful Things', one of the more serious pieces in the sisters' first book, *Original Poems for Infant Minds*. *Rhymes for the Nursery* contained Jane Taylor's famous 'Twinkle, twinkle, little star', and was suited for rather younger children. Their satirical and comic contribution to nonsense verse has been mentioned earlier in this chapter.

In more solemn mood the sisters emulated Dr. Watts with their book *Hymns for Infant Minds* in 1808. These religious verses are gloomy and purposeful, much concerned with wickedness and sin, and even easy language could not redeem them from oblivion. The Taylors' more cheerful secular rhymes had over a century of popularity. But today most of their verses are forgotten. Only occasionally does one of their best or most characteristic compositions – such as 'Meddlesome Matty', 'The Cow', 'The Baby's Dance', 'The Star' – add a touch of old-world charm to modern anthologies.

The third contributor to *Original Poems*, Adelaide O'Keefe (1776–1855), was a writer of many poems for youth which pleased her generation. She never wrote anything better than the verses she composed for this volume made famous by her more able contemporaries. Like them she did not bring a moral lesson into everything. She could be dramatic, instructional and sometimes naïve, as in 'Birds, Beasts and Fishes', first published in *Original Poems*, and later issued by Darton and Harvey as a separate work with illustrations.

> 'The Dog will come when he is called,
> The Cat will walk away.
> The Monkey's cheek is very bald,
> The Goat is full of play.'

Jeffreys Taylor (1792–1833), a younger brother of Ann and Jane Taylor and the reputed 'wag' of the family, wrote many books for youth, and included at the end of his *Aesop in Rhyme* (1820) some original fables in satirical and humorous vein.

The taste for the new style in verse for children was much exploited by enterprising publishers, among them William Godwin. It was to compete in this market that he or Mrs. Godwin invited Charles and Mary Lamb to compose a book of poems for children in the winter of 1808–1809. Charles Lamb described it as 'Task-work', and he was responsible for about a third of the whole. But it seemed that his lighter verse trifles were more appreciated than this joint work in two volumes. It was published in 1809 and then was completely lost until its re-issue in 1872. In it there is not much of real interest to children, although there is much fanciful thought about childish ways and some true tenderness of feeling. It is too contemplative in tone to be successful as verse for children, and Mary Lamb, especially, could not match the technical skill of the Taylors. In this work, the Lambs are much more the prisoners of their time than in their other writings for the young, and therefore few of their verses are known today.

A more popular successor to the Taylor sisters was Elizabeth Turner (d. 1846), who wrote simple rhymes for small children, although never too young for warnings about bad behaviour. *The Daisy; or, Cautionary Stories in Verse* (1807) was designed for children from four to eight years old. Two years later this was followed by *The Cowslip; or, More Cautionary Stories in Verse*. There is a very sing-song beat to most of Mrs. Turner's rhymes, most of them concerned with lessons about good conduct, although the author could make a pleasant jingle about very little without labouring any moral, as in 'Pretty Puss'.

> 'Come, pretty cat,
> Come here to me,
> I want to pat
> You on my knee.

Go, naughty Tray,
By barking thus,
You'll drive away
My pretty Puss.'

A hundred years later echoes of Elizabeth Turner's more didactic style are to be found in the mirthful parodies of this school of persuasive verse by Hilaire Belloc.

Much verse of the period was very pedestrian and uninspired. *Simple Stories in Verse*, an anonymous little work published by Tabart in 1809, and possibly by Eliza Fenwick or Elizabeth Sandham, is typical in seeking to infuse a larger share of entertainment into moral teaching. Kindness for the donkey the children ride, going away to school, gifts for a poor boy, a Bible-reading young shepherd, coming home for Christmas, an evening hymn are some of the themes. Imitation of the Taylors led to much humdrum verse-making. Mary Belson (later Elliott) was a prolific writer of verses as well as moral tales in the early nineteenth century, and sometimes invented pleasing little pieces, but also much that was trivial or insipid. For example, there were such banalities as resulted when she copied the metre used by Ann Taylor for her well-known 'My Mother' (based on William Cowper's model for 'My Mary'),

'Mamma, said Julia, as she took
From off her mother's knee a book,
Say, shall I like a woman look,
    By reading?'

This appeared in *Simple Truths in Verse* (1812).

A more able practitioner of the art of simple verse for boys and girls to follow in the wake of the Taylors was Sara Coleridge (1802–1850), whose *Pretty Lessons for Good Children* came out in 1834. She believed in fantasy for children, and thought much of the Taylors' verse gloomy, and the sentiments false. Yet her efforts, inspired by her own children, do not mark a great advance. Benign and happy in tone, they mingle instruction with playful reflections on everyday things. Perhaps her most enduring rhyme is one that many generations of children must have learnt by heart – 'The Months', beginning

'January brings the snow
Makes our feet and fingers glow'.

One of the most popular of versemakers of the 1820s and 1830s, whose work was to be famous for many years, was Mrs. Felicia Hemans (born Browne, 1793–1835). Fluent, overflowing with sentiment, often dramatic in form, her poems had much appeal and influence throughout the nineteenth century, particularly among ordinary people and young reciters. Her *Hymns for Children* (1833), originally published in America as *Hymns on the Works of Nature for the Use of Children* in 1827, are characterised by fervent and hope-ful religious faith and an enthusiasm for nature in its revelation of divine power. Sorrow is banished, for death only leads to happiness beyond the grave. But it was the favourites for recitation, such as 'The Stately Homes of England' and 'Casabianca', which kept her fame alive. One of her truly pathetic little poems, 'The first Grief', can be found in *Come Hither*, the famous modern anthology compiled by Walter de la Mare.

The work of William and Mary Howitt is considered in the next chapter, but their verse should be mentioned here. Mrs. Howitt once described Mrs. Hemans' poetry as 'luscious', and for her part, she followed a quieter, more homely path, expressing sympathy with the poor, and delight in nature and simple pleasures. Best remembered today are her verses 'The Spider and the Fly' (*Sketches of Natural History*, 1834), and 'The Fairies of Caldon Lowe' (*Ballads and other Poems*, 1847). A typical and charming piece, 'The Sale of the Pet Lamb', has been rescued from oblivion by Walter de la Mare and included in his anthology mentioned above. William Howitt's chief claim to fame as a writer of verse for youth rests upon the lively lines, 'The Wind in a Frolic,' put into his *Boy's Country Book* (1839).

Fairy folk came dancing into children's verse with the Irish poet, William Allingham (1824–1889), whose 'The Fairies' (1850, re-issued 1855) is still familiar in modern anthologies. Touched with the Celtic magic of his native Donegal, it tells of human fears of the wee folk, trooping altogether in their

> 'Green jacket, red cap
> And white owl's feather!'

and of the child Bridget they stole away, and the old Fairy King supping with the Queen of the Northern Lights. Most of his other verses did not equal its captivating power. There is an aura of moonlight and romance about his verse drama, *In Fairyland* (1870), written to accompany some exquisite pictures in colour by Richard Doyle, and printed by Edmund Evans, but it does not match the delicate and fanciful invention of the artist.

William Brighty Rands' lighter verse has already been mentioned. His poems have a wide range, and many are nimble and gay, showing much understanding of childish interests and fancies. There are Christ legends, fairy lore, cheerful trifles like 'The Cuckoo in the Pear Tree', and serious little histories about goodness or deserving poverty among his subjects, as well as comic and playful notions. He handled contrasting themes with skill and variety. In 'The Rising Watching Moon' he vividly expresses the child's tendency to invest ordinary things with his own fears and imaginings.

> 'Ah, the moon is watching me!
> Red and round as round can be.'

The anonymous *Lilliput Levee* (1864) contained some of his best verse for youth. He wrote much for magazines, and a volume of *Lilliput Lyrics*, issued in 1899 under his own name after his death, included poems from periodicals and from his published books.

Rands' best writing for children is to be found in his verses, but two other Lilliput books, issued anonymously, and chiefly prose, *Lilliput Lectures* (1871) and *Lilliput Legends* (1872), had a vogue in their day.

With Christina Rossetti (1830–1894) the children's muse found the crystal springs of true poetry. There had been nothing of the quality of her lyrics for the young since *Songs of Innocence*. Finest of all is her fairy poem, *Goblin Market* published with six other poems in 1862. This introduces the ancient motive of evil fairy creatures who tempt mortals to their undoing, and here the conquest of their spell is achieved through the human love of sister for sister. Both the theme and the style are fascinating, expressed with a lilt and pace new in children's verse.

> 'Come buy our orchard fruits,
> Come buy, come buy:
> Apples and quinces,
> Lemons and oranges ...
>
> Currants and gooseberries
> Bright-fire-like barberries,
> Figs to fill your mouth,
> Citrons from the South,
> Sweet to tongue, and sound to eye;'

cry the goblins. These wicked folk are likened to creatures with tails and whiskers, full of antics.

> 'Chuckling, clapping, crowing,
> Clucking and gobbling,
> Mopping and mowing,
> Full of airs and graces,
> Pulling wry faces ...'

Laura eats the fruit of the goblin men and so is brought to misery and near to death, but she is saved through the love of Lizzie, who braves the creatures to get the 'fiery antidote' to bring her sister back to life and happiness.

Sing-Song, nursery songs for children, came out ten years afterwards in 1872, with charming drawings by Arthur Hughes. These are jingles in the nursery rhyme tradition.

> 'Bread and milk for breakfast,
>   And woollen frocks to wear,
> And a crumb for Robin Redbreast
>   On the cold days of the year.'

Some of the rhymes have a deeper feeling and a haunting sadness, but there is also much joy and laughter. Lessons of conduct, when they come, can be given with playful brevity.

> 'Seldom can't
>   Seldom don't
> Never shan't
>   Never won't.'

Christina Rossetti was a fine lyric poet of sensitive and devout feeling, and other verses, besides those she wrote for children, are often put into their anthologies. One of the best known is 'Uphill', beginning

'Does the road wind uphill all the way?
   Yes, to the very end.'

She also wrote a prose fairy tale, *Speaking Likenesses* (1874), illustrated by Arthur Hughes, and inspired by *Alice's Adventures in Wonderland*, but it lacks the charm and power of her poetry.

The artistic picture-books of the 1870s and 1880s were to bring new life in exciting form to some of the old ballads and verses. The humorous ballad poem, 'John Gilpin', by William Cowper (1731–1800), first published in 1782, and 'An Elegy on the Death of a Mad Dog' and 'Mrs. Mary Blaize', by Oliver Goldsmith, were the subjects of picture-books by Randolph Caldecott. It was not the first time these works had been issued in a form to appeal to children. There was an edition of 'John Gilpin' with vigorous illustrations by George Cruikshank in 1828. Harris published an illustrated 'Mrs. Mary Blaize' in 1808, and 'An Elegy on the Death of a Mad Dog' was issued by Hodgson about 1810.[1] Caldecott's contemporary, Kate Greenaway, wrote her own verses for some of her picture books, but she also interpreted the work of others, including Robert Browning's *The Pied Piper of Hamelin* in 1888. This had first been published in *Dramatic Lyrics* by the poet in 1842.

By the second half of the century the discovery was being made that much poetry never written specially for children was suitable for them, and anthologies for youth begin to reflect this changed viewpoint. A landmark in this development was made by Coventry Patmore (1823–1896), who compiled, with his first wife, *The Children's Garland from the Best Poets* (1862). In the preface the editor stated that he hoped the volume would be found 'to contain nearly all the genuine poetry in a language fitted to please children'. His object was to make a book 'which shall be to them not more nor less than a book of equally good poetry to intelligent grown persons'. He excluded nearly all verse written expressly for children, and he took the liberty of abridging pieces or substituting a word occasionally.

Among the 173 poems, which begin with Blake's 'The Piper' and end with Wordsworth's 'The Rainbow', there are old and modern ballads, nursery rhymes, Shakespeare songs, story poems, like 'John Gilpin' and 'The Pied Piper', shorter poems by Wordsworth and Tennyson, Allingham's 'The Fairies' and 'Robin Redbreast', some of Gay's *Fables*, and 'La Belle Dame sans Merci' by Keats. It is the real beginning of the exploration for children of the whole realm of poetry, now a feature of all their good anthologies.

[1] *N.B.L. Catalogue*, 601a, 651, 649 (Bibl. 42). For Caldecott see p. 197.
Mrs. Mary Blaize was first published in *The Bee* (1759) and *The Elegy* in *The Vicar of Wakefield* (1766).

Retellings from epic poetry and long poems beyond a child's understanding were also bringing something of the greatness of the poetic heritage of the ages into children's books. Versions of Homer have already been mentioned. The 'Home Treasury' series included *Tales from the Faerie Queene* (1846), retold from Spenser by Charles Cole, and there had been a version of two of the tales by Eliza W. Bradburn in *Legends from Spenser's Fairy Queen for Children* in 1829. In 1833 Charles Cowden Clarke (1787–1877), inspired by the example of the Lambs' *Tales from Shakespeare*, produced *Tales from Chaucer* for young people. An authority on his subject, he put into easy prose twelve of the better-known stories, including 'Palamon and Arcite', 'Griselda', and 'The Fable of Chanticleer and Partlet', from *The Canterbury Tales*. His wife, Mary Cowden Clarke (1809–1898), prompted by a love of Shakespeare, wrote an imaginative reconstruction of the early life of fifteen of the great dramatist's noblest women characters in *The Girlhood of Shakespeare's Heroines* (1851–1852), tracing adventures as might be supposed to shape their future lives.

For younger children, however, rhymes and jingles and verses written to delight them continued to flourish, and found new distinction towards the end of the century. Robert Louis Stevenson (1850–1894) drew on memories of his childhood for his 'rimes for children' published in 1885 as *A Child's Garden of Verses*. To the author they were 'a little ragged regiment', but they have captivated old and young ever since their first appearance by their happy expression of childhood's moods and fancies, joys and imaginings.

'Now my little heart goes a-beating like a drum,
    With the breath of the Bogie in my hair;
And all round the candle the crooked shadows come
    And go marching along up the stair.'

'Being good' is a part of every child's upbringing, but R.L.S. can see it with a child's eye view.

'A child should always say what's true
And speak when he is spoken to,
And behave mannerly at table,
At least as far as he is able.'

Few books have stimulated so many different styles of illustration as *A Child's Garden of Verses*, but the first edition was unadorned. Its success and influence needed no help from pictures, however. These little poems, fashioned by a craftsman of words, make articulate some hidden depths and delights of the young child's world and invade the romantic and limitless realm of a child's imagination. Here are starry solitudes, visions in the fire, dreams of far places,

'Where the Great Wall round China goes
And on one side the desert blows'.

Modest flowerets they may be, but they are rhymes from the slopes of Parnassus.

Much trifling verse in sentimental mood followed in imitation of Stevenson's little masterpiece. A typical end-of-century example, reflecting its period, which is intensified by the *Art Nouveau* drawings by Helen Stratton, is Norman Gale's *Songs for little People* (1896). But fine poetry for the young, transcending fashion and sentimentality, was not to be lacking as the Edwardian era opened. Rudyard Kipling (1865–1936) had introduced vigorous and rhythmical chants and songs to prefix the tales in his *Jungle Books* in 1894 and 1895, and in the Puck stories of the next decade he set down some of the most haunting verses he ever penned for youth, expressive of the mystery and magic of England and her history. 'A Tree Song' refers to the leaves which Puck uses to put a spell upon the two children he takes into the past.

> 'Of all the trees that grow so fair
>   Old England to adorn,
> Greater are none beneath the Sun
>   Than Oak, and Ash, and Thorn'.

The true successor of Blake, Christina Rossetti, and Stevenson, however, in the development of poetry for children is Walter de la Mare. He really belongs to the twentieth century, but some of his best poems for children were published before 1914. *Songs of Childhood* (1902) – his first volume of poems – is a delightful garland of verses, showing some nineteenth century romantic influences, but also reflecting the light of moonshine and elfin magic with individual grace and style. In 1913, with *Peacock Pie*, De la Mare produced perhaps his finest book of lyric poems for youth. The range is wide, and there is a masterly skill in the handling of metre and melody. He explores the land he made especially his own – the country between wake and dream, sometimes bordering on oddity and the macabre, sometimes flashing out into daylight and child's play and jollity. His versatility and vision place him in the first rank of lyric poets for children – the greatest since William Blake.

DRAMA

The origin of drama for children, like their stories, lies in the shared experience of young and old – especially in the folk plays and religious performances of the Middle Ages. But when secular drama and the rise of the theatre removed plays from the market place, folk entertainment became less widespread, and children had very little designed for them for public performance until the nineteenth century brought the heyday of the Christmas pantomime, spectacle and extravaganza. Children saw many plays never written for them – we know that the Lambs were spellbound by the theatre from the age of six – but a drama of their own with pretensions to literary quality was long in coming.

Acting and taking on a different identity are a natural part of children's play, and it was with some understanding of this predilection of youth that drama was enlisted in the service of moral and religious teaching. In the eighteenth century, with the spread of publications which attempted to instruct by amusement, the practice of putting stories and histories into dramatic form increased. The purpose was school or home performance or reading aloud. Schoolboys had long performed classical plays, often in Latin, at their grammar schools, but the moral and uplifting scenes now presented were intended for wider dissemination. Arnaud Berquin put many of his stories into dialogue in his *L'Ami des Enfans*. More notable was a work which preceded Berquin's publication, *Le Théâtre d'Education*, by Madame de Genlis, published in 1779 (English edition 1781). Twenty-four comedies were set out in four volumes, chiefly intended for performance by girls. 'Odious characters have been excluded', declared the author in her preface. Only 'growing errors' susceptible of being corrected are depicted. One of Madame de Genlis' earliest delights was theatricals, but here the activity is firmly allied to moral education. She carefully explained that the fourth volume, which included the popular 'Rose of Salency', was intended 'solely for the education of children of shopkeepers and mechanics; but people even of a lower rank may find useful instruction in it.' The plays were often performed in academies for girls both here and abroad, but they were also read as stories.

More to the taste of Mrs. Trimmer and the orthodox were the *Sacred Dramas* of Hannah More, published in 1782. The author in her dedication to the Duchess of Beaufort describes 'her little work as written with a humble wish to promote the love of piety and virtue in young persons.' Hannah More had had plays produced by David Garrick, and was no beginner to the art of play-writing, but here successful stage composition was not the intention. Religious education was the object by private performance. She used Biblical themes – Moses, David and Goliath, Belshazzar, and Daniel – and reflected with awe 'that the place whereon I stood was holy ground'. The diction of the unrhymed verse is very much of its period, and the plays lack action. The last piece, Hezekiah, is a monologue.

Typical of the moral school of drama and intended for reading as much as for presentation was *Dramas for Children: imitated from the French of L. F. Jauffret*, and published by M. J. Godwin in 1808 (p. 88). The little plays all embody lessons about conduct or warnings against wrong-doing, as some of the titles convey – 'The Dangers of Gossiping', 'The Fib found out', 'The Spoiled Child', and similar designations. Maria Edgeworth also used the dramatic form for some of her tales, for example 'Old Poz' and 'Eton Montem' in *The Parent's Assistant*. Most of these plays of the moral school are little different from stories, and were probably chiefly intended for reading aloud, not for performance.

Home acting and charades greatly increased in popularity among young people in the Victorian age and more interesting material began to find its way into their plays. In the middle years of the century the firm of Dean were publishing series of plays, often on fairy tale or romantic themes. A well-known writer of such plays was Julia Corner (1798–1875), who justified the use of acting such plays in education 'if selected carefully and constructed to give moral lessons'. Miss Corner's *Little Plays for little Actors* were issued in series between 1854 and 1863, chiefly by Dean and Son. They were all intended for home performance and titles included 'Beauty and the Beast', 'Whittington and his Cat', and 'Cinderella'. These three plays were also made into one volume with illustrations by Alfred Crowquill (A. H. Forrester). A little later came the plays of Kate Freiligrath-Kroeker. She made two plays from the *Alice* stories, and invented fairy tale themes as well as using traditional tales such as the Grimms' 'Snowdrop'. *Alice and other fairy tale plays for Children* was published in 1879, and was followed by *Alice thro' the Looking Glass and other Fairy Tale Plays* in 1882.

These versions of *Alice's Adventures* were neither comprehensive nor for the commercial stage. It was not until December 1886 that the first London production of *Alice in Wonderland* opened at the Prince of Wales Theatre. The story had been adapted by Henry Savile Clark, with music by W. Slaughter, as a comedy-opera, and the same author and composer also wrote the stage version of Thackeray's *The Rose and the Ring* produced in 1890. Other famous stories – among them that resounding stage success, *Little Lord Fauntleroy* (1888) – were from now on often adapted for the stage, to join the nursery stories which had been transformed from the simplicity of their originals to make glittering pantomime for youthful audiences. *Aladdin, Cinderella, Little Goody Two-shoes, Dick Whittington, Jack and the Beanstalk,* and many others were turned into much-loved Christmas entertainments of this kind. But as yet there was little of quality invented for the children's theatre.

The influence of the Toy Theatre, which originated between 1810 and 1820, must have stimulated interest among young people in the drama and in home acting. By the middle of the nineteenth century, the publishing of 'Juvenile Drama' sheets of characters and scenes, with books of words, usually founded upon actual stage productions, was a thriving concern. Very soon magazines for youth, including Brett's *Boys of England*, vied with each other in offering cheap and attractive series to their young subscribers. The history of these wares is a bypath outside the scope of this work, but it may be traced by interested readers in the excellent book by Mr. George Speaight (Bibl. 206). It is only relevant here to mention that many of the dramas had their origin in pantomime, or in melodrama, and many were based on children's traditional tales and favourite stories, such as *Robinson Crusoe* and *Robin Hood*. Travesties they might be of their literary originals, but their circulation in this form for paste board miniature dramatics may have had something of the same stimulating effect on the young imagination as the products of the chapbook makers a century earlier.

Writing for full-size live performance by young people was a frequent occupation of Victorian authors. Yet few plays of real value have survived. One of the more interesting is the traditional Christmas Mumming play, *The Peace Egg*, by Juliana Horatia Ewing, founded on her story of the same title. It first appeared in *Aunt Judy's Magazine* in 1884, and in 1887 both the story and the play were published in one volume. It is based on various versions of the old folk play, and Mrs. Ewing also drew on her memory of performances she had seen or heard of, for many of these mumming plays were not written down, and were often varied to suit the characters available and the national events of the day. The author added some lines of her own to this verse play of old times – 'a *bludgy* play' as she termed it – with nothing in it about peace or eggs, but plenty about St. George and the champions who fight the pagans.

Up to the end of the nineteenth century the achievement in drama for children, represented in their literature, is not impressive. But before the death of Queen Victoria, Peter Pan had already come to life in Kensington Gardens in the stories invented for the Davies boys by J. M. Barrie (later Sir James, 1860–1937). He introduced this baby Peter into a strange medley of novel, whimsy and romance – *The Little White Bird* (1902). Peter, like all other children, was once a bird, and he is only a week old when he flies away to the Gardens to join the birds and the fairies. The chapters telling of Peter's adventures (as a tale told to the boy David) were to form the book *Peter Pan in Kensington Gardens* (1906), beautifully illustrated by Arthur Rackham. But this was not the Peter who was to endear himself to millions of children in the famous play *Peter Pan* first produced in December 1904. Peter in the play is the boy who would not grow up, symbolising escape and joy. It is theatre entertainment of a high order, blending nursery sentiment, magic and fairy-lore, pirate and Red Indian adventure, in a way to delight young audiences ever since its first success.

The play was put into story form by Barrie himself as *Peter and Wendy* in 1911, but it has also been retold in many other versions. The text of the play as acted was not published until 1928. A major innovation in children's literature, its whimsical make-believe allied to exciting incident and heightened emotion, was a powerful force in the making of books for children for many years. Not least it proved to be a starting point for plays written for children that were worthy of a permanent place on the child's bookshelf as well as excellent stage entertainment. One of the most notable fairy plays to follow *Peter Pan*, showing something of the influence of the *fin-de-siècle* experimental theatre and a range of ideas beyond Barrie's scope, was *L'Oiseau bleu* (*The Blue Bird*), by Maurice Maeterlinck, published in England in 1909. This moving fantasy tells of the search of two peasant children for the Bird of Happiness, and has something of the visionary power of religious allegory. But neither *The Blue Bird* nor other plays that followed have ever rivalled the popular and perennial appeal of Barrie's masterpiece.

No type of story is more firmly anchored to its period than the domestic tale for young people. Methods of education, social habits, prevailing attitudes, are all deeply imbedded in it, and few of these stories possess sufficient creative life to prolong their existence for more than a generation. The moral tale described earlier might be assigned to this branch of writing for children, but this tended to present what was to be emulated or avoided rather than to reflect actual life. Its unnatural formula rather than its moral purpose was its weakness. The story which has neither fantasy, romantic background, nor faraway scenes to entice the reader, has to rely more than ever upon character-drawing, and living characters in stories before the accession of Victoria are scarce indeed.

Catherine Sinclair (1800–1864), one of the 'six and thirty feet of daughters' of John Sinclair of Edinburgh, felt that something was wrong about this lack of individuality among the children depicted in stories for youth. Children's books, she considered, should both appeal to the heart, and excite the fancy – and to do this they must portray real children. In *Holiday House* (1839) she determined to describe 'noisy, frolicsome, mischievous children', believing that these were true to life, and that young people were once truly more like 'wild horses on the prairies rather than well-broken hacks on the road'. It is this creation of character, rather than anything new in the construction or meaning of her story, which marks it as the real breakaway from the stock didactic pattern. Moral teaching is not left out of this account of the two natural and naughty children, Harry and Laura, but it never detracts from their living qualities. Although there is sadness and serious reflection towards the end, when Harry and Laura, tamed at last, are at the deathbed of their revered and virtuous sailor brother, Frank, the earlier chapters are full of fun and high spirits. Some distinction, also, is made between naughtiness and real wickedness. The brother and sister who get into so many scrapes have the virtues of truthfulness and loyal affection as well as a natural urge for mischief. There is a dragon of a nursery governess, Mrs. Crabtree, and a sympathetic Uncle David (who tells them the fantastical story about Master No-Book), and he and the kindly grandmother manage the children far better with their cajoling and persuading than Mrs. Crabtree does with blows. This book, like many of the moral tales, is more a series of incidents than a continuous story, but it has many excellent qualities, and it demonstrated that the long domination of the moral tale was at an end.

By the time *Holiday House* was published in 1839, the tales and verses of Mary Howitt (born Botham, 1799–1888) were becoming known. She and her husband, William Howitt (1792–1879), had published their first joint work in 1823, a volume of poems entitled *The Forest Minstrel*, and in 1834 Mary Howitt had produced some poems for her own children, *Sketches of Natural History*, referred to in the previous chapter. Two years later came her *Tales in Prose*, with a companion volume, *Tales in Verse*, both like her former publication under the imprint of the Quaker firm of Darton. Mary and William Howitt were Quakers, although they were later to sever their connection with the Society, and Mary, six years before her death, became a Roman Catholic.

The Howitts put into their books something of their quiet faith, their love of the countryside, and the life and scenes and people they knew. William Howitt came from Heanor, and was familiar with Sherwood Forest and the country of the Nottinghamshire-Derbyshire border. Mary was brought up at Uttoxeter, but came to Nottingham soon after her marriage in 1821, and lived there until 1836. After that the Howitts went to London, and then abroad for a time to Heidelberg. They finally lived abroad from 1870. They were interested in all the intellectual and social movements of their day, yet they were basically sincere and unaffected, working and writing ceaselessly, sometimes in collaboration, but more often separately. Mary Howitt became interested in German and then in Scandinavian literature, and it has already been recorded that she was the first translator of the Hans Andersen stories into English. But in her own writings she made little excursion into fantasy, except in a few of her poems. Most of her fiction for children is about family life. Sometimes she creates poignant little studies of honest and suffering poverty, for to her earnest spirit the poor were no class apart, but persons for whom she felt true compassion. Her aim was to promote goodness, truth and kindness, as well as social betterment, and she did it in a pleasant and unobtrusive way. In the 1840s she wrote a series of tales 'to illustrate household virtues' for Tegg's project, 'Tales for the People and their Children'. One of them, possibly by William Howitt, or with his collaboration, *My Uncle the Clockmaker* (1844), is an old-world tale about a carrier, who worked between Nottingham and a Derbyshire village. Another story was born of her experience of the Nottingham riots in 1831, *Little Coin and Much Care* (1842). But all her stories, well-founded on real life and genuine feeling as they were have little merit beyond their contemporary appeal. She created no child characters with the liveliness of Catherine Sinclair's Harry and Laura.

William Howitt wrote less for children than his wife. His best work is perhaps that autobiographical account of rural life and pursuits – *The Boy's Country Book; being the real Life of a Country Boy, written by himself* (1839). He also wrote a story for boys founded on experiences in Australia, which he visited with his son – *A Boy's Adventures in the Wilds of Australia* (1854). This is only partly fictional, and is perhaps more valuable as a description of conditions in the country than as a tale.

The Howitts belonged to an age that was passing, and few of their writings for boys and girls are now remembered. The creator of the domestic story in England with a real attraction for girls was Charlotte M. Yonge (1823–1901). Leadership in the field of the tale of family life was soon to pass to the United States, notably on the publication of that much-loved classic, *Little Women* (1868). Charlotte Yonge, however, had a great vogue in the nineteenth century. She was a born storyteller, and wrote many best-selling novels, widely praised in her day. The book which made her famous was *The Heir of Redclyffe* (1853), a novel for the general public, but especially enjoyed by older girls. Filled with strong sentiment, it perfectly expressed the author's staunch faith in the Church of England as regenerated by the Oxford Movement. John Keble, one of its leading figures, and author of *The Christian Year*, was an important influence in her life, mostly spent in the quiet Hampshire village of Otterbourne, where Keble became a near neighbour as parish priest of Hurley. Charlotte Yonge's first publication for young people was a French tale, *Le Château de Melville* (1838), written when she was only fifteen years old. Soon afterwards she began to write for Sunday School scholars, and from 1846 her tales of 'Langley School' appeared in *The Magazine for the Young*, edited by Anne Mozley for her brother, the publisher. A collection of the stories was issued as *Langley School* in 1850, but further volumes of these little-known stories of village boys and girls were not published until the 1880s. Perhaps this was because Miss Yonge had become much occupied with her new duties as editor of the magazine the Mozleys intended for Anglican young ladies, *The Monthly Packet*, founded in 1851.

The author's first family chronicle for young people, *The Daisy Chain*, appeared in its pages before being published in book form in 1856. It is a long, skilfully told, delightful narrative about a Victorian middle-class family, the Mays, and their daily lives. Dr. May, a medical man, much respected in the old country town of Market Stoneborough, has eleven children, the youngest six weeks old, the eldest a young man at Oxford, when the story opens. What scope for diversity and interest such a family provides! The opening chapter takes the reader straight into the schoolroom of Dr. May's house, and very soon into the activities of his industrious, affectionate family, before long to be overwhelmed by the tragedy of a carriage accident, in which the mother is killed, and the eldest girl, Margaret, is made a helpless invalid. The Mays are a clearly defined and energetic group of young people – most of them much guided by their own or their elders' sense of discipline and ideals of service. Especially vivid is Ethel May, the clever, clumsy, noble-hearted heroine, who at fifteen years old keeps pace with her elder brother Norman, in Latin and Greek, all on her own, then gives it all up, after the tragedy, when she realises that more womanly duties are required of her. She and her younger brother, the manly Harry, who goes away to sea, are perhaps the best drawn of all the very convincing personalities in the book.

Service to the Church and to the community plays a large part in the lives of the Mays. Much of the story centres on the dream of the lanky, plain Ethel for a church to be built in the poor, neglected district of Cocksmoor, where she has helped to establish a school.

High ideals animate most of these young people, as well as family affection. Selfishness and glory for oneself are to be despised. The hard path of Christian duty means self-denial and concern for others, but this is a way to happiness and joy, when the sorrow felt at the loss of their mother begins to fade. The book is a mirror of Victorian life in High Church circles, but its claim to excellence lies in its life-like characters and their development and relationships. Charlotte Yonge continued the story of the Mays in *The Trial* (1864), but this did not equal the popularity of the earlier book.

One of the writer's best stories for younger readers is *Countess Kate* (1862), reissued in 1948 with illustrations by Gwen Raverat. The young orphan heroine, Kate, is said to possess some of the traits of her creator. Excitable, imaginative, naughty, yet upright, the child inherits a title, and goes to live with two aunts in London, who are to bring her up in a fitting manner for her new role as Countess Caegwent. Kate finds out that this is by no means as pleasant as she expected, and her life is told with much understanding, with any moralising made part of the story in the author's expert way. Another family story for young people which is very enjoyable, and which was reprinted in a collection of stories in 1960,[1] is *The Stokesley Secret* (1861). This concerns the Merrifields, a naval captain's family, and the difficulties a young governess has with them in the absence of their father and mother. Again problems of conduct are made an integral and interesting part of the story, and the young people are like the Mays in being very much alive. Charlotte Yonge wrote many other books, including historical tales for young people, to be mentioned in a later chapter.

Meg March one day found her sister Jo 'eating apples and crying over *The Heir of Redclyffe*', and Charlotte Yonge's books, as well as other literary influences from Europe, had much influence on Louisa M. Alcott and the writing of *Little Women* (1868). Innovations by American authors in the story for girls had already found much popularity over here when this famous publication arrived to win the hearts of girl readers. Life and manners in America were more democratic and free-and-easy than for Victorian young-ladyhood, although moral and religious fervour was just as widespread, as the stories of that very popular American author, 'Elizabeth Wetherell', make plain. This was the pen-name of Susan Warner (1819–1883), a native of New York. Her stories were much read by girls in Britain as well as in her own land, and the first to win success, *The Wide, Wide World* (New York, 1850), was one of the best and most characteristic. It is in the tradition of the pious and tearful tales of the mid-Victorian age, but it is less hampered by the conventions and stratification of that society. Ellen Montgomery, the young heroine, who soon becomes an orphan, is very intense in her feelings, and much pre-occupied with religion, but she has some natural traits. There is an interesting contrast shown in the early

---

[1] In *The Sapphire Treasury for Boys and Girls*, edited by Gillian Avery. Gollancz 1960.

chapters between Ellen's sheltered existence with her mother in New York City, and the more primitive life she endures after she has reached the home of a Puritanical and unfeeling aunt in the backwoods of New York State. Farm life, cooking, country ways, and the beauty of an open landscape make this part of Ellen's story memorable and evidently the author was drawing upon her own knowledge. Later the heroine's vitality flags as she grows up into a young lady and becomes perfected in her Christian faith. *The Wide, Wide World*, like other books of its kind, succeeded because the reader could identify herself with Ellen, and share her trials and experiences, and the many religious passages heightened its emotional appeal. It was followed by other works by the author in similar vein, of which *Queechy* (1852) and *Melbourne House* (1864) are perhaps the best known. Other American writers were also producing stories for girls about this time, but none came anywhere near the standard of *Little Women*.

The author of this best-loved tale for girls, Louisa May Alcott (1832–1888), was the daughter of a New England teacher and philosopher, Amos Bronson Alcott, a progressive who admired Emerson. Her mother was no less cultured, and Louisa drew upon a spiritually rich if materially austere home background for her story. The March sisters and 'Marmee', their mother, are true-to-life portraits. 'We really lived most of it', the author wrote, 'and if it succeeds, that will be the reason for it'. It did succeed becoming known and loved all over the world, and its success has never faded. Its secret lay in Louisa Alcott's ability to present lovable characters, brimful of life and personality, and to weave around them a compelling story. The four sisters, Meg, Jo, Beth, and Amy, so close in affection, so different in temperament and character, are real beings. Most popular with many generations of readers is Jo – quick-tempered, clever, tomboyish, generous Jo who, like her creator, wants to be a writer. Moral and religious teaching of a liberal and basic nature is an integral part of the tale, made as necessary and natural in the lives of the young Marches as the air they breathe.

There is an unconfined and happy atmosphere in the home into which the reader is admitted. The friendship with Laurie, the boy next door, especially between him and Jo, is something which could scarcely have been depicted by the more conventional pen of Miss Yonge. This less self-conscious attitude to human relationships, outside class-ridden Victorian society, brought a welcome transatlantic vigour into books for girls at this period. *Little Women* was followed by a sequel, *Good Wives*, originally published in 1869 as *Little Women, Part 2*, and Louisa Alcott continued to chronicle the activities of the March family, as well as to invent other tales of domestic life. The first two books, however, were to become the acknowledged classics of their kind.

In England a writer of much artistic promise was publishing her first stories in the sixties. In Charlotte Yonge's *Monthly Packet* for July 1861 there had appeared a moralistic story with a style out of the common – *A Bit of Green*. The twenty-year-old author was

Juliana Horatia Gatty (1841–1885), five years later to marry Major Alexander Ewing. Her mother, Mrs. Margaret Gatty, was a writer of children's stories notable for their gentle and cleverly presented moral truths, and something more will be said about her later. Mrs. Ewing was born at Ecclesfield in Yorkshire, where her father was clergyman, and she had several younger brothers and sisters for whom she invented her early stories. After her marriage she travelled a good deal, and became interested in army life, as her later writings reveal.

Mrs. Gatty had published several volumes of her own *Aunt Judy's Tales* – using Juliana's nursery name of Judy – and in 1866 she started a monthly periodical, *Aunt Judy's Magazine*. This publication was devoted to excellent aims, and it was to be the means of putting into circulation most of the charming and versatile stories of her gifted daughter. Some of Juliana Ewing's books have already been noted with fairy tales, and she was much influenced by Hans Andersen, and other writers of fantasy. But the majority of her stories deal with real life, presented with a sensitive feeling for time and place, a delight in the old-world, and a literary grace rare in writing for youth. She took great pains in framing her stories, and into them she put a good deal of her own personality, her love of gardens and dogs and ordinary folk, her aspiration after noble ideals, her admiration of brave conduct, her generosity of spirit and sense of fun. The stories have a wide range, but their appeal is not immediate or universal. For some discriminating young readers, however, their spell has something of the fragrance of old lavender.

One of Mrs. Ewing's finest tales is *Six to Sixteen* (1875), serialised three years earlier in *Aunt Judy's Magazine*. This is the history of a girl, a supposed autobiography, beginning with her early life in India, where her parents die, and then describing her experiences with distant relations in a Yorkshire vicarage, which might be Ecclesfield itself. The activities of Margery, the heroine, and her friend Eleanor evidently reflect the zest of the Gatty family for learning and doing. There are some interesting glimpses of life at a 'non-progressive' boarding school for girls, where existence is much hedged about with petty restrictions and prim propriety. The two girls pine for better things, for air and exercise and true education, and they devise their own discipline for their conduct at home and at school. There is much wisdom and humanity in this story, which captivated the young Kipling at ten years old. 'I owe more in a circuitous way to that tale than I can tell', he wrote towards the end of his life in his autobiography (Bibl. 259). 'I knew it as I know it still, almost by heart.'

Her stories have often a sad, but never a pessimistic character. Always at their core is deeply felt religious faith. One of her more sorrowful tales, *The Story of a Short Life* (1885), has a military background. It is set within the camp at Aldershot, and relates how a boy, crippled through saving his dog's life, finds consolation by living up to the ideals of military conduct as 'a wounded soldier' until his early death. The more famous *Jackanapes*

(1884) is also concerned with army life, and it unites heroic action with a village setting. The theme sounds trite. Jackanapes, the son of an officer killed at Waterloo, is brought up from infancy by a maiden aunt living in a remote part of the country. He goes into the army and dies in saving a companion's life on the battlefield. In Mrs. Ewing's hands it becomes a little gem of imaginative writing, if over-sentimental by modern standards. It was illustrated by Randolph Caldecott, whose work Mrs. Ewing greatly admired, and the excellent drawings added much to its appeal. Caldecott also worked with her for *Daddy Darwin's Dovecot* (1884), a country tale about an orphan boy and an old man and his pigeons. *A Flat Iron for a Farthing* (1872), 'some passages in the life of an only son', recalls childhood memories of the seaside and a quaint shop where two little girls buy tiny irons and meet the hero of the tale. *Jan of the Windmill* (1876), one of her best stories, describes the life of a foundling, half-Dutch, who is brought up by a miller in the West country, and becomes a great painter. *Mary's Meadow* (1886) reflects the writer's love of flowers and growing things, and was inspired by John Parkinson's seventeenth century *Paradisus*. Also in the first rank is *Lob-lie-by-the-Fire*, illustrated first by Cruikshank in 1874, and by Caldecott in 1883. It is another village story, this time of the English Border country of the north, and it hinges on an old legend that a 'Lob-lie-by-the-Fire' or 'Lubber-fiend' once haunted and helped the family at the old Hall of Lingborough. Here now live two little old ladies, and the story tells how they found and cared for an abandoned gipsy boy, and how eventually he became their 'Luck of Lingborough'.

A more popular and prolific writer for young people, without Mrs. Ewing's refinements of artistry, was Mrs. Molesworth (Mary Louisa Stewart, 1839–1921). Some of her tales of fantasy have already been mentioned, but she also produced many stories of family and everyday life, both for younger and older readers. Her work in this field is more deeply tinged with the sentimentality of the period than her fairy stories, and there is rather too much feeling and 'namby-pamby' softness about these stories to please modern taste. Nevertheless, she was a most capable storyteller, and her great success was in revealing very young children and their feelings, although their baby talk becomes at times a little tiresome. Her most famous tale about the very young is *Carrots* (1876) and this gives a vivid picture of the young child's world in the days of the Victorian nursery, when Papa, very much the head of the family, is rather remote behind the study door, Mama is loving but delicate, and the children live mostly with their nurse. The book came out under Mrs. Molesworth's pseudonym, 'Ennis Graham', which she ceased to use after 1877, and it was illustrated, like many of her later books, by Walter Crane. The blend of playful tenderness and clever storytelling centred on the little but very important things in the life of a four or five-year-old is also a characteristic of *The Adventures of Herr Baby* (1881). *Us: an Old-fashioned Story* (1885) is again about the very young, this time with the most exciting theme of two little twins kidnapped by gipsies.

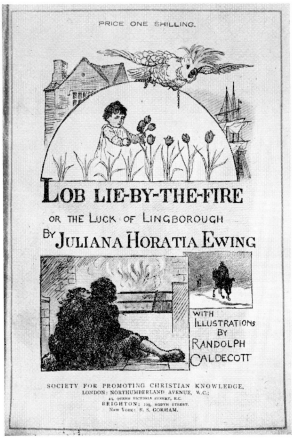

PRICE ONE SHILLING.

LOB LIE-BY-THE-FIRE
OR THE LUCK OF LINGBOROUGH
BY JULIANA HORATIA EWING

WITH
ILLUSTRATIONS
BY
RANDOLPH
CALDECOTT

SOCIETY FOR PROMOTING CHRISTIAN KNOWLEDGE,
LONDON: NORTHUMBERLAND AVENUE, W.C.;
43, QUEEN VICTORIA STREET, E.C.
BRIGHTON: 129, NORTH STREET.
New York: E. S. GORHAM.

17. *A typical late Victorian pictorial cover by Randolph Caldecott*

Outstanding among all Mrs. Molesworth's books about everyday life, however, is the moving and convincing *Carved Lions* (1895). This is told in the first person by a little girl who lives with her brother and her parents very happily in a northern industrial city (no doubt Manchester, which the author knew well), until they must all be parted when her father and mother go to South America. The lions are two great carved beasts in a shop they visit, and Geraldine and her brother come to think of them as real friends. She is very unhappy and lonely at the school to which she is sent, and these chapters are not only a most understanding revelation of a child's feelings, but throw light on the kind of education provided for girls in those days. It was a school 'where no story-books were permitted, except such as were read aloud in the sewing afternoons'. The lonely and misunderstood child runs away, and eventually she comes to the shop and finds the lions again. In a dream, the only fantastical episode in the book, she and her brother are taken by the lions over the sea, and she meets her mother. After this experience things improve for Geraldine, and she never goes back to the school where she suffered such unhappiness. The author perhaps put into this lifelike story some of her own memories and experiences, for it has the genuine ring of truth.

Mrs. Molesworth was the author of over a hundred books which vary a great deal in their standard. Her novels and books for older girls now have little value, but at her best, as in *The Carved Lions* and the fantasies already described, she reached a high degree of excellence.

A very popular contemporary of Mrs. Molesworth was Mrs. Frances Hodgson Burnett (1849–1924), whose most famous story for youth, *Little Lord Fauntleroy*, appeared in 1886. It had first been serialised in the American magazine *St. Nicholas* (1885–1886) and was illustrated by Reginald Birch. It soon won a great vogue, and fully exhibits the tendency towards the end of the century for stories of everyday life to become more dramatic and highly-coloured in sentiment. The little Lord Fauntleroy of the title is the American-born Cedric Errol, who at seven years old finds that he is the heir of his English grandfather, the embittered and lonely old Earl of Dorincourt. Cedric comes from America with 'Dearest' his mother, and goes to live with the Earl, winning his heart by his trustfulness, courage, and kindliness. Many boy readers have found the little lord a prig, and loathed his long curls, velvet suit, and lace collar, especially when this style was adopted for them by fond mammas. But for all the criticism the book has received in a more cynical age, it has much merit. Mrs. Burnett, an Englishwoman who married in America, where she went as a girl, knew both her transatlantic worlds, and was a splendid storyteller. Like most writers of her day she indulged in sentiment, and made an idol of goodness. But not all her books were so lavishly supplied with emotional feelings as *Little Lord Fauntleroy*. *Sara Crewe* (1888), later dramatised and published under the title by which it is now known, *The Little Princess*, is better in quality, if no more compelling than its predecessor. Best of all is her tale of the unhappy and disagreeable Mary, as invigorating as the Yorkshire moorland air of its setting – *The Secret Garden* (1911).

Through the cloud of emotionalism which enveloped domestic stories for youth at the end of the century a new light began to break in the last decade. A glimmering is visible in the stories by Frances E. Crompton (1866–1952), a Cheshire writer, whose most famous tale *The Gentle Heritage* (1893) is among recent revivals. Told by one of the characters, this narrative about nursery life forecasts a style to be adopted by greater writers in the near future. 'There *is* such a person as Bogy in the house', Patricia said, 'for Mriar says there is. So he must live somewhere, and the thing is where is it?' After dark this knowledge that a Bogy is in the house made it very disagreeable. The children then discover that Bogy has come to live next door. But he turns out to be quite unbogyish, and he has a wonderful garden. Blind, gracious, sympathetic, he becomes their friend, and he tells them about 'the Gentle Heritage', how anyone who tries can find it, for it is not a matter of birth or privilege, but a precious thing in itself. So the children begin to seek for it with his help.

The real milestone of the new era, when sentimentalism begins to give way to a realistic perception of the feelings and experiences of young people in their books, is the appearance of the first volume of Bastable stories by Edith Nesbit. The author, already introduced as the teller of tales of fantasy firmly allied to everyday life, was becoming known for her stories and poems, when a story featuring this famous family was printed in the *Illustrated London News* for Christmas 1897. More tales about the Bastables came out in other periodicals and in 1899 their fame flashed into the world of children's books as *The Story of the Treasure Seekers*.

It was the first volume of Nesbit tales to establish the author as a master of the craft of writing for children. The style is new, vigorous, free-and-easy, familiar, just the kind of narrative to be written 'from the inside', if not in the first person. Very soon the reader has guessed that it is Oswald Bastable telling the history of the family and their efforts 'to restore the fallen fortunes of the House of Bastable'. With humour and uncanny insight into how things appear when one is fourteen or twelve or younger, E. Nesbit wrote in a captivating and highly individual way, and followed this first book with other tales about the Bastables to delight children then and now – *The Would-be-goods* (1901) and *The New Treasure Seekers* (1904). Another of her family stories, without the introduction of magic, which has always been one of the most popular with young readers, is *The Railway Children* (1906), perhaps because of its more conventional and exciting plot.

The books by E. Nesbit at the beginning of the twentieth century look towards the future. They show that a revolution in the making of family stories had taken place, and that something more than a new century had now dawned in writing for children.

THE SCHOOL STORY

The story of school life closely follows the pattern of education, and in the pages of school tales over the years there is much to be gleaned about educational practices and history. The origin of this form of writing for the young lies in the tale, largely consisting of episodes to illustrate moral truths, centred on the small boarding establishments, which were often little more than large private houses in the eighteenth or early nineteenth century, where a few pupils were taken by the master or mistress.

The earliest of such productions (also notable as the first continuous piece of fiction written for children) was *The Governess; or, Little Female Academy*, by Sarah Fielding (1710–1768), the sister of the famous novelist, Henry Fielding. It was published in January 1749 by A. Millar and it is as significant in its way as Newbery's *Little Pretty*

Pocket Book issued five years earlier. The 'Governess' is Mrs. Teachum, a gentlewoman and widow of a clergyman, who has nine young ladies under her roof. The narrative extends over nine days, and includes the story of the life of each pupil recited by herself, and various readings of fairy tales. Jenny Peace, the leader of the girls, begins the latter with 'The Story of the cruel Giant Barbarico, the good Giant Benefico, and the pretty little dwarf Mignon'. At this Mrs. Teachum is a little alarmed, notwithstanding the excellent moral intention of the tale. 'By no means let the Notion of Giants or Magic dwell upon your Minds', she warns her charges. Such were 'high-flown things' not to be reconciled with matters of simplicity, fact, and taste, which she is trying to inculcate. But she allows the fables and fairy tales to go on, and they are interpolated with the lives of the girls and the activities of the school. Formal and rational as it is, in spite of the fairy tales, the characters are not quite puppets, but have individual characteristics. Very early in the book they show the danger of giving way to their passions. They fall out over an apple, and in the ensuing battle, 'the ground was spread with rags and tatters, torn from the backs of the little inveterate combatants'. Mrs. Teachum, however, is able to promote love and friendship after this fearful affair, with Jenny Peace throughout as her exemplar.

Most early tales with a school setting follow this model although few authors were as enlightened as Sarah Fielding in bringing in fables or fairy tales to brighten instruction. Episodes were usually confined to the children's own conduct and experiences, although the interpolated history or episode was a favourite eighteenth century device. *The Governess* reached its seventh edition in 1789, and in 1820 Mrs. Sherwood brought out an 'improved edition', omitting the fairy tales and other elements which she disapproved of, and altering and amending the original considerably.

An interesting example describing a rural dame school of the period is *The Village School* (ca. 1783), by Dorothy Kilner. Here Mrs. Bell, 'a very good woman', teaches little boys and girls to read, and the girls 'to spin, knit stockings, and to hem, fell, stitch and mark'. The clergyman, Mr. Right, is much in evidence. He helps to pay for the poor children's schooling, plays with the scholars at cricket, and helps them to fly their kites. The tale is full of awful incidents about naughtiness, with moral histories added to show how bad actions lead to worse, but all these artificialities do not destroy the tale's claim to be 'a nursery Crabbe'.[1]

Many writers of moral tales, including Maria Edgeworth, tried their hand at stories of school life or brought incidents at school into their stories. Elizabeth Sandham wrote several improving tales in the style of the day, centred on typical middle-class boarding establishments, including *The Boys' School; or, Traits of Character in Early Life* (1800), and *The Schoolfellows* (1818), an equally purposeful work about girls at school. She had little

---

[1] Barry, pp. 127–8 (Bibl. 3).

humour, and these books, and others like them, merely displayed their characters as examples and warnings to young readers. The school background was often quite incidental.

The best example of the story set within the framework of school in this early period is *Mrs. Leicester's School* (1808), by Mary Lamb, with a little help from her brother Charles. It is no school tale in the modern sense, but a little volume giving 'the history of several young ladies related by themselves' – in this following the model of *The Governess*. Ten little girls have all just arrived at Amwell School, and 'to divert the solitary young strangers' their teacher gathers them in front of the fire and suggests that they tell the story of their own lives. The writers' own memories are drawn upon in the invention of some of the tales. Mary Lamb recalls her visits to Hertfordshire, and there are glimmerings of the future Elia in his three pieces – 'The Witch Aunt', 'First going to Church', and 'The Sea-voyage'. The tales by Mary Lamb are less meditative and a little closer to childish understanding. There is an attractive picture of rural life in 'The Farmhouse', with its closing scene of a sheep-shearing supper, and old Spot, the shepherd, in the chimney corner. Another of her tales is 'The Father's Wedding-day', which treats the stepmother theme most sympathetically, and there is true pathos in 'The Sailor Uncle', where sad little Elizabeth Villiers uses her mother's tombstone as primer and spelling-book, and is transformed into a happy child by the coming of a naval uncle who tells her stories and takes her for walks. The school setting is merely a pretext for the stories.

The first genuine story of school life, which for all its limitations, looked upon the experience from the child's point of view, was *The Crofton Boys* (1841), by Harriet Martineau (1802–1876). She had already written several tales for youth, including a work about the home education of two sisters, *Five Years of Youth; or, Sense and Sentiment* (1831). This new story of boys at school was part of her 'Playfellow' series of four stories published by Charles Knight, and in spite of its sermonising, shows some advance on her earlier works for youth. Eight-year-old Hugh, the central figure, is a likable, imperfect little fellow, who finds learning at first exceedingly difficult. At home he envies his brother away at Crofton School, and longs to go there, where he thinks life will be easier. Soon his hopes are realised, but school is not quite as delightful as he imagined. And soon the story becomes more sad and earnest, for Hugh has an accident at play which makes him a cripple for life. It sounds rather grim, yet there is much that is really pleasant and sensible in this story about a small school, staffed only by a headmaster and an usher. The tale held its place throughout the nineteenth century and it may be regarded as a pioneer in the development of the modern story of school life.

The reform and extension of the public schools in the middle of the nineteenth century was the mainspring of the public school tale for boys. The work and influence of a great headmaster, Doctor Arnold, at Rugby, inspired an old boy, Thomas Hughes (1822–

1896) to create a first-class book founded on his schooldays there – *Tom Brown's School-days* (1857) – the evergreen classic among all stories of school. Tom Brown is a new kind of hero – the typical English boy of yeoman stock, with nothing smug or introspective about him. It was he and his like 'who for centuries have been subduing the earth in most English counties, and leaving their mark in American forests and Australian uplands'. After the wax figures of the moral tales, Tom is splendidly alive. The story describes the influence of Dr. Arnold at Rugby chiefly through his effect on the boisterous Tom, his friend East, and the other boys. Tom in his early days gets into plenty of mischief, but in a year or two he is given the charge of a younger boy, the delicate and sensitive Arthur, and this proves a steadying influence. Tom does a great deal for Arthur, who finds school life rough and frightening, and Arthur, in more spiritual ways, does much for Tom. There are high spirits and rousing scenes in this energetic tale, and also much Christian idealism. The British boy must not only be brave, self-reliant, and good-natured. He must have faith and serve God. The serious purpose is a vital part of the book, part of Tom's life at school within its confines of the elms, the close and the Great Field, and also in the world outside to which he belongs.

Through hero worship, such as the boys at Rugby had for their headmaster, the author believed that young men win their way 'to the worship of Him who is King and Lord of Heaven'. The book lives on, not because of the preaching or its tribute to a great head-master, but because of its convincing life and exciting scenes. Tom's first going to school and his ride on the box of the stage coach, the revolt of Tom and his friend against the bully Flashman, the fight with Slogger Williams, the final cricket match, are some of the episodes which stand out. And it was not a story of a school cut off from the world of men, as so many later examples were to be. Tom's background is inherent, and the book has the invigorating air of the downs of the White Horse country where he was bred.

Even more popular in its day than *Tom Brown's Schooldays* was a boys' school tale which faded into a term of derision – *Eric; or, Little by Little* (1858). The author F. W. Farrar (1831–1903), taught at Marlborough and then at Harrow before becoming Dean of Canterbury in 1895. The background of his tale is the Isle of Man, where he was once a pupil at King William's College. Farrar knew much about boys and public school life, but his story is too heavily imbued with emotion and pre-occupation with sin, guilt and death to win lasting success. Its immediate appeal was great, due not only to its strong religious message for youth but to its able narration. The tone of the book is now likely to displease or amuse the reader, but the story has power, with absorbing incidents such as that of the Stack Rock, when Eric and his companions are in danger of being drowned by the tide. The soul-searching allusions and death-bed scenes, however, make it morbid reading in an age which eschews highly-charged emotionalism and guilt feelings. As long ago as the

1870s, Kipling and his schoolfellows were pouring scorn on its attitudes according to the pages of *Stalky and Co.*

Farrar wrote another story of public school life, *St. Winifred's; or, the World of School* (1862), and a tale of university life, *Julian Home* (1859). Both works are much concerned with the struggle between good and evil, but they are less harrowing and more idealistic than their more famous predecessor. All three books were frequently printed until the early part of the present century, and *Eric* is among recent revivals (Bibl. 217).

Both Thomas Hughes and Dean Farrar had written school stories marked by strong individuality. A little later a stock pattern was adopted for this type of tale, and its creator was Talbot Baines Reed (1852–1893). He wrote his tales for the *Boy's Own Paper*, which had been launched as a weekly in January 1879. In 1881–1882 there was serialised in its pages the most famous of his stories of school life, *The Fifth Form at St. Dominics*, published in book form in 1887. G. A. Hutchison, the editor of the *B.O.P.*, wrote a prefatory note declaring 'there is a breeziness about it calculated to stir the better life in the most sluggish'. The author was assistant editor and his story fitted in perfectly with the *B.O.P.* aim to provide healthy, wholesome fare, Christian in tone, without any over-stressing of the emotions. In this miniature world, with its conventions and rules, school-boys have an importance of their own, and their actions have more significance than in the adult world outside the gates. From now onwards for about fifty years this type of literature was to have a great attraction for young Britons, whose education was mainly of Board rather than boarding school brand. Its fascination for them probably lay in the vision of a society from which adults – except for a few fleeting and often unimportant masters – were excluded.

Other tales by Talbot Baines Reed followed, including *The Willoughby Captains* (1887), *The Cockhouse at Fellsgarth* (1893), and *The Master of the Shell* (1894). By the end of the century, the story of boarding school life for boys had become almost as popular as the adventure story. Harold Avery began to publish his long series of school tales with *Frank's First Term* in 1896, others followed suit, and the way was prepared for the stereo-typed concoctions of the early twentieth century and the coming of Billy Bunter and his set in that famous weekly, *The Magnet*, in February 1908. Talbot Baines Reed's stories were rarely surpassed by later writers, and although his characters are types rather than individuals, his aim to foster a spirit of truth, courage, and self-reliance among his readers, gives his writings a value not yet quite forgotten.

The antithesis of the conventional school story and its accepted *ethos* is to be found in *Stalky and Co.* (1899). Rudyard Kipling used his own boyhood experiences at the United Services College at Westward Ho in Devon for his startling, unsentimental presentation of schoolboy adventures. He is the verse-making 'Beetle' of the famous trio, who delight in defying official attitudes and devise with much ingenuity their revenge on masters and boys. The hard, amoral quality of boyish thinking is clearly expressed, and the book was not greeted with anything like universal approval. The younger generation tended to revel in it, but many elders frowned. 'A more odious picture of school life can seldom have been drawn', wrote Somerset Maugham.[1] But its realism founded on actual experience and set down by a great writer has given it enduring life, while the books it ridiculed, such as *Eric*, were forgotten.

The story about girls at school developed much later than its counterpart for boys, chiefly because home education with a governess was for long considered the ideal practice for girls of the middle and upper classes. A change came about as higher education for women made its impact in the latter part of the nineteenth century, and the first public school for girls, Cheltenham Ladies College, was founded in 1858. Its establishment was followed by others in the 1870s under the Girls' Public Day School Trust, and good schools for girls began to increase slowly but steadily. Schools like Mrs. Goddard's, 'where girls might be sent to out of the way, and scramble themselves into a little education, without any danger of coming back prodigies', or 'Miss Pinkerton's Academy', were too lacking in freedom and real education to provide the background for stories which might rival in interest those written for boys. The vividly depicted 'Lowood' in *Jane Eyre* (1847) was modelled on Charlotte Bronte's experience at The Clergy Daughters' School at Cowan Bridge, but *Jane Eyre* was far more than a story of school life.

As higher education for girls advanced, and examinations and then university degrees became open to women, the girls' school was transformed. Then the modern school tale could find roots. Its beginnings are glimpsed in some of the stories of L. T. Meade (Mrs. Elizabeth T. Smith, 1854–1914), and with *A World of Girls* (1886) she was the pioneer in a *genre* to be widely developed early in the twentieth century by Angela Brazil and many other writers. From the present writer's own knowledge, L. T. Meade's old-fashioned yet significant tale was still being read to tatters in one school in the 1920s. It has the seriousness and emotional appeal of its period, but there are auguries of things to come. Lavender House is no large establishment, but the story is told with a new excitement of plot centred on the girls' activities and characters. Misunderstandings play a large part, and there is an exciting climax, when the suspected Annie rescues the young heroine's sister, and nearly dies. An important figure is Mrs. Willis, the silver-haired headmistress, who believes in discipline and character-training above everything for her girls. She is averse to cramming for examinations, already casting their shadow. 'The great motto here', she tells the new girl, Hester, 'is earnestness – in work and in play'. The girls are carefully shielded from temptation, including the reading of *Jane Eyre*. But notwith-

[1] Charles Carrington, p. 244 (Bibl. 257).

standing these signs of Victorianism, this book marks the beginning of a spate of school stories for girls, often for all their modernity to prove more trivial and incredible than this heartfelt portrayal of the girls of Lavender House.

v   THE TALE OF ADVENTURE

'It happen'd one Day about Noon going towards my Boat I was exceedingly surpris'd with the Print of a man's naked Foot on the Shore, which was very plain to be seen in the Sand: I stood like one Thunder-struck, or as if I had seen an apparition . . . ' This was the kind of writing to set a boy's imagination aflame, and the book from which it comes needs no introduction. *The Life and Adventures of Robinson Crusoe* (1719), still famous all over the world, marks the true beginning of the adventure story for young people, although Daniel Defoe wrote his novel for a larger public. He intended this tale about a mariner 'who lived eight and twenty years all alone in an un-inhabited island on the coast of America near the Mouth of the Great River Oroonoque . . . ' not merely as a piece of fiction, but as a guide to living. He founded his story on fact, the marooning of Alexander Selkirk on the Island of Juan Fernandez from 1704–1709, and put into it so much convincing detail and such effective writing that it reads like fact. The young reader is spellbound by Crusoe's isolation and his building of a life in the wilderness, described with such practical and exact particulars. He can never believe, like the castaway, that it could be 'an Island of Despair'. He skips quickly over Crusoe's soul-searchings, not realising that these enforce the credibility of the narrative. Excitement and action accelerate in later chapters, after the mysterious footprint incident, the arrival of man Friday, and the fight with the cannibals. *Robinson Crusoe* has irresistible qualities to charm young hearts, and very soon after its publication abridged and chapbook editions were on the market, with crude cuts showing the island hero in his skins and goatskin cap, with umbrella, parrot and dog.

Robinson Crusoe brings the reader face to face with the elemental problems of making a living in the wilderness, and Rousseau extolled the book as he believed that to live close to nature is the best education. The moralists also seized upon the story, especially after the great writer had commended it, and most of them adapted the captivating Crusoe theme to expound their theories. 'Robinsonades', as these imitations of Defoe's creation were styled, became a regular feature in improving literature for the young in the eighteenth century, both here and abroad.

One of the earliest examples is *The Hermit; or, the unparallell'd Sufferings and surprising Adventures of Mr. Philip Quarll, an Englishman, who was lately discovered by M. D - - -*

upon an uninhabited Island in the South Sea (1727). This was very different in spirit from *Robinson Crusoe*, although similar in theme. Quarll has a monkey for his man Friday, and becomes a moralising philosopher who loves his solitude. The ship which finally comes to rescue him is hailed as 'an unlucky invention'. Unlike Crusoe, he elects to stay on his island where he has found salvation and strength. The authorship has been ascribed to Peter Longueville, the preface being signed P.L. The book was put into chapbook form and remained popular for a century. It was issued as *The English Hermit; or, The Adventures of Philip Quarll*, by John Marshall (circa 1790), and later it was revised and corrected under the same title by Mary Elliott (William Darton, 1822).

More popular than Quarll's history, which was not addressed to children, was *Robinson der Jüngere* (1779), a work by the German writer and educationalist, J. H. Campe (1746–1818). It was published in English in Hamburg in 1781, but best-known in England as *The New Robinson Crusoe*, an adaptation published by Stockdale in 1788. It never had the vogue here, however, that it enjoyed on the continent. Campe, a disciple of Rousseau, attempted to simplify the story and to make it more instructional and suitable for youth. His Robinson has not the advantage of tools from a wrecked ship upon his island, and the author uses the device of a father telling the story to his children to give opportunities for much explanation and advice.

The most popular and enduring of all the earlier imitations of the Crusoe story is the still famous *Swiss Family Robinson*. *Der Schweizerische Robinson* (Zurich, 1812–1813) was the work of Johann David Wyss (1743–1818), a pastor of Berne. He wrote it to give instruction and entertainment to his own four sons, and it was edited and published by his son, Johann Rudolf Wyss. The story relates the experiences of a father shipwrecked with his wife and four sons on an uninhabited island, where every opportunity exists, not only for pious living, but for lessons in natural history, so profuse and amazing are its flora and fauna. Part one appeared in a first English edition under the title *The Family Robinson Crusoe*, issued by William Godwin in 1814. The same year Madame de Montholieu translated the book into French and later adapted and expanded it very considerably. In 1818 Godwin issued a second edition, this time of the complete story, apparently based on the German version, under its now familiar title. Various editions were in circulation in the nineteenth century, but probably the most widely known was the version by W. H. G. Kingston (1814–1880), published in 1879 (not 1849 as sometimes given). Kingston explains, in a note prefixed to the first edition, that his family translated it from the German 'with the omission of the long, sententious lectures found in the original, and some slight alterations calculated to enliven the narrative'. Another version was published in 1878 by H. Frith, a translator who 'made a serious attempt to return to the French and German sources'. This was the basis used by Audrey Clark for an excellent rendering of the tale in Dent's 'Children's Illustrated Classics' in 1957, and the position of this much-loved tale as a classic of junior literature is well-established. It seems to be one of those rare excellent books which have endeared themselves to children, but which adults find tedious.

Moral tales which treated the castaway theme as a device for admonition in the style of the day soon perished. Among the many examples of the early nineteenth century were *The Rival Crusoes* (1826), by Agnes Strickland, *The Young Crusoe; or, The Shipwrecked Boy* (1828), by Mrs. Hofland, and a rather more natural invention, *Leila; or, the Island* (1839), by Ann Fraser Tytler. Bernardin de St. Pierre's little masterpiece of Rousseauist sentiment, *Paul et Virginie* (1788), was more renowned than any of them and had a longer existence. It was a sad idyll of young love and simple living on the island of Mauritius, and drew inspiration from the author's early delight in *Robinson Crusoe*. But it is scarcely in the tradition of the adventure story for young people.

Life on a desert island continued to be a favourite subject for new tales of adventure of a more robust type, after the moralists began to unfasten their hold upon it in the 1830s. But other fascinating and fertile material was becoming available for the making of books to excite boyish fancy as the century advanced and the boundaries of Empire and exploration of the globe extended under the reign of Victoria. Before the proper adventure story for youth came into being, the young reader had found powerful stimulus in the romances about pioneers and redskins in the settlements of America, by James Fenimore Cooper (1789–1851). Cooper, inspired by Sir Walter Scott to do for his native America what the great novelist had done for Scotland, began to write novels about frontier settlements and the life of the wilds in the 1820s. His most famous work is *The Last of the Mohicans* (1826), a tale of action and Indian fighting with touches of greatness. The Indian, Uncas, is drawn as a noble figure whose death presages the decline of the Indian races. The most notable character to appeal to boy readers, however, is the white hunter, Natty Bumppo, alias Leather-stocking and Hawkeye. The first of the series of Leatherstocking tales to introduce this denizen of the wilderness was *The Pioneers* (1823), but in chronology of events it comes fourth in the series. Others, in addition to *The Last of the Mohicans*, are *The Prairie* (1827), in which Natty's death as an old man occurs, *The Pathfinder* (1840), where the hunter is at the height of his powers, and *Deerslayer* (1841), a tale of Glimmerglass or Otsego Lake, and Natty's youth.

Cooper wrote other novels, including sea tales, and a Crusoe story with political implications, *The Crater* (1847), published in England as *Mark's Reef*. It is the five Leather-stocking tales, however, centred on the experiences of the great hunter among white settlers and Indians and the wilds of virgin forest, which opened up a new world to youthful imagination, and marked the true beginning of the mass of redskin and cowboy reading matter of later generations. Cooper did not address his books to youth but to men and women for whom he wrote from his own knowledge against a background of wild landscape and simple morality.

Real experience rather than theories was to be an increasingly important factor in the making of the story of adventure, and the first writer of genuine adventure tales for youth to draw upon it fully was Captain Frederick Marryat (1792–1848). He began his naval career at the age of fourteen with Lord Cochran, and his life at sea was as crowded with events as any of his novels or his tales for children. After a brilliant and adventurous career, in which he showed much ability and valour, he was chiefly on shore after 1830, and already launched upon his literary activities. He wrote his many stories of naval life and the sea for the general reader but older boys seized upon them eagerly, especially the picaresque *Peter Simple* (1833–1834) and the humorous *Mr. Midshipman Easy* (1836). The ocean was a new sphere for the writer of romance who could bring to his task real knowledge. 'He is the enslaver of youth', wrote Joseph Conrad of Marryat, 'not by the literary artifices of presentation, but by the natural glamour of his own temperament'.[1]

Marryat became more and more absorbed in literature, and after travelling on the continent and to America and Canada, he settled down with his large and growing family, at first near London and later at Langham in Norfolk. It was early in the forties when he planned his first story for children, through the request of his own family for a continuation of the *Swiss Family Robinson*, which they had much enjoyed. The Captain felt that this work had its limitations, being wanting in seamanship and filled with incongruities. He intended to do better. 'Fiction, when written for young people', he wrote in the preface of this first story, 'should at all events be based on truth'. *Masterman Ready; or, the Wreck of the Pacific* came out in three volumes in 1841 and 1842. The author had added to the alluring desert island theme authentic detail, racy narrative, and a convincing if over-pious character – the old man Ready who, for all his moralisings, is knowledgeable in all the things dear to a boy's heart. Without this old seaman, who shows the Seagrave family how to build a house, how to find water, how to fish and catch turtles, how to blaze a trail, and in fact how to keep alive, the story would lose much of its interest. For the Seagraves are rather dull and the female part nonentities. Marryat mingled religious teaching with his story, and Mr. Seagrave, like other Britons of his kind, is always careful to see that Sunday is observed as a day of rest. There is here, and in other books Marryat wrote for the young, an implicit belief in an omnipotent God who watches over those who serve him, and whose will they must accept in humility.

The success of the story lay in its realistic scenes and its engrossing plot which maintains suspense until the last chapter. An attack on the stockade by the savages is foiled at the very last moment by the rescue ship, but it is too late to save the heroic Ready, mortally wounded while fetching water for the besieged. 'Happy are they who die in the Lord!'

[1] *Tales of the Sea.* In *Notes on Life and Letters.* 1921.

declares Mr. Seagrave earnestly, when Ready is buried. And with feelings of sorrow at their loss, which many young readers must have echoed, the Seagraves leave the island. Unprofitable as the religion in the book may strike the reader of today, it helped to make Ready, the Seagraves, and their creator what they were.

For his next book for children, *Settlers in Canada* (1844), Marryat used his knowledge of the New World gained on his travels. The theme has something of kinship with life on a desert island, for the Campbell family are uprooted from their estate in England, and have to find their living in the wilderness, this time surrounded by virgin forest not salt water. The character of the old hunter, Malachi Bone, the Indian girl named The Strawberry Plant, the storming of Angry Snake's camp – these are reminiscent of the pages of Fenimore Cooper. Next came *The Mission; or, Scenes in Africa* (1845), the least successful of Marryat's works for youth. Two years later he made up for its deficiencies by the splendid *Children of the New Forest*, described with the historical story in the next chapter. Finally came *The Little Savage* (1848–1849), completed after Marryat's death by his son Frank. This is a strange, serious book, with the same remarkable narrative power of all the author's work. The subject is again a desert island, where a young boy is cast away with an old man who proves to be his enemy. There is much Christian teaching as well as some conventional features in this story, but certain episodes have imaginative power, particularly where Frank, the boy, is alone on the island, with only the wild creatures as his friends, after he has forgiven the dying man who wronged him.

Before Marryat died in 1848, there were other signs of the development of the sea tale of adventure. In *Rattlin the Reefer* (1836) E. G. G. Howard had produced a realistic and probably autobiographical account of life at sea, edited by Marryat, a friend and former shipmate. Other ocean sagas enjoyed by older boys were *Tom Cringle's Log* (1833) by Michael Scott, a wild sort of novel about a midshipman's exploits, full of gusto, sudden death, and bright West Indian scenes. It was followed by *The Cruise of the Midge* three years later. These were not books for children, although *Tom Cringle's Log* was put into the hands of Edmund Gosse at ten years old, as his first book of fiction. 'For the sake of the descriptions' – so he records in *Father and Son*.

In children's books with a faraway or foreign background there was an innovation of a different nature in these formative forties. This was *Feats on the Fjord* (1841), the third and best-known volume in the 'Playfellow' series, by Harriet Martineau (1802–1876). This is remarkable as a pioneer attempt to found a story for boys and girls on the ordinary life and customs of another country – Norway. Although written from secondhand sources, the background is painted with such skill that it is hard to believe this. The *milieu* is a peasant community living within the Arctic Circle, and the story reveals the part tradition and superstition play in their lives. For all its serious undertone, there is a good deal of pleasurable excitement in the tale – bear-hunting, mysterious disappearances, threats of pirates, a secret cave, escapes by water, with some folk believing in demons and water-sprites to make for terrors where none need exist. The herd-boy, Otto, is perhaps the most sympathetic character, not least because of his youth, and he braves superstitious fears to rescue his friend from an 'enchanted' islet. To add to the charm of this not yet forgotten story, there is much delight in nature and the march of the seasons in this land where the midnight sun and the move to summer pastures are the crown of the year.

Feats on the Fjord is the forerunner of the story which reflects the actual life of the people of other lands, a rare product until the twentieth century. William Howitt's *A Boy's Adventures in the Wilds of Australia* (1854) might have been worthy to place beside it if it had been a more closely woven tale. It was in the United States, however, that the next first-class example of this kind of book for children was to appear. This was *Hans Brinker; or, The Silver Skates* (1865), a delightful and still famous story about two poor children and other boys and girls in Holland, by the American, Mary Mapes Dodge (1831–1905).

The development of the popular tale of action for boys was to be carried on by two writers, who were the first to produce such material in quantity – Mayne Reid and W. H. G. Kingston. Captain Thomas Mayne Reid (1818–1883), a native of County Down, began his romances of adventure in 1850 with *The Rifle Rangers; or, the Adventures of an Officer in Southern Mexico*, which was founded on his experiences with the American army during the war between the United States and Mexico. He followed this the next year with *The Scalphunters; or, Romantic Adventures in Northern Mexico*. Like the first book, it was full of hair-raising incidents and depicted the wild life of pioneering days in the Southern States and encounters with hostile Indians. Neither was addressed to youth, although later both books were included in series for boys. After the success of these two publications, the publisher David Bogue suggested Reid should write a series for boys, and the first appeared for Christmas 1851. This was a story set in the Mexican desert – *The Desert Home; or, English Family Robinson*, a variant on the Crusoe theme. More famous was his next book for youth, *The Boy Hunters of the Mississippi; or, Adventures in search of a White Buffalo* (1852). In writing for young people Reid laid special stress on genuineness of scenery and accuracy in natural history, and he frequently interrupts the narrative to give scientific information rather in textbook style. More rarely does he offer any other advice and his stories are essentially of action. In this famous tale about three boy hunters, three young brothers sent into the wilds by their father to hunt for a white buffalo skin, there is an exciting novelty about the scenes described, so soon to vanish. The impact they had in their own day can be well understood. At the end of the tale there is real suspense when the boys are captured by Indians, and only saved from death by their possession of a pouch containing a pipe, which the Indians recognise as once belonging to a great chief. Many other works for boys followed, including *The Young Voyageurs* (1853), *The Bush Boys* (1855, dated 1856), and the sequel to this South African tale, *The Young*

Jagers (1856, dated 1857). Nearly forty books by Reid are listed in Routledge's Juvenile Catalogue in the 1880s.

W. H. G. Kingston (1814–1880), almost exactly Reid's contemporary, was an even more prolific and popular writer for boys. His earliest book for youth, and one of his best, was *Peter the Whaler* (1851). It is a story told in the first person, by the son of a clergyman of Southern Ireland, Peter Lefroy, nearly sixteen when the book opens. He is sent away to sea because of a poaching escapade, and his life becomes fraught with catastrophe, amazing escapes, and salutary experiences. The Arctic scenes and the marooning of Peter and his companions among the Esquimaux are perhaps the most vivid in the book, and there is much practical knowledge about making and contriving to add realism to this chronicle of adventure. The evil in the world and suffering are faced bravely, but there is no dwelling on horrors. The keynote is optimism. 'Always keep your presence of mind, Peter, and never despair' is the advice of one seaman friend, who escapes death by his own exertions. Courage and cheerfulness in situations of danger are the qualities to be cultivated, and religion is an underlying force and support, especially seen in the character of Andrew. His faith gives him an inner strength which the others respect, so he is chosen as their leader. Such features exhibited in *Peter the Whaler* were to be characteristic of many adventure stories which captured the imagination of Victorian youth. At the end Peter comes home, as poor as he went away, but he tells his father he is infinitely richer. 'I have learned to fear God, to worship him in his works, and to trust to his infinite mercy. I have also learned to know myself, and to take advice and counsel from my superiors in wisdom and goodness'. This intermingling of exciting events with ethical or religious feeling pervades most of Kingston's excellent yarns. He wrote over a hundred books, edited several papers for boys, and won the appellation 'the boy's Marryat'. Many stories were of the sea, but he also wrote 'of redskin and buffalo, Africa and the Australian bush', and adventure in many parts of the world.

Youths, far away from ever-watchful tutors or parents, now find out the dangers and realities of life on their own, often far from home, and this marks the great difference between Reid, Kingston and Ballantyne, and the stories which had gone before. R. M. Ballantyne (1825–1894) was to make the boy hero more natural, cheerful and convincing, and so his tales have outlived those of his contemporaries. He is the great purveyor of adventure for boys in this pre-Stevenson era, and his best stories are still in print. Born in Edinburgh, he went to Canada at the age of sixteen as a clerk in the service of the Hudson's Bay Company. During six years he travelled a great deal in the North of Canada, and then on his return to Scotland he joined the publishing house of Constable.

His first story for boys came out in 1856 under the title *Snowflakes and Sunbeams; or, the Young Fur-traders*, but it was soon to be known by its sub-title. Into it he put his experiences of Canada, the stark beauty of the wilderness, the rigours of the life and climate, the ways of pioneers, *voyageurs*, and '*Injuns*', and descriptions of hazardous journeys by canoe over lake, river and rapid, or on snow-shoes over ice and snow. The two heroes personify the ideal young Briton abroad – the honest manly type, ready for a practical joke, sentimental but never soft, despising desk-work and full of zest for an open-air life, with high spirits curbed by memories of womenfolk or a devout home far away. This world of Ballantyne is the Empire in the making – the white man opening up the wilderness and bringing trade, medicines, rough justice and, above all, Christianity to the savage.

Ballantyne introduced feminine interest and romance into his stories, but woman is regarded as the ministering angel rather than the active partner, although she can show high courage when danger threatens. In *Ungava*, published for Christmas 1857, and one of his finest tales, again set in northern Canada, he gives a more heroic and active role to a female character – the ten-year-old Edith, who saves the young hero from death, and is carried off by Esquimaux. His most famous book, probably inspired by an American tale, *The Island Home*, by James F. Bowman, issued in 1851 and in England the following year, is undoubtedly the beloved *Coral Island*, which came out at the same time as *Ungava*. Perhaps this should not be rated as highly as its success might warrant, but the desert island theme, always a powerful attraction, is here made more alluring by a new type of cast-away. A trio of young friends, full of good humour and jollity, are marooned upon a little South Sea paradise, where they find everything provided by nature for their needs. Ballantyne declared in his introduction that the book was not intended for the morose and melancholy but 'for those who can enter with kindly sympathy into the regions of fun'. The humour and characterisation may be rather simple, but at last we have boy heroes who are not old beyond their years. The author's sincere Christian faith is introduced into all his books in some degree, but it does not hold up the narrative, told here in the first person by one of the three friends, Ralph Rover. The later chapters of *The Coral Island* are much concerned with natives, cannibalism, and Christian missionaries, and the author succeeds in mingling many thrilling incidents of narrow escape and rescue with appreciation of mission work in the South Seas. Even the pirate captain, who carries Ralph away from the island and his two companions, approves of missions. 'The captain cares as much for the gospel as you do (an' that's precious little)', says one of his men, 'but he knows and everybody knows, that the only place among the southern islands where a ship can put in and get what she wants in comfort, is where the gospel has been sent to. There are hundreds o' islands at this blessed moment, where you might as well jump straight into a shark's maw as land without a band o' thirty comrades armed to the teeth to back you'.

For most of his stories Ballantyne was careful to seek first-hand information, lacking for this island tale, but potent and convincing in his Canadian settings. He explored various activities to portray plucky young heroes showing their mettle. For example, he spent a fortnight in the Bell Rock lighthouse for his book *The Lighthouse* (1865), and travelled on the footplate of the Scottish express to learn about railways for *The Iron Horse* (1871), a story about the Grand National Trunk Railway. Deep-sea diving, fire-fighting, tin-mining in Cornwall, the hazardous work of the lifeboat service – these were a few of the other indigenous materials he used, but he also ranged far afield, into Africa and the far West as well as the icy north. Nearly all his works were intended for boys, but he also wrote some trifles for younger children under the pen-name 'Comus', and he had the versatility to illustrate these and other tales of his own. In all he published about eighty books for young people, of which *The Coral Island* and *Ungava* and *The Dog Crusoe* (1861), an excellent tale set in the Far West of America, are now perhaps the best known.

Ballantyne and his contemporaries were soon joined in the production of books for boys by George Manville Fenn (1831–1909), whose first book, *Hollowdell Grange*, was issued in 1866. Exploration was a favourite subject for his tales, but he also wrote some adventure stories with a historical background. One of the best of his stories is *Nat the Naturalist* (1882), set in Borneo and New Guinea. This reflects the writer's belief that 'the boy who loves nature goes on loving nature to the end' and, unlike many other books of its period which introduce wild life, it is not entirely absorbed with useless slaughter. Nat and his uncle do not only shoot strange and savage beasts and birds. They collect specimens. Dangers and breath-taking incidents are here in plenty, but there is also presented in simple fashion a world of nature of some value apart from forming a quarry for the hunter.

Five years after Fenn's debut as a writer for youth, there appeared on the scene the more striking personality of G. A. Henty (1832–1902). His first story for boys, *Out on the Pampas; or, The Young Settlers*, was published at the end of 1870, two years after it was written. Like most Henty publications it was dated for the forthcoming year, but unlike many of his later tales it depicted the contemporary scene and not the military exploits of the past which became his speciality. Another typical example of an adventure story set in his own time is *Maori and Settler* (1891), a tale of the New Zealand war. This is a world where natives are regarded as wild and uncivilised beings, a menace to peaceful and superior white settlers, an extrovert and unimaginative attitude of mind that was not Henty's alone but a reflection of the white man's early encounters with races of an alien or primitive culture. Henty became famous, however, as 'the boy's historian' – for his ability to combine a tale of action with a vivid historical background, and his work is therefore considered in more detail with the historical story. But he has much in common with Ballantyne and other writers for boys in the late Victorian period. Like them, he featured the boy hero, and he used first-hand experience gained as a war correspondent for the background of some of his contemporary tales of adventure.

By the seventies a new type of fiction was enthralling young readers, created by the Frenchman, Jules Verne (1828–1903). His scientific stories were – in his own words – '*voyages extraordinaires dans les mondes connus et inconnus*'. The first of them, *Five Weeks in a Balloon* (1863), was inspired by the experiments of a friend, who like the author, had a mania for 'aerial navigation', and it describes the exciting experiences of a trio, led by a scientist, Dr. Ferguson, in crossing Central Africa, then a relatively unknown and savage continent. It was the publisher Jules Hetzel who encouraged Verne to write fiction rather than works of popular science, and most of his tales were serialised in Hetzel's review, *Magasin d'Éducation et de Récréation*, after it started in March 1864. An English translation of Verne's first story came out in 1870, but it was also published as a serial in *Youth's Playhour* in 1871. From this time onwards amazing fictional excursions into regions of earth and ocean, air and outer space, by means of wonderful inventions, as yet only existing in the dreams of scientists, astonished and captivated readers, young and old, at home and abroad. Jules Verne is the first and greatest master of science fiction. His style is quick and energetic with a reporter-like precision, except when he holds up the narrative for an exposition of technical or geographical details, which some modern translations curtail or omit. But this factual information adds to the verisimilitude of his tales and the quality of his achievement, and it can be skipped by the reader anxious to get on with the story.

Verne's books are more than thrilling excursions into strange realms. They exhibit a feeling of wonder for nature's secrets and marvels, and the possibilities dormant in their conquest by man, always regarded as less than his Creator. Humanity is not dwarfed by technical invention, and Verne's characters are more than puppets. In the words of I. O. Evans, he endowed science fiction 'with humour, idealism, and vivid, if rather improbable, characterisation'.[1] Verne also made it 'austere', avoiding the vulgarity and undue violence and horror to be found in the work of some of his modern followers.

His finest work is perhaps *Twenty Thousand Leagues under the Sea* (1870), dominated by its powerful central figure, the mysterious Captain Nemo, and remarkable for its de-lineation of the underwater realm penetrated by his submarine vessel. Another very popular tale was that about a wager accepted by the imperturbable and taciturn English-man, Phineas Fogg – *Around the World in Eighty Days* (1873). Captain Nemo reappears in *The Mysterious Island* (1875), an unusual desert island tale about the escape of five Americans to a Pacific island at the time of the American Civil War. Jules Verne wrote many other types of stories, as well as science fiction, but it is this which has survived to delight young readers who live in the more marvellous scientific world of the space age.

[1] *Jules Verne and his Work.* (Bibl. 247).

No other writer in the *genre* of science fiction has rivalled Verne's output, immense readability, or uncanny insight into the future. The more political and social tinge of the stories of H. G. Wells (1866–1946) in this field give them a depth and literary merit Verne cannot rival, but they do not surpass the Frenchman's fecundity of invention. *The Time Machine* (1895) began a fascinating series of tales of the unusual and unexpected, but in more Vernian tradition was *The First Men in the Moon* (1901), which it is interesting to compare with his predecessor's account of imaginary lunar flight, *From the Earth to the Moon* (1865), and its sequel, *A Trip round it* (1870).[1]

Sensation for its own sake was already an important ingredient in the boy's adventure story in the 1870s, particularly in the cheap, popular weeklies such as *The Boys of England*. Spine-chilling incidents, stock situations, carelessness of style – these were the characteristics of the penny dreadfuls which had become the successors of the chapbooks. If blood-curdling excitement was what boys craved for in their reading, it was soon to be demonstrated that such fare could be raised to the level of literature by literary genius. *Treasure Island* (1883) is, in Harvey Darton's words, 'the apotheosis of the penny dreadful'. Robert Louis Stevenson (1850–1894) had been charmed in his youth by 'Kingston, Ballantyne the brave, Cooper of the wood and wave', and he drew inspiration from this early reading to create an entirely original tale, the acknowledged masterpiece among adventure stories for youth. It was first serialised in *Young Folks* from October 1881 to January 1882 under the pen-name 'Captain George North', and it was the editor who changed its original title, *The Sea Cook*, to *Treasure Island*. In atmosphere and suspense this tale of a quest for pirate treasure has few rivals. Romance is afire on the first page with the arrival of the scarred old sea dog at the 'Admiral Benbow' Inn, and the fearful fascination of his refrain:

> 'Fifteen men on the Dead Man's chest
> Yo-ho-ho and a bottle of rum!'

A livelier array of rogues than these ex-pirates, Billy Bones, Black Dog, Israel Hands,

---

[1] Dates given for Verne's works are for first publication in France. A list of the French titles follows, with the date of first publication in English.

Cinq Semaines en Ballon (*Five Weeks in a Balloon*) 1870.

De la Terre à la Lune.

Autour de la Lune (*From the Earth to the Moon . . .*, and *A Trip round it*) 1870.

Vingt Milles Lieues sous les Mers (*Twenty Thousand Leagues under the Sea*) 1873.

Le Tour du Monde en quatre-vingt Jours (*Around the World in Eighty Days*) 1874.

L'Île Mystérieuse (*The Mysterious Island*) 1875.

Many of Verne's stories were serialised in the *Boy's Own Paper*.

Ben Gunn, and the incomparable, one-legged schemer, Long John Silver, the cook, can hardly be imagined. The tale, narrated by the young hero, Jim Hawkins, possesses all the elements dear to youth – a dangerous voyage, fighting and stratagems, and an island, not for a Crusoe existence, but as a battle-ground for hidden treasure. Most important of all was the style of the telling, which heightened the dramatic effect and wrought from these blood and thunder materials a piece of first-rate literature.

Stevenson's historical tales of adventure are considered with the historical novel for children in the next chapter. All his books for young people, including *Treasure Island*, appealed to a far wider circle, and 'statesmen and judges and all sorts of staid and sober

No. 565.]   YOUNG FOLKS.

TREASURE ISLAND;

OR,

THE MUTINY OF THE HISPANIOLA.

By CAPTAIN GEORGE NORTH.

PROLOGUE.—THE ADMIRAL BENBOW.

CHAPTER I.

THE OLD SEA DOG AT THE ADMIRAL BENBOW.

SQUIRE TRELAWNEY, Dr. Livesey, and the rest of these gentlemen having asked me to write down the whole particulars about Treasure Island, from the beginning to the end, keeping nothing back but the bearings of the island, and that only because there is still treasure not yet lifted, I take up my pen in the year of grace 17—, and go back to the time when my father kept the Admiral Benbow Inn, and the brown old seaman, with the sabre cut, first took up his lodging under our roof.

I remember him as if it were yesterday, as he came plodding to the inn door, his sea-chest following behind him in a hand-barrow; a tall, strong, heavy, nut-brown man; his tarry pig-tail falling over the shoulders of his soiled blue coat; his hands ragged and scarred, with black, broken nails; and the sabre cut across one cheek, a dirty, livid white. I remember him looking round the cove and whistling to himself as he did so, and then breaking out in that old sea-song that he sang so often afterwards:

"Fifteen men on the dead man's chest—
Yo-ho-ho, and a bottle of rum,"

in the high, old tottering voice that seemed to have been tuned and broken at the capstan bars. Then he rapped on the door with a bit of stick like a handspike that he carried, and when my father appeared, called roughly for a glass of rum. This, when it was brought to him, he drank slowly, like a connoisseur, lingering on the taste, and still looking about him at the cliffs and up at our signboard.

"This is a handy cove," says he, at length, "and a pleasant sittyated grog-shop. Much company, mate?"

My father told him no, very little company, the more was the pity.

"Well, then," said he, "this is the berth for me. Here, you, matey," he cried to the man who trundled the barrow, "bring up alongside and help up my chest. I'll stay here a bit," he continued. "I'm a plain man; rum and bacon and eggs is what I want, and that hill up there for to watch ships off. What you mought call me? You mought call me captain. Oh, I see what you're at there;" and he threw down half a dozen gold pieces on the threshold. "You can tell me when I've worked through that," says he, looking as fierce as a commander.

It was odd how big and round his voice was when

walking the plank, and storms at sea, and the Dry Tortugas, and wild deeds and places in the Spanish Main. By his own account he must have lived his life among the wickedest fiends of men that ever sailed upon the sea; and the language in which he told these stories shocked our plain country people almost as much as the crimes that he described. My father was always saying the inn would be ruined, for people would soon cease coming there to be tyrannized over and put down, and sent shivering to their beds; but I really believe his presence did us good. People were frightened at the time, but on looking back they rather liked it; it was a fine excitement in a quiet country life; and there was even a party of the younger men who pretended to admire him, calling him a "true sea-dog," and a "real old

salt," and such like names, and saying there was the sort of man that made England terrible at sea.

In one way, indeed, he bid fair to ruin us; for he kept on staying week after week, and at last month after month, so that all the money had been long exhausted, and still my father never plucked up the heart to insist on having more. If ever he mentioned it, the captain blew through his nose so loudly that you might say he roared, and stared my poor father out of the room. I have seen him wringing his hands after such a rebuff, and I am sure the annoyance and the terror he lived in must have greatly hastened his early and unhappy death.

All the time he lived with us the captain made no change whatever in his dress but to buy some stockings from a hawker. One of the cocks of his hat having fallen down, he let it hang from that day forth, though it was a great annoyance when it blew. I remember the appearance of his coat, which he himself patched up stairs in his room, and which, before the end, was nothing else but patches. He never

TREASURE ISLAND.—"THE CAPTAIN AIMED AT THE FUGITIVE ONE LAST BL[OW]
WAS STOPPED BY THE SIGN BOARD."

last broke out wi[th]
there, between dec[ks]
"Were you add[ing]
and when the ruf[fian]
oath, that this was
to you, sir," repl[ied]
on drinking rum, th[e]
dirty, low scoundr[el]

The old fellow's
feet, drew and op[ened]
balancing it open o[n]
to pin the doctor to

The doctor never
him, as before, ov[er]
tone of voice; rath[er]
hear, but perfectly

"If you do not pu[t]
pocket, I promise, u[p]
next assizes."

Then followed a b[rief]
the captain soon kn[ew]
and resumed his seat

"And now, sir,"
now know there's s[uch]
may count I'll have
I'm not a doctor on[ly]
catch a breath of co[urage]
for a piece of inciv[ility]
effectual means to h[ave]
out of this. Let the

Soon after Dr. Liv[esey]
held his peace that e[ver]
come.

C[HAPTER]

BLACK DOG A[PPEARS]

It was not very lo[ng]

18.   *The story by R. L. S. as it first appeared as a serial in 1881*

men became boys once more . . .'[1] Adults could annex books designed for their juniors as well as the reverse, and it was at last becoming plain that great books written for boys and girls, such as the *Alice* books, and Stevenson's adventure stories, were universal in their interest. Now that the younger branch of literature had come to maturity, might not the grown-up sometimes find as much wisdom and entertainment on the child's bookshelf as on his own?

The success of *Treasure Island* challenged an untried writer to try his hand as a spinner of tales, and soon another type of adventure story came into being – *King Solomon's Mines* (1885), by H. Rider Haggard (1856–1925). 'Dedicated to all the big and little boys who read it' this is a story of vivid power, founded on the author's knowledge of South Africa and the Zulu wars. Again the theme was a search for treasure, this time through a wild and savage continent. The book was much praised by Andrew Lang, who helped the author to find a publisher, and another admirer was Robert Louis Stevenson. Haggard had little of Stevenson's consummate style and mastery of words, but he had imagination and the ability to tell a story in such a way that it reads like true exploration rather than fiction. Another popular African story was his *Allan Quatermain* (1887), featuring the hunter and explorer already introduced in *King Solomon's Mines*. Haggard ranged far in time and place for his many spectacular and fanciful novels, but these two African romances have had most attraction for the young reader.

Some of the adventure stories and historical romances of Sir Arthur Conan Doyle (1859–1930) are enjoyed as much by young people as their elders, but probably his Sherlock Holmes stories of detection are their favourites. With the publication of *A Study in Scarlet* in 1887, readers met for the first time the remarkable, keen-eyed figure of 221B Baker Street, Mr. Sherlock Holmes, private detective, and his colleague and friend, the faithful and genial chronicler of his adventures, Dr. Watson. With the coming of Sherlock Holmes the popular tale of detection had arrived, and thereafter came a steadily widening torrent of fiction about crime and its detection, chiefly addressed to an adult public, but sometimes intended for younger readers, as, for example, in all the Sexton Blake fabrications of the cheap press. In spite of a mass of later competitors, however, Sherlock Holmes has kept his attraction for older boys and girls, who perhaps find a piquant difference in the old-fashioned atmosphere of hansom cabs, gaslight, and Victorian manners.

The tale of espionage was soon to rival the detective novel, and *The Riddle of the Sands* (1903), by Erskine Childers, has a claim to be considered as the first modern classic in this field. It is a superb tale of sailing as well as of secret service, and recounts the adventures of two Englishmen in their boat among the Frisian Islands and shoals of the North German

---

[1] Balfour, Graham. *The Life of Robert Louis Stevenson*. Vol. 1, p. 211 (Bibl. 239).

coast, where they come upon evidence of German naval secrets and preparations for a possible invasion of Britain. In a little more than another decade came the first of the Richard Hannay tales, by John Buchan (1875–1940), another investigation into German war secrets, *The Thirty-nine Steps* (1915). Already known as the writer of historical adventures and a powerful story in the Haggard tradition, set in Africa, *Prester John* (1910), Buchan's novels have since become more and more young people's reading rather than books for the older public for whom they were written.

The story of detection is usually adventure near home, while the tale of adventure plunges the reader into unfamiliar scenes, either in the past or the present. Among the stories for youth, which may be grouped with those of adventure, a few developed during the nineteenth century of rather different texture. For they recreated a boy's own world and made a story about real or imagined adventures, using nothing more than his home environment. The origin of these more realistic and domestic tales for boys, as of the best family stories for girls, is to be found in the United States. Mark Twain (Samuel Lang-horne Clemens, 1835–1910) gave to this branch of writing a distinction, humour, and realism never surpassed, in *The Adventures of Tom Sawyer* (1876), and its sequel, *The Adventures of Huckleberry Finn* (1885). These were stories of a fascinating liveliness and vigour born of real experience, chiefly founded on the boyhood memories of the author and his schoolfellows. 'The odd superstitions touched upon', he writes, 'were all prevalent among children and slaves in the West at the period of the story: that is to say thirty or forty years ago'. Tom Sawyer is a typical boy, who hates civilised ways and wearing his best clothes, and his background is the genuine life of an essentially American community on the banks of the Mississippi in the 1840s. In one episode, the three boys, Tom, Huck, and Joe, decide to run away and be pirates and they return just in time to attend their own funerals – for they are believed to be drowned. There is a villain to be outwitted in 'Injun Joe' and plenty of adventure, all firmly rooted in the boys' activities around this little town by the great river. Huckleberry Finn is the real 'hobo', and in the second and greater book, he tells in American idiom his own story of his wanderings and adventures.

These robust recreations of real boyhood experiences were something entirely new for young English readers. Nothing of the kind was invented for them over here until Richard Jefferies (1848–1887) used his early memories for the creation of *Bevis: the Story of a Boy* (1882). This, however, is a book of a very different spirit. Bevis had already appeared in an earlier book by Jefferies, *Wood Magic* (considered later with the tale about animals), and in this second tale the author tells of a rather older Bevis making and doing, imagining and contriving, often with his friend Mark, in the Wiltshire countryside around his father's farm near a great reservoir. This was based upon Jefferies' childhood home at Coate, near Swindon. Bevis and Mark sail the craft they have built themselves and live on their island, 'New Formosa', with Pan the dog, and towards the end, a female 'slave', Loo, a labourer's child, who plays the role of despised and adoring femininity. Jefferies was a naturalist, and the book is full of the close observation and love of natural things – the sky, the sunlight, the grass, the wind, and the living world of out-of-doors. In the midst of it the boys create their own realm of make-believe, engendered by their reading, and the jungle they explore and the seas they sail are filled with the terrors and excitements of their own imagining. These are the long, long days of youth on holiday, in halcyon summer weather, nearly always in the open-air. *Bevis* is a lengthy story, packed with detail, and it may be rather formidable for some young readers today. Nevertheless it is a rewarding and fascinating book, full of realism, beauty, and sincere feeling. And it hints of things to come, looking forward to the Swallows and Amazons fifty years ahead, and the holiday stories of sailing and exploring by Arthur Ransome. It also gives the reader a new version of the Crusoe theme, for here the 'castaways' play the part not far from their home.

Very different, depicting a boy's background of an unfamiliar kind, is Kipling's story about India – *Kim* (1901). This absorbing tale, 'full of Eastern sunlight', is in a class by itself. The hero, a white boy who is part of both the world of the Sahibs and that of the native bazaars and wild places, accompanies a simple and wise old lama on a quest which leads them to the hills. The old man seeks the River of Life and Healing, but Kim has a more practical purpose. The intertwining of these themes, and the vivid Asiatic diversity of characters and scenes, make *Kim* an impressive saga. It was intended for a wide public, not for young readers, but many older boys and girls have found a compulsive magic in this tale about a vanished Imperialist India.

By the end of the nineteenth century the adventure story for girls was making hesitant progress, and the first stories by a popular writer who featured girls having adventures in far places were in being by 1900. Bessie Marchant (1862–1941) continued to write many such stories during the Edwardian age and after, and gradually others followed her example. But there was little of value in this field, and girls who wanted more dynamic fare than the tales of home and school thought suitable for them usually turned to the books intended for their brothers. Female characters began to take a more prominent part in some of these books, but fiction which portrayed girls as active explorers or pioneers in true adventure style was as yet a rarity.

The careful separation of stories into series, which publishers and librarians could complacently label 'Boys' or 'Girls', had in fact become a minor oppression of young readers in the later nineteenth century. The emphasis on female reading was on home and family duties. But many of the young ladies who now rode bicycles and struggled to get a college education were becoming rebellious. The wiser of them ignored any such literary demarcations.

171

The turning back to the past during the nineteenth century for all kinds of traditional and medieval lore was only part of the new interest in history, both for its own sake and as a source for romantic fiction. The great pioneer in making the past live again for the reader's entertainment was that genius of the north, Sir Walter Scott (1771–1832) – the creator of the historical romance for old and young. Lord David Cecil, in an asssesment of Scott as 'a great novelist' in 1933, pointed out that his reputation had so much declined as a serious writer that E. M. Forster rated him as little more than 'a glorified writer of children's books'. It is true that he is still more read by young people (sometimes compulsorily) than by adults, and an increasing number of his books are issued in series for children, but at last he is regaining something of the stature and popularity he enjoyed in his own day and for long afterwards.[1]

One of Scott's great achievements was to reveal for the first time how vividly a sense of the past, with its famous figures, its strangeness, its colour, its romantic associations, might be used to create novels of dramatic interest, and historical fiction as we know it today may be said to date from the publication of *Waverley* in 1814. Scott also showed the way in the delineation of living and robust characters, and so his romanticism never became tenuous or artificial. Though sometimes tedious or careless in style, he was a master in his self-created field, and after that first novel about the 'forty-five rising, a stream of romances flowed from his pen until his death. He covered many historical periods, and depicted some memorable persons, especially in his Scottish tales, acknowledged to be his greatest. South of the Border, however, young readers have perhaps enjoyed most the novels less notable for their characters than for their action and their more highly-coloured background, especially those set in feudal or Tudor times – *Ivanhoe* (1819), depicting the England of Richard I and introducing Robin Hood, *Quentin Durward* (1823), a story about a young Scottish archer in the France of Louis XI, *Kenilworth* (1821), centred on the court of Queen Elizabeth and the history of Leicester and his wife, the ill-fated Amy Robsart, and *The Talisman* (1825), a tale of the Crusades, remarkable for its portrait of Saladin.

The only work which Scott addressed to children was *Tales of a Grandfather* (4 series, 1827–1830), inspired by his love of Scottish history and written for his six-year-old grandson, John Hugh Lockhart. It is a long book, certainly formidable for the ordinary six-to-eight year old, yet it presents a great country's past in a fascinating way for able young readers who like history. The story of Scotland is related from earliest times to the 1745 Rebellion, this later period being described in much detail, with reports of

---

[1] Cecil, Lord David. *Sir Walter Scott* (Bibl. 253).
Devlin, D. D. editor. *Walter Scott: modern judgments* (Bibl. 254).

first-hand experiences of persons whom Scott had known. The last volume deals with the history of France.

In children's literature Scott is most important as an influence and an originator. He excited in his admirers and followers a keen interest in the life of the past and a love of romance, eventually to take the prominent place in books for children they were never to lose. Writers of adventure stories were to find that they could add effect and unusual background to their plots by a historical setting, but few were to reveal a genuine feeling for the past like Scott, and in the 1820s and 1830s when Scott's novels were delighting people everywhere, children's books showed little evidence of their influence. A few writers of moral tales might be encouraged to set their stories about exemplary conduct or warnings against evil-doing in former times, and introduce historical facts into their pages, but these features made little difference to the finished product. For example, *Adelaide: or, The Massacre of St. Bartholomew* (1822), by Mrs. Hofland, combines details about Henry of Navarre and French history, with the story of a young girl who possesses all the qualities highly rated by the contemporary didactic school. Setting a tale in the past could be a device, rather than an imaginative interpretation of events, and the tale which was to follow Scott's pattern had to wait, with other manifestations of romance and imagination in children's books, for the emancipating middle years of the century.

Signs of the new era are visible in the forties, especially in two historical tales written by Harriet Martineau for her 'Playfellow' series in 1841. The second volume of the four in the series was *The Peasant and the Prince*, a narrative in two parts, both concerned with the French Revolution. The first episode introduces Marie Antoinette on her way at the age of fifteen to be married to the future Louis XVI, and describes the fortunes of a French peasant family for whom she intervenes on her journey. The second part deals with the life and death of the child Dauphin, the ill-fated Louis XVII, and evokes sympathy for the Royal family in their sufferings, so forming a contrast to the earlier pages, where the hardship and misery of the peasants are stressed.

The author indulges in a good deal of reflective comment, but tells a plain tale, and she makes a real effort to show exactly what was happening in these days of revolution, with facts well-blended into the narrative. But Miss Martineau had no taste for romantic fabrications, and she shows her firm belief in democratic principles and moderation, so that *The Peasant and the Prince* is a little too much weighted with meaning to appeal to a less earnest age.

Also little known today is her other historical tale in the 'Playfellow' series, the more exciting, less sombre *Settlers at Home*, the first volume to be issued in 1841. This is a story about the Isle of Axholme, and the Dutch and French Protestant settlers there on land reclaimed from the fens. It takes place during the Civil War, but is more concerned with local feuds of families in the area at a time of flood and disaster, than with national affairs.

Three children are marooned, finding asylum in a church tower, after they have saved their enemy, a bad boy, who at last turns out well. Much of the interest of the story concerns the practical details of how they live, cut off by water on every side. Christian teaching of an unsectarian kind is a part of the tale, and sadness intrudes with the death of little Geordie, the youngest child, 'so innocent he was fit to go to God'. Boys and girls here share responsibilities in an unusual story with some interesting features, but its rather heavy tinge of didacticism has prevented its survival.

Early stories for children which used a historical background were usually sedate rather than colourful, more intent on teaching lessons from history than arousing the imagination. An interesting example of this type of story in the 1840s is Mrs. Sinnett's *A Story about a Christmas in the Seventeenth Century*, issued in 1846 by Chapman and Hall in exactly the same format as *Wonderful Stories for Children* (the first volume of Andersen to appear in English). Both volumes have delicately tinted prints by Vizetelly. Mrs. Sinnett's tale is set in Germany at the time of the Thirty Years' War, and relates the experiences of a Lutheran merchant's family and their escape from the Catholic armies of Wallenstein. It is by no means as exciting as this may indicate, but there is one sensational episode – an escape by means of a secret passage – foreshadowing a stock ingredient of much juvenile adventure to come.

The following year, 1847, saw the publication of a much loved favourite about Cavaliers and Roundheads, *The Children of the New Forest*, by Captain Marryat, whose other stories have already been mentioned. This was just as much an adventure story with a 'castaway' theme as an excursion into the past. The romantic background was well-exploited, however, and the plot had a powerful attraction, being concerned with the fortunes of a family of four Royalist children, who go into hiding and make a living in the forest, disguised as the grandchildren of a faithful forester. Housekeeping in strange or primitive surroundings is again the Crusoe theme, with its never failing lure for young readers, and here Marryat's mastery of practical detail and narrative skill make his story of absorbing and perennial interest. It is also one of the few stories sympathetic to the Royalist cause, where the Roundheads are depicted without prejudice. Edward, the eldest of the children, comes into his own at the Restoration, and marries his childhood friend, the daughter of the Roundhead Intendant, who is a moderate and 'no great friend of Cromwell'.

The romance and pageantry of history, especially of a rose-coloured Middle Ages, tinted by High Church sympathies, first appear for children in the stories by Charlotte M. Yonge. She had always delighted in the novels of Scott and the more rhapsodical tales of De La Motte Fouqué, and these influences are strong upon her historical writing. She may have invested medieval Christendom with her own vision of ecclesiastical Gothic, but all writers look on the past with the eyes of the present, and Miss Yonge's genuine interest, painstaking study, and competent storytelling resulted in a series of deeply interesting historical tales for the young. The first, usually considered the finest, is *The Little Duke*, published serially in *The Monthly Packet* in 1851, and in book form in 1854. The central figure is Richard the Fearless, Duke of Normandy, when a child of eight years old. His story is told in an exciting narrative, with one episode of real suspense, when the boy is smuggled out of the French court in a bale of straw. It is much concerned with the principle of Christian forgiveness, and the little Duke and the tenth century are somewhat idealised. Richard becomes 'the Fearless' because there was but one thing he feared, and that was to do wrong.

Charlotte Yonge wrote about thirty historical tales, not all of them for children and young people. One of the most typical is *The Prince and the Page* (1865), in which the chief characters are Prince Edward (later King Edward I), and Richard de Montfort, fourth son of the great leader, Simon de Montfort. Richard enters Edward's service as a page, although the Prince is hated by the other De Montfort sons. The boy finds out that Edward is not the enemy he once believed, but a fine, generous soul, who did not wish for the death of their father. The story tells how Richard sacrificed himself to save the Prince during an expedition to the Holy Land on the last crusade. Rich detail is mingled with reflections that death is not tragic if suffered for a righteous or selfless cause. Another favourite still remembered is *The Lances of Lynwood* (1855), inspired by Froissart's *Chronicles*. *The Dove in the Eagle's Nest* (1866) recalls Fouqué's more Gothic style. Intended for rather older readers, it describes the life of a young girl among robber barons near Ulm in the days of Kaiser Maximilian. Charlotte Yonge was also fond of the Tudor and Stuart periods. *Unknown to History* (1882) appealed to older girls, and introduced a supposed daughter of Mary, Queen of Scots, and Bothwell, in the days of the Queen's captivity in England. Another sixteenth century story, and one of her best for young people in their teens, is *The Chaplet of Pearls* (1868), set in France in the period of the massacre of the Huguenots in 1572. The historical stories by Charlotte Yonge bear many marks of their day, but they are well constructed narratives revealing a genuine enthusiasm for the past, and a few of the best have endured to please readers of the present generation.

The 1850s and 1860s were almost as rich in historical romances to be taken over by young people as their own, as in those addressed to them. Charles Kingsley wrote *Westward Ho!* (1855) as a novel for the general public, but it has all the attributes of a book for youth, with its heroic action and splendid scenes set in Elizabethan days. Kingsley's love of Devon and its seacoast, his reading of Hakluyt, his delight in bold endeavour and bravado were poured into a fine tale, although it is marred for some by its anti-Catholic bias. For his second great historical romance, *Hereward the Wake* (1866), which also has much attraction for young readers, he drew upon his childhood memories of the Fen country and made his own theatrical interpretation of ancient sagas to create in this 'last of the English' a stalwart warrior, in keeping with his own views of muscular Christianity. Other historical novels of this period which have found a home on the shelf for young readers are *The Cloister and the Hearth* (1859), by Charles Reade, a story about the Renaissance in Europe, and the parents of Erasmus, and that rousing romance about Exmoor in the seventeenth century – *Lorna Doone* (1869), by R. D. Blackmore.

Boys and girls had no need to borrow the historical tales intended for their parents however. As well as the stories by Charlotte Yonge, there were the books for boys by J. C. Edgar (1834–1864), who began by writing short biographies of heroes and great men, and excerpts from history. Much of his work appeared in the pages of Beeton's *Boy's Own Magazine* (established in 1855), including one of his best tales, *Cressy and Poictiers* (1865). This is largely based on Froissart, and tells the story of the Black Prince, with fiction interwoven with actual events, chiefly relating to the life and prowess of the Prince, especially in the French wars. Edgar was much swayed by Scott, and he delighted in chivalry and battles. His tendency to use old-world language rather heavily is a handicap but it does not obscure the vigour of his spirited scenes of action.

At the beginning of the seventies the real founder of the historical adventure story for boys appears – George Alfred Henty (1832–1902). He began his career with *Out on the Pampas* (1870), mentioned in the preceding chapter. This was a tale about an English family who emigrate to the Argentine, not dissimilar in some of its features from Marryat's *Settlers in Canada*. But very soon the author's interest in history, which was to be the most prominent trait in his books for boys, became apparent. Yet he continued to put much of his own experiences, gained as a war correspondent in many parts of the world, into books reflecting action, adventure and war of his own times. Many of these topical stories were directly founded on his first-hand observations – as, for example, in *The Young Franc-Tireurs* (1872), based on events in the Franco-Prussian war, and in *Out with Garibaldi* (1900), for which he drew upon knowledge gained with the hospital service in Italy at the time of Garibaldi's struggle for Italian freedom and unity. But most of his books show that he explored the past for material to make his tales, which also utilised wide geographical knowledge and study. They range as far back as the days of ancient Egypt in *The Cat of Bubastes* (1888), and the early days of Britain in *Beric the Briton* (1892), considered to be one of his best books, and *Wulf the Saxon* (1894).[1]

Nearly every country and every period come within the orbit of his yarn-spinning, with military history and strategy his speciality. In thirty years he produced more than seventy volumes, dictating them rapidly to his secretary when the necessary research had been done.

The tales, for all the diversity of scene and period, follow a stereotyped pattern, featuring

---

[1] Actual dates of publication are given, the books usually being dated for the forthcoming year.

the same kind of hero, the manly British youth eager to serve his country, always imperturbable, and usually unscathed in the most dangerous situations. These deficiencies, however, do not detract from Henty's remarkable achievement and long popularity. He shared with Ballantyne and similar writers of his time a deep influence over the youthful, and often not so youthful readers, who eagerly awaited each new volume. Courage, resourcefulness, cheerfulness in adversity, good-nature, truthfulness, magnanimity towards the enemy, were some of the qualities which Henty and his contemporaries held up for admiration and emulation, and the output of these 'manly' tales helped to foster the needful spirit of adventure and service as Britain enlarged her territories under the ageing Queen.

Many boys owed to Henty an interest in history which school or textbooks would never have inspired. 'He taught more lasting history to boys than all the schoolmasters of his generation', affirmed G. M. Fenn, in his biography of Henty.[1] 'Who of us who write the historical adventure stories of today, can deny our debt to him?' asked Geoffrey Trease, in an article in the *Junior Bookshelf* fifty years after his death.[2] The vogue for Henty persisted well into the present century, although it was fading fast in the 1930s. Since the expiration of copyright in 1952, there have been signs of some revival of interest, and many Henty titles have been reissued, but Henty is likely to remain a 'giant' only for his own generation.

Henty stands midway between storytellers who carefully strive for historical accuracy and scholarship in their books, and the school of romancers who use the past as a backcloth for cloak and dagger fabrications. There can be no clear division between tales of adventure and tales of history, as the reader well knows, and many writers, including Ballantyne and Fenn, sometimes found inspiration for a stirring yarn by turning to history. Ballantyne did so in his stories of the Norse sea kings – *Erling the Bold* (1869) and *The Norsemen in the West*, (1872). And before the end of the century writers for girls, notably L. T. Meade (Mrs. E. T. Smith, 1854–1914), and E. Everett-Green (1856–1932), were moving from the world of the present to that of the past for some of their romantic tales, reflecting the widening scope of reading material being offered to British girlhood.

The classic example of the historical adventure story for young people is that masterly Scottish tale, *Kidnapped* (1886), by Robert Louis Stevenson, not quite matched in quality by its sequel, *Catriona* (1893). *Kidnapped*, like *Treasure Island*, first appeared in the periodical *Young Folks*, and *Catriona*, which had a feminine interest, was serialised in *Atalanta* as *David Balfour: Memoirs of his Adventures at Home and Abroad*, from 1892–1893. Stevenson was not so adept with his young women characters, and Catriona, the heroine of the second book, never has the life of David Balfour, the Lowland Scot of Whiggish

[1] *George Alfred Henty* (Bibl. 249).
[2] Vol. 16 No. 2 (Bibl. 251).

sympathies, who tells his own adventures in both volumes. Stevenson went deeper into reality in these Scottish tales than in the purely sensational *Treasure Island*, and in *Kidnapped* he wove a superb story of suspense from many strands, putting into it his heartfelt knowledge of Scotland and her people and traditions, the feuds and troubles after the 'forty-five, the wild grandeur of mountain, moor, and glen, and Scottish folk as real as the earth they tread. He founded the plot upon a historical incident, the murder of Campbell of Glenure in Appin in 1751. His young hero, after escape from other dangers, becomes a witness of the murder, and is suspected of complicity, with Alan Breck Stewart, a Jacobite agent. This daring, quarrelsome, vainglorious Highlander and loyal supporter of the Stuart cause is a striking foil to David, the dour young Lowlander, and their flight together through the heather pursued by the redcoats is one of the great escapes of fiction.

Kidnapped never falters from first to last, but its continuation, *Catriona*, is more unequal. Another historical story for boys and girls by Stevenson, *The Black Arrow* (1888), first issued in *Young Folks* in 1883, does not match the David Balfour books in its sense of the past or in narrative power. Yet this tale of Tunstall Forest at the time of the Wars of the Roses was most successful as a serial. The young subscribers who sent in comments to the paper used pseudonyms taken from characters in the story, a sure sign of its appeal. *Treasure Island* had awakened no such interest when it had appeared in the same periodical, although 'in the other court' the verdict was reversed, and *The Black Arrow* never rivalled in book form *Treasure Island* or *Kidnapped* in popularity. This romance of fifteenth century England has very often an air of contrivance and conscious invention absent from the other books, although it has all the elements to appeal to youth – a boy's fight for his inheritance against powerful enemies, a maid in disguise and in peril, friendly outlaws and a mystery, frequent battles and encounters by sea and land, and a finale which introduces Richard, Duke of Gloucester, to settle affairs. Lawless, leader of the outlaws, is a likeable rogue, a hybrid of Little John and Friar Tuck, who might have stepped from the pages of *Ivanhoe*. But the breath-taking magic of Stevenson at his best is missing.

More scholarly recreations of the past in fiction, without the creative spark which illumined everything penned by R.L.S., came from Alfred J. Church (1829–1912) in the 1880s and onwards. Church was a classical scholar and teacher, and his versions of Homer for children have already been mentioned. He also retold episodes from other ancient writers, including Livy, Thucydides and Josephus, and made a version of the Charlemagne romances, *Stories of Charlemagne and the Twelve Peers of France* (1902). Most of his historical tales for youth depict the ancient world, and one of the best is *The Count of the Saxon Shore; or, the Villa in Vectis* (1887), written in collaboration with Ruth Putnam. The scene is Britain at the time of the departure of the Roman legions early in the fifth century. The book contains a good deal of information about the ways and customs of Roman and

Briton at this date, and its appeal to lofty ideals recalls Miss Yonge. Founded on exact study, it nevertheless possesses much excitement, and the undercurrent of realism beneath the romantic strain of the narration is significant. The style of composition dates it, however, and the book is nearly forgotten. Rather less absorbing, but equally based on careful study is *The Chantry Priest of Barnet* (1885), which recounts the story of a monk of St. Albans Abbey, and experiences at the Battle of Barnet in 1471.

Church's historical tales are important in that they show a new trend towards realism and historical scholarship in fiction for young people, but he was not as capable a story-teller as Henty and other writers with a more popular following. Another writer who gave to boys and girls an interesting story of a rather different kind was Mark Twain (Samuel Langhorne Clemens), whose books for boys have already been described. In *The Prince and the Pauper* (1881), the staunch American republican turned his attention to English history, and made a serious though never solemn tale from an old legend that the boy Prince Edward (soon to become King Edward VI) changed places for a while with a poor beggar of his own age, Tom Canty. Such a theme provided much opportunity to contrast the luxury of the Court and the aristocracy with the harsh existence of the underprivileged. Out of perspective as it may be in some of its details and conclusions, this is a compelling story, with a refreshing difference of viewpoint.

The more piquant and colourful school of romantic writers, who tended to glamorise the past, at the end of the century, included Henry Seton Merriman (Hugh Stowell Scott, 1862–1903) and Stanley J. Weyman (1855–1928), and some of their best novels still appeal to present-day youth. Less known is S. R. Crockett (1860–1914), once famous as the author of four rather precious and over-sentimental stories about childhood, of which the best is *Sir Toady Lion* (1897). He is now better remembered for the historical romances he wrote, inspired by his native Galloway and Scottish history. His success, however, was soon to be eclipsed by that of a rising new writer and fellow-countryman, John Buchan (1875–1940).

Much influenced by Stevenson, John Buchan's early novels were historical tales with a Scottish background, written in a mannered style reminiscent of his greater predecessor. *Sir Quixote of the Moors* (1895) was his first essay in the art, followed by *John Burnet of Barns* (1898) – both first-person narratives echoing *Kidnapped* or *Catriona*. Finer than either of them is *Salute to Adventurers* (1915), another of Buchan's 'grown-up boys' books' in similar vein, where much of the action takes place in Virginia. His later historical novels reached more adult literary status, but his long series of adventure stories, whether set in the past or the present, carried on the romantic spirit into the twentieth century to delight readers of all ages. And in the same tradition were the excellent historical tales for boys by John Masefield (1878–1967) – *Martin Hyde* (1910) and *Jim Davis* (1911).

Trends towards realism and careful research into facts, with increasing interest in the social background of history, had already shown themselves in stories about the past, but only rarely. In the years ahead the widening scope of history would bring some profound changes into this kind of fiction for youth. Yet boys and girls often care more for the raptures of high adventure, heroic deeds, suspense, and vivid pageantry, than for factual background in their reading. So it was unlikely that the banners of romance would be overthrown, or that those grand storytellers of the nineteenth century, Scott and Stevenson, would cease to be read and imitated in a more enlightened age, when the study of the past was to concern itself as much with the everyday life of the people, as with the kings, battles, and great events, which spelt history for Charlotte Yonge and most of her contemporaries.

VII   THE ANIMAL STORY

The story about animals is among the most primitive fictions of the human race and an intrinsic part of folk-lore all over the world. Fables and anecdotes about talking birds and beasts, who are only thinly disguised human beings with animal attributes, go back to Aesop and earlier, and something about their development has already been given. Fairy tales, myths and other inventions about the supernatural, also introduce furred and feathered creatures of a fabulous or a familiar kind. There was Bellerophon's winged horse, Puss-in-boots and other marvellously endowed quadrupeds to aid human beings in traditional lore. Another commonplace of the faery world is the frequent metamorphosis of mortals (and immortals) into animals, plants, and other forms of life. The vast part that animals have played in fantasy and fables, however, is not the subject of this chapter. An attempt will only be made to trace some of the stories which have presented beasts and birds more or less in their natural form. Such realistic treatment of animals has been far less common than the fabulous or magical in stories for the young, and it was not until comparatively recent times that writers began to look at living creatures objectively, and try to picture their lives in their natural surroundings.

The domestic animals, the friends of man, make an appearance in their own character in books for children long before wild and untamed creatures. Dick Whittington's cat is a famous example.[1] No wielder of magic, this, but a mouse-catcher who brings his master riches by very catlike prowess in a rat-ridden Barbary palace. Argos, the old dog who recognises his master, Odysseus, on his return, and dies, and Gelert, the faithful hound

---

[1] Printed as a Ballad, *The Vertuous Life and Memorable Death of Sir Richard Whittington*. (Register of the Stationers' Company, 16th July, 1605.)

of the old folktale, best known in its Welsh version, are more ancient, but they are merely dogs possessing only canine powers, and they and others like them have come into children's books in devious ways. To find stories invented for boys and girls, treating animals in a natural way, without using them to provide lessons in morality, or making them agents for good or evil, is rare before the nineteenth century.

The attraction of animals for the young mind has always been exploited by religious teachers and moralists, as the history of the fable makes clear. In the eighteenth century, however, a new bent concerning animals appears in children's books – the encouragement of kindness towards them. It is a marked feature of the books published by John Newbery, particularly so in *The History of Little Goody Two-shoes* (1765), where Mrs. Margery rescues various creatures and trains them to help her run her school, and in *The Valentine's Gift* (1765). In this there appears the character of 'old Zig-Zag' with a horn which enables him to understand the language of birds and beasts. Zig-Zag becomes convinced that 'Man, proud, imperious, cruel Man, is the most unjust of the Animals', for on his journey he has seen or heard of many wrongs inflicted on the brute creation. There is the goaded ox, the goldfinch's nest cruelly destroyed by wicked boys, the cock murdered by stone throwing, and many other sufferers. Happier, if no less admonitory, is the incident about the rooks learning to fly. 'Hustle, my boys, hustle', says the old rook, 'and learn to get your bread'. At the end 'Zig-Zag, out of humour with all he has seen and heard, either burnt his horn, or gave it to Mr. Newbery, who daily employs it in writing the conversation of birds, beasts and other animals . . .'

Another book concerned with animals published by Newbery is *A Pretty Book of Pictures for Little Masters and Misses; or, Tommy Trip's History of Birds and Beasts* (1752). This contained 'a familiar description of each in verse and prose, to which is prefixed the History of Tom Trip himself, of his dog Jouler, and of Woglog, the great Giant'. Jouler is an unusual dog, for he serves Tommy also as a steed. 'Tommy, when he has a mind to ride, pulls a little bridle out of his pocket, whips it upon honest Jouler, and away he gallops – *tantivy*!' The author of this bit of spirited invention may have been Newbery himself, as Goldsmith indicated in *The Vicar of Wakefield*. Doctor Primrose, it may be recollected, meets at an inn 'the philanthropic bookseller of St. Paul's Churchyard, who has written so many little books for children . . . at the time actually compiling materials for the history of one Mr. Thomas Trip'.

This trend of encouraging kindness to animals continued, and gradually became allied to a more naturalistic treatment of their behaviour in children's books, although moral instruction for long played a dominant role. Animals began to act more like themselves, although they were often given the mental powers of human beings. One of the best animal moralities, very popular at the end of the eighteenth century, is *The Life and Perambulation of a Mouse* (1783), by Dorothy Kilner, whose work under the initials

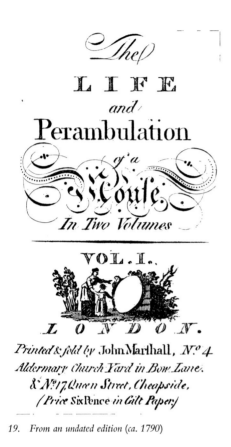

The
LIFE
and
Perambulation
of a
Mouse.
In Two Volumes
VOL. I.

LONDON.

Printed & sold by John Marshall, N.º 4
Aldermary Church Yard in Bow Lane,
& N.º 17 Queen Street, Cheapside,
(Price Six Pence in Gilt Paper)

19. *From an undated edition (ca. 1790)*

'M.P.' has been introduced in a former chapter. This shows a real attempt to depict the animal's world, not merely to use its history to the full to persuade the child to good behaviour.

The preface describes how the story came to be written. Everyone at a house party is to write the story of their lives, but the author taking up her pen, says aloud that she cannot do it. 'Then write mine, which may be more diverting', says a little squeaking voice. It is the mouse, Nimble, the hero of the tale. The language is precise and formal, and the mice, Nimble and his brothers, are given some very superior feelings, but they do live like mice. Their troubles naturally result from disobeying the advice of their mother, who has left them to fend for themselves. Longtail, Softdown, and Brighteyes, all come to a sad end in various ways, but Nimble has survived to tell his story and to comment on human conduct. At the end, the friend now of his amanuensis, he takes refuge from the cat in a tin canister. The author is careful to add to her introduction an apology for her invention, declaring as the mouse is about to begin its history, 'I must beg leave to assure my readers, that, *in earnest* I never heard a mouse speak in all my life . ..' The tale is entertaining and certainly likely to put small readers of the day into the right humour to receive 'all the advice the mouse has been giving them' – the principal object of the author.

The duty of being kind to animals is part of the mouse's admonitions, and this sentiment also inspired Mrs. Trimmer to write two books: one for her own children, *Fabulous Histories* (later known as *The History of the Robins*,) and *The Two Farmers*, 'designed to instruct the poor about the treatment of the brute creation', both published in 1786. The *Robins* was popular all through the nineteenth century, and lingered on in abridged versions until the first World War. Its attraction as a story does not seem to have suffered from the heavy weight of morality contained in its pages, or the chastening lessons such as Frederick's mother gives her six-year-old son, when he feeds the birds in the morning before addressing her. 'Remember, my dear', she says, 'that you depend as much on your

182

papa and me for everything you want, as these little birds do on you; nay, more so, for they could find food in other places; but children can do nothing towards their own support; they should therefore be dutiful and respectful to those whose tenderness and care they constantly experience'.

Mrs. Trimmer expressed herself with great clarity and with plenty of moralising in this strain. She saw animals very much in human perspective. Yet she had something of a deeper insight too. For she could look at the world of the little robins with understanding and love. The names of the fledglings – Robin, Dicksy, Pecksy and Flapsy (the last two also belong to two of the young rooks in *The Valentine's Gift*) – are endearing, and each bird has its own characteristics. Father Robin is very much the human Papa, but there is at times a real sense of sharing in the life of the birds. When the little robins leave the nest and see the orchard for the first time, it seems to them the whole world. Flapsy at length cries out, 'What a charming place the world is! I had no conception it was half so big!' There is a more striking description of the impact of things on the fledglings, when the apparition of a 'monster' frightens them in their nest. This turns out to be only the friendly gardener.

Other stories about birds succeeded *Fabulous Histories*, but none rivalled its long popularity. Among the more notable were the books by Edward Augustus Kendall (1776–1842), including *The Crested Wren* (1799) and *The History of a Goldfinch* (1807). The latter was a pleasing narrative about 'little Goldy' written to impress upon young readers the evil effect of cruelty to animals. Kendall's outstanding work for youth, however, is a tale about a dog – *Keeper's Travels in Search of his Master* (1798). Mrs. Trimmer described this story in *The Guardian of Education* (I, 393) as 'a very interesting and entertaining history of a poor dog, who met with a variety of adventures and disasters, in consequence of his giving his attention to a basket of fowls in the market, when he ought to have been following his master', before she went on to criticise the author's religious principles. Notwithstanding the strong moral purpose and asides, this is a very good story, and Keeper is no talking animal, but a real dog, one who behaves according to his nature. At the end Keeper is united once again with his master, who finds that his dog has brought him romance in the person of a young lady who had befriended him on his travels.

There had been dog stories before *Keeper*, including the popular *History of Pompey the Little; or, The Life and Adventures of a Lap-Dog* (1751), ascribed in the British Museum Catalogue to F. Coventry. This was more concerned with satirising fashionable life and human folly than amusing boys and girls. A later example, *The Dog of Knowledge; or, Memoirs of Bob the Spotted Terrier* (1801), cannot compare with Keeper for credibility. The unknown author also wrote *Memoirs of Dick the Little Pony*, published either 1799 or 1800. He made his 'petty volumes' for his own children, but Bob's adventures are too much manipulated to point out the vagaries of human life to make him much of a children's pet.

M

183

Cats were equally popular in moral tales for the young at this period. One of the more interesting is *Felissa; or, The Life and Opinions of a Kitten of Sentiment*, an anonymous work with some style and humour, published by Harris in 1811, and once ascribed doubtfully to Charles Lamb. The author has now been identified as a Mrs. Ludlow. Two more typical tales of the time were *The Adventures of Poor Puss* (1809), by Elizabeth Sandham, an affecting history in two parts, the second being 'The History of Tib . . up to her death', and *Marvellous Adventures; or, The Vicissitudes of a Cat* (1802), an even more serious tale by Mrs. Pilkington where the feline narrator shows up the weaknesses and virtues of the human beings she encounters, but is not permitted to sacrifice her life by springing into the grave of her mistress at the end. She must 'anxiously await the final blow of death'.

Donkeys have much attraction for the young, and very soon there was a donkey hero telling his story. *The Adventures of a Donkey* (1815), by Arabella Argus, is an animal morality with some very pleasing features. Jemmy Donkey follows the example of most of the animals in these improving tales by relating his own story, but he exhibits more cheerfulness and good-humour. Sincerity is his motto, and he confesses that his chief fault is vanity. 'Surely an ass may look at a horse', he comments, when a horse and a mare treat him with disdain. He has many experiences, but finally comes back to his old home. He ends with an apologia for his kind, and an appeal for indulgence, signing himself 'the most respectful and humble of donkeys'. Jemmy's history was continued in *Further Adventures of a Donkey* (1821).

Stories about wild creatures are much scarcer than those about pets and domestic animals, although the mouse was a favourite subject. By the end of the eighteenth century there was at least one tale about a hare, as well as Gay's popular fable, 'Hare and many friends'. *The Hare; or, Hunting incompatible with Humanity* (1799), a little work without an author, was 'an instructive fable for the human race' according to Mrs. Trimmer in her *Guardian of Education* (I, 323). A little later came a less solemn work about a squirrel, *The Life of Brushtail the Squirrel, that could play and not quarrel* (1806), adorned with twelve hand-coloured plates.[1] Purposeful as all these early animal stories were, the range of interest widens considerably in the first decade of the nineteenth century.

This century was to bring marked progress in knowledge of the natural world, and the increased importance given to scientific observation and field studies was soon to be reflected in books for children. Something about the development of natural history books for the young will be given later, but the new attitude to animal life also affected children's fiction. This is seen especially in the books written for youth by two devoted observers of nature – Mrs. Gatty and Richard Jefferies. Margaret Gatty, born Scott (1809–1873), was the mother of Mrs. Ewing, and the editor of *Aunt Judy's Magazine* from

[1] *N.B.L. Catalogue*, 580 (Bibl. 42).

its inception in 1866 to her death. She was an able naturalist and the author of a standard work on British seaweeds, among other accomplishments. She had begun to publish tales for children in 1851, and from 1855 to 1871 there appeared her most famous work for them, *Parables from Nature*, in five series. These are fables interpreting in simple, sometimes poetic fashion, truths of life, but the descriptions of creatures are based on the writer's accurate knowledge of the *minutiae* of nature. Mrs. Gatty's caterpillars, star-fish, snow-flakes, robins, spruce firs and other living things may interpret duties and meanings in human fashion, but their histories also unveil the fascination of the life of the natural world.

Richard Jefferies (1848–1887) has already been introduced as the author of *Bevis*. His earlier book for young people, *Wood Magic* (1881), is much more a story about the wild, although the subject is treated with fantasy. It is an ill-constructed, unusual tale about Bevis as a child, and his adventures with the things of nature, the winds and the trees, as well as animals and birds. The creatures are personified, with Kapcheck, a tyrannical old magpie, as their king. Much of the story is concerned with the struggle of the animals and birds to overthrow Kapcheck, and to elect another king. There are intimations here of more powerful tales to come in this vein from Kipling. Realism is depicted alongside fancy, for Jefferies reveals the harshness of the life in the wild, the preying of one creature on another, the fight to survive. Imperfect as it is through its lack of form, *Wood Magic* has fine qualities, and running deep through it there is intense and understanding feeling for nature. This reaches a climax at the end, when 'Sir Bevis' hears the wind telling him of the wonders the earth will bring him, if only he will not listen to the foolish people who live in houses.

New knowledge and realism, however, were rarer in animal stories in Victorian days than sentiment, and this was especially so in tales about horses and dogs. A not over-sentimental popular book of its generation about a dog was *The True, Pathetic History of Poor Match* (1863), by 'Holme Lee' (Harriet Parr, 1828–1900). With some humour and much feeling the author tells the history of the life and death of the pet belonging to a family of children who live in York. Match is a mischievous terrier, endowed with no more than canine faculties, and his history makes a pleasant story about things which could have happened, and very likely did happen, in a Victorian family. The book came out in two editions the same year, published by Warne and Smith Elder, perhaps in conjunction, as both have illustrations by Walter Crane. More vigorous and exciting was the story of the Newfoundland companion of a young hunter in Western America, told by R. M. Ballantyne in *The Dog Crusoe and his Master* (1861). Saved from a cruel death when a puppy, Crusoe becomes his rescuer's faithful friend, sharing many dangers, and proving his courage and intelligence in many exploits in the wilderness.

Mrs. Ewing was a great lover of animals, and she introduced dogs into many of her stories. In a clever fantasy, *Benjy in Beastland*, a short tale which appeared in *Aunt Judy's Magazine* in 1870, she holds up to scorn an unpleasant boy, who is carried off to Beastland (in the moon) to face the judgment of the animals, for his persistent ill-treatment of them on earth. As animals are not so cruel as human beings, the judge of the assembly, the lion, decrees banishment. Benjy, back on earth, is rescued from drowning by the retriever, Nix, a return of good for ill, and the boy becomes a reformed character. This fanciful and warm-hearted tale has some affinity with a much earlier publication, *The Biography of a Spaniel* (1804), where the hero, departed after life to the world of animal spirits on the moon, tells of his terrestrial pilgrimage.[1]

The variety of the animal story is well in evidence in the second half of the nineteenth century, and it was this period which produced perhaps the best loved animal tale yet to be written – *Black Beauty* (1877). This imaginary history of the life of a horse by Anna Sewell (1820–1878) also presents a vivid social picture of the days before the internal combustion engine. But its success was due to its sincerity and powerful feeling. The author was lamed from an accident as a child, and may have felt on that account more sympathy for suffering. She began to write her story in 1871, always struggling against illness, and it was the only book she ever wrote. A note found after her death records that its special aim was 'to induce kindness, sympathy, and an understanding treatment of horses . . .', and she put into her book practical advice as well as moving incidents. Black Beauty, like the animals in earlier, more purposeful tales, tells his own story, thus making it more poignant, although he must step out of horse character. In spite of sentimentality and the device of narration, this is a most convincing, well told story, with many features to endear it to children. Beauty's descent in the world, his work as a cab-horse, his eventual rescue, his recognition by an old friend, Joe, once a stable lad, and his final return to happiness and security, have something of the sequence of a fairy tale. Few books have won from young readers such lasting and heartfelt allegiance.

In the 1890s the old fabulous inventions about animals were to be shaped afresh in the dynamic, soon to be world-famous, *Jungle Books* by Rudyard Kipling (1865–1936). Kipling had written some stories about childhood in *Wee Willie Winkie and other Stories* (1888), in which he recalled unhappy early years spent in England, when his parents were still in India, his birthplace. After his schooldays were over, he returned to India and became a journalist. Soon he began to make a name for himself with ballads and tales of army life and India. It was later, after his marriage, when he was living in New England, that he began to write the stories (at first printed in magazines), which were to enthral a wide public – *The Jungle Book* (1894) and *The Second Jungle Book* (1895). Into them he put

[1] *Toronto Catalogue*, 233 (Bibl. 46).

inspiration drawn from many sources, including the Jataka tales of the Buddhist scriptures and his knowledge of the life and lore of India.

'It chanced', he wrote in his autobiography, 'that I had written a tale about Indian Forestry work which included a boy who had been brought up by wolves. In the stillness, and suspense, of the winter of '92, some memories of the Masonic Lions of my childhood's magazine, and a phrase in Haggard's *Nada the Lily*, combined with the echoes of this tale. After blocking out the main idea in my head, the pen took charge, and I watched it write about Mowgli and animals, which later grew into the Jungle Books'.[1] The origin for the theme of a human child brought up by wolves goes back to Romulus and Remus, and probably earlier, but here the idea is developed into stories revealing a unique and startling genius.

The first three tales in *The Jungle Book* take the reader into a world of wild creatures, who keep a Law of the Jungle all must obey. Among them is reared the child, Mowgli, saved as an infant from Shere Khan, the tiger, and brought up by a Father and Mother Wolf with their cubs. Mowgli learns much from the wiser of the jungle folk, but he is cast out by his own kind when he goes back to help them, slaying his enemy and theirs, the tiger. There is something more than action and originality in Mowgli's history, something which belongs to the deeper mysteries of life. Mowgli finds out that he is two beings, as he declares in his song – 'a song without any rhymes, a song that came into his throat by itself', when he leapt upon the striped hide of his dead enemy. 'Ahae'! he cries amid his triumph, 'my heart is heavy with things that I do not understand'.

Verses preface and conclude the tales with a rhythmic energy echoing the prose. Not all the tales are about Mowgli. In the first book there are three more Indian stories, including *Toomai of the Elephants*, and the mongoose story, *Rikki-tikki-tavi*. And there is one tale about the cold grey north, *The White Seal*. The second book shows no slackening of creative power. Most of the eight stories and accompanying verses concern Mowgli and the Jungle folk. One of them, *Red Dog*, is full of violence, a fearful tale of the battle of Mowgli and the wolves against the terrible *dhole* hunting packs of the Deccan. At the end of the book, Mowgli, no longer a man-cub, but 'master of the jungle' goes back to man, 'hearing a double step upon his trail'. Like the first book, the *Second Jungle Book* contains one episode about the far north – *Quiquern*, a tale about 'the people of the elder ice'.

Kipling's stories blended realism and fable in a new way. More ordinary earthbound efforts to present wild life in fiction for the young were also being made in this last decade. One of the best was *The Story of a Red Deer* (1897), by J. W. Fortescue (later Sir John Fortescue, 1859–1933). It was dedicated to his nine-year-old nephew, and the author put into his preface some wise words about writing for children.' . . . if men would write

---

[1] Kipling, *Something of Myself*, p. 113 (Bibl. 259).

books to be read of the young, they must write them, not after particular study, but from the fulness and overflowing of their knowledge of such things as they have dwelt withal and felt and love beyond all others'. His own tale is the result of such feeling and knowledge. In it he describes the life of a red deer of Exmoor from its earliest years until it is hunted to death as an old stag.

The year after Fortescue's book was published there came an important innovation from across the Atlantic. This was *Wild Animals I have Known* (1898), by the English-born, Canadian-educated Ernest Thompson Seton (1860–1946), an able artist, who had specialised in wild life. Thompson Seton had been contributing to periodicals since 1884, and some of his early animal tales were known to Kipling. This first collection of them contained some of the best, including 'Lobo, King of Currumpaw', and 'Raggylug, the Story of a Cottontail Rabbit'. It had an immediate success, and was followed by *The Trail of the Sandhill Stag* in 1899, and more stories in the new century. The author also wrote and illustrated an excellent 'Crusoe' tale of boys camping and fending for themselves in the woods, based on his own boyhood experiences in the forests of Ontario – *Two Little Savages* (1903).

The first book by Ernest Thompson Seton can be claimed as a landmark as well as the beginning of a new kind of animal story. For these 'personal histories' of woodland creatures in the New World were a breakaway from familiar patterns, and showed that the realistic animal story was from now onwards to be an important part of children's literature.

VIII PICTURE-BOOKS AND BOOKS FOR YOUNG CHILDREN

The subject of illustrations is very scantily treated in these pages, but it is a vital part of the making of books for children deserving much fuller attention. And when it comes to books for very young children, pictures are more important than text. References have been made already to various attempts to make books more attractive or more useful by illustrations. Caxton's *Aesop* was adorned with crude woodcuts, but even this use of visual aids was not general in books for the young until the eighteenth century. Comenius had shown the way in 1658 with his *Orbis Sensualium Pictus*, pleading for pictures the natural inclination that children 'willingly please their eyes with such sights'. But his example was not widely followed for many years.

Pictorial alphabets and riddles as well as uncouth cuts in the style of the chapbooks were becoming increasingly common when John Newbery began to make illustrations take an active part in the narrative. Bad pictures could be made to suit the story, and were better than none. The need for cheapness ruled out quality, but when the Bewicks transformed the art of wood-engraving towards the end of the eighteenth century, and their woodcuts began to appear in children's books, then the movement towards a higher artistic standard had begun.

An early use of pictures in instructional books for children is the illustrated alphabet already mentioned, which appeared in *A Methode or comfortable Beginning for all Unlearned, whereby they may be taught to read English, in a very short Time with Pleasure . . .*', a little manual by John Hart, published in 1570. But the first books intended for young children, designed for their amusement rather than their instruction, were the nursery rhymes and jingles which began their appearance in the eighteenth century. These, with their tiny cuts, were intended for the delight of infancy before reading began, and after their debut

20.   *The Victorian image of 'A Child's Picture Book' (1865)*

in 1744, they became a regular feature of books for the young. Something about their development has already been given earlier in this book. By the early nineteenth century, at least, separate rhymes were being issued with a more plentiful use of pictures. For example, *The House that Jack Built, Cock Robin,* and *Humpty Dumpty.*[1]

A landmark in the approach to the reading of the very young child is the little work Mrs. Barbauld composed for her infant nephew – *Lessons for Children* (1778–1779). Part one was for children between the ages of two and three, the next two parts for those of the riper age of three, and the fourth for children of four years old. It was perhaps less intended for infants to read, and more as a book to be read to them, although at the very beginning Charles is bidden 'Make haste, sit in Mamma's Lap. Now read your Book'. Simple little phrases are intended to arouse interest in everyday things a tiny child might observe or understand – things to eat, animals, playing in the hay, the snow, the seasons, the sun, the moon, the butterfly, feeding the robin, and similar matters. Yet there is a sense of delight about it which makes it far from trivial.

Mrs. Barbauld's tender understanding of infancy was something new in books for the very young. Other writers also were beginning to make little reading books for the under-

[1] *N.B.L. Catalogue*, pp. 64–67 (Bibl. 42).

189

fives, if less attractively. There was Lady Fenn's *Cobwebs to catch Flies* (1783), which she wrote as 'Mrs. Teachwell'. The first volume consisted of 'easy lessons in words of three letters up to six letters' for children of three to five years old. 'Be good, and you will be happy' is her advice to these mites. Mrs. Barbauld had used no pictures in her little book – only large type, but Lady Fenn's had the attraction of cuts. Under another *alias*, 'Mrs. Lovechild', Lady Fenn showed her reliance on pictures in the cause of learning by compiling *A Book of 336 Cuts for Children* (1799).[1]

Madame de Genlis and Mrs. Trimmer, two leading pedagogues of their day, had put into practice their firm belief in pictures as an aid to instruction, and by the beginning of the nineteenth century the part played by illustrations in children's books was becoming much more prominent. More easy stories and verses, too, were being published for the youngest readers. The issue of *The Infant's Library* (ca. 1800–1801), by John Marshall, in a miniature set of sixteen tiny volumes in a box resembling a minute bookcase, shows that the presentation of facts in suitable form for the very young was also exercising publishers' ingenuity. The first volume is a pictorial alphabet, and the other volumes, full of simple engravings, deal with games, flowers, animals, everyday scenes and objects, usually with a few words only on each midget page.

William Godwin and his wife brought out several books of easy stories for infants, including his own *Fables, ancient and modern* (1805), intended for children of from three to eight years. Other examples of the Godwin firm's productions for this age are *Six Stories for the Nursery in Words of one or two Syllables* (1824), by 'A Mother, intended for her own Children', and *Stories for little Boys and Girls in Words of one Syllable* (ca. 1820), by the author of *Stories of Old Daniel*. The house of Darton also issued simple stories for young children. *Little Prattle over a Book of Prints*, issued in 1804 by William Darton and J. Harvey, was in large type, with pictures in the centre of the text. Another popular little work was *The Story of Little Mary and her Cat*, by Mrs. Fenwick, first issued by Tabart and Co. in 1804,[2] and later reprinted by William Darton and Son.

The simple verses by Ann and Jane Taylor have been described in a former chapter, also those intended for younger children by Elizabeth Turner. Her trifles in rhyme, *The Daisy* (1807) and *The Cowslip* (1809) were intended for children from four to eight years old. The Taylors' *Rhymes for the Nursery* (1806) were suitable for the same age.

Although more and more regarded as an essential feature, pictures in children's books were generally poor in quality. But after the Bewicks had made the work of the artist important for the first time in books for boys and girls, his contribution won steady recognition, until by about the middle of the nineteenth century the name of a popular or

[1] *N.B.L. Catalogue No.* 746 (Bibl. 42).
[2] *Spencer Collection Cat.* p. 119 (Bibl. 45).

well-known artist was an asset to sales. After the Bewicks had become known, there appeared the early work of William Mulready (1786–1863) in the children's books published by Godwin and John Harris, perhaps best known for the pictures in the famous *Butterfly's Ball* (1807), although his name did not appear. A little later children's books had an able and vigorous artist in George Cruikshank (1792–1878), the illustrator of the first English version of *Grimm's Fairy Tales*.

Hand-colouring became an important feature of children's books at the beginning of the nineteenth century, coloured copies being a good deal dearer than plain alternatives. About the same time there began the production of what Percy Muir has termed 'Nick Nacks' – an offshoot of book publishing for youth, comprising Harlequinades, turn-ups, Juvenile Drama sheets, paper doll and movable books, panoramas, peepshows and games.[1] These were contrivances for the delight of younger children, but scarcely come within the scope of this survey. Perhaps there is most kinship between the ordinary picture-book and the paper-doll or 'cut-out' book, which consisted of a figure or series of figures with interchangeable costumes or heads. These were first put on the market by S. and J. Fuller at their 'Temple of Fancy' in Rathbone Place, between 1810 and 1815. The cut-out illustrations usually accompanied little stories in verse.

In the twenties and thirties, while the reading of their older brothers and sisters was much dominated by morality and instruction, young children were fortunate to have a series of cheerful if inelegant picture-books and easy stories, published by Dean and Munday, later Dean and Co. Thomas Dean had set up business in Threadneedle Street at at the end of the eighteenth century, but it was after he had taken Munday into partnership, sometime before 1820, that the firm began to specialise in cheap and attractive books for younger readers. It was associated at this date with A. K. Newman and Co., and books were often issued under a joint imprint, or simultaneously by both firms. Munday seems to have left the establishment about 1830, when it became Dean and Co., and after 1847, Dean and Son. The chief claim of this long established firm to importance lies in its activities in these pioneer years, when publishing for children, after the bright promise of the first decade of the century, fell into a rut.

Dean and Munday produced alphabet books, nursery rhymes and tales, books of games and riddles, and many small volumes of simple stories, at sixpence or a shilling. They were usually in large print, with plenty of pictures coloured by hand. Among this nursery lore was *Dame Wiggins of Lee*, *A Apple Pie*, *The Gaping Wide-mouthed Waddling Frog*, *Aldiborontiphoskyphorniostikos* (a kind of nonsense alphabet inspired by the *Arabian Nights*'), *Jack-the-giant-killer*, *The Children in the Wood*, and other old favourites. There were bits of nonsense, and also original verses, for example, those by Susanna Strickland in

[1] Muir. *English Children's Books* Ch. 8 (Bibl. 17).

The Flower-basket, and by J. Bishop in *Pleasing Tales for Little Folks*. None of the publications is dated, but they may all be assigned to the decade 1820–1830. One little book, with very large type, was *The Evergreen*, by Mrs. Martin, 'containing stories about Ellen and her fawn, Sleepy Francis, etc.'.[1] Easy-to-read, pictorial books of no high quality continued to be issued by the firm of Dean throughout the century, widening in scope to include toy books, moveable books, plays, and other amusing literature. By the fifties there were many series of Dean's picture-books and publications for young children, series under such engaging promoters as 'Papa Lovechild'. 'Grandpapa Easy', 'Brother Sunshine' and 'Aunt Affable'. Productions were ephemeral, but the enterprise of this publishing house in providing picture-books in quantity for young children, especially before 1850, both filled a need and stimulated the trade.

Hand-colouring was used by Dean and by some other firms well into the 1860s and even later, although by the time of the Great Exhibition of 1851 colour printing was coming into general use in children's books. The first successful colour printing by wood blocks and metal plates was the work of George Baxter (1804–1867), whose process was patented in 1835. It was used by the firm of Darton for frontispieces for three of their children's books that year – Mrs. Sherwood's *Caroline Mordaunt*, and Mary Elliott's *Tales for Boys* and *Tales for Girls*. But Baxter's process and that of Charles Knight which soon followed, were too complicated and expensive for general use in juvenile books, and it was not until the middle of the century, when cheaper adaptations of Baxter's process became available, that the Leighton Brothers, Kronheim, and others began to make rather more garish coloured illustrations for children's annuals and other books.

Lithography had been introduced into this country in the first years of the century and by the 1830s chromolithography was the rival of wood block colour printing. Much chromolithography was done in Germany, and in children's books especially colours tended to be oily and crude. The influence of Germany penetrated more happily into children's book-making about the middle of the century with the arrival of one of the earliest and most successful author-artist picture-books for the very young – widely known as 'Shock-headed Peter'. It was published anonymously in 1845 in Frankfurt-am-Main as *Lustige Geschichten und drollige Bilder*. Its creator was a Frankfurt physician, Dr. Heinrich Hoffmann (1809–1894), and his book, made for his three-year-old son and his little patients, consisted of much exaggerated awful warning verses ('Shock-headed Peter' or Struwwelpeter, who never cut his hair or his nails, 'The Dreadful Story of Harriet and the Matches', 'Fidgety Philip' are three of them), accompanied by wildly comical drawings. In the third German edition the title became *Der Struwwelpeter*, and very soon foreign editions were printed in Leipzig, including the first English edition of

[1] Tuer. *Forgotten Children's Books* pp. 459–478 (Bibl. 27).

1848 – *The English Struwwelpeter; or, Pretty Stories and Funny Pictures for Little Children* (based on the sixth German edition).

The printing was at first done by colour lithography, but in 1868 the illustrations were re-drawn and engraved on wood. The book maintained its wide circulation, and its comic awfulness became very familiar in English nurseries, delighting and affrighting generations of young children up to the present day. Hoffmann made other picture-books, but nothing with the enduring power of *Struwwelpeter*. One of them was *König Nüssknacker und der arme Reinhold* (1851), a picture-book about Christmas toys and a poor boy. It was freely adapted by J. R. Planché, as *King Nutcracker; or, The Dream of Poor Reinhold* (1855). In it 'Shock-headed Peter' and his companions make a brief appearance to show 'that naughty people are still to be found'.

The general standard of colour printing was low in the middle of the nineteenth century, and the best artists preferred to do book illustrations in black and white, particularly as the standard of engraving, notably by the Dalziel brothers, was of excellent quality. Until the seventies most of the best pictures in books for children are in black and white. Examples which readily come to mind are the illustrations by John Tenniel for the *Alice* books, Richard Doyle's drawings for *The King of the Golden River* (1851), and the work of Arthur Hughes. One of the most charming books ever made for young children is *Sing-Song* (1872), nursery verses by Christina Rossetti, most sympathetically illustrated by Hughes.

In the 1870s, however, the art of wood-engraving began to decline as more mechanical methods came into use, and much of the black and white illustration in later Victorian books for children is mediocre. This regression coincided with, and may have been influenced by, the transformation of the coloured picture-book for boys and girls in the sixties, mainly due to the craftsmanship of the engraver and colour-printer, Edmund Evans (1826–1905). It was his skill and collaboration with the three great picture-book artists, Walter Crane, Kate Greenaway, and Randolph Caldecott, which gave children coloured books of real excellence.

By the time that Edward Evans achieved his triumphs in colour-printing in books for children, there was a large range of picture-books on the market, many printed in colour, but others still coloured by hand. There were the series of Dean and Son, described above, Routledge's 'Aunt Mavor's Toybooks' (from about 1855), and among others, those issued by Griffith and Farran, the successors of John Harris. Warne entered the field with 'Aunt Louisa's London Toybooks', about 1865, with Mrs. Laura Valentine as editor. The list of Griffith and Farran publications in 1863 included picture-books written and illustrated by Thomas Hood the younger (1835–1874), and also stories he illustrated for his sister, Mrs. Frances F. Broderip (1830–1878). His work is clever but typical of its period. There is a good deal of fussy comicality, pictures of large, bouncing children, and amusing caricature-like drawing. Hand-colouring is still in evidence, giving a rather unfinished and amateurish appearance. But at least one of Tom Hood's picture-books, *The Loves of Tom Tucker and Little Bo-peep* (1863), had a cover printed in colour by Edmund Evans.

There is nothing very remarkable about this work of Evans in 1863. In children's books he had scarcely yet made his mark, although he had been experimenting with printing in colour since early in the 1850s. But his name did not become famous or his results in books for boys and girls achieve success until he began to produce the series of *Toybooks* by Walter Crane (1845–1915) about 1865. Evans was introduced to the young artist in 1863, but it was not until about two years later that work began on the *Toybooks* to be published by Routledge. Crane did three Toybooks for Evans printed for Warne, and then followed the first two in the Routledge series in 1865 – *A Railroad Alphabet* and *A Farmyard Alphabet*.[1] Other artists and engravers contributed to the series, but it was the work of Crane in co-operation with Evans which marked a new artistic standard. With *Sing a Song of Sixpence* in 1866 it was apparent that children's picture-books had reached an unsurpassed achievement, to be firmly established in the many Crane *Toybooks* which were to follow in this Routledge Sixpenny Series until 1873. Old and new themes were used, and one of the most interesting is a little contemporary piece, *Annie and Jack in London* (ca. 1868). Steadily the *Toybooks* became more lavishly decorated and richer in colour, the newly invented items usually being plainer in style than the old fairy tales. In 1873, a further series of Walter Crane *Toybooks* came out in a new Shilling Series, with one to be rated among his best, *Goody Two-shoes* (1875). Another short series of Crane *Toybooks*, chromolithographed and issued by Marcus Ward, came out in 1886, but although the Crane inventive style is there, they do not match the quality of the Evans' productions. None of the *Toybooks* by Crane had the vitality to endure far beyond their generation, but they set a standard of excellence important for the future of the picture-book.

Walter Crane's strength as an artist lay in his power of design, but he also had versatility. He had begun to illustrate children's books about 1863, with some drawings for *The True, Pathetic History of Poor Match*, and he was also to illustrate many of Mrs. Molesworth's stories. After the Routledge *Toybooks* series came to an end, he continued to collaborate with Edmund Evans, and designed three small, square picture-books in rather different style, whose charm continues to please young children today. They were *The Baby's Opera* (1877), *The Baby's Bouquet* (1879), and *The Baby's Own Aesop* (1887). Published in large editions by Routledge, these picture-books had a great success. The first contained nursery songs, with music arranged by Crane's sister, Lucy. The third

---

[1] *Reminiscences of Edmund Evans* p. xvi, 32 (Bibl. 271).

consisted of some of Aesop's Fables put into simple verse by W. J. Linton. Unity of design, delicate colours, and decorative borders enclosing the text are special features of these distinctive little books.

In 1882 there appeared a fine example of Walter Crane's art of book illustration in the *Household Stories* of the brothers Grimm, translated afresh by Lucy Crane. The influence of the Pre-Raphaelites and William Morris is visible in the decorative but spirited treatment of the old stories. Crane's most beautiful book is doubtless the little known expensive gift-book, *The First of May* (1881), a fairy masque in verse, by E. J. Wise, embellished by Crane on every page in exquisite pencil drawings expressing the daintiest rustic and fairy lore. This Maytime revel in art was inspired by the visits of author and artist to Sherwood Forest. What a pity that a work of such charm was published in a form which kept it out of children's hands!

Some of Crane's later picture-books for children, such as *Legends for Lionel* (1887) and *Flora's Feast* (1890), show his love for Japanese art, also revealed in some of the later *Toybooks*. They are more mannered and fanciful than the 'Baby' books, and more marked by their period.

Kate Greenaway (1846–1901) began her career as an artist with the design of Christmas cards and similar wares, and about 1870 she did some not very well reproduced work for Warne's 'Aunt Louisa's Toybooks', and for other publishers about this date. It was through her engraver father's acquaintance with Edmund Evans, and his showing the colour-printer some of his daughter's drawings and verses, that she was given the chance which brought her fame. Evans persuaded Routledge to accept a book of her pictures and rhymes, and he printed 20 000 copies, apparently on his own initiative. His faith in Kate Greenaway was soon proved to be right. For this first picture-book, *Under the Window* (1878), brought its creator immediate renown, not only in this country, but in Europe and America.

Kate Greenaway is the most beloved, if not the greatest of the trio of picture-book artists of the seventies, and her work maintained a quiet popularity after its dazzling contemporary success faded. She created with her pen and brush a realm of her own for children's delight, an Arcadia where tidy little boys in pantaloons and prettily dressed little girls in frilly gowns and sunbonnets played games, gathered flowers, or took tea in cottage gardens. Kate Greenaway's engaging infants are always spotless and neat, even when they climb apple trees or go fishing. Flowers were her joy, and her pages are much devoted to them. Occasionally something more fearful appears, such as the witch and the queer old man who runs away with Billy in *Under the Window*, but such darker aspects are rare.

Criticism has been made of Kate Greenaway for her technical faults, but her charming, original style more than outweighs any such deficiencies. Ruskin, a great admirer, with

Ring-a-ring-a-roses,
A pocket full of posies ;
Hush ! hush ! hush ! hush !
We're all tumbled down.

21. *From Kate Greenaway's* MOTHER GOOSE *(1881)*

whom she corresponded in his declining days from about 1880, wanted her to draw more from nature and life. 'Draw things as they are', he urged her. 'You should go to some watering place in August, with fine sands, and draw no end of bare feet – and what else the Graces unveil in the train of the Sea Goddess'. He asked for 'flowers that won't look as if they had been in curl papers all night' and 'girls with limbs as well as frocks'. And 'no more round hats.'[1] Ruskin thought that her best work was her illustrations for *The Pied Piper of Hamelin* (1888), but he was also greatly impressed with the baby in the basket of roses on the titlepage of her *Mother Goose* (1881), a version of some of the old nursery rhymes.

[1] Spielmann, M. H. and C. S. Layard. *Kate Greenaway* pp. 115, 119 (Bibl. 273).

Kate Greenaway was both author and illustrator of what is perhaps her most attractive book, *Marigold Garden* (1885), as she was for her first success, *Under the Window*. Although there is nothing remarkable about her simple verses, they are so harmoniously interpreted in line and colour that the whole book is a triumph of artistic skill. Other picture-books she made include a setting for some of the verses of the Taylors, *Little Ann and Other Poems* (1883), rather more robust illustrations for Bret Harte's *The Queen of the Pirate Isle* (1886), and a new adornment of the old rhyme, *A Apple Pie* (1886). It was this last production which caused Ruskin to criticise her drawings of feet, here becoming, he declared, 'literal paddles or flappers'.[1]

Today some of Kate Greenaway's picture-books still please young readers, although they may have lost some of the fascination they once possessed for their great-grand-mothers. Her work has been imitated, but never equalled in the style she created. She gave to boys and girls not merely some picture-books of real charm, but her own vision of innocence and happy childhood, a world 'seen through golden spectacles'. It is appropriate, therefore, that her name should have been chosen for the annual award established in 1955 by the Library Association to the artist who has produced the most distinguished work in the illustration of children's books first published in the United Kingdom during the preceding year.

The United States had already honoured in the same way the third and perhaps the greatest artist of the three picture-book makers who worked with Edmund Evans – Randolph Caldecott (1846–1886) – for the 'Caldecott' Medal award was established there in 1937. Caldecott had begun his career as a bank clerk, but at twenty-six he decided to make art his profession, and left Manchester for London. It was about 1877 or 1878, when he was already a successful illustrator, that he began his series of picture-books for children, encouraged by Evans. The first two, *The House that Jack Built* and *John Gilpin* (the ballad by William Cowper), were issued by Routledge in the autumn of 1878. Fourteen more shilling picture-books followed until Caldecott's early death in 1886. They brought a new quality into such publications for young children, for the artist was not merely illustrator, but a storyteller with a pencil like quicksilver. He had a great power of line, a keen sense of humour, and a love of dogs, horses and the countryside, especially evident in that racy and vigorous work, *The Three Jovial Huntsmen* (1880). Most of his subjects were traditional, such as *Sing a Song of Sixpence* (1880) and *Hey Diddle* and *Baby Bunting* (1882), but he also illustrated two of Oliver Goldsmith's ballads, *Elegy on the Death of a Mad Dog* (1880) and *Mrs. Mary Blaize* (1885), and that nonsensical piece of eighteenth century prose by Samuel Foote, *The Great Panjandrum* (1885). These lively,

[1] *Ibid.* p. 142.

clever picture-books have lost little of their savour with the years and are regularly re-printed.

This trio of artists with Edmund Evans created the picture-book of real quality. The achievement did not arrest the acceleration towards the cheap and mediocre in illustrated books, but it ensured that henceforth children would never lack an aristocratic, widely-influential minority of artistic merit. Other excellent illustrators were also contributing to the improvement of books for boys and girls in the later Victorian age. Among them were Harrison Weir (1824–1906), pre-eminent for his animal pictures, and artists specialising in fine line drawings (a characteristic of the last decades of the century encouraged by improved photo-engraving), including Linley Sambourne (1844–1910), Gordon Browne (1858–1902), who illustrated many of Mrs. Ewing's books, H. J. Ford (1860–1941), famous for his designs for the Lang Fairy Books, and John D. Batten (1871–1932), illustrator of the Jacobs series of Fairy Tales. From across the Atlantic came the Dürer-like work of Howard Pyle (1855–1911), the author-illustrator, whose *Merry Adventures of Robin Hood* was introduced with ballad literature. From France came some delicate and charming flat-colour drawings by Maurice Boutet de Monvel (1850–1915) who contributed to *Little Folks* towards the end of the century.

New processes were transforming the appearance of children's books as the reign of Victoria drew to its close, notably the half-tone block for monochrome, and the three colour process. Both methods required art or coated paper for reproduction, so that the 'tipped in' illustration, often of inferior quality, now became common. But the three (or four) colour process also made possible the reproduction of delicate water-colours as seen in the work of three outstanding artists who succeeded the Crane-Caldecott-Greenaway trio – Beatrix Potter, Arthur Rackham, and Leslie Brooke.

L. Leslie Brooke (1862–1940) began to illustrate children's books about 1892, including some later tales by Mrs. Molesworth. In 1897 he made his mark by an attractive *Nursery Rhyme Book*, edited by Andrew Lang, but he is perhaps most famous for his amusing and genial pictures and verses for his Johnny Crow series, which began in 1903 with *Johnny Crow's Garden*. More renowned as a twentieth century illustrator is Arthur Rackham (1867–1939). Among the earliest work he did for children's books are twelve drawings for the Lamb's *Tales from Shakespeare* in 1899, re-issued with additional illustrations in 1909. But more successful and characteristic were his pictures for *Grimm's Fairy Tales* the following year, better known in its revised edition of 1909. Illustrations for other well-known classics (and new books) soon followed, and two of the best and most enduring examples of his work in the Edwardian period are *Rip Van Winkle* (1905), and *Peter Pan in Kensington Gardens* (1906), where he visualises Barrie's whimsies in very apt style. These and others have been continually reprinted, including his *Alice's Adventures in Wonderland* (1907) and *Aesop's Fables* (1912). A versatile fancy, ranging from the ethereal to the grotesque, an intensive use of expressive, vibrant line, a subdued, disciplined handling of colour are features of the work of this fine artist.

Pre-eminent among makers of picture-books for the very young is Beatrix Potter (1866–1943). She was no mere illustrator, but a creative author-artist whose series of nursery classics is still greatly treasured by the under-fives (and by others). 'I don't know what to write to you', she began a letter to little Noel Moore, the sick child of a friend, on 4th September 1893, 'so I shall tell you a story about four little rabbits whose names were Flopsy, Mopsy, Cottontail, and Peter'. Full of delightful scribbled drawings it was to take final shape as the first of the miniature picture-books which have since delighted young children in many parts of the world. *The Tale of Peter Rabbit* was published by Warne in 1902, after being privately printed the previous year. In 1903 came a rather different story about a mouse, *The Tailor of Gloucester*, again after private printing, and very soon *The Tale of Squirrel Nutkin* was in being. Sixteen more little books followed in the next ten years up to Beatrix Potter's marriage in 1913, when she became devoted to her home and farm at Sawrey in the Lake District, and her chief creative period came to an end.

The secret of the fascination of these exquisite little books lies in their maker's loving observation of animals and country scenes, and a fusion of artistic fidelity with a playful invention which merges the world of her animal characters with that of human beings. 'Under the petticoats and aprons there are real pigs and hedgehogs', and fantasy becomes a part of solid country ways and realistic surroundings. Unsurpassed, inimitable, the Beatrix Potter books still reign supreme – modest, and unassuming as they may seem besides many splendid newcomers.

Books for young children were to be produced in large numbers in the early years of the twentieth century, and the success of the Beatrix Potter books showed the trend and demand. But before Victoria's reign was over, there are one or two more publications to note of special interest. One of them, showing that stories as well as pictures were considered to be important, was *The Nursery Alice* (1889). This was C. L. Dodgson's own version of *Alice's Adventures in Wonderland* for the young child, with Tenniel illustrations printed in colour by Edmund Evans. Dodgson with his passion for perfection found the first edition unsatisfactory, so, like its more famous original, he had the book withdrawn, and another edition issued the next year. 'My ambition *now* . . .', he wrote in his preface to 'Any mother', 'is to be read by children from nought to five. To be read? Nay, not so! Say rather to be thumbed, to be cooed over, to be dog's eared, to be rumpled, to be kissed, by the illiterate, ungrammatical dimpled darlings . . .' Such phrases reveal the attitude to the 'dimpled darlings' in this late Victorian age. But although Lewis Carroll told the story very simply, was it really possible to present such a fantastical tale to babies?

In the 1890s there was an innovation in picture-books significant for the years ahead.

This was the 'Golliwogg' series of large, flat, oblong picture-books, designed by Florence Upton (1873–1922), with stories in verse by her mother, Bertha Upton (1849–1912). The arresting, sometimes ugly pictures, are done in lithography, and show a utilisation of white space and unconfined outlines suggestive of a style to come. These productions also introduced the character of 'Golliwogg' into children's books in England. The first was *The Adventures of Two Dutch Dolls and a Golliwogg* (1895), and it was succeeded by *The Golliwogg's Bicycle Club* in 1896, with some very colourful scenes of Japan and the South Seas. Other volumes of Golliwogg's adventures followed up to 1909. The verses were amusing, but not up to the standard of the illustrations, and being sprinkled with topicalities, these 'new-look' picture-books quickly went out of fashion, although there are now signs of some revival of interest in them.

More familiar during the twentieth century than the much-travelled Golliwogg and his wooden companions is the little negro boy whose history was told by Helen Bannerman (1863–1946) in *The Story of Little Black Sambo* (1899). This is an uproarious piece of nursery fun, with striking coloured illustrations by the author, about an amazing encounter with tigers, who come to a 'buttery' end. More little picture-books of the same kind were to follow, but this first publication has remained the favourite.

The Edwardian era was a rich and varied period in books for young children. One of the most overwhelming successes for them was the famous *Just-So Stories* (1902), written and illustrated by that master of originality, Rudyard Kipling. This made no concessions to babyism or the sentimentality of the age, for it presented in reverberating prose a series of astonishing fables about 'How the Camel got his Hump' and similar histories. Its enormous vogue was a pointer to the future and a coming change in taste less favourable to the sugared dainties in fashion for the very young.

IX   BOOKS OF KNOWLEDGE

Religion, morals and manners – apart from purely scholastic tuition – were the subjects thought sufficient in books for children for centuries. But as man's quest for knowledge changed its course after the Renaissance towards the direct observation of nature and practical experiment, and away from the accepted authorities of the medieval world, then the direct ancestors of modern books of information began to make their appearance.

H. S. Bennett, in his survey of the English book trade from the first days of printing to the death of Queen Elizabeth I (Bibl. 47), has shown how the demand by the citizen for practical manuals and books of information to help in daily living was steadily being met in the sixteenth century. But there was an absence of any suitable adaptations for children, and books for them about people and things lagged sadly behind such productions for grown readers.

The first attempt to show the world in all its diversity to youth was by Comenius in his *Orbis Sensualium Pictus* (1658). This 'brief of the whole world' was 'a little encyclopaedia of things subject to the senses', and as one of its principal aims was the easier teaching of Latin, all objects depicted were given both their Latin and vernacular terms. Above all it was a picture-book of general knowledge. Perhaps that earlier, native, unillustrated publication, *Dives Pragmaticus* (1563), should not be overlooked, for this also was a book of information, a catalogue in rhyme naming everything that could be merchandise.

These pioneer works for youth about the world of things are only isolated examples at this early date. Seventeenth century books for children (and those issued earlier) usually confined factual information to religious biography and martyrology, and secular history penetrated into them only slowly. In the later years of the Stuart period it was introduced in some of the compilations of 'R.B.' or 'Richard Burton', the pseudonym of Nathaniel Crouch. Doctor Johnson thought 'R.B.'s books very proper to allure back-ward readers', according to a letter written to Dilly the bookseller on 6th January 1784. Many of these popular wares were religious in their purpose, but there were also 'hashed-up' histories, for example *The English Hero; or, Sir Francis Drake, England's Monarchs* ('with pictures of every monarch from William the Conqueror to Charles the Second'), and *The English Empire in America* (with information for intending emigrants), all published about 1685.

As yet natural history was seldom introduced into books for the young, although there had long been illustrated bestiaries and herbals for grown people. A well-known seventeenth century work which was to have some influence later on children's books was Edward Topsell's *Histories of Four-footed Beasts* (1607), and this was also likely to fascinate young readers who came upon it. Probably it was one of the sources used by the compiler of an illustrated natural history book for children published in 1730 – *A Description of Three Hundred Animals: viz. Beasts, Birds, Fishes, Serpents and Insects . . .* The three publishers were Richard Ware, Thomas Boreman and Thomas Game. A supplement was issued in 1736 entitled *A Description of a Great Variety of Animals and Vegetables; viz. Beasts, Birds, Fishes, Insects, Plants, Fruits, and Flowers*. This was published by Boreman on his own, and he had now moved from the corner of Clement's Lane to St. Paul's Church-yard.[1] Both volumes were illustrated with numerous copper-plates, and vestiges of the fabled world of the bestiary may be traced in their pages, especially in the first volume, which included the human-faced manticora and the unicorn. The plants and vegetables

---

[1] Both works have been ascribed to Boreman as compiler, but according to *Notes and Queries*, 19th June 1926, the author was a Mr. McQuin.

in the supplement are those yielding commodities from abroad – tea, sugar, spices, tobacco, etc., except for 'the sensible plant', put in, one assumes, because of its oddity.

William Sloane records an earlier and more comprehensive outline of the natural world for boys and girls, with the secondary object of teaching French (Bibl. 74, No. 261). This is *A Short and Easie Method to give Children an Idea or True Notion of Celestial and Terrestrial Beings . . .* , published in 1710, and reproducing hundreds of figures in thirty-eight copper-plates. Sloane terms it 'a very early science for children combined with French textbook'. It seems to owe something to Comenius, for it aimed 'to teach the names of most things that are useful and necessary to human life; as also of arts and sciences, plants, fruits, and living creatures; as fishes, birds, and four-footed beasts', giving terms in French and English.

The mechanistic universe disclosed by Sir Isaac Newton and the elements of scientific knowledge of the day were described for the entertainment of youth in John Newbery's

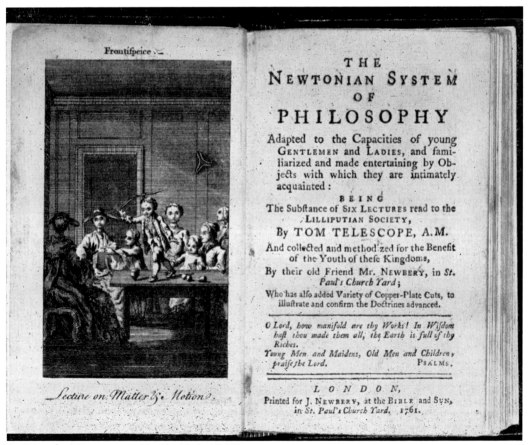

22. *Science for children as presented by John Newbery (1761)*

publication, *The Newtonian System of Philosophy* (1761). This contained 'the substance of six lectures read to the Lilliputian Society, by Tom Telescope, A.M.', and it was advertised and sometimes known under its alternative title, *The Philosophy of Tops and Balls*. Authorship has been attributed to Oliver Goldsmith, and there is an air of enjoyment and playful good-humour about these lectures which suggests his hand. The little gentry gathered at the house of the Countess of Twilight cannot agree how to amuse themselves, so Master Telescope, objecting to the suggestion of playing at cards for money, takes them to the Marquis of Selstar's abode, where they may have the use of proper instruments for his lectures on natural philosophy, as science was then termed. Tom is something of a prig, and gives advice and information in conceited fashion, until put in his place on the arrival of the Duke of Galaxy. There is a good deal of conversation and lively discussion upon Tom's expositions, which cover the solar system, properties of matter and motion, physical features of the earth, and natural history. He ends with a lecture on man and his five senses, taking the opportunity to give sober reflections on morality in true Newbery style.

Out of date as all books of knowledge must soon be, this little work is important as an early attempt to convey scientific facts to children in an interesting and attractive way. It also follows the practice of combining fact and fiction – a mode much to be adopted in children's books for the next half-century and more.

Topographical books for boys and girls probably begin with the tiny 'Gigantick Histories' brought out by Thomas Boreman. They included in addition to *The History of the Two Famous Giants* (1740), *The History of St. Paul's* (1741), *Curiosities of the Tower of London* (1741), and *Westminster Abbey* (1742–1743). Less original in format and not so well designed for youth (although dedicated to 'the least son of the Prince of Wales, Prince William Henry', an infant of three years old) was *The Travels of Tom Thumb over England and Wales*, issued by M. Cooper in 1746. Ostensibly written by the well-known midget of folk-lore, the style is jocular and sometimes boastful, but much of the book consists of guide-book information, county by county.

John Newbery seems to have been the first publisher to have produced a suitable compendium of knowledge for boys and girls, so beginning a perennial feature of publishing. His *Circle of the Sciences* was completed in ten volumes from 1745 to 1748. It covered the subjects of Grammar, Writing, Arithmetic, Rhetoric, Poetry, Logick, Geography and Chronology – solid educational matter, although the advertisement expressed the hope that 'the Whole will seem rather an Amusement than a Task'. Two volumes, a *Spelling Book* and a *Dictionary*, originally planned for inclusion in the ten volumes, were issued separately. Dialogue, a common feature in books for youth, was often used to impart knowledge, taken over from the age-old method of the catechism. It was to be a favourite device in instructional works for another century and more, and it reached its apotheosis in such frequently reprinted manuals as Richmal Mangnall's *Historical and Miscellaneous Questions* (1798). A similar compilation to rival this instructor of youth was *A Child's Guide to Knowledge*, which was first published in 1825 as *262 Questions and Answers*, by 'A Lady'. The anonymous author was not Mrs. R. Ward as often stated, but Fanny Umphelby (1788–1852). Later editions, which reached the fifty-eighth in 1899, had new matter added by her nephew, Robert Ward.

Newbery's list of publications in 1766 (appended to the third edition of *Goody Two-Shoes*) included several volumes of history, including *No. 21 A New and Noble History of England, 6d.*[1] Might this have been an abridgment of a work Goldsmith wrote for the publisher, once ascribed to Lord Chesterfield – *An History of England in a series of Letters from a Nobleman to his Son* (1764)? It was later ascribed to other persons of rank, but there is no doubt about the poet's authorship, as the receipt for a payment of £21 for the work is now in the Philadelphia Public Library. Another significant, though uncompleted work, which Goldsmith is known to have compiled for Newbery, is a version of *Plutarch's Lives*, published from 1762–1763 in seven volumes. This famous classical work of the first century A.D. was much used as a source for anecdotes and extracts in children's books (and others), since Sir Thomas North had made the first English translation from the French in 1579. Plutarch was fond of putting stories and experiences not always supported by evidence in his lives of famous Greeks and Romans, but his biography is a noble work, permeated by a high moral tone much to eighteenth century taste.

Newbery had in mind, according to Forster's *Life of Goldsmith*, 'A *Compendium of Biography*, or History of the lives of those great personages, both ancient and modern . . . likely to inspire young gentlemen and ladies with a love of virtue'. It was to begin with an abridgment of Plutarch, but Goldsmith having finished the first four volumes fell ill, and the last three were completed by Joseph Collyer. Then the whole project was abandoned probably due to competition from a rival work launched by Dilly.

Goldsmith wrote these compilations in haste as a bookseller's hack, but his pleasing literary style in the service of history and biography for youth is a noteworthy event in their development. Many more miscellaneous scribblers as well as amateur educationists were to enter the field, but the talent of a Goldsmith was rare.

The range of non-fiction books offered to children by John Newbery and his successors, for their entertainment not merely their instruction, indicates that this branch of their literature was developing steadily in the latter part of the eighteenth century. Rousseau and the Romantic writers who followed him were soon to stress a new feeling for the wonders of nature. Towards the end of the century this appreciation of the natural world

---

[1] Roscoe. 254 (Bibl. 104) has traced an advertisement for this in 1763 but no copy has been discovered bearing the title.

began to invade children's books. Histories and biographies for youth, largely inspired by classical antiquity or religion, were by then numerous and well established, but nature books introducing a sense of wonder and reverence for the work of creation were more of an innovation. Mrs. Trimmer linked scriptural knowledge and divine revelation with information about the natural world in her first book for children, *An Easy Introduction to the Knowledge of Nature* (1780), and used narrative and conversation to render it more appealing. It was partly inspired by Mrs. Barbauld's *Lessons for Children*, published in 1778–1779, but it may also owe something to the *Histoire Naturelle* of Buffon, which came out in Paris in thirty-six volumes from 1749 to 1789. This renowned work had much style and learning, and was frequently used as a source book for natural history at this time. Mrs. Trimmer purchased it, but recorded in her Journal that she found 'so many improper descriptions in it', that she could not put it into the hands of her family.

The art of the wood-engraver, Thomas Bewick, in delineating animals and birds and other creatures for the delight of young and old, has been mentioned in a former chapter. His realistic, finely-detailed pictures gave a special distinction to popular works of natural history at the turn of the century, and stimulated the production of others where the role of illustrations was all-important. Many simple compilations for youth about animals and birds, often with attractive, hand-coloured copper-plates, appeared in the first decades of the nineteenth century, no longer showing traces of the bestiary, but still relying much on anecdote and fable, sometimes with a complacent air of rational superiority.

An interesting work of a pioneer kind, which attempted to create a general interest in nature for children, was *The Calendar of Nature* (1784), by Dr. John Aikin (1747–1822), dedicated to his sister, Mrs. Barbauld. In the fashion of the time, the author included poetical quotations, with details of natural history, month by month throughout the year.

The great progress made by science in the latter part of the eighteenth century is reflected in publications for children after 1800. The first decade of the nineteenth century, in fact, is as rich in books of information for youth as in more fanciful works. A notable publication, setting out scientific knowledge with rather more system than Tom Telescope, is the *Scientific Dialogues* (1800–1805), a work in six volumes by Jeremiah Joyce (1763–1815). Joyce, much impressed by the Edgeworths' *Practical Education*, drew upon R. L. Edgeworth's chapter on mechanics, and expressed his indebtedness both to him and to the more gifted Maria. He became Secretary to the Unitarian Society and a Unitarian minister, but earlier in his career he was tutor to the two sons of Lord Stanhope, to whom he dedicated the first two volumes of his book. It covers the main branches of pure science – Mechanics, Astronomy, Hydrostatics, Pneumatics, Optics and magnetism, Electricity and galvanism. Frequently revised and reprinted it remained a standard work for many years. Smaller, separate works on scientific matters were also being published for children, for example about the telescope and astronomy, the microscope, chemistry, mineralogy, and various aspects of nature. An example of a more general book is *The Natural History of the Earth* (1802), by 'N.E.', a work commended by Mrs. Trimmer (*Guardian of Education*, I, 271) as 'not among the instruments which have been employed to invalidate the mosaic history of the world', implying the old chronology of the Bible was already being assailed. Little readers are told by 'N.E.' not to concern themselves with 'curious theories', for 'the great outlines of nature are themselves the most improving to the mind that meditates upon them'.

The boundaries of the globe were fast falling back as new discoveries and explorations shed light on many unknown territories, and in the eighteenth century these began to penetrate into books for boys and girls. The great source for earlier voyages was Richard Hakluyt's splendid compilation, *The Principal Navigations, Traffiques, and Discoveries of the English Nation . . .* (1589). Borrowings from this for children's books rarely acknowledged the debt, however, and the earliest named 'Stories from Hakluyt' appear to belong to the twentieth century. Incidents and information about the finding and settlement of new regions can be found in children's books from the latter part of the seventeenth century, but one of the first writers to make the history of exploration really interesting to youth was the German, J. H. Campe (1746–1818). He used his favourite method of a father telling events to his children in his trilogy on the early voyages to America (*Die Entdeckung von Amerika*, 1780–1782) comprising the lives and explorations of Columbus, Cortez, and Pizarro. The separate volumes became available in English translations from about 1799. Campe followed this work with a series of twenty-two travel episodes for rather older children. From this is taken the well-known *Polar Scenes*, available in English in 1821, where Campe tells the story of the voyage of the Dutchmen, Heemskirk and Barenz, to the far North, and some experiences of four Russian sailors on the Island of Spitzbergen.

Versions for children taken from the accounts of the voyages of Captain James Cook, published between 1772 and 1784, became available from 1800, when an edition adapted for children was issued by John Marshall, following an abridged edition of 1785. A more popular work for youth resulting from explorations of the Pacific was *The History of Prince Lee Boo* (1789), founded on *An Account of the Pelew Islands* (1788), by George Keate. It told the story of a young Prince from the islands, who was brought to England in 1783 and died of smallpox the next year.

Books giving more factual geographical knowledge tended to accentuate national characteristics, costume, and peculiarities, rather than describe physical features or commodities. Newbery had included a book on these lines as Volume six of *The Circle of the Sciences* in 1748 – *Geography made familiar and easy to young Gentlemen and Ladies*. Much of it was conveyed in question and answer form. The vast unknown of Central Africa is referred to as 'Negroland, or the Country of the Blacks', an area ruled by ten or twelve absolute kings, where there are English and French settlements on the coast. 'Gold, slaves, elephant's teeth, bees-wax, and some drugs' are listed as the chief commodities. Other compendiums of knowledge included the subject a little later, but an early and interesting separate publication is a little work entitled *Moral Geography* (1789). Filled with earnest purpose, it begins with 'a short view of the modern astronomical system', explains various geographical terms, and then proceeds to give piecemeal information under countries, with moral comments. The French are gay and sprightly, but vain, the Italians are effeminate, the Chinese learned and industrious, the English noted for spleen and whims, but 'justly accounted the most spirited and judicious people in Europe'. The newly-discovered Botany Bay, apparently all of the Antipodes known to the writer, is referred to as 'now a part of the world allotted for civilisation'.

Books of less formal instruction often presented information in the form of letters, conversations, or fiction. Priscilla Wakefield (1731–1832) was responsible for a variety of instructional works intended to inform in a pleasing and effortless way, and she used the form of letters between young people to convey enlightenment about botany, the sagacity of animals, and accounts of various parts of the world. The use of the story form to impart knowledge to children without them being aware of it was also very much favoured. Madame de Genlis was a great believer in this method, and she had a faithful disciple in Maria Edgeworth. The latter, with some help from her father, uses narrative more cleverly than many of her contemporaries in *Early Lessons* (1801 and 1821–1825). In the *Harry and Lucy* part of this, which was begun by Edgeworth *père*, she tried to teach children something about science and useful inventions. Episodes range rather haphazardly from the barometer to gaslight and electricity, from canals to the printing press. The little heroine, Lucy, has sometimes a Rosamond-like capacity for impulsive or unladylike behaviour, and she is told by her mother that eagerness for knowledge is no excuse for getting her hands dirty, or tearing her frock. 'It is more necessary that a girl should be clean and neat, than she should try experiments' is a warning that summarises the prevailing view, but Lucy, like Rosamond, was not easily suppressed.

A typical example of the fact-presenting tale of this period, among many similar publications, is *The India Cabinet Opened* (1821), by 'A Mother' (Mrs. S. Wilson, born Atkins), published by John Harris. This puts into the frame of a story explanations of the contents of a cabinet full of shells and other museum objects. Ellen and Charles learn that a bit of ash has come from Mount Vesuvius, and this leads to a long description, punctuated by the children's comments and questions, about the volcano, and a recent eruption. And so it goes on, mingled with other happenings, for various exhibits.

Rapid industrial advancement and the achievements of the age of steam and railways were to be vividly revealed to the nation in the Great Exhibition of 1851. This stimulated wider interest in scientific and technical knowledge, and also enshrined the matter-of-fact spirit of the age, which pervaded many books for children as persistently as smoke in the manufacturing towns. Romanticism and sentiment were not yet overriding elements in Victorian children's books. There were also powerful forces behind the Gradgrind idea of education. 'Teach these boys and girls nothing but facts' was not merely a Dickensian invention, but a real threat. Useful and informative matters in books for youth were in danger of taking the dominant place that moral education had formerly occupied. Factual fare was often advocated as the only proper material for children's reading, as in the innumerable Peter Parley books. The idea that the child needed a variety of reading matter to satisfy the many needs of his growing mind, with stimulus for his imagination no less vital than training in useful knowledge, was not to be fully accepted for another generation – not until *Alice* and the sixties.

Useful books on the work of the world were a welcome innovation when they first began to appear for children at the beginning of the nineteenth century. Perhaps the earliest books to introduce trades to boys and girls were the various little publications on London 'Cries'. How far these go back in print in children's literature the writer is uncertain, but Francis Newbery (nephew of John Newbery) advertised a copy in January 1771, and there are copies dated 1775 extant.[1] By the first decade of the next century there were various books about industries and commodities. In 1803–1805 the firm of Tabart and Co. produced *The Book of Trades; or, Library of Useful Arts* for youth in three volumes, and a similar work was also issued by Darton, called *Little Jack of all Trades* (1804–1806). Dr. John Aikin dealt with food, shelter, and clothing in the three parts of his book, *The Arts of Life* (1802), and this appears to be one of the earliest descriptions of economic subjects for the young reader.

Agriculture was one of the first occupations to be described in books for children. John Harris, a pioneer in publishing non-fiction for children as well as other branches of their literature, included in his 'Cabinet of Amusement and Instruction' a volume entitled *The Progress of the Dairy* (1808?).[2] According to the advertisement in the book there were companion volumes on wheat and wool. A more general description of country pursuits was compiled by Ann and Jane Taylor in *Rural Scenes* (1801), a companion to their *City Scenes* issued the same year and describing London.

Series of volumes on scientific and practical subjects soon became a feature of publishing for children. John Harris issued a 'Little Library' in the 1820s, with contributions by the male members of the Taylor family. Isaac Taylor (1759–1829) was a nonconformist clergyman who had already written for Harris a cheerful if pious little travel series begin-

---

[1] Roscoe 86 (Bibl. 104).

[2] The book also bears the imprint of J. Wallis and may have been first issued by this firm. The date on the B.M. copy is obscured, but must be after 1807 if Harris' 'Cabinet' began that year with *The Butterfly's Ball*.

ning with *Scenes in Europe* (1818), and it is likely that it was he rather than his son Isaac, another author, who wrote *The Mine* (1829), and *The Ship* (1830) for the publisher's new 'Library'. Jefferys Taylor, another son, contributed 'a new account of rural toils and produce' in *The Farm* (1832). Both Jefferys and his father, like his more famous sisters, had a flair for presenting facts and ideas in a simple and attractive way to children.

Writers for youth were much in the habit of turning easily from one subject to another in these early days when specialisation in knowledge was less advanced. Mrs. Marcet (1769–1858, born Jane Haldimond) was one of these versatile exponents of different aspects of knowledge for the young. She produced a series of easy-to-understand 'Conversations', which won great praise in her day. Best-known are *Conversations on Chemistry* (1806) and *Conversations on Political Economy* (1816), the latter making much impression on Harriet Martineau. Mrs. Gatty found Mrs. Marcet a bore, but she was not so to everyone. Michael Faraday (1791–1867) venerated her, for long before he became a great scientist, when he was a bookbinder's apprentice, it was her *Conversations on Chemistry* that set him on the road to his life's work.

In 1826 Faraday began his series of Christmas lectures for young people at the Royal Institution, which he continued until 1862. From these lectures came two volumes which may be hailed as the first 'classics of science' for youth – *The Chemical History of a Candle* (1861) and *On Various Forces of Nature* (1863). 'If every writer of learning and imagination made it his happy privilege to write but one book for the young on his own beloved subject, and put his *whole mind* to it, just as Faraday wrote his *History of a Candle* – what joy there would be for children yet unborn', wrote Walter de la Mare in one of his notes in *Come Hither*. It was an ideal rarely to be reached, but already in the middle of the nineteenth century Faraday was showing the way. 'There is no better, there is no more open door by which you can enter into the study of natural philosophy, than by considering the physical phenomena of a candle . . . ' he tells 'my boys and girls', to whom he speaks 'as a juvenile myself'. Simply, with practical illustrations and experiments, he takes his young audience through the mysterious world of phenomena, combustion, gases, electricity, all founded on this single theme of a candle and its flame.

In 1828 had come the opening of the Zoological Society's Gardens in London, with a consequent spate of publications on the subject for children, especially picture-books. Modern geology was also making strides early in the century with the work of Lyell and others, and Mrs. Trimmer's mosaic chronology was fast crumbling. As exciting new knowledge was disclosed, science and natural history became more specialised, but in the nineteenth century much was still to be done by the devoted amateur. And it was an amateur enthusiast for natural history, Charles Kingsley, who gave Victorian children two outstanding books on the subject – *Glaucus; or, The Wonders of the Shore* (1855) and *Madam How and Lady Why* (1869).

Superseded as these books are now, in their day they marked an important stage in the development of books for the young about the physical world. Startling discoveries were being made about the origins of life and the age of the earth. Kingsley saw in these revelations only fresh manifestations of divine glory and power, and he reconciled in his contemplation of Nature the God of Scripture with the God revealed in his creation. In *Glaucus* he explores the coast of Devon, as he had often done since childhood, drawing upon such authorities as Philip Gosse. He gives some fascinating details about the creatures of the shore and the ocean, but the work is too weighted with opinions and irrelevancies to escape criticism. Towards the end there is some useful advice about the building of an aquarium, and a guide to further reading. Among the books Kingsley recommends are four small S.P.C.K. works by Philip Gosse on Mammals, Birds, Reptiles, and Fishes, 'dear old Bewick for ornithology, *passé* though he may be in a scientific point', and the botanical works of the Rev. C. A. Johns (1811–1874), another devoted amateur of natural history, whose *Flowers of the Field* was published in 1853. Johns when a master at Helston Grammar School had inspired Kingsley with a love of botany, and it was to his later school at Winton House, that Kingsley sent his son Grenville Arthur, to whom *Madam How* was dedicated. *Madam How and Lady Why; or, First Lessons in Earth Lore for Children* appeared serially in the first issues of *Good Words for the Young* in 1868 and 1869. It is a livelier and more interesting work than *Glaucus*. 'Madam How' is Nature, the force which moulds the earth and its creatures. 'Lady Why' is 'the mistress of Madam How, and of you and me; and, as I think, of all things that you ever saw, or can see, or even dream'. 'Why' things happen we cannot tell. 'How' is to be perceived through long and patient observation. Kingsley writes his book as a kind of conversation – but how differently from the stiff and formal style of many of his predecessors! He roams through all kinds of earth lore, recreating everything from the things seen near at hand. This is no dull record of facts, but an exciting exploration of the secrets of water, rocks, ice, and earth changes over vast tracts of time. Didactic the author may be, but never tedious. He impregnates the book with his feeling, showing that Nature was for him the teacher of wisdom and truth.

These books by Kingsley indicate how the growing emphasis on imagination, entertainment, and new avenues of fiction for the delight of boys and girls, were affecting books of a factual kind. In history and biography the effect was just as potent. After Sir Walter Scott had shown how fascinating history might be unfolded for youth with his *Tales of a Grandfather* (1827–1830), other writers began to present the subject in more interesting ways than lessons, catechisms, or letters. In 1835 there appeared that long popular little work by Lady Callcott (1783–1842), *Little Arthur's History of England*, a great advance on most of its contemporaries, only rivalled by Mrs. Markham's *History of England* (1823), written by Elizabeth Penrose, 'with conversations at the end of each chapter'. Both were easy narratives, and Lady Callcott succeeded quite brilliantly in her aim to be intelligible, simple, and interesting. *Little Arthur's History* was written for a real child, and the style is conversational. Lady Callcott, like others, brought her principles into her writing, and she liked to label monarchs and their actions 'good' or 'wicked', but the short chapters really bring the past alive. Not the least of her achievements was to make plain difficult ideas such as 'freedom', 'feudalism', 'Parliament'. Dates she relegated to her chapter headings.

Charlotte Yonge also made simple versions of historical events for young readers in a series, *Aunt Charlotte's History Stories*, separate volumes covering *English, Bible, Roman, Greek, German, American* and *French History*, between 1875 and 1895. She also wrote four series of *Landmarks of History* (1852–1883) and *Cameos of History* (1868) for children a little older. Although like other Victorian writers, she tended to dwell on the more romantic and dramatic aspects of the past her enthusiasm for her subject and able presentation gave life to her historical writings for the young. Best known of all her factual books, however, is that mixture of history and biography, *A Book of Golden Deeds of All Times and Lands* (1864). This was intended as a treasury for young people where they might find 'soul-stirring deeds that give life and glory to the record of events' in more detail than in their history books. She included spiritual heroes and heroines, as well as many other examples of sacrifice and selfless duty. Selflessness rather than valour was her measure of a golden deed.

J. C. Edgar also advanced the writing of history and biography, especially for boys, by his more robust accounts of heroes 'who added to the national greatness' in such works as *The Heroes of England* (1853). He wrote other volumes of biography for boys, largely inspired by his love of the past and the heroic. Much of it appeared first in *The Boy's Own Magazine*, and also in the periodical for which he was the first editor, *Every Boy's Magazine*, in 1862.

Charles Dickens was to put all his narrative skill and feeling for the dramatic into his *Child's History of England* (1852–1854), first serialised in *Household Words* at various intervals from January 1851 to December 1853. He told the story of England in a series of splendid or grimly painted scenes, with no hiding where his sympathies lay. Henry VIII was 'one of the most detestable villains that ever drew breath', and as for Elizabeth, 'on the whole she had a great deal too much of her father in her to please me'. He ends his vivid chronicle which stresses personalities and action, with 'the great and glorious revolution of 1688'. He and Scott had certainly proved that history could be made as interesting as any romance, and other writers followed their lead.

In the last decades of the nineteenth century the production of fiction and other imaginative literature had become more and more prominent in reading for youth, although there was a steady widening of the range of non-fiction also. Much factual material, it must be remembered, was by now included for young readers in their many magazines, especially information about sport, hobbies, pastimes, and natural history. There is a growing tendency to make factual books more alluring to enable them to compete with the wiles of fiction. In 1879, when Arabella B. Buckley (1840–1929) brought out the first of her popular science books for youth, she almost apologises that it is not a fairy tale, so completely had children by this time taken possession of the citadel of pleasure in their reading. But science, she tells her youthful audience (the book arose from lectures for them), has fairies of her own, 'tales equal to the old fairy tales we all know so well'. *The Fairyland of Science*, this first book, and other volumes which followed, set out to please as well as instruct, and the wonders and truths of nature are set forth in an imaginative though systematic fashion. 'No-one can love dry facts', the writer avers. 'We must clothe them with real meaning, and love the truths they tell, if we wish to enjoy science'. At last the child's need to have information presented in fascinating and simple ways is recognised. Pleasure in reading need not be restricted to adventure, fairy tales, and romance.

Religion, for all its importance in books for the young over the centuries, seems to have produced few masterpieces for them, except for that great treasure store, the *Bible*, *The Pilgrim's Progress*, and some much-loved hymns and carols. Charles Dickens wrote a simple and sincere *Life of Our Lord* for his own children in 1849, but it was written without thought of publication, and it has not become well-known since its first appearance in print in 1934. Just before the Victorian era was over, however, a new kind of religious biography for youth must be noted. This was *A Child's Book of Saints* (1898), by William Canton (1845–1926). He wove into these legends told 'under the pressure of an insatiable listener', his own W.V., a gleaming thread of poetry and romance. With them began the development of religious books for boys and girls of high artistic and literary quality – a notable feature of the century ahead.

With the Edwardian period there came into being a new kind of compendium of knowledge for children, as much concerned with stories, poetry, religion, and wonder, as with information about the world around us. Self-educators in cheap periodical parts had by now become a feature of publishing for the masses, and on 17th March 1908 there appeared the first number of a new publication of this kind designed for boys and girls, *The Children's Encyclopaedia*. For Arthur Mee (1875–1943), its Editor, it was 'The Book of my Heart', and many children lucky enough to have been brought up with it in the house will echo this with feeling. The fifty fortnightly parts were later published in eight volumes, and so there was added to the child's bookshelf a book full of inspiration as well as every kind of knowledge and information, presented in attractive, well-illustrated fashion. A new edition came out in ten volumes (again after periodical publication) from 1922–1925, and in spite of competition from more orderly and up-to-date rival cyclopaedias of knowledge, Mee's creation has continued as one of the great and influential books of this century for children.

Books of knowledge are the most ephemeral of all, for science and other branches of human knowledge make giant strides forward in every generation. The subject in children's literature has been little explored, but it is hoped that this brief glance at a few of the obsolete and pioneer productions of a former age may have shed a little light on the relationship between the two linked hemispheres of the child's reading – Poetry (and Imagination) and Science (and Reason).

x   PERIODICALS

The first juvenile periodical to be published in this country is apparently the venture advertised by John Newbery in the *General Evening Post* for 9th–12th February 1751 and noticed in an earlier chapter – *The Lilliputian Magazine*. No copy of the three separate issues in which it was launched have survived, but Jill E. Grey has now shown from evidence in the ledger of the printer, William Strahan, that 4000 copies of No. 1 and No. 2 were printed early in 1751, each with a separate printed cover (Bibl. 286).

Mary Cooper had advertised a *Penny Medley; or, Weekly Entertainer* in the *General Advertiser* for 7th August 1746, but this seems to have been more a series of little chapbooks rather than a magazine for children. So that Newbery's publication is a pioneer of its kind. It remained in print as a collected volume from about 1752 until the 1780s.

The annual for children was born in Switzerland in the form of *Neujahrsblätter* or *Neujahrsstücke* (New Year sheets) in the year 1645, when the children of Zurich found at the town library, with their parents' greetings, an engraving with verse beneath it. But it was in Germany that the first weekly journals for children were founded early in the 1770s, the most famous being *Der Kinderfreund* of C. F. Weisse (1726–1804), which ran from 1775–1782. It was this periodical which inspired Arnaud Berquin to bring out his *L'Ami des Enfans* (already described with the moral tale) in Paris in twenty-four monthly issues from 1782–1783. But all these early periodicals, including Newbery's, were more like miscellanies than journals for youth in the modern sense.

In England John Newbery's first successor was Madame Le Prince de Beaumont (1711–1780). Her famous work, *Le Magasin des Enfans*, however, probably owes more of its inspiration to Sarah Fielding's *The Governess* (1749) than to Newbery's *Lilliputian Magazine*. It was not a true periodical, for it was published by subscription as a collected edition only, in four volumes, at first in French (London, J. Haberkorn, 1756), and the following year it came out in English with the title, *The Young Misses Magazine*, (J.

Nourse, 4 vols, in 2).[1] Madame Le Prince de Beaumont was a French writer on education who spent much of her life in England, and this *Magasin* was more of a medley than a journal for youth. It consisted of *'dialogues entre une sage gouvernante et plusieurs de ses élèves'* – young ladies of quality between seven and thirteen years of age. The improving conversations were interspersed with tales, the whole intended to promote the author's plan 'to inculcate the spirit of geometry in children'. Some of the stories, like the popular *Beauty and the Beast* and *Prince Désir* (the original of Lamb's Prince Dorus), were delightfully ungeometrical, but others were more shaped to the writer's purpose. *Le Magasin des Enfans* was followed by three sequels intended for rather older readers. The most suitable for youth was *Le Magasin des Adolescentes* (1759), published in 1760 in an English version, *The Young Ladies Magazine*. The dialogues here introduce characters of from five to eighteen years of age.

The second publisher to attempt a periodical in monthly parts for boys and girls in Great Britain was the enterprising John Marshall of Aldermary Churchyard. He brought out the first number of a *Juvenile Magazine* in January 1788. It was intended for children from seven to fourteen years of age, and designed to be 'an instructive and entertaining miscellany for the youth of both sexes'. Each monthly number was embellished with two plates, and the contents include easy geography (with maps), serials in the form of improving tales and dramas, 'familiar letters' sometimes from schoolboy or schoolgirl readers, instructive puzzles, and verses, some of these signed 'S.S.' (Mary Kilner). In the first number the editor, apparently Lucy Peacock, invites young readers to take advantage of her advice by consulting her about the overcoming of any unruly passion, or for guidance in situations where they were at a loss as to how to conduct themselves. She also made an appeal for contributions from young people, and there is the semblance if not the actuality of young readers participating in this short-lived journal which is important in the development of magazines for children.

Marshall evidently found that monthly publication brought insufficient returns, but eleven years after the demise of this interesting venture at the end of December 1788, he tried again with *The Children's Magazine; or, monthly Repository of Instruction and Delight*, which ran for two years from January 1799 to December 1800. His third effort which may have been a continuation under a new title, *The Picture Magazine*, lasted only from 1800 to 1801. By this time another publisher had appeared on the scene – Elizabeth Newbery – with no more lasting success than her rival. *The Young Gentleman's and Young Lady's Magazine* which she sold consisted of twelve monthly issues from 1799 to

[1] *Toronto Catalogue*, p. 128 (Bibl 46).
Grey, Jill E. *The Governess* pp. 64–66 (Bibl. 218).

1800. It was not dissimilar in contents from Marshall's first effort, but it has special significance for its inclusion of notices about children's books.

These journals very much resembled the usual reading material offered to youth in the books of the day, being largely moral in purpose, but enlivened with pictures, narrative, puzzles, and other attractions. More enduring was a publication apparently brought out each year as an annual by William Darton, under the title of *The Minor's Pocket Book*, from about 1798 to 1810. It was in this work that Darton introduced some of the early writings of Ann and Jane Taylor. But Jane Taylor, writing as 'Q.Q.', was probably better known later as a contributor to *The Youth's Magazine*, an evangelical journal established in 1805. Her *Contributions of Q.Q.* were published in book form in 1824.

This magazine was an early example of the many religious and Sunday School periodicals, which were to be the first really successful and cheap periodical publications for the young. The recently established Sunday Schools were much in need of suitable reading matter to exercise their scholars' newly acquired skill and also to further their religious education. At first this need was met by tracts, published at a penny or a halfpenny by the Religious Tract Society from 1799, but there was an opportunity for more regular circulation of material as the number of scholars steadily multiplied. So the Sunday School magazines for children came into existence. Two of them were successfully launched in the 1820s – *The Child's Companion; or, Sunday Scholar's Reward*, and *The Children's Friend*. The first was a Religious Tract Society publication started in January 1824. The first number of this small thirty-two page journal reveals an intensive religious purpose, conveyed more often in simple stories, hymns and verses, than in direct sermonising. There are snippets of information about countries abroad, chiefly relating to missionary activities, and a serial, 'The History of Joseph Green: a Sunday Scholar'. Reading the Bible and the searching out of texts are continually encouraged, but this proves to be a little journal not too over-weighted with theology for childish understanding. It endured, becoming less severe in its piety, and more in touch with the general interests of children, as the years passed. In 1846 it became *The Child's Companion and Juvenile Instructor*, and it lingered on in various forms until the 1930s.

The second journal, *The Children's Friend*, was of sterner mould. It was another penny monthly, inaugurated in 1826 by the Rev. W. Carus Wilson, a well-known Evangelical clergyman, perhaps now better remembered as the literary character of Mr. Brocklebank, the founder and inspector of Lowood Institution in *Jane Eyre*. Charlotte Bronte drew upon her own memories of him and her experiences at the Clergy Daughters' School at Cowan Bridge for the perhaps overharsh portrait she delineated. But in his periodical for Sunday scholars he does little to redeem this severe judgment, showing himself very much the disciple of Janeway in his approach to the religious training of youth. There are frequent warnings against sin and the pleasures of the world, and many examples of holy dying. Such puritanical strictures and gloom, however, did not seem to detract from the appeal of this monthly paper, and it continued to circulate until 1860. It should not be confused with another periodical of the same name started in the fifties of rather more secular and cheerful nature, and continuing as an annual into the twentieth century.

These two popular examples are chosen from a flood of cheap religious journals for the young, which came out from the 1820s onwards. A Baptist magazine for children was in circulation before 1830, and there were several Methodist periodicals for youth, including *Early Days; or, the Wesleyan Scholar's Guide*, started in 1846. By this time most sects had their periodical for young readers, and there were also missionary magazines, Band of Hope journals, and similar organs, most of them marketed at a penny or a halfpenny to bring them within reach of the poor children for whom they were chiefly designed. Sometimes the title was the brightest thing about them – for example, *The Sunbeam: a Little Luminary to Guide the Young to Glory* (1858–1861) – but, whatever their defects, these cheap productions were the means of bringing to boys and girls of the poorer classes reading matter which had some standard of values, if narrow and harsh in our estimation today. Without them children would have been left exposed entirely to the tawdry and sensational matter being supplied increasingly by commercially unscrupulous publishers to exploit the expansion of literacy.

In genteel social circles young readers in the 1820s and 1830s were enjoying their first annuals – junior editions of the miscellanies and 'keepsakes' for fashionable drawing-rooms. For 1828 and 1829 they had *The Christmas Box*, 'an annual present for children' edited by T. Crofton Croker (author of *Fairy Legends and Traditions of the South of Ireland*). The elegant *Juvenile Forget-me-not*, edited by Mrs. S. C. Hall (Anna Maria Hall, 1800–1881), came out each year from 1829 to 1837, intended to be a Christmas or New Year Gift, or a birthday present. The ubiquitous annual for the young was now in being, but as yet in very superior and expensive form. Like their senior counterparts these productions for youth were finely bound and embellished with steel engravings, but their pages lacked sparkle, elegance and sedateness being considered more important than vitality.

This precious type of annual soon gave place to others of a more popular and cheaper kind, and towards the middle of the century annual volumes associated with periodicals became a general feature of publishing for children. There was *Peter Parley's Annual* from 1840, the outcome of *Peter Parley's Magazine*, which ran from 1840 until 1863, and then continued as an annual for another thirty years. It was at first published by Darton, and edited by William Martin, one of the English 'Peter Parleys'. All Peter Parley publications stressed the matter-of-fact, and the *Magazine* and *Annual* brought together much diverse information for the benefit of young minds, lightened by an occasional realistic tale breathing exhortation towards cheerful industry and duty. 'Be merry, but be wise, my friends', is the message of Peter Parley in the rhymed preface to his *Annual* for 1851. The subjects of the rather condescending articles range from astronomy to discoveries in Assyria, and there are two expositions of the folly of superstitions and legends. One deals with witches, wizards, ghosts, and hobgoblins, expressing satisfaction that children need fear them no more, 'for the days of superstition are on the wane'. The other exposes the falsehood of many of the legends about King Arthur, though it praises him as a historical figure.

More fanciful and fictional was *Green's Nursery Annual*, another Darton production, published between 1847 and 1858. A 'new edition' of 1849, apparently a reprint of an earlier one, is distinguished by an attractive Victorian format, with each square page adorned with a border, alternating in colour, and pleasant black and white illustrations. It contains little else but stories and verses by Mrs. S. C. Hall, Mrs. Sherwood, and other writers. Most outstanding is a charming tale about Germany by Mary Howitt – *The Christmas Tree*. Both the *Peter Parley Annual* and *Green's Nursery Annual* have a frontispiece and title-page printed in colour – a sign of the advancing use of the art.

A step forward was made in the range and quality of cheap periodicals and annuals for the young in 1866, when the Rev. J. Erskine Clarke of Derby launched *The Chatterbox* as a counterblast to the evergrowing 'blood and thunder' (his own words). Its price was competitive for it came out as a halfpenny weekly, as well as a threepenny monthly, and annual. It persisted far into the twentieth century, and in its long life changed surprisingly little in form and contents. Its promoter kept its pages free of violence, bloodshed, and the supernatural, used bold black and white engravings, mixed religious advice with pleasing patter, and printed stories and serials with plenty of action, if rather too much sentiment. Clarke was also responsible for a Sunday School magazine called *The Children's Prize* (later *The Prize*, 1863–1931). This had the distinction of being selected by Ruskin for furious castigation in his *Fors Clavigera*, as an example of all such pious literature of poor quality, preaching the wrong kind of morality, encouraging apathy and class-consciousness among poor children, and thus bringing 'ruin – inevitable and terrible, such as no nation has yet suffered . . .'

Cheap sensation in print in the form of 'penny dreadfuls' was no doubt as great a menace (if not greater) as the wrong kind of Sunday School literature. The history of this escapist reading matter has been most divertingly and fully outlined by E. S. Turner in *Boys will be Boys* (Bibl. 287), and will only receive scant mention here. The lurid penny dreadfuls of the early Victorian period displaced the chapbooks to a large extent, going back for inspiration to the Gothic novel and its stock ingredients of murder, horror, and supernatural terrors. From these melodramatic and horrific productions, not primarily intended for youth, arose the cheap periodical for boys. This may be said to begin its career with *The Boys of England*, a penny weekly established in 1866. From No. 10 onwards the editor was Edwin J. Brett, who had already been concerned with more ferocious, low-cost productions. The paper offered 'wild and wonderful, but healthy fiction, with sport, fun, and instruction', not merely sensation. Not the least of its attractions were the prizes offered – an astounding array including ponies, dogs, pigeons, watches, volumes of Shakespeare etc., usually in fifties. It also presented sheets of Juvenile Drama, with the first one taken from its serial 'Alone in the Pirate's Lair'. It was by no means as worthless as

23.   *Picture by Harrison Weir for the cover of* CHATTERBOX, *14th September 1878*

later publications of the kind might lead the reader to expect. It contained notes on garden-ing, sport, and military matters, and an early serial was a historical story founded on 'Chevy Chase'. In 1871 the first 'Jack Harkaway' story by Bracebridge Hemyng made its appearance, and thereafter credibility was to know no bounds.

Other cheap weeklies for boys were soon competing in the market, and standards seem to decline in inverse proportion to the increase in sales. Brett's various productions for boys were rivalled by those of the Emmett firm and Charles Fox. And in the last decade of the century, Alfred Harmsworth (later Lord Northcliffe) entered the arena with the watchword 'No more penny dreadfuls!' to undercut all rivals with his *Halfpenny Wonder* (1892), *Halfpenny Marvel* (1893), *Union Jack* (1894) and *Pluck* (1894). The hawklike sleuth Sexton Blake began his career with the Harmsworth group, finding fame in the early issues of *Union Jack*.

By 1900 the cheap periodical for boys had achieved huge sales, a trend continuing well into the new century. In its first decade there appeared a new personality in the field, under the name of 'Frank Richards' – one of the many pen-names of Claude H. St. J. Hamilton (1876–1961). He was responsible for *The Gem*, launched as a weekly in 1907. The next year came an even more famous weekly series about boarding school life, *The Magnet*, introducing Greyfriars School, and the astonishing 'Fat Owl of the Remove', Billy Bunter. Both these popular weeklies from the pen of 'Frank Richards' continued to depict their coterie of boys in a familiar pattern of far-fetched and lively adventure based on school life and its comradeship – perhaps the secret of their appeal – until the early years of the second World War. But the endearing buffoon, Billy Bunter, lives on to haunt some popular productions of the present day.

Most of the cheap papers published for boys were of low quality, featuring easy-to-read sentences or short expressions, no paragraphs, remoteness from real life, sensation and incident *ad nauseam*, and similar defects. But they certainly attracted readers, and in their day must have brightened many dull young lives by a sterile and short-lived pleasure, unfortunately seldom leading to any progress towards a more rewarding exploration of literature.

But not all periodical literature for boys was of this nature. Other magazines followed aims beyond sensationalism and soaring circulation figures. In 1855, Samuel Orchard Beeton (1832–1877) started a twopenny monthly, *The Boy's Own Magazine*, 'an illustrated journal of fact, fiction, history and adventure'. This contained some good and solid fare in its closely printed columns, and J. C. Edgar wrote many of his historical and biographical articles for it. The price was later raised to sixpence, thus making it into a middle-class magazine, rather than a rival of the cheap weeklies. It ceased publication in 1874, by which date another paper of a similar kind had been established, Routledge's *Every Boy's Magazine* (1862–1889), with an F.R.G.S., Edmund Routledge, as editor for much of its existence.

Its fate was not inglorious for it was eventually amalgamated with a more famous competitor, which almost reached the status of a British institution – *The Boy's Own Paper*. This highly prized periodical for youth first came out on 18th January 1879 as a penny weekly. It was published by the Religious Tract Society under the direction of Dr. James Macaulay, M.A., and M.D., but the man who guided the paper's destiny for the first thirty-four years was its editor, George Andrew Hutchison (1841–1913). Under him

219

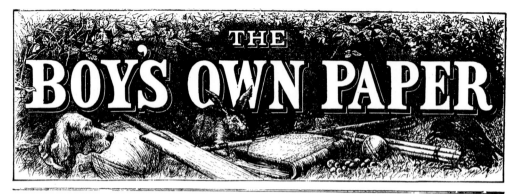

No. 1.—Vol. I.   SATURDAY, JANUARY 18, 1879.   Price One Penny.
[ALL RIGHTS RESERVED.

MY FIRST FOOTBALL MATCH.

By an Old Boy.

IT was a proud moment in my existence when Wright, captain of our football club, came up to me in school one Friday and said, "Adams, your name is down to play in the match against Craven to-morrow."

I could have knighted him on the spot. To be one of the picked "fifteen," whose glory it was to fight the battles of their school in the Great Close, had been the leading ambition of my life—I suppose I ought to be ashamed to confess it—ever since, as a little chap of ten, I entered Parkhurst six years ago. Not a winter Saturday but had seen me either looking on at some big match, or oftener still scrimmaging about with a score or so of other juniors in a scratch game. But for a long time, do what I would, I always seemed as far as ever from the coveted goal, and was half despairing of ever rising to win my "first fifteen cap." Lately, however, I had noticed Wright and a few others of our best players more than once lounging about in the Little Close where we juniors used to play, evidently taking observations with an eye to business. Under the awful gaze of these heroes, need I say I exerted myself as I had never done before? What cared I for hacks or bruises, so only that I could distinguish myself in their eyes? And never was music sweeter

"Down!"

24.   The earliest appearance of a famous periodical for boys

220

it became a journal read in many quarters of the globe outliving all the other boy's magazines of its day. Throughout the nineteenth century and early twentieth century it remained a weekly, changing to a monthly in 1913. It provided much healthy and wholesome fare. Information about sport, hobbies, and nature accompanied full-blooded serials featuring young Britons battling triumphantly against immense odds in jungles and other wild places, imperturbable and confident when in the tightest of corners, as sons of the Empire were expected to be. It was the *B.O.P.* which fixed the pattern of the boy's school tale, with its serialisation of the stories of Talbot Baines Reed. Other authors which contributed to its pages include Ascott Hope (Ascott Hope-Moncrieff, 1846–1927), Dr. Gordon Stables, R.N. (1840–1910), who specialised in sea tales and conquering Scottish heroes, and those famous story-spinners already introduced here in an earlier chapter, R. M. Ballantyne, W. H. G. Kingston, G. A. Henty and Jules Verne. The turning away from introspection and sentimentality is much in evidence in the pages of this new magazine for boys. The emphasis is on action, open-air activities, and sport, and not even the approval of schoolmasters and parents could dim the *B.O.P.*'s success. It had at least one rival of its kind later in the century, when *Chums* was published by Cassell in 1892, with Sir Max Pemberton as its first editor. But the *B.O.P.* was unassailable. Sadly transformed as it may have seemed in some elderly eyes it endured until 1967, dispensing advice and help as well as entertaining readers. Its disappearance with the February number according to *The Times* on 11th January 1967, 'is a nostalgic social landmark...'

Attempts to promulgate magazines of quality for youth had been made before the prolific seventies and the *B.O.P.* One of the earliest was *The Monthly Packet*, edited by Charlotte M. Yonge from its inception in 1851 until 1893, five years before its demise. It was intended for young ladies, rather than children, 'as a companion in times of recreation ... to make them more steadfast and dutiful daughters of our beloved Catholic Church of England'. Many of the editor's stories for young people were first printed in its pages. Less thriving but more ambitious was *The Charm*, published by Addey and Co. from 1852 to 1854. This magazine for boys and girls was a brave attempt to provide a well-illustrated literary periodical with charm of three kinds, 'variety, novelty and art'. It contained much of merit, with articles about the zoo, history and science, but it lacked such popular journalistic features as serials and competitions, and its excellent format was not enough to keep it alive. It admitted fairy tales, but on the whole its virtues were down-to-earth rather than imaginative. Yet it deserves praise as a pioneer of its kind.

The 1860s saw a spate of new journals, and above all, two of real merit. One of them – *Aunt Judy's Magazine* – has been mentioned several times in previous chapters. This was a monthly periodical issued by Bell and Daldy, and edited by Mrs. Margaret Gatty. It began its existence in May 1866 and continued until 1885, being edited after Mrs. Gatty's death in 1873 by one of her daughters, H. K. F. Gatty, at first with the help of another, the more famous Mrs. Ewing. Most of this writer's excellent stories appeared in this magazine, which treated its young readers as intelligent beings with versatile interests. It was educational in its purpose, but pleasure was to be the means, and all was imparted with such skill and warmhearted enthusiasm that *Aunt Judy* stands apart from all other juvenile periodicals. Its book review features have already been mentioned, and Mrs. Gatty's literary judgment and her appreciation of the writings of Hans Andersen and Lewis Carroll, both contributors to her journal, gave it true distinction.

The other periodical of quality started in November 1868, proving less popular, but no less excellent in its way, than *Aunt Judy's Magazine*. This was *Good Words for the Young*, a junior companion of *Good Words*, both edited by Norman Macleod, a Scottish minister and friend of George Macdonald, who followed him as editor of the junior publication from 1870–1872. A monthly sixpenny, like *Aunt Judy*, it contained contributions by Charles Kingsley, Mrs. Craik, W. B. Rands, and other first-rate writers of the day, but never printed anything finer than the serial in its first volume, *At the Back of the North Wind*, by George Macdonald, with illustrations by Arthur Hughes. Literary and artistic merit could not ensure success, however, and after changing its name to *Good Things for the Young of all Ages*, it came to an end in 1877.

The seventies brought another sixty or more periodicals upon the ever-expanding market, and two are worth a fanfare, besides the *Boy's Own Paper* in 1879. The first is a journal for younger children, *Little Folks*, published in 1871 by Cassell, Petter and Galpin. Its principal features were short tales, bold black and white illustrations, and such joys for small readers as picture puzzles and models for painting. At first both a weekly and a monthly this pleasing magazine deserved its steady success and long existence which terminated in 1931. The second magazine to be hailed with special delight is the American *St. Nicholas*, conducted by Mary Mapes Dodge, who addressed a frank and friendly opening letter to 'dear Girl and Boy' in the first number in November 1873. This magazine had as its aim the true welfare of children. It provided varied fare, with stories of excellent quality, and very soon a correspondence column was begun, where young readers could give their views as well as receive answers to their enquiries. Contributors included Louisa M. Alcott, W. C. Bryant, Susan Coolidge, Mrs. Dodge herself, Lucretia P. Hale, Bret Harte, and other notable writers. Many famous stories first appeared in its pages, among them *Little Lord Fauntleroy*, by Mrs. F. H. Burnett, and some of the tales by Kipling afterwards included in *The Jungle Book*.

Another periodical launched in the seventies was James Henderson's *Our Young Folks Weekly Budget* in 1871 (continued under varying titles until 1897), and deserving mention for its serialisation of the stories of Robert Louis Stevenson in the 1880s, when it was known as *Young Folks*. This production catered more for the excitement-loving tastes of young readers, but *Treasure Island*, which ran from 1st October 1881 to 28th January 1882, made no great mark as a serial. *Kidnapped* appeared from 1st May to 13th July 1886 with little more effect. The most successful of the three Stevenson stories to be published in this weekly journal was *The Black Arrow*, from 30th June to 20th October 1883, perhaps because it has the regular fluctuations of suspense and the more episodic character needed for a serial.

Younger children not only had *Little Folks* in the seventies. In 1875 came Mrs. Lucy Sale-Barker's *Little Wideawake*, a monthly issued by Routledge, and very much a Victorian mamma's composition for her own nursery. There are neither fairies nor fantasy in its pages, but short, well printed tales about pets, children, and everyday things suitable for a six-to-eight year old. It was also issued as an annual, and at least one frontispiece (for 1880) was the work of Kate Greenaway. Its existence came to an end in 1892. But by then the youngest readers were served by more mediocre, easy-to-read magazines, with the emphasis on plenty of pictures, like *The Little One's Own Coloured Picture Paper* (1885–1894), *Our Little Dots* (1887–1923) and *Tiny Tots* (1899–1948).

Little has been said about periodicals for girls, for the very good reason that for a long time little was specially addressed to them. Many of the better magazines intended for both sexes – such as *Aunt Judy's Magazine* and *Good Words for the Young* – probably pleased more girls than boys. Young ladies in Anglican circles had their *Monthly Packet*, and there was a *Young Ladies Journal* from 1864, but nothing much was done to put a cheap periodical of some quality into the hands of poorer girls until *The Girl's Own Paper* started as a penny weekly in 1880. This was brought out by the Religious Tract Society as the female complement to *The Boy's Own Paper*, but it never matched its success. Perhaps it was that while many girls rushed to get hold of the new issue of the *B.O.P.* before their brothers, the reverse was unthinkable! Nevertheless the *G.O.P.* filled a real need, and brought innocuous fiction and useful knowledge to many girls who had little opportunity for education or self-improvement.

The religious tone of the paper was stronger than in the *B.O.P.* Fiction usually promoted the ideals of dutifulness, control of temper, usefulness in the home, and other feminine virtues. The emphasis throughout was on the practical and useful, with articles on cookery, needlework, making clothes, sketching and similar activities, but gradually its scope widened to give more space to literature, the arts, and music. Literary competitions were a feature from the start, as in its masculine counterpart. It also emulated the *B.O.P.* by having a correspondence column, the agency for much advice to young enquirers, especially about health and hygiene, etiquette and behaviour. 'Kindness is the foundation of all good breeding' is one bit of sensible advice. The cold or tepid bath every morning is offered as a panacea for complaints ranging from clamminess of the hands to sleeplessness. There is no nonsense about glamour, and romance walks in very sober garb. Later *The Girl's Own Paper* was to turn its attention more and more to young women rather than to girls in their early teens, and it ceased to be a juvenile periodical in Edwardian days.

More distinguished from a literary viewpoint was *Atalanta* (1887–1898), a monthly journal which incorporated Routledge's *Every Girl's Magazine*, published since 1878. L. T. Meade (Mrs. E. T. Smith) was one of its first editors, and it set a high standard, with material not exclusively of interest to girls. The first volume had an African tale by Rider Haggard, a serial by Mrs. Molesworth, and an article on classical drama by Professor A. J. Church. From December 1892 until September 1893, *Catriona* by R. L. Stevenson was serialised under the title – *David Balfour: Memoirs of his Adventures at Home and Abroad*. But like other periodicals of merit this valiant effort to provide firstclass reading matter for girls lasted little more than a decade.

This short outline can only sketch the main features of the rise and decline of periodicals for boys and girls during a century of great activity. Achievement in quality probably reached its peak in the seventies. By the 1890s the likelihood of finding masterpieces serialised in juvenile magazines was fading, although the editor of *Chums* had the sensible idea of repeating a good thing by reprinting *Treasure Island* as a serial in 1894. On the other hand periodicals of mass circulation and appeal were increasingly thriving. Among the more than commonplace only *Little Folks*, *St. Nicholas*, *The Boy's Own Paper*, and *The Girl's Own Paper* lived on into the twentieth century.

Of nearly a hundred papers being published at the close of the nineteenth century, many were Sunday School magazines and other pious or purposeful journals, to which Dr. Barnardo added a halfpenny monthly, *Father William's Stories*, in 1866. In 1868 this Bible-teaching mixture of the serious and lively, which also set out to reveal something of the plight of the destitute children Barnardo was rescuing, became *The Children's Treasury*. It continued from 1881 as *Our Darlings* for about another forty years.

But the majority of papers for youth were now the commercially successful 'circulation-chasers', chronicling with monotonous repetition the deeds of dareall supermen like Jack Harkaway, Sexton Blake, and Deadwood Dick. How different the situation had become in the opulent and literate Edwardian age from the tentative beginnings of journals for youth a hundred and more years earlier. It would seem that periodical literature had been developed mainly to satisfy a new mass of undiscriminating young readers, ready and eager for regular halfpenny or pennyworths of vicarious excitement, if no better material could be put within their reach.

5 Childrens' Books Abroad

'Every country gives and every country receives – and so it comes about that in our first impressionable years the universal republic of childhood is born', wrote Paul Hazard in *Books, Children and Men* (Bibl. 12). Each nation, he affirmed, reveals its own characteristics in its literature for children, but children have always ignored national or other manmade frontiers in their reading. From the beginning their books have been more translated or transplanted than any other writings. So claimed M. Pierre Bouet in his preface to the first edition of the booklist and report, *Children's Books and International Goodwill*, published by the International Bureau of Education in Geneva.[1] From this report it can be gleaned how widely books for children have travelled. Little Mexicans have found delight in the tales of Perrault and Grimm, Yugoslavian children have enjoyed Jules Verne, *Little Lord Fauntleroy* and the works of the Comtesse de Ségur have been read in lands as far apart as Roumania and Brazil. *Robinson Crusoe* has roamed all over the world, fascinating the Indian poet, Rabindranath Tagore, in his youth, when he read it in Bengali.[2] Stories by the much-loved Hans Andersen have found their way into eighty languages – including Turkish and Chinese.[3]

It is not the purpose in this chapter to attempt a survey of the rise of children's literature in various parts of the world. Such an undertaking is beyond the scope of this work or the capacity of its writer. There is much research to be done before an authoritative general history of children's literature can be compiled, and as yet facilities in Britain for such a study are uncoordinated and inadequate. An added difficulty is that very little on the subject of the history of children's books in other languages has yet been translated into English. But some advances to aid the better investigation of the subject can be reported within the last decade. An important contribution to sources of information was made in 1968 by Anne Pellowski in her bibliographical survey, *The World of Children's Literature* (Bibl. 44). Unfortunately references to books and articles on literature and its history are not separated from those on more general aspects of book provision and

[1] Quoted in foreword of 2nd edition 1932 (Bibl. 306).

[2] Tagore. *The Religion of Man* 1931 Ch. 12.

[3] *Catalogue of the Hans Christian Andersen Jubilee Exhibition*, 1805–1955 (Bibl. 173).

library activities, but a wide range is covered – over eighty countries, including many in Latin America and Africa – each section prefaced with useful comments.

Another advancement with much promise for the study of children's literature on the widest basis has been the growth of institutions concerned with children's books, past and present, national and international. A Children's Books Section of the Library of Congress in Washington was established in 1963, and the Swedish Institute for Children's Books opened in Stockholm in 1967. Resources for the study of children's books in many countries exist at the International Youth Library in Munich (founded 1949), and the extension in reference material there is much to be welcomed.

The aim of the short survey which follows is to fill in a little of the background and to introduce some foreign contributions to our own literature for youth. Some have already been described. This was inevitable for many classics from abroad have become natural-ised and scarcely seem to belong to their country of origin. What is not well-known is the pattern of development surrounding them, or the influence of contemporary trends in different lands.

A two-way exchange of ideas and publications for children across the Channel and across the Atlantic has been a feature since the beginnings. Because of this relationship the following account is limited to two main areas – Western Europe and North America, with the addition of another English-speaking country with a flourishing literature for youth – Australia.

1 NORTH AMERICA

In the New World children's books, like the literature for their parents, were to be much affected by ideas from Europe, not only through importations and translations, but by the traditions and culture of various immigrant races. But for a long time influences were chiefly British. When the Pilgrim Fathers settled in New England in the early seventeenth century they took with them, besides their steadfast courage and intense religious convictions, their literary treasures, above all the *Bible* and Foxe's *Book of Martyrs*. Very soon other Puritan books from the old country were added to these basic works read by the children of the new settlers. And it was not long before the young colonists had their first books produced on their native soil.

The first printing press, introduced at Cambridge, Massachusetts, was in operation early in 1639. In 1656 Samuel Green printed there, for Hezekiah Usher in Boston, what is probably the first book for children to be printed in North America, an edition of *Spiritual Milk for Boston Babes in either England . . .*, by John Cotton (1585–1652), a

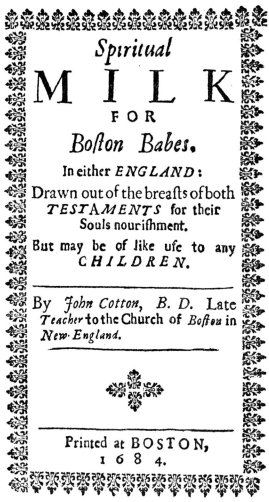

Spiritual
MILK
FOR
Bofton Babes.
In either *ENGLAND* :
Drawn out of the breafts of both
TESTAMENTS for their
Souls nourifhment.
But may be of like ufe to any
CHILDREN.

By *John Cotton,* B. D. Late
Teacher to the Church of *Bofton* in
New-England.

Printed at BOSTON,
1 6 8 4.

25. *A later edition of the first children's book to be printed in North America in 1656*

minister who had come from Boston in Lincolnshire. It was chiefly concerned with indoctrinating the child with theological knowledge in the question and answer form of the catechism.[1] After 1674 printing in New England became centred at Boston, for long a flourishing centre of the book trade, but closely followed towards the end of the century by Philadelphia and New York.

The most favoured and ubiquitous work for American children in these early days, and for many generations, known among its readers as 'the little Bible', was *The New England Primer.* Probably first published at Boston sometime between 1685 and 1690, its publisher

[1] Evans 42 (Bibl. 292). It was first issued in London in 1646 as *Milk for Babes.* See also Bibl. 299.

and very likely its compiler was Benjamin Harris. It may have been inspired by a work he had already issued in London in 1679, *The Protestant Tutor*, which was as much a piece of anti-Catholic propaganda as a work for youth. The main link between the two works is that they both both contained the verses ascribed to John Rogers (actually by Robert Smith), entitled *The Exhortation that a Father gave to his Children, which he wrote a few Days before his Burning*, the farewell message of a Protestant martyr, first published in 1559.[1] *The New England Primer* was intended to be a means of instruction in reading as well as a gateway to holy living and salvation. In its hundred and fifty years of life its religious purpose was always dominant, although its contents and theological emphasis varied in the many succeeding editions. Permanent features were the ABC and syllabary, admonitory rhyming alphabets often with scriptural message, and woodcuts. Calvinistic tenets and religious teaching became more marked in the middle of the eighteenth century, evidently the result of the efforts by conservative theologians to stem the rising tide of liberalism by the 'Great Awakening' evangelical revival then taking place in America.

For example, in an edition of 1762 the Deluge that drown'd takes the place of the Dog that will bite and the prophet Elijah fed by ravens the Eagle's flight in the rhyming alphabet. Other contents over the years include the Lord's Prayer, the Ten Commandments, verses by Isaac Watts, *Spiritual Milk for Babes*, and *The Shorter Catechism of the Westminster Divines*. An account of the *Primer* is given by Cornelia Meigs in *A Critical History of Children's Literature* (Bibl. 15), where it is described as 'perhaps the first work of American literature to be current abroad, for Puritan children in England and Scotland were set to read it'. The earliest extant copy of this little mirror of American attitudes to youth, learning and religion is an edition of 1727 now in the New York Public Library.

Other primers were made for children in America, but none rivalled this first publication. In 1753 came *The Royal Primer Improved*, issued by J. Chattin in Philadelphia, founding this on Newbery's *Royal Primer* of 1751, with some deviation from the original.[2] John Woolman, the Quaker, also produced *A First Book for Children* in Philadelphia in 1766.[3] But the *New England Primer* outlived them all.

The earliest narrative book to be published in America for boys and girls was the already popular importation, *A Token for Children*, by James Janeway (p. 26). This was printed in Boston in 1700, and to the two parts of Janeway's histories of thirteen model

[1] Sloane 2 (Bibl. 74). The verses were also in Foxe's *Book of Martyrs*.
For *The New England Primer* see Sloane 163, Evans, 494, 573 also Bibl. 299.

[2] Rosenbach 40 (Bibl. 296).

[3] Meigs. p. 117 (Bibl. 15).

In *Adam's* Fall
We Sinned all.

Thy Life to Mend
This *Book* Attend.

The *Cat* doth play
And after flay.

A *Dog* will bite
A Thief at night.

An *Eagles* flight
Is out of sight.

The Idle *Fool*
Is whipt at School.

26. Alphabet verses from the earliest surviving copy of the NEW ENGLAND PRIMER *(1727)*

English children and their early and pious deaths, was added *A Token for the Children of New England; or some Examples of Children in whom the Fear of God was remarkably budding before they dyed: in several parts of New England* . . .[1] The anonymous author was the renowned divine and writer, Cotton Mather (1662–1728), grandson of John Cotton. In similar vein to Janeway he chronicled the lives and deaths of seven children he had known, taking one or two examples from works already published. In 1690 he had included in his *Addresses to old Men, and Young Men, and little Children* a section 'The Little Child's Lesson; or a Child wise unto Salvation. A Discourse instructing and inviting little children to the exercises of early piety'. Here he refers to Janeway's book, and gives the history of an uncle, and of Ann Greenough, who appears again in the *Token*.[2] The

[1] Welch 607.1 (Bibl. 298).

[2] Sloane. 203 (Bibl. 74).

books Mather addressed to youth are typical of their place and period, and indicate that there was more uncompromising and God-centred teaching in the books fashioned for the new colonies of the north than in England.

Reprintings or amended versions of English books for children formed the main substance of children's books printed in America for many years. Piracy was a common practice in these days before international copyright, and this may have discouraged American writers. But the book trade thrived, especially after the Revolution, and the number of original works for youth increased. Something of their history (as well as details of many English children's books printed in America) can be traced in the valuable record made by the late Dr. d'Alté A. Welch in his *Bibliography of American Children's Books printed prior to 1821* (Bibl. 298), also most useful for information concerning English editions from which American versions were taken.

The earliest known 'non-Biblical child's book in America' according to Dr. Welch is *A New Gift for Children* (1756?), printed by D. Fowle of Boston. It contained 'delightful and entertaining stories for little Masters and Misses' and was evidently founded on an English original also used by John Marshall for *The Careful Parent's Gift* published in London around 1787.[1] It marks the beginning of a new era and the lifting of the ban on fiction and secular reading for youth under the influence of the genial spirit of the age of reason which in England produced John Newbery. A little later in 1767, Mein and Fleeming in Boston printed two tales of a more fanciful kind, *The Story of the cruel Giant Barbarico* (from *The Governess*, by Sarah Fielding), and *The Adventures of Urad*, from *Tales of the Genii*, by James Ridley.[2]

In 1768 the same firm issued an American edition of John Newbery's famous story-book, *The Renowned History of Giles Gingerbread*, only four years after its publication in in London.[3] But children had not had to wait so long for their introduction to Newbery's pleasing little books. Benjamin Franklin in Philadelphia had imported some of them in the 1750s, and a decade later Hugh Gaine was selling Newbery volumes regularly at his 'Bible and Crown' bookshop in New York. In 1775 Gaine produced the first American edition of the most famous of all the Newbery books – *The History of Little Goody Two-shoes*.[4] The same year he brought out in shortened form that work most appealing to youth – *Robinson Crusoe*.[5]

---

[1] Welch. 848a. 848.1. The ten stories were expanded to fifteen in a second edition in 1762.

[2] Welch. 381 and 1002.

[3] Welch. 417.1

[4] Welch. 427.1

[5] Welch. 260.1

These pioneer activities, among others, were only a prelude to much greater achievement, the publishing enterprise of that famous American in the trade, Isaiah Thomas (1749–1831). In 1775, because of political troubles, he moved his press from Boston, where he had supported the rebel cause, to Worcester, Massachusetts. After the storms of the Revolution subsided in the 1780s and the new American nation was born, Thomas had a flourishing printing, publishing and bookselling business, and in 1785 he began his important work of publishing books for children. Newbery was his chief inspiration, and the American purloined many of his little publications, copying their gay and small format as well as their contents. He began his numerous series for young readers in 1785 with *The Beauty and the Monster*, a version of the old fairy tale taken from a comedy by Madame de Genlis in her *Théâtre d'Éducation*, and perhaps the same year an edition of *Mother Goose's Melody*, which only survives (except in fragmentary form) in a second edition of 1794.[1] In 1786 came the first Worcester editions of the many Newbery titles. Two of the earliest were *Nurse True-love's New Year's Gift*, and that less engaging collection of jests compiled by 'Tommy Trapwit', *Be Merry and Wise*.[2] The next year was more prolific. Among Thomas's Newbery items were two of the English publisher's most famous publications, *A Little Pretty Pocket-Book*, his earliest venture in 1744, and the second American edition of *The History of Little Goody Two-shoes*.[3]

Not all Isaiah Thomas publications for boys and girls were Newbery books, although these were his speciality. For example in 1788 he printed the first American edition of *A Curious Hieroglyphic Bible*, invented for the improvement and diversion of English children in 1783 (p. 23), and he also had the good sense to issue the little nursery rhyme book published by Mary Cooper in 1744 – *Tommy Thumb's Song-Book* (p. 46).[4] Isaiah Thomas, however, was more than a printer who traded in children's books. 'He spread his products over the entire nation, catered to every taste and established himself in every field of printing', wrote Clifford K. Shipton in his biography (Bibl. 301). But today, like Newbery, who was also active in many branches of publishing, he is best remembered for the many attractive little volumes he made for children, nearly all founded on importations from England, and diffusing Newbery friendliness and good humour for the delight of the young citizens of the new republic. Pages in his account book listing his stock of printing materials in 1796 show that he held cuts for over fifty children's

---

[1] Welch. 399, 825.1, 825.2. For John Newbery see Chapter 2, ii.

[2] Welch. 866.1, 1178.1

[3] Welch. 717.2, 427.4

[4] Welch. 468, 737.2

books he had printed or published.[1] By then his activity was declining, although his son carried on the business. Most of his initial publishing for youth was completed by 1790.

Sometimes Thomas amended his texts a little to make them more suitable for small readers accustomed to American ways, referring to Governors rather than to Monarchs or Lord Mayors, but on the whole he changed Newbery's pages very little. In one instance he certainly increased the admonitory flavour of the original by adding to *A Little Pretty Pocket-Book* a hundred and sixty-three 'Rules for Behaviour in Children'. These maxims cover many aspects of the child's life, beginning with 'At the Meeting House', and they were apparently taken from a very popular courtesy book circulating in eighteenth century America, *The School of Good Manners*. This was first published in London in 1685, but was amended by a schoolmaster in Boston, Eleazer Moodey, to suit young colonists.[2] Etiquette and social behaviour are as important as morality in these rules. 'Approach not thy parents at no time without a bow' is one precept indicating that discipline in the home was as much a part of American family life as it was in Georgian England. Newbery preferred in his books to intersperse any such moral advice and maxims with more amusing fare.

Amusement allied to instruction might now be advancing rapidly in reading matter provided for boys and girls, but this did not mean that the importance of religion was forgotten. It received fresh impetus with the evangelical revival in America as it did in Britain. The *New England Primer* still sold in its thousands, and Thomas himself issued several religious books for youth, including those favourite works of piety, *The History of the Holy Jesus* and the *Divine Songs* of Isaac Watts, both already published in American editions.[3] At the end of the eighteenth century tracts and Sunday School literature from England also began to invade America, and to encourage similar products there.

The first Sunday Schools were established in America in 1791, Tract Societies from 1803. At first literature circulated was mainly of British origin, but soon home publication became the aim of the larger Sunday School Unions and Tract Societies. Many of the 'Cheap Repository Tracts' (pp. 61–2) were reprinted in American editions from about 1800 onwards, but later tracts of American composition more suitable for their readers' needs were issued by the larger Tract Societies. Sunday School literature was also prolific in the early nineteenth century. By 1830, six years after its foundation, the American Sunday School Union had circulated through its Committee on publications over six million copies of works. Two early popular items were *Little Henry and his Bearer*

---

[1] Reproduced in Shipton (Bibl. 301).

[2] Rosenbach. 41 etc. (Bibl. 296). Welch. 794.1

[3] Welch. 532, 1240.1

(p. 63), and Legh Richmond's best-selling tract, *The Dairyman's Daughter*, first published in England in 1809.[1]

The American Tract Society was formed in 1825 by an amalgamation of the two largest societies, those of New York and New England. Many of the first tracts issued were reprints of those already circulated by the New England Tract Society, which had seventy-five children's tracts when the merger took place. The literature produced was didactic and uninspiring, but an attempt was made to compete with the chapbooks and other secular wares by imitating the format used by Isaiah Thomas and other publishers especially by using cuts and decorative borders. In 1834 more ambitious works for youth were projected 'by authors of some reputation and experience'. Jacob Abbott's offer of three of his books was accepted by the Society – *The Young Christian* (first published in 1832), and two books written in collaboration with his brother, John S. C. Abbott, *The Child at Home* and *The Mother at Home*. Another writer, Thomas Hopkins Gallaudet, provided seven volumes of scripture biography from 1835 to 1843, beginning with *The History of Joseph*. Other series of books followed. By 1850 there were 207 tracts and 69 other volumes being issued by the Society, fiction now being admitted if it preached the correct morality within the confines of a narrow religious outlook. This purpose to indoctrinate completely overshadowed the need for true literary quality and imaginative understanding to promote religion. Like their English counterparts, these tracts and Sunday School books were fabrications for a purpose, fulfilling an immediate need, but lacking enduring life.

Instruction was conveyed in more secular and less proselytising style in the long series of books by 'Peter Parley', the pen-name of Samuel G. Goodrich (1795–1866), whose widespread and popular productions started in the 1820s (p. 98). Goodrich's fellow New Englander, Jacob Abbott (1803–1879), was soon to rival him in his success. Religion influenced Abbott's writings, but it was not sectarian or evangelical in spirit. His contributions to Tract Society literature have already been mentioned, and he became an even more prolific writer than Peter Parley with a total of 180 volumes to his credit at the end of his life. Religion was no all absorbing interest, although never far away from his thinking. He was deeply interested in science, mathematics, education and other subjects, and after teaching at college and being head of a girls' school in Boston, he devoted himself to the ministry and to writing for youth. His earliest work was *The Little Philosopher; or, The Infant School at Home* (1830). In 1834, the same year as the Tract Society issued his already popular *Young Christian* came the inception of his very successful Rollo series. Early volumes describe a scheme for the learning and amusement of Rollo as a young child, but later on when a little older he goes with his uncle on various travels abroad,

[1] Rice, E. W. *The Sunday-School Movement and the American Sunday School Union.* (Bibl. 116).

and explores other subjects especially those concerned with making and doing and scientific experiment. These are cheerful and matter-of-fact little books gaining interest by featuring a small boy at the centre of events and information, and they reveal Abbott's sympathy and understanding for the young, though they lack power and vision. His best work is to be found in the ten volumes of *Franconia* stories (1850–1854), where he describes in a natural and convincing way the activities of a group of young people in a simple rural community. Some of their experiences were founded on his boyhood memories in Maine, and it seems that he put something of himself into the character of the boy Phonny, impulsive, likeable, and often finding himself in difficulties. These tales point to the future and the achievements to come in the American story for children about everyday adventure and family life.

The first truly creative spark of imagination in children's literature in America is to be found in a book written for adults – a not uncommon event in the history of books for young people. Washington Irving (1783–1859) was the first American man of letters – James Fenimore Cooper closely following – to gain international repute. An entertaining writer, who pleased English readers as much as his own countrymen, Irving was a native of New York, and interested in American history. He travelled much in Europe, and on a second visit, when he met Sir Walter Scott, he set down impressions in a series of essays published from 1819–1820 as *The Sketch Book of Geoffrey Crayon*. Most of them deal with British life and traditions, but several relate to America, including two legendary stories of the Dutch-settled district of the Catskill Mountains and the Hudson River. Both these tales now rank as children's classics, especially *Rip Van Winkle*. Irving founded this on a German original, but gave it a new setting, telling of the experiences of a Dutchman who meets strange beings on the mountains, and falls into an enchanted sleep, seemingly for a night, but in reality for twenty years. The second narrative, *The Legend of Sleepy Hollow*, is a ghost story about a headless rider, with a hint of rational explanation at its close. Both narratives are enhanced by their style and setting and vividly recreate old traditional ways of life in a little known region.

Irving's duties took him later to Spain, and among the riches of Spanish history and romance he introduced to English-speaking readers were the Moorish legends he presented in *The Alhambra* (1832). Part folklore, part invention, these stories of the Moors in Spain have from time to time been published in editions for children, but they are not so well-known abroad as Irving's two famous American stories.

The New World made its real invasion into Europe with the 'Leatherstocking' romances of James Fenimore Cooper (1789–1851) (p. 159). A conventional view of the simple sublimity of the Indian had been presented by Irving in one of his *Sketch Book* essays, but Cooper was to have a powerful impact with his dramatic and romantic novels about the American wilderness. They had a wide influence abroad, and from the time his first tale, *The Pioneers*, appeared in 1823, there opened up before young minds exciting vistas of wild forests and prairies inhabited by a fascinating and unfamiliar race. Cooper's romances were to inspire, at home and abroad, a long line of sensational some-times meretricious tales featuring braves and pale-faces. The best writers of American tales of adventure for boys, soon to develop, were not always those best-known abroad, and one of the lesser but more popular writers of adventure stories of frontier and forest to have a following in Britain was Edward S. Ellis (1840–1916), a 'dime novelist' who used several pen-names. His stories began to appear in the 1860s, and his 'Deerfoot' series was still delighting boys in urban England in the days between the wars.

A more romantic and literary concept of the redskin became familiar to children on the publication of *Hiawatha* in 1855. Henry Wadsworth Longfellow (1807–1882) has been criticised in this modern age as a poet with the weaknesses of the over-refined 'Brahmin' literary coterie of New England. But he has also been termed 'the children's poet, 'and his ballads and narrative poems have in the past been much to the taste of young people. His long narrative poem, *Hiawatha*, was inspired by various accounts of Red Indian history and customs, but it also seems to owe something to the great Finnish epic, *The Kalevala*, for Longfellow used its metre, and looked back to an idealised Indian past in a similar legendary spirit. His poem has been much parodied, but it is filled with scenes of vivid appeal for young readers, many of whom have come to know it through retellings rather than in its original verse. The genuine lore and legends of the Indian races were not to be edited or retold for children until the 1920s.

The negro in America and elsewhere had also begun to appear in books for children. A popular tale of unknown authorship – *The Adventures of Congo in search of his Master* – was advertised in a Boston edition in 1818[1], and published in London in 1823. Said to be based on fact it tells of a slave's effort to find a benevolent master after a shipwreck. Slavery, especially in British territories, had already been attacked in various publications for youth, notably by Mrs. Barbauld and her brother John Aikin, and there was at least one tract on the subject, *The Sorrows of Yamba*, by Hannah More. How far the negro was introduced into early American books for children the writer does not know. But the abolitionist message and the plight of the slaves soon were to break upon the world like a thunder-flash in an American novel of intense power. Harriet Beecher Stowe (1811–1896) had no idea of addressing *Uncle Tom's Cabin* (1852) to youth, yet it has become annexed to children's literature especially in Europe. She intended it for men and women everywhere, and whatever bitter feelings it aroused in a divided nation, its impact abroad was tremen-dous. After the fires of controversy had died down and the end of the Civil War brought freedom to the negroes, it continued to be read, mainly by children. Young readers who

[1] Welch 6a.

235

knew nothing of America found in it an unfamiliar and fascinating difference. They could feel deeply with the negro characters, the simple, pious Uncle Tom, the desperate Eliza who escapes over the ice-floes with her child, the mischievous young limb Topsy. Mrs. Stowe's book has been criticised as giving an unrealistic picture of the negro, but children find its excitements and strong contrasts spellbinding.

Unlike the equally famous *Uncle Remus* plantation stories, by Joel Chandler Harris (p. 122), *Uncle Tom's Cabin* cannot be regarded as part of the main stream of American literature for children. It points the way, however, to what was to be the outstanding contribution of the American genius to books for youth – the creation of fiction about everyday life full of vitality and sympathetic understanding of the nature of young people and their elders.

It is perhaps little-known outside America that Mrs. Stowe wrote tales for children and older girls, of much less intensity than her famous novel about slavery. One of them which came out in a London edition was *Little Pussy Willow* (1871), where a simple country heroine is contrasted with a sophisticated young lady from the city. This type of domestic story for girls had already begun twenty years earlier. At first it was much concerned with religion and pathetic sentiment, and heroines were pious and earnest, like Ellen Montgomery in *The Wide, Wide World* (1850), one of the earliest and most popular tales of its kind, and the first of many by Susan Warner (1819–1885), who wrote under the name of 'Elizabeth Wetherell' (p. 145). Almost as famous was *The Lamplighter* (1854), by Maria Susannah Cummins (1827–1866), a tale set in Boston about an orphan girl from her childhood as a destitute waif to her rise in the world and her perfection in virtue.

In the 1860s a new kind of family story for girls came into being. The trend towards the creation of more natural young characters is visible in the New England tales for girls by Mrs. A. F. Whitney, but all forerunners were to be eclipsed when the March sisters arrived – four of the most convincing young people in fiction. Meg, Jo, Beth, and Amy March belong to a real home circle, and they are depicted as real beings with foibles, weaknesses, joys, heartaches, affections, and other human qualities. Louisa M. Alcott (1832–1888) brought the best qualities of an enlightened New England background and 'freedom from the trammels of schools and sects' to the writing of *Little Women* (1868) (p. 146). This first-rate story has never been surpassed in its own field, and has been enjoyed by generations of girls all over the world. The sequel, *Good Wives* (*Little Women, part 2*) (1869), has been almost as great a favourite, but Louisa Alcott's many later stories about family life, which avoided the pitfall of long series about the same characters, never reached the standard of these two classics.

Jo March, the endearing and lively heroine of the March family stories, has something of the tomboy in her make-up. From henceforward a more robust and less introspective type of heroine was to invade American books for girls, the rebellious harum-scarum who may climb trees and get into scrapes, but who never behaves in mean or vulgar fashion, however much she may flout the proprieties revered by her more sedate predecessors. Katy, eldest of the Carr children, is an example. She hated sewing, and cared little for being thought 'good'. Her adventures, begun in *What Katy Did* (1872), by Susan Coolidge (Sarah Chauncey Woolsey, 1845–1905), both entertained her compatriots and the girls in the more confined circles of Victorian England. In *What Katy did at School* (1873) readers were to have a pioneer school tale looking to the future. Another attractive heroine of mischievous and rompish nature began her series of exploits in *Gypsy Breynton* by Mrs. Elizabeth Stuart Phelps Ward (1844–1911) in 1866. Long series of books featuring a young heroine from childhood through marriage and sometimes to days as a grandmother were to the taste of the period, but vitality was often lacking. One of the most popular sequences was that featuring 'Elsie' – termed by some critics a tiresome prig. Martha Finley (1828–1909) began the many volumes with *Elsie Dinsmore* in 1867.

Such American tales had much popularity and influence in Britain. One of the most famous writers with a transatlantic following was Mrs. Frances Hodgson Burnett (1849–1924) (p. 150). She wrote domestic stories of rather wider scope, but perhaps appealing more to girls than boys. The world-renowned *Little Lord Fauntleroy* (1886) delighted many types of readers, young and old, but Mrs. Burnett's other books have perhaps a less universal attraction. Her *Secret Garden* (1911), an English tale set in Yorkshire, is a little masterpiece. Mrs. Burnett is English as much as American, but another writer at the turn of the century, Kate Douglas Wiggin (1856–1923), was to continue the American achievement in creating books for girls with a genuine American background. A favourite not yet forgotten is her *Rebecca of Sunnybrook Farm* (1903).

Excellence in the writing of stories based on everyday life was not to be confined in America to books intended for girls. Family stories for younger children were in existence in the sixties with the first series of tales by 'Sophie May' (Rebecca S. Clarke, 1833–1906), and the realistic novel for boys was soon to find distinction with the publication of a minor classic in 1869 – *The Story of a Bad Boy*. Thomas Bailey Aldrich (1836–1907), seven years before the advent of *Tom Sawyer*, drew upon memories of his childhood at Portsmouth, New Hampshire, to create a story about 'a natural, actual boy engaged in the natural, actual escapades of boyhood'. William Dean Howells greeted it enthusiastically as 'a new thing . . . in American literature'.[1] It is still much praised in its own country but little known abroad, unlike the world-famous books in similar vein by Mark Twain. Samuel Langhorne Clemens (1835–1910), using this well-known pseudonym, featured the less familiar region and more vigorous idiom of the Mississippi and the Middle West in *The Adventures of Tom Sawyer* (1876) and *The Adventures of Huckleberry Finn* (1884)

[1] Darling. *The Rise of Children's Book Reviewing in America, 1865–1881*. p. 31 (Bibl. 168).

(p. 170). He introduced a new kind of realism and humour into these books for boys, and they remain outstanding classics, especially *Huckleberry Finn*, a universal novel on the theme of escape from civilisation as much as an adventure for youth.

The American book trade expanded rapidly in the middle of the nineteenth century, and as more and more indigenous writers of ability turned to the creation of books for children, the flow of publications between Britain and America became increasingly an affair of mutual exchange. Fortunate indeed was this for English-speaking children everywhere, for they could enjoy a much wider range of good literature than either country could produce by itself. So the close relationship between the old and new nations entered a more rewarding phase in the expansive era now dawning for them both.

Fantasy, a theme less congenial to the temper of American letters than real life, was a popular importation from Britain. A famous example is *Alice's Adventures in Wonderland*, for which the firm of Appleton secured the withdrawn copies of the first English edition of 1865, and issued them in the United States the following year. Yet widely popular as magic and fairy lore from abroad proved to be, there was not entirely a dearth of home invention. Nathaniel Hawthorne in the early fifties had retold twelve of the Greek myths in an imaginative way in *A Wonder Book* (1851) and *Tanglewood Tales* (1853) (p. 112). Soon afterwards came a fanciful, rather sad tale about a good giant and his wife discovered on an island – *The Last of the Huggermuggers* (1855). The author-illustrator was Christopher Pearse Cranch (1813–1892), one of the New England transcendentalists who lived much in Europe. He followed the story with a sequel – *Kobboltozo* (1856) – about an evil dwarf concerned in the giant's fate. Other American writers were to write tales of wonder and magic, notably Frank R. Stockton (1834–1902), but few became well-known abroad. Howard Pyle is the greatest American writer for children to recreate the realm of faery and romance, and his work is described below. A book which has won much fame at home and abroad, more so than it deserves and largely through its stage and screen presentations, is *The Wonderful Wizard of Oz* (1900), by L. Frank Baum (1856–1919), the first of a number of stories about a strange land, where he sought to produce a new kind of wonder tale omitting 'disagreeable incident'.

The advance of publishing for children in the United States and the increase in books of quality led to a wider interest in their criticism and selection. Reference (p. 103) has already been made to the survey by Dr. Richard L. Darling, *The Rise of Children's Book Reviewing in America, 1865–1881* (Bibl. 168). Dr. Darling outlines the part played by criticism and reviews in a significant and productive period, and analyses and quotes from many reviews of children's books in thirty-six leading literary and other periodicals examined for the purpose. He also gives some interesting information about the growth of juvenile publishing in America, and he illustrates the development of serious criticism of children's books by an examination of four contributions made between 1865 and 1879. They comprise an article by Samuel Osgood, 'Books for our Children', published in *The Atlantic Monthly* for December 1865, a series of articles 'The Literature of our Sunday Schools', by a Presbyterian minister, George R. Bacon, in *Hours at Home* (February to April, 1870), the lists and comments issued by the Unitarian Ladies' Commission on Sunday School books from 1867 to 1873, and the papers presented on the subject of children's books at the Boston Conference of the American Library Association in 1879.

Writers on the history of American literature for children are unanimous in their recognition of the important role played by the best periodicals for children in disseminating and encouraging first-rate reading material. Two outstanding figures involved are Horace E. Scudder (1838–1902), critic, editor, and writer of the 'Bodley' books, a series of travelogue tales for young people, and Mary Mapes Dodge (1831–1905), famous as the author of *Hans Brinker* (p. 162). In 1867 Scudder launched the excellent though short-lived *Riverside Magazine for the Young*, publishing in it stories by Andersen, Frank R. Stockton, and other notable writers. In his column 'Books for Young People' he set down regular comments on books, old and new, interpreting books for children not as those expressly written for them, but those 'worth giving to a child'. Mary Mapes Dodge was to produce perhaps the finest magazine ever issued for children in *St. Nicholas*, which started in November 1873. Her editorial aims combined the practical and useful with high ideals. She expressed them clearly and kept to them steadily, so that *St. Nicholas* offered its readers varied and excellent fare in many fields, both fictional and factual. Many enduring classics first appeared in its pages, and other entertaining stories, fulfilling the promise she made in the first number that 'the ideal child's magazine is pleasure ground'. Alice M. Jordan has declared that within the bound volumes of this much-loved monthly 'lies the very kernel of American books for children.'[1]

Preceding these two outstanding journals, *The Riverside Magazine* with four years of life, and *St. Nicholas* which survived up to the 1940s, there had been other American periodicals for youth, going back to the 1820s. One of the first to mark the mid-century breakaway from didacticism (however disguised) was *Our Young Folks*, a junior venture of the *Atlantic Monthly* started in 1865. There was an editorial board of three – John T. Trowbridge, Gail Hamilton, and Lucy Larcom. Famous serials printed include *The Story of a Bad Boy* in 1869, and *A Holiday Romance*, by Charles Dickens in 1868. A very popular series by Trowbridge, beginning with *Jack Hazard and his Fortunes*, also first appeared in this magazine. The author drew on his boyhood knowledge of the country of the Erie Canal for these out-of-the-common adventure tales with a genuine American

[1] *Good old St. Nicholas...* in *From Rollo to Tom Sawyer* (Bibl. 293). see also p. 222.

background. *Our Young Folks* came to an end after nine years when ownership passed to Scribners of New York, the publishers of *St. Nicholas*.

By the 1880s children's literature in America had achieved true distinction, and both imaginative works and books of information had widened in range as impressively as in Britain. This decade, however, was to bring forth a yet richer flowering of art and creative power, as there arose a new interest in the past and the lore and legend of Europe. James Baldwin (1841–1925) explored the realm of saga for *The Story of Siegfried* (1882) and *The Story of Roland* (1883), putting these ancient hero tales into an attractive form for young readers. Sidney Lanier (1842–1881) interpreted medieval romance with equal skill, shaping Malory faithfully into a simpler text in *The Boy's King Arthur* (1880), and giving new life to the ancient bardic tales of Wales in *The Boy's Mabinogion* (*Knightly Legends of Wales*) (1881). But the peak of American attainment in the recreation of legend and the world of the fabulous in books for youth was to be reached in the books written and illustrated by Howard Pyle (1853–1911).

Since the 1840s children's book illustration had developed steadily, very much through the medium of the best children's magazines in the latter part of the century. Pyle's contemporary, Reginald Birch (1856–1943) became well-known abroad for the characteristic drawings he made for *Little Lord Fauntleroy*, and he was only one of a number of American artists enhancing the attraction of books for children. Among them was A. B. Frost (1851–1928), whose subtle and sympathetic pictures for the *Uncle Remus* stories, from 1892, have become part of the life of Brer Rabbit and his fellow creatures. But no American illustrator reached the status or wielded the influence of Howard Pyle.

Pyle had contributed some fables to *St. Nicholas* from 1877 with illustrations marked by vigour and individuality. Although he illustrated the work of others, including Baldwin's *Story of Siegfried* in 1882, he devoted most of his career to the twofold art of illustrating his own writings. 'Howard Pyle was to become more than a great illustrator', wrote Robert Lawson. 'He was to become an American institution . . .'[1] Both in his writing and in his pictures he brought new splendour and creative power into the realms of history, fairy-land, and romance. Long versed in folk literature he used both traditional themes and original material in his stories and retellings, decorating them with faithful and detailed drawings. Both the attitude of the Pre-Raphaelites in their search for truth and the nervous realism of Dürer inspired his art. His love for the Middle Ages is woven into his books, above all expressed in that romance of a blithe and sunlit Sherwood, *The Merry Adventures of Robin Hood* (1883) (p. 19), regarded in America as his finest work. More poetic and diffusive were the four volumes founded on the cycle of King Arthur romances, beginning in 1903 with *The Story of King Arthur and his Knights*, the last being issued in 1910. Pyle

---

[1] Mahony and others. *Illustrators of Children's Books* p. 105 (Bibl. 14).

Queen Morgana loses Excalibur his sheath:

27. *Illustration by Howard Pyle for* THE STORY OF KING ARTHUR (*1903*)

also brought new renown to the craft of historical fiction for youth with two original tales set in the later Middle Ages, *Otto of the Silver Hand* (1888), a tale of the Germany of the robber Barons, and *Men of Iron* (1892), an adventure of fifteenth century England. In Britain the most popular of his works have been his volumes of fairy tales, *Pepper and Salt* (1886), and *The Wonder Clock* (1888), where he sought to revive 'queer forgotten things laid away in time's attic'. Both these works were based on stories and drawings first published in *Harper's Young People*, another magazine of quality for children.

A great craftsman, a romantic who expressed his idealism in a robust style, Howard Pyle is not merely the greatest American author-illustrator. He is a pioneer of international importance in the history of children's books, and his work crowns a century of great development in his own country. It also heralds a new era ahead of richness and diversity in the making of books for children not only in the United States but throughout the world.

CANADA

The earliest books to be printed for children in Canada were primers, catechisms and alphabets, mainly for the French settlers' children. After British ascendancy books for English-speaking children consisted largely of importations from England, and a Canadian literature for children did not develop until the middle and later years of the nineteenth century. It was foreshadowed by a book written by a Canadian immigrant before she left Britain, Mrs. Catherine Parr Traill (1802–1899)—*The Young Emigrants; or, Pictures of Canada* . . . This was published in England by Harvey and Darton in 1826, and founded by the author upon information sent to her by an emigrant family. Mrs. Traill, a member of the famous Strickland family, went to Canada in 1832, but did not produce her first book there for children for another twenty years. This was a tale about three young people lost in the wilderness of Ontario entitled *Canadian Crusoes* (1852), and it was re-issued later as *Lost in the Backwoods*. Her later Canadian books for boys and girls did not reach the standard of this first realistic Crusoe tale by a Canadian writer for youth.

Books by British writers with first-hand knowledge of the country, notably by Frederick Marryat, who had written *Settlers in Canada* in 1844 (p. 161), and by R. M. Ballantyne (p. 163), had introduced Canadian scenes into tales of adventure, preceding the genuine product by native authors. One of the earliest series of Canadian adventure stories for boys was written by James de Mille (1833–1880), beginning with *B.O.W.C.* (*Brethren of the White Cross*) in 1869. The sentimental tale for girls popular in Britain and America materialised a little later in Canada, and the outstanding example is *Anne of Green Gables*, by L. M. Montgomery (1874–1942), published in 1908, and very soon a great success abroad. Set in Prince Edward Island this story about an attractive red-head has a distinct charm, but the many later volumes about Anne's experiences never equalled it. In the words of Sheila Egoff they show an increasing 'sentimental dishonesty'.

The greatest Canadian contribution to literature for the young has undoubtedly been the creation of the naturalistic animal story based on real knowledge of the wild, and already described at the end of the chapter about the animal story (p. 188). At first by Ernest Thompson Seton (1860–1946), and quickly followed by his contemporary, Sir Charles D. G. Roberts (1880–1943), with his *Kindred of the Wild* in 1902, the stories heralded a new type of tale founded on objective and sympathetic understanding of animals in their native habitat. A well-known contribution from Canada to the more emotional type of story, in the tradition of *Black Beauty*, is to be found in *Beautiful Joe* (1894), a popular dog story, by Margaret Marshall Saunders.

Sheila Egoff in her critical survey of Canadian children's literature, *The Republic of Childhood* (Bibl. 302), points out that Canadian writing for children has concentrated on the outdoor adventure story or the historical romance. Fantasy was for long an unexplored realm, although books of this kind from Britain had a wide popularity. The picture-book and illustrated book were also slow to develop. An interesting early example, which remained as a pen-and-ink manuscript until first printed in 1966, is *An Illustrated Comic Alphabet* (1859), done for her pupils in Canada by an Englishwoman, Amelia Frances Howard-Gibbon. This is a typical Victorian treatment of the old rhyme beginning 'A was an Archer and shot at a frog', and there is little Canadian influence to be found in it. The original is now in the Toronto 'Osborne Collection of Early Children's Books' (Bibl. 46).

II AUSTRALIA

The first children's book to be published in Australia was a series of evening conversations between a lady and her four children in typically Victorian style entitled *A Mother's Offering to her Children: by a Lady long resident in New South Wales*, published by the Sydney Gazette in 1841. Authorship was ascribed to Lady J. J. Gordon Bremer, but according to Marcie Muir in her *Bibliography of Australian Children's Books* (Bibl. 304) this is now considered doubtful.

Books for children about Australia go back to the earliest retellings for youth of the *Voyages of Captain Cook* published around 1800, but a truly native literature for children produced by Australian writers was not to be developed until the second half of the nineteenth century. English writers were to set adventure stories in this little-known continent, sometimes without much knowledge of its realities, sometimes concentrating too much on unusual or exotic features of the Australian scene. One of the best early accounts by an English visitor was *A Boy's Adventures in the Wilds of Australia* (1854), by William Howitt (p. 143). Rosemary Wighton in her account of early Australian literature for children (Bibl. 305) considers that one of the more faithful presentations of the country in an English adventure tale for boys, especially for its treatment of the aborigine, is *The Dingo Boys* (1892), by G. Manville Fenn.

In the later nineteenth century books for children by Australian writers began to appear regularly, but few became known abroad until the first of the family stories by Ethel Turner (Mrs. H. R. Curlewis, 1872–1958), *Seven Little Australians*, was published in Melbourne and London in 1894. 'It was Ethel Turner', writes Rosemary Wighton, 'from 1894 onwards who gathered together the existing picture of the freedom and pathos of the motherless Australian child, and popularised them for Australian readers as well as English ones . . .'[1] Motherless families were Ethel Turner's favourite theme, and *Seven Little Australians*, which pictures a genuine background of life in and around Sydney, was followed by other popular if sentimental tales featuring orphans or stepchildren. These stories delighted English boys and girls, as well as those at home, and the first of them still survives at the time of writing. Equally popular a little later on were the Billabong series by Mary Grant Bruce, beginning with *A Little Bush Maid* in 1910. Not so well-known were the schoolgirl stories by Louise Mack, whose *Teens* was issued in Sydney in 1897. The greatest Australian achievement in this field, however, though scarcely to be classed as a book for children, is that female counterpart of *Stalky and Co., The Getting of Wisdom* (1910), by Henry Handel Richardson (Ethel Florence Robertson, born Richardson, 1870–1946). This is a powerful and satirical account of a self-centred and unpleasant child, Laura, at a superior school for girls, and was founded on the author's experiences at a school in Melbourne.

Legendary stories and tales of the aborigines for children go back at least to 1891, when Mary Anne Fitzgerald produced *King Bungaree's Pyalla and Stories illustrative of Manners and Customs that prevailed among Australian Aborigines*, a Sydney publication. In 1896 came *Australian Legendary Tales*, by Kate L. Parker, with an introduction by Andrew Lang, and another example in this decade is *Australian Fairy Tales* (1897), by Atha Westbury. Original works of fantasy were rare so far in this fast-developing country, but the twentieth century was to show Australian aptitude for the magical and nonsensical in an outstanding and enduring contribution by Norman Lindsay – *The Magic Pudding* – first published in Sydney in 1918. By that date a vigorous and distinctive national literature for young readers in Australia was coming into being founded on the sturdy if meagre beginnings in the old days of Empire.

---

[1] *Early Australian Children's Literature* (Bibl. 305).

The culture of the west, deeply rooted in Mediterranean civilisation and the classical heritage of Greece and Rome, is reflected in the kinship of children's books throughout Europe. English children's books have shared this common inheritance, and like their neighbours exhibit a continental as well as a national trend in their development.

After the invention of printing made possible the wide dissemination of reading material for children and the general public, something of the spirit of medieval Christendom survived in the attitude to children's reading, in spite of rising nationalism, and the increasing use of the vernacular in place of Latin. The tradition of the past lingered after the Reformation in the continued domination of the Church in education and books for youth, both Catholic and Protestant. In the Protestant north the emphasis on the reading of the Bible in the vernacular was a powerful influence, but everywhere catechisms, works of piety, primers for learning, and manuals of behaviour were the main mental fare provided for the young, long after Gutenberg and his fellows ended the era of the hand-produced book. Entertainment in reading was for long discouraged or condemned.

The cult of the fairy tale in France at the end of the seventeenth century was an isolated but significant episode. By that time the age of religious strife was giving way to a more tolerant era, and the age of Enlightenment based on reverence for reason was dawning. But fairy lore was not to be admitted as fit reading for youth for another century. Boys and girls on the continent, as over here, had to rely for the wonders and marvels they craved on old nurses' tales, or the flimsy wares of the *colporteur* – the equivalent of the chapman. Goethe records how he found at a dealer's door in Frankfurt, when a child in the 1750s, 'some precious remains of the Middle Ages' – among them versions of the old romances, *The Fair Melusine* and *Fortunatus*. Such trafficking in 'sub-literature' was rife in many countries.

There were other common features in the history of books for children in Western Europe. The fable was universally popular, books of manners or courtesy spread far beyond their beginnings in Italy and France, 'Robinsonnades' followed everywhere in the wake of Defoe's *Crusoe*, and moral tales inspired by the doctrines of Rousseau were perhaps even more popular on the continent than in England. A widening range of literature for youth becomes apparent in the early nineteenth century as the prejudice against fairy lore and fantasy gave way before the forces of Romanticism. And the increasing importance given to social conditions and their improvement affects the realistic tale. Sentiment played a major role in the creation of pathetic tales, often religious in aim, about poor, pious children, triumphing over misfortune.

A secular literature for youth, though still didactic in purpose, began to emerge in most countries in the eighteenth century. But John Newbery's series of gay little books in easy and cheerful style seems to have been purely an English affair, and his books were little-known abroad, except in America. But children's book publishing was growing fast in the second half of the eighteenth century in Europe, as recorded by a regular visitor to the Leipzig Book Fairs in 1787. Friedrich Gedicke, a Berlin schoolmaster, wrote in the programme of his *Gymnasium* that year some observations about schoolbooks and other works for children, stating that no form of literary manufactory had become as common as the making of books for youth, often of inferior quality. 'At every Winter and Summer Fair at Leipzig', he wrote, 'there flows in, like the flood of the sea upon the shore, a countless number of books . . .' Few 'pearls or amber' were to be found by the rush of buyers – 'it was mostly mud, or at best painted snail-shells'. Every kind of publication for children was there – children's newspapers and journals, stories, poems, plays, histories, travels, and much more for children, and also reading books in every tongue. Gedicke decried the practice of enticing fond parents and relations by labelling worthless items 'Christmas Gifts for Good Children'.[1] The exploitation of the Christmas trade is evidently a long-standing practice.

Much of this miscellaneous fare still combined instruction or moral purpose with entertainment until well into the nineteenth century. A genuine imaginative literature emerged in the latter part of this century, but by no means simultaneously. Germany was in the van with the collection and printing of *Märchen* – traditional fairy tales – and their consequent inspiration to writers to invent original stories of fantasy. Before the middle of the century, however, an invigorating breeze from the West began to affect European children's books, as the novels of Fenimore Cooper brought the wilderness of the redskin far beyond his native shores. Other admired writers abroad to bring new visions of far places or adventures at sea were Captain Marryat and R. M. Ballantyne. Under these major influences – German, American and British – first the fairy tale, then the boy's story of adventure, were to take an important place in every country's books for youth.

Although the general pattern of the history of children's books in Western Europe has many basic similarities to its history in these islands, there are also some sharp differences. Each nation has its own marked characteristics. Paul Hazard analysed some of these tendencies with clarity and understanding. He yields to the North superiority over the South in this matter of books for boys and girls – if in nothing else – and finds it so because the Latin races seek after the rational and put a bridle on the imagination. 'The Latins', he wrote, 'lack a certain feeling for childhood . . . understood as a fortunate island where happiness must be protected, like an independent republic living according to its own

---

[1] Koster. *Geschichte des deutschen Jugend literatur* p. 386 (Bibl. 325).

laws, like a caste with glorious privileges'.[1] Nevertheless, as he points out, each country, north or south, has given something distinctive to the international treasure house of children's books, whatever they may have received from it. 'Every country gives and every country receives – and so it comes about that in our first impressionable years the universal republic of childhood is born'.[2]

ITALY

Italy, centre of Renaissance humanism and the rediscovery of the classical literature of Greece and Rome, had much early influence on the writing of books for youth, notably on those for instruction or the teaching of manners. It was in Italy also that the first emblem books originated in the sixteenth century. The *Emblemata* by Andrea Alciati in 1531 inspired the English emblem writers, and so this style of writing for youth when it was adapted for them later in the seventeenth century. More significant for the eventual development of imaginative literature for children were the early Italian collections of fairy tales. Giovanni Francesco Straparola brought out *Le Notte Piacevoli* (*The Pleasant Nights*) in Venice in 1550–1553. The stories – like the more famous *Decameron* of Boccaccio – were set in a frame story, and the scene was the island of Murano during the carnival season. About twenty of the seventy-three tales, taken from many sources, were folk-tales. Among them were versions of Beauty and the Beast, Puss-in-Boots, and other familiar examples. There was a French translation in 1585, and it is very likely that Perrault knew this.

The *Pentamerone* (*Lo Cunto de li Cunti*), by Giambattista Basile (1575–1632), published in 1634–1636, is a richer and livelier work than its predecessor. It consisted of real fairy tales, told in exuberant Baroque style in the Neapolitan dialect, and set against a background of early seventeenth century Neapolitan life. Again there is a fictional setting for the telling of the stories – ten ladies amuse the wife of a prince, with fifty tales in all spread over five days. The Sleeping Beauty appears here in the guise of 'Sun, Moon and Talia'. Another familiar is 'The Cat Cinderella', where the heroine finds herself with six stepsisters when she is put among the ashes. A magic date tree with a fairy serves instead of a fairy godmother. In another well-known tale, the Puss who helps Gagliuso to trick the king into believing him a fine lord is female and has no boots. Many other fairy-tale themes are met with in flamboyant style, with ogres and ogresses to add terror and sensation. But Basile's book was not really intended for children, and the Neapolitan dialect and ornate style were barriers to youthful reading. But, like Straparola's work, it

---

[1] *Books, Children and Men* p. 109 (Bibl. 12).

[2] Ibid. p. 146.

was influential and popular, and may have influenced Perrault. An English edition of Basile was published in 1674, but the first version edited for children is probably that made in 1848, when thirty of the stories were published, translated by J. Edward Taylor, and illustrated by George Cruikshank. But Basile's book is now chiefly of interest to students and folklorists.

Italian literature was rich in early prose fiction, but little of it was intended for boys and girls. Soon after printing was introduced there was an Italian *Aesop*, and fables on the John Gay or La Fontaine model were popular in the eighteenth century. Vezio Melegari in his article 'Children's Books in Italy before Pinocchio' (Bibl. 312) has stated that the story of Italian literature for young people begins in 1776 with the publication of some short stories by Father Francesco Soave (1743–1806). These tales, together with some verse narratives by Gaetano Perego, written for the same competition in Lombardy won by Soave's work, mark the beginning of an era when a new style of writing suited to the capacity of young minds developed. The purpose of the stories was both educational and literary, and the moral emphasis was strong. Francesco Soave was a philosopher, pedagogue and translator, and his *Novelle Morali* were agreeable examples of their kind which made their way abroad. An enlarged edition came out in 1786, and there was an English version by P. R. Rota in 1802. Twenty-eight stories appear in this volume, very much in the moralistic fashion of the day, but covering historical incidents and eastern tales to add piquancy.

Soave's stories and others like them served an immediate purpose, and opened the way to the creation of living books in the century ahead, books better able to serve the youth of a country struggling to throw off oppression and to become one nation. In 1837 there came another prize-winning work to win acclaim – *Giannetto*, by Luigi Alessandro Parravicini (1799–1880). The competition had been organised by the Florentine Society of Primary Education, and the book to be chosen was a little encyclopaedia of knowledge, conveyed in simple fashion. It centred interest on the boy, Giannetto, a paragon of a boy, always eager for instruction. He is more a device than a living character. It was rewritten in a more lively style in 1877 by 'C. Collodi' as *Gianettino*, and so it became the ancestor of the famous puppet, Pinocchio.

Publishing for children increased steadily in the nineteenth century but, like *Giannetto* most works were tinged with moral or educational purpose. Pietro Thouar (1809–1861) was very active in extending children's literature, expecially to the poorer classes, and he wrote many appealing tales. He was devoted to the cause of education and Italian freedom. A little later Jules Verne had an Italian imitator – Emilio Salgari (1862–1911) – to provide Italian youth with more exciting fiction.

The Risorgimento and the birth of the Italian nation in 1870 greatly stimulated historical and patriotic literature for young and old. Love of country and the fight for freedom inspired some fine novels with an appeal for older boys and girls. The cult of the hero and the exploits of the outstanding leader, Garibaldi, were also reflected in literature for the young in the nineteenth century.

But the first Italian children's book to win international fame was something quite different – a fantasy about a puppet. *Storia di un Burattino* (*The Story of a Puppet*) began to appear in a children's newspaper, *Giornale per i Bambini*, in Rome, in July 1881. It continued as a serial until January 1883, the later instalments being entitled *Le Avventure di Pinocchio*, and it came out in book form early in 1883 with this title. It was an event to be celebrated. Here was the final blow to didacticism in Italian children's literature and the birth of a world classic. The author was Carlo Lorenzini (1826–1890), already known as the writer of many books for boys and girls. But nothing of his was to win the immediate and outstanding success of *Pinocchio*. He wrote the story under the pen-name of 'C. Collodi', the name of a Tuscan village he had known in his childhood, now a name to travel all over the world.

The first English edition was issued in 1891 as *The Story of a Puppet*, but the title was soon to be changed to *The Adventures of Pinocchio*. It was plain that here was a story of universal appeal, a concoction of ingenious fantasy and humour, brisk as a circus and light as a bubble. What an amazing series of adventures befall this little wooden creature who has come to life in the making by old Geppetto to face a strange world full of danger and magic! Pinocchio may be only a puppet, but he has feelings to captivate the reader's sympathy. He tries hard does Pinocchio but rarely fulfils his good intentions. So a note of realism makes itself heard beneath the whirl of make-believe. Finally Pinocchio learns how to become a real boy when he has gained from his many escapades and experiences something of a practical philosophy of life. This blending of reality with high-spirited fantasy is perhaps the secret of the book's great success.

Less universal in its appeal, intensely nationalistic yet idealistic in spirit, is another famous book of the same decade – *Cuore* (*Heart*), by Edmondo de Amicis (1846–1908). This was published in 1886. De Amicis had served in the army, and he was already a well-known writer when he called one day for his son after school, and was impressed by a moving incident. He saw his boy coming along with another pupil, a poor youth dressed in clothes too large for him, but such was the affection between the children that they embraced on parting. It inspired De Amicis to write his book in the form of a diary of a young schoolboy, depicting school life at a time when there was a great need to foster a spirit of unity and comradeship between boys from different Italian provinces and varying backgrounds to make them true citizens of the new united nation. '*Si* Pinocchio *est amusant*, Cuore *est beau*', wrote Paul Hazard.[1]

---

[1] *La Littérature enfantine en Italie* (Bibl. 311).

Cuore was translated into English as *Heart* in 1895, and there was also a version entitled *Enrico's Schooldays* in 1899. But the book was too Italian in its feeling, too much of its own period, to win enduring life outside its own nation. Much was published for children in Italy and much has been written about Italian children's books, but little else has become known abroad except these two fine examples – *Pinocchio*, a tribute to the Italian gift of imaginative story-telling, and *Cuore*, much less known, revealing the youthful spirit of Italy at a time of challenge and promise.

FRANCE

Source and centre of medieval romance, France has contributed much fabulous lore to children's literature. Caxton and other early printers raided these stores for many translations into English, although the books they circulated were intended for the ordinary reader rather than his offspring. Many of these fictions came into the chapbooks – English and European – and later were revived and put into children's books. French romance also provided the main sources for that great classic of Arthurian legend by Sir Thomas Malory, which Caxton printed as *Le Morte D'Arthur* (pp. 13–14).

But in France as elsewhere romance and fabulous material were for long not thought fit for young minds. Primers and ABC books, catechisms, manuals of deportment or devotion, fables – these were the books provided for children. Besides Aesop, there was also the *Roman de Renart*, a vaster compilation of the *Reynard the Fox* beast epic than the Flemish version used by Caxton. Dating from the last quarter of the twelfth century this compilation of tales about the crafty fox and his enemies indicates a trend to come in children's literature in France which was to be enriched with animal fables of more than ordinary quality.

Little Pierre and Marie, however, were soon to find out more alluring material than the books given to them. Early in the seventeenth century Jean Oudot, a bookseller of Troyes, began to fashion from the *chansons de gestes*, romances, chronicles, and other old texts, the *Bibliothèque bleue*, a series of cheap little books, making them available for sale in town and country. So tales about the prowess of Roland, *Les Quatres Fils d'Aymon*, *Melusine*, *Griselidis*, and similar lore, began to circulate among the people and their children. And at the end of the century came the temporary liberation of the fairies with the publication of that great classic we know as Perrault's *Fairy Tales* (p. 35). Other more sophisticated *contes de fées* came out during this brief, bright interlude before the spirit of rationalism, under the sway of Voltaire and the Encyclopaedists, firmly led the children away from fairyland.

French children, perhaps more than others, have tended to read books addressed to a wider circle. When Jean de La Fontaine (1621–1695) vivified the Aesopian fable by putting

some of the old incidents into pithy and polished verse, he did not address himself specifi-
cally to youth, although the first fables in his *Fables Choisis* (1668) were addressed to the
seven-year-old Dauphin. More fables, becoming more complex and adult in meaning,
followed in 1678–1679 and in 1694. These little pictures of life, cleverly using animal
characters and founded on acute observation, have ever since held a leading place in
French literature for boys and girls. In England they have tended to be used more as a
French language text in school than read in translation. English versions of the best
known fables, attractively illustrated, have appeared from time to time, and one of the
best was *Select Fables of La Fontaine* (1893), with illustrations by Maurice Boutet de
Monvel, taken from the French original of 1888.

The seventeenth century in France towards its close is also notable for the writings of
Fénelon (pp. 68–9). He recognised that children long for fairy tales, and he believed in
profiting by this. So fairy tales should not be forbidden, but utilised or adapted to effect the
right impression, emphasising the moral of the story. He adapted the 'impure heathen
mythology' as the basis for *Les Aventures de Télémaque* (1699), written for his pupil, the
grandson of Louis XIV. His *Fables* (1718) show a similar aim to encourage virtuous ideas
in his young pupil through the use of stories. Gods and goddesses and other mythical
beings play a part, but magic is always carefully treated to reveal the error and misery of
wrong behaviour. Some of the best fables follow the Aesopian style – such is 'The
conceited owl', who thought himself fit to mate with an eaglet. Fénelon's writing was
intended for the son of a prince, not for general circulation, but it is important. For the
first time the realm of ancient poetry and myth was made the background for stories for
youth.

'France, the mid land, stands for a rational interpretation of art', wrote Esther Averill, in
a preface to a catalogue of French children's books (Bibl. 314). She agreed with Paul
Hazard that order and moderation rather than flights of pure imagination are most
congenial to the French *esprit*. In the age of reason – the eighteenth century – this tendency
was at its height. The '*Grande Encyclopédie*' inspired the production of little books of
instruction for children, elucidated by pictures, but moral teaching was to win the
ascendancy under the influence of Fénelon and Rousseau. Madame Le Prince de Beaumont
was one of the earliest French writers to present in fictional form a system of moral education, inserting fairy tales to further her purpose in *Le Magasin des Enfans* (1756) (p. 213).
The principal aim of her writing was to serve the cause of education, particularly the
'correction of bad habits'.

The moral tales by Madame de Genlis and Arnaud Berquin were widely popular
outside France (pp. 67–9), and there was much interchange with English writings of a
similar pattern. Arnaud Berquin translated Mrs. Trimmer's *Easy Guide to the Knowledge
of Nature* and the works of Thomas Day into French, and other popular English writers

to be read in French were Mrs. Barbauld, Maria Edgeworth and Mrs. Hofland. Another French writer to follow the teachings of Rousseau was his friend and benefactress, Madame d'Épinay (1726–1783). In her *Conversations d'Émilie* (1774), translated into English in 1787, she created a female Émile always under the guidance of a perfect mother. The moral tale also owed something to Jean-Francois Marmontel (1723–1799), whose *Contes Moraux* came out from 1758 to 1761.

Progress towards a more natural type of story than the artificial contrasts of the moral tale can be seen in the work of Madame Marie or Sophie Cottin (1773–1807). A writer of talent, she produced serious descriptive tales, utilising historical events as the background for the encouragement of virtue. Her best known book, *Élisabeth; ou, les éxilés de Sibérie* (1806), translated into English in 1808, tells of a young girl's difficult journey from Siberia to St. Petersburg to procure a pardon for her father from the Tsar.

Marie-Thérèse Latzarus in her thesis, *La Littérature Enfantine en France dans la seconde moitié du xixe siècle* (Bibl. 317) has written a thoughtful and penetrating study of the history of French children's books up to the beginning of the twentieth century. She claims that a proper literature for children did not develop until about 1860, and then it was much under the influence of '*la vie bourgeoise*' and the materialistic ideas of that society. Yet in an earlier decade, about 1830–1840, publishing activity for youth was extending considerably. In 1833 the first real periodical for boys and girls was established, *Le Journal des Enfants*, chiefly by Eugénie Foa (1799–1853). She was a Spanish Jewess of Bordeaux and one of the first French writers to bring to children something of their national heritage of history and legend. The magazine began with a flourish, for it serialised what was to be a famous story, *Les Mésaventures de Jean-Paul Choppart* (1834), by Louis Desnoyers (1802–1868), about a boy who runs away from a good home to join a circus troop. Desnoyers' later story, *Les Aventures de Robert-Robert* (1839), described by Jean de Trigon as '*un essai satirique*', recalling *Gulliver's Travels*,[1] was also popular. Adventures further from home were also to be a feature a little later. The Indian and cowboy tale was the main concern of Gustave Aimard (1818–1885), but the pinnacle of power and originality in the field of sensation was achieved in the world-famous stories by Jules Verne (p. 166).

Tales imitative of *Robinson Crusoe* preceded the true adventure story. Two favourites were the French version of *The Swiss Family Robinson* by Madame de Montholieu in 1814, and the island tale of a different kind, the fresh and sentimental *Paul et Virginie*, by Bernardin de St. Pierre, long popular since its publication in 1788.

Tales of fantasy and old legends began to make their way into books for children in the 1840s, not to be obscured by a more favoured realistic approach to children's books.

---

[1] *Histoire de la Littérature Enfantine* ... p. 48 (Bibl. 319).

Charles Nodier (1780–1844) went back to the material used for the *Bibliothèque bleue* for his *Légendes populaires de France* (1840), and he also wrote original fantasies, including *La Fée aux Miettes* (1832), a blend of fairy tale and wild Gothic imagining. Alexander Dumas the elder (1803–1870) founded his fairy tale, *Les Aventures d'un Casse-Noisette* (1845) on a German tale by E. T. A. Hoffmann (p. 259), and there was an English version in 1875. Another fanciful tale of this period to be popular in England was *Monsieur Le Vent et Madame La Pluie* (1846), by Paul de Musset, brother of the more famous Alfred de Musset. It came out in English as *Mr. Wind and Madam Rain* in 1864. Inspired by Ossian and the legends of Fingal, De Musset found part of his tale in old Breton legends. He describes the efforts of a poor miller to avert ruin, with magical intervention by the Wind and the Rain, and this is interwoven with the fortunes of the miller's son who helps Duke William at the time of the Conquest.

The historical story, foreshadowed by Madame Cottin, was developed further by Eugénie Foa and Julie Lavergne (1823–1886). 'Legends are the flowers of history', wrote Madame Lavergne in one of her prefaces. She admired and emulated Walter Scott and wrote many tales and legends of French history. Among French historical romances the best known and enduring are the stirring novels written for a wide public by Alexandre Dumas *père*, especially the trilogy featuring the famous musketeers, D'Artagnan, Porthos and Aramis, which began with *Les Trois Mousquetaires* in 1844. Another Dumas favourite with youth was *Le Comte de Monte-Cristo* (1845).

A little later came the tale of pathos and *l'enfance malheureuse*. The most outstanding example in France is *Sans Famille* (1878), by Hector Malot (1830–1907), a tale about a foundling who is sold to the manager of a troupe of performing animals, but who finally wins his inheritance. It appeared in English under various titles up to 1938, when it came out as *Nobody's Boy*. Older children in France have also enjoyed the simple rustic tales by George Sand (Aurore Dupin, 1804–1876) such as *La Mare au Diable* (1846) and *La Petite Fadette* (1848).

Periodical literature was important in the nineteenth century. In 1864, Pierre Jules Hetzel (1814–1886) launched his famous journal, *Le Magasin d'Éducation*, and maintained in it a high standard of writing, production and illustration. Its purpose was far more recreational than the title suggests, and most of the works by Jules Verne appeared for the first time in its pages. Another outstanding publisher was Hachette. He began to issue the famous series, *La Bibliothèque Rose*, about the middle of the nineteenth century, as well as *Le Journal de la Jeunesse* in 1873. Attractively bound in crimson gilt-embossed covers the *Bibliothèque Rose* gave to little French readers some of their loved fairy tales and stories as well as interesting new works. Among the new titles were the books by the Comtesse de Ségur (1799–1874). These 'miniature novels of real life written for and about her own grandchildren' began to appear towards the end of the fifties. The author was the daughter of a Russian general named Rostopchine and became a Frenchwoman on her marriage. At the age of fifty-seven she started to write stories for the young children of her family and friends, beginning with *Nouveau Contes de Fées* in 1857. The two small girls for whom this was written appear in her next book, *Les Petites Filles Modéles* (1858) as Camille and Madeleine. The story to win the most fame was *Les Malheurs de Sophie* (1859), said to be partly founded on the writer's own childhood. It is centred on a naughty four-year-old girl contrasted with her good cousin Paul. Sophie, like most of Madame de Ségur's characters is of good family, and her misdemeanours are diverse and amusing. She walks through lime because it looks pretty, stands in the rain to make her hair grow, and cuts off her eyebrows, among other exploits. For all this mischief there are punishments to fit the crimes. One of them is to have the remains of a bee attached to a ribbon around her neck as a penalty for her wanton killing of it.

Another popular tale is about the donkey, Cadichon, who tells his own history and judges human nature in *Mémoires d'un Ane* (1860). Madame de Ségur's books reflect the upper class life of her day and the prevailing attitude to children, but they introduce living characters and lively incidents, and they had a wide appeal. This little '*comédie humaine*' of the nursery has now faded away like the social mileu it reflected, but many of the twenty volumes in their red covers were long in demand and found their way into English nurseries.

The place of art in children's books gained importance in the second half of the nineteenth century. Famous artists illustrated editions of the classics, notably J. J. Grandville (Jean-Ignace Isidore Gerard, 1803–1847), who illustrated *Robinson Crusoe*, La Fontaine's *Fables*, and *Gulliver's Travels*, and Gustave Doré (1832–1883), whose sombre and extravagant drawings (1867) for the Perrault tales heightened fantasy but ignored their vernal gaiety.

No outstanding picture-book maker of the quality of Walter Crane or Kate Greenaway came upon the scene in France until Maurice Boutet de Monvel (1850–1913) began to produce his charming illustrations towards the end of the century. He depicts a childhood of carefree innocence in flat pure colour and delicate outline. Boutet de Monvel was influenced by the English illustrators of picture-books, but he was also inspired by the *Images d'Épinal*, large picture sheets in bright colour giving the gist of famous stories or incidents, popular since their beginnings in the seventeenth century. They were revived and extended by Pellerin at the beginning of the nineteenth century, and increasingly aimed at a youthful public. Boutet de Monvel's finest work is perhaps *Jeanne d'Arc* (1896), where he captures the pageantry and action of battle as well as scenes of quiet idealism. His illustrations for the *Fables of La Fontaine* are among his livelier pictures. More playful and gentler in mood are the decorative scenes for *Les Chansons de France* (ca. 1890), and the tales of child life he illustrated for Anatole France, *Nos Filles et Garçons* (1900) and *Nos Enfants* (1887).

The work of Boutet de Monvel is the prelude to the excellence of the French picture-book of the twentieth century. In the 1920s both Madame Latzarus and Paul Hazard felt that the state of children's books in France was in decline. They were not to know that the books from abroad and the treasures from the past would soon be enriched by a resurgence of native talent and invention in the making of books for youth.

SPAIN

'Spain is brimful of imagination', affirmed Paul Hazard, 'but she does not possess any literature for children'.[1] It was an opinion echoed by Eva Maurice Fromkes in an article in the *Horn Book* in 1934 (Bibl. 322), but since these pronouncements new light has been shed on the subject of children's books and their history in this colourful and mysterious peninsula by Carmen Bravo-Villasante. She has illustrated her *Historia de la Literatura Infantil Española* with a two volume anthology (Bibl. 320). This begins with some fables from a very early work of Spanish prose in 1251, *Calila e Dimna*, and it covers many aspects of books read by or written for children up to the 1950s.

Oriental influence was strong in Spain in the Middle Ages through her close contact with the Moorish invaders. This early collection of fables is older than Aesop, and it was taken from an Arabic version of the *Panchatantra* (also known as the *Fables of Bidpai*) of ancient India. Two lynxes, Calila and Dimna, are the main characters, and the framework of their history allows the introduction of many edifying little anecdotes resembling those of Aesop. Proverbs in verse, holy songs, and legends, lives of the saints were other works shared by children and adults before the days of printing. There was also much traditional lore and many romances and ballads, the most popular featuring that national hero in the fight against the Moors, Le Cid. After printing was introduced in the 1470s the romances and ballads circulated more widely, including the famous *Amadis de Gaul*, printed in 1508. The sixteenth century was to be the golden age in Spanish literature.

Devotional and religious works were chiefly favoured for the young, however, and they continued to reflect allegiance to the Catholic faith during the Reformation and after. One of the earliest books printed for children in Spain – and a very early example of its kind in Europe – was a 'Little Bible', *Biblia Pequeña*, printed in Barcelona in 1492.[2] The Renaissance had more effect in Spain than Protestantism and it is represented in the works of Luis Vives (1492–1540), philosopher and educationalist, who wrote some

[1] *Books, Children and Men* p. 77 (Bibl. 12).
[2] *Pierpont Morgan Library Exhibition Catalogue* (Bibl. 43).

popular Latin colloquys, and some dialogues in their own tongue for little Spaniards, *Dialogos Escolares* (ca. 1530).

Spain's claim to importance in the sphere of literature for young people rests principally on that immortal novel of universal appeal – *Don Quijote de la Mancha*, familiar in England as *Don Quixote*. The writer, Miguel Cervantes Saavedra (1547–1616) intended a satire on the romances of chivalry (still widely read), and he achieved a masterpiece by his humanity and vision, combining in his long and fascinating novel laughter at their absurdities with respect for the nobler ideals of these outworn tales of a vanished age. Burlesque hinges upon tragedy, humour is allied to understanding, and the wealth of incident never obscures the realism of the many characters. The novel appeared in 1605 and was an immediate success. Children, particularly those entering their teens, found it much to their taste. It was translated into English in 1612 by Thomas Skelton, but the lengthy original has usually been given to boys and girls in abridged form. F. Newbery, nephew of John Newbery, issued an abridgement in 1778 as *The Life and Exploits of the Ingenious Gentleman Don Quixote*,[1] and many English versions followed in the next century, often accompanied by spirited or splendid illustrations. *Don Quixote* has become, like *Robinson Crusoe*, universal in the world's literature as well as part of children's books in many lands.

Spain in the past has been dependent on other countries for many of her children's books. But there also seems to have been a good deal of activity at home, little known as it rarely crossed her borders. Popular literature circulated in the familiar form of picture-sheets or broadsides, in Spain called *Santos* or *Aleluyas*, from their origin in religious subjects. Intended for the unlettered rather than children, they were gradually extended to all kinds of secular subjects, and increasingly enjoyed by younger readers. In the eighteenth century there were the usual moral tales and verse fables. This didactic form of literature, spiced with a little amusement, characterised the first periodical to be issued for boys and girls in Spain, *La Gaceta de los Niños*, in 1798.

More romantic and imaginative material penetrated into books for children in the nineteenth century. Fernán Cabellero (the pseudonym of Cecilia Bohl de Faber, 1796–1877) was a writer of regional novels and deeply interested in peasant lore. She retold some traditional tales for children, which were published in the periodical, *La Educacion Pintoresca*. Gradually through such magazines, often well-illustrated, a less didactic if undistinguished literature for children developed.

Poetry has always been the medium of the best literature for children in Spain from the

---

[1] Roscoe 50 (Bibl. 104).

About the same time a German edition for youth was included in Prestel's *Lustige Kinderbibliotek. Vol. 1. Leben und Thaten des weisen Junkers Don Quichote* 1767.

time of the early ballads. Some great poets have dedicated or addressed certain of their compositions to children. Among them is Ruben Dario (1867–1916) of Nicaragua. He was inspired by the holy legends, *Flos Sanctorum*, to make some charming little verses for the young. Drama has also been one of the finest literary arts in Spain, and early this present century, Jacinte Benavente (1866–1954) founded 'the children's theatre', and wrote some fairy tale plays. Little of this literature reached children outside Spain, however. This land remains known in the realm of children's books chiefly through some of her romances and legends and that immortal work of prose fiction – *Don Quixote*.

GERMANY

Across the Rhine an extensive and varied literature for children had come into existence by the end of the nineteenth century. In Germany the tendency has been for children's books to be more closely associated with teaching and pedagogic movements than in Britain, and didacticism and purpose played a leading role. Writings for youth in Germany have also reflected the diversity of regional life and traditions in a country of many small states, not united as a nation until 1870.

As elsewhere the earliest reading material for children revealed a strong preoccupation with religion. A very early work of piety for youth belongs to the beginning of the fifteenth century. This was *Der Seele Trost* (*The Consolation of the Soul*), a composition containing histories and episodes from many sources illustrating the ten commandments. Fables, of course, were much approved. Printed versions of Aesop in German go back to 1477, when Steinhöwel's edition was issued. After the Reformation the emphasis was on reading the Bible, and Martin Luther (1483–1546), the great leader of Protestantism, gave the German people a literary and religious treasure in a living and vigorous translation all could understand. Luther believed in fables to teach the young, and he translated a selection from Aesop in 1530. These fables were included in *Hundert Fabeln aus Esopo* (1571) with examples translated by Nathaniel Chytraeus and others. Some of the best original fables to be enjoyed by children in Germany were the verse fables written in the eighteenth century by C. F. Gellert (1715–1769), although these were not specially intended for them.

Instruction and moral guidance continue to dominate German literature for children as it took a more secular form in the age of reason. But it was in this land of Teutonic thoroughness and purpose that imagination in children's reading first found true expression, and a magic light from a realm unknown to rationalism penetrated into their books. The Romantic movement at the end of the eighteenth century affected children's books in Germany earlier than elsewhere. The rebellion against the rule of reason brought a liberating power to the imagination, and the turning back to the past to discover legends and traditional lore led to the greatest landmark in German literature for youth – the publishing of the *Fairy Tales* collected by the brothers Grimm in 1812–1815 (pp. 90–1).

By the time that Jakob and Wilhelm Grimm had begun to preserve these old stories still current among peasant storytellers, and writers of *Märchen* were active, a thriving literature of a prosaic and useful nature was well established for young people. It was the outcome of the new interest in education and ideas about human perfectability generated by the '*Aufklarung*' and the theories of Rousseau. As Gedicke testified in 1787 publishing for children in Germany (and Europe) was by then extensive. One of the best features in Germany was the early use of good illustrations. The *Orbis Pictus*, by Comenius, that harbinger of the picture-book, had been first printed at Nuremberg in 1658, and its influence in Germany was strong. It inspired Johann Bernhard Basedow (1723–1790) and other teachers to produce texts with pictures to illustrate everyday objects and living things. Basedow had founded a school on enlightened principles at Dessau in 1774, known as 'Philanthropin', and he believed with Comenius that knowledge can best be conveyed to the child through his delight in pictures. His *Elementarwerk* (1770–1774) was a picture-book of knowledge and an early example of a well-illustrated children's book, for the hundred copper-plates appended were the work of the gifted artist Daniel Chodowiecki. In 1790 a more impressive and costly production of a similar kind was published, *Das Bilderbuch für Kinder* (*Picture-book for Children*), edited by F. J. Bertuch (1747–1822) of Weimar. It presented natural history and other subjects in twenty-four volumes, twelve of text, twelve of hand-coloured copper-plates. Illustrated ABC or simple reading books were also a feature of this period. One attractive example from the *ABC Buch* (1773), by C. F. Weisse, reproduced with many others from old German children's books is included by Dr. Kunze in his *Schatzbehalter* (Bibl. 326).

The moral tale of the time had some able practitioners in Germany, and two of the most famous to present information and moral truths in easy and agreeable style were J. H. Campe (1746–1818) and C. G. Salzmann (1744–1811). Their writings became known in English and something about them has been set down in the chapter on the moral tale. The pioneer children's newspapers show the same endeavour to mingle serious purpose with mild amusement, carefully avoiding any attempt to awaken the child's sense of wonder. By the time of the Napoleonic Wars new currents were to disturb these placid waters – bubbling up from underground. As in England and in other lands the wonder tales and romances had been kept alive by the chapbook makers in the seventeenth and eighteenth centuries. In Germany this lore circulated to ordinary folk through the *Volksbücher*. Much matter came from the old romances, but there was a wealth of other *Stoff* – legends, history, lives of the saints, jest books, stories of varying lineage, such as *Dr. Faustus*, fables including *Reineke Fuchs* (the German *Reynard*), and more lurid and trivial fare. The *Volksbücher* deteriorated in format in the eighteenth century and increasingly appealed to the younger reader. Goethe's tribute to their value in his early reading has already been quoted.

A fresh interest was taken in this old material by the Romanticists, who brought to German letters nationalistic and idealistic sentiments strongly allied with nostalgia for the past. For children's books the new interest in native lore and legend, more barbaric and macabre than in the Latin countries, was to be all important. Already before the end of the eighteenth century some of the old traditional tales were being put into literary form. J. K. A. Musaeus (1735–1787) brought out his *Volksmärchen der Deutschen* (*German Folktales*) in 1782, but these were romanticised stories, not the pure source presented by the Grimm brothers. A German edition of these tales was made for children, and they were put into English in 1791. Mark Lemon (1809–1870) used this 1791 version for his *Legends of Number Nip* (1864).

The Grimm brothers began to collect their stories around 1806, seeking always to find living examples of the storyteller's art. This great classic of fairy-lore marked a revolutionary change in the development of children's books. Traditional material in every country would soon be prized – not merely for children's reading – and it would inspire writers, like Hans Andersen and many others, to create *Kunstmärchen* themselves. By the second decade of the nineteenth century the fairy tale in Germany was firmly launched.

E. T. A. Hoffmann (1776–1822) wrote richly fantastic tales of the supernatural, many for adult rather than junior readers. Three of his stories became well-known as the themes of Offenbach's opera. The best known of his children's stories is *Nüssknacker und der Mäusekönig* (*Nutcracker and the King of the Mice*), first published in a collection of tales, *Kindermärchen* (1816), by C. W. Contessa, Friedrich de la Motte Fouqué, and Hoffmann. Hoffmann believed that children possess a vision beyond adult understanding and his tale about Fritz and Marie, their adventures with the toys, the great battle between Nutcracker and the evil sevenheaded King of Mice, with visions of a land of marzipan castles and sweetmeats at the end, overflows with invention and magic.

The Gothic and somewhat superficial romances by Fouqué have been mentioned in an earlier chapter (p. 107). His most famous story *Undine* (1811) is about a watersprite who gained a soul by her marriage with a Christian knight. A writer under the spell of the *Arabian Nights'* as much as the folklore of Swabia and the Black Forest was Wilhelm Hauff (1802–1827). His *Märchenalmanach* came out in three volumes from 1826 to 1828. The first two books contain *Die Caravane* and *Der Scheik von Alexandria*, Eastern tales set within a framework for their telling. The third volume, *Das Wirtshaus im Spessart* (*The Inn in the Spessart*), contains stories more in the Grimm tradition, including a tale of the glass-makers and charcoal-burners of the Black Forest, *Das Kalte Herz* (*The Cold Heart*). This was included in a collection of *Popular Tales* in an English series in 1844, 'The Juvenile

Englishman's library'. Hauff's Tales have been revived in English in various editions in recent years.

The poet, Clemens Brentano (1778–1842), wrote fairy tales in lyrical and fanciful vein, founding some on Italian sources and some on Rhine and other legends. His finest story for youth is considered to be his elaboration of a traditional theme with much humour and poetical fancy – *Gockel, Hinkel, und Gackeleia* – first published in 1838, but written much earlier. Brentano is not so well-known in England as some of the other German writers of *Märchen*, but his tales were translated by Kate Freilegrath Kroeker, and issued as *Fairy Tales from Brentano* in 1884, followed by another volume in 1887, *New Fairy Tales from Brentano*. This second collection contained a shortened version of *Gockel, Hinkel and Gackeleia*.

Another collector of traditional stories was Ludwig Bechstein (1801–1860), who followed the example of the Grimms in searching for tales still existing in oral form. In 1823 there appeared his *Thüringischen Volksmärchen* (*Thuringian Folktales*), and later came the *Deutsches Märchenbuch* (*German Fairy Tale Book*) (1845) and *Neues Deutches Märchenbuch* (1856). The style did not equal the excellent simplicity of the Grimms, but the stories remained popular. Mrs. Ewing in *Aunt Judy's Yearly Volume* for 1875 testified to the delight the tales had given her in her childhood, recalling a version entitled *The Old Storyteller*, issued with pictures by Richter, by Addey and Co. in 1854. She was reviewing a new edition of Bechstein stories, *As Pretty as Seven* (1872), again with Richter illustrations.

The foregoing are a few examples only from the rich store of German fairy lore. Other traditional material was not being forgotten, including the hero tales, sagas, and myths. An important landmark was the publication of folk-songs and traditional verses collected by Achim von Arnim (1781–1831) and Clemens Brentano in *Des Knaben Wunderhorn* (*The Boy's Wonder-Horn*). This was issued in Heidelberg in three volumes from 1806 to 1808, and the last volume contained *Kinderlieder* or songs for children. They have been well described by Bettina Hürlimann in her survey of European books for children (Bibl. 307), and they formed a precious store in print of some long familiar rhymes of infancy. Their joyous and unfettered spirit was to inspire future original verse for children. Didactic poems, hymns, and moralised fables were no longer to monopolise poetry for the young.

Picture-books were also to advance in quality and diversity often to the accompaniment of light-hearted verses. Most famous among nineteenth century picture-book makers in Germany was Dr. Heinrich Hoffmann (1809–1894), who produced a new style of entertainment by guying the moral type of warning verse in his world-renowned *Struwwelpeter* in 1845 (p. 192). Its chronicle of amusing and horrific catastrophe has fascinated children in England and elsewhere ever since.

BIRD AT THE WINDOW.

It raps at the window light and low;
" Open to me a moment, or so;
The snow falls thick, the wind blows strong,
I've nothing to eat; shall freeze ere long!
Dearest people, oh, let me in,
Well-behaved I have ever been !"

They let him in in his distress,
With crumbs of bread made his hunger less;
He staid in joy while the weeks went on;
But when the sun through the window shone,
Mournful he sate the long day through;
They opened the casement—and off he flew !

15

2. Vogel am Fenster.

An das Fenster klopft es: pick! pick!
Macht mir doch auf einen Augenblick.
Dick fällt der Schnee, der Wind geht kalt,
Habe kein Futter, erfriere bald.
Lieben Leute, o laßt mich ein,
Will auch immer recht artig seyn.

Sie ließen ihn ein in seiner Noth;
Er suchte sich manches Krümchen Brod,
Blieb fröhlich manche Woche da.
Doch als die Sonne durchs Fenster sah,
Da saß er immer so traurig dort;
Sie machten ihm auf: husch war er fort!

28. *A page from the English edition of Hey's* PICTURE FABLES, *illustrated by Speckter, and translated by Mary Howitt in 1844, contrasted with the same fable in the original German edition of 1833*

Other German illustrators became well-known abroad, especially Otto Speckter (1807–1871) and Ludwig Richter (1803–1884), whose pictures for the Bechstein fairy tales have been mentioned. A favourite work illustrated by Speckter was the verse fables by Wilhelm Hey (1789–1884). This Thuringian pastor believed that a love of animals could lead to a love of God, but he put no sermonising into his charming little anecdotes in rhyme about familiar creatures. They were published in two volumes, *Fünfzig Fabeln* (*Fifty Fables*) (1833), and *Noch Fünfzig Fabeln* (*Fifty More Fables*) (1837). An attractive English edition, with pictures drawn on wood by Speckter and engraved by the Dalziel brothers, was brought out by Routledge in 1858. But the illustrations vary a good deal from the originals, and from those in an earlier French-German-English version by Mary Howitt, *Otto Speakter's Fable Book* (1844). Many other artists made notable contributions to children's books, including Oscar Pletsch (1830–1888), whose books featured winsome and round-cheeked boys and girls. The silhouette illustration became popular in the latter part of the century especially in the work of Paul Konewka (1840–1871) and Karl Frohlich (1821–1898).

Cheap and universally appealing graphic material existed in the form of *Bilderbogen* – picture-sheets – which came into being not long after the invention of printing. They were not specially intended for youth, any more than the *Volksbücher* – at least not until the nineteenth century when their sale greatly expanded. Among the most famous of these *Bilderbogen* were those issued at Neuruppin from about 1825 onwards. All kinds of subjects were utilised, among them abridgements of famous stories and fairy tales. For children perhaps the most fascinating sheets were the series issued in Munich. This was started in 1849 by Kaspar Braun of the famous Braun and Schneider publishing house. Talented artists were employed in delineating a wide range of subjects – fables, lands and peoples, costume, *Märchen*, history and much else. Among the most gifted were Franz von Pocci (1807–1876) and Wilhelm Busch (1832–1908). Pocci, poet as well as illustrator, entered the child's world to create simple, living picture-books, sometimes adding melody as well. Wilhelm Busch is distinguished for his racy and comical narratives, above all for *Max and Moritz* (1865), a history of two bad boys, their many scrapes, and their dreadful end. Delightful incredibilities are presented in a caricature-like style which prefigures the art of the cartoon film.

Fiction for young readers also expanded in many ways in the nineteenth century. As elsewhere the influence of the adventure story from Britain and America was important, at first in imitation of Defoe's *Crusoe*, and then through the works of Marryat and Fenimore Cooper. But German writers were soon to find inspiration to create their own tales of adventure for boys. One of the most popular, if not to be rated among the best, was Karl May (1842–1912). Begun in the 1870s, his meretricious adventures about the Far

West, centred on the characters of 'Old Shatterhand' and Winnetou, an idealised Indian hero, proved to be best-sellers.

More thoughtful and homely stories also flourished. A popular writer of tales with a religious purpose was Johann Christoph von Schmid (1768–1854), a Roman Catholic priest and teacher in Augsburg. Probably the best-loved tale in his own country is *Die Ostereier* (*Easter Eggs*) (1816), but in English the favourite has been *Das Blumenkörbchen* (*The Basket of Flowers*) (1823), the history of the wrongfully accused and much abused Mary and her gardener father. Romance and sentimentalism were making headway, and the story for girls also developed. Other tales with a religious or moral aim, with a new flavour of pathos, found favour. Books were reaching a wider circle of readers as the century advanced, and many mediocre though readable narratives were penned with children of poorer circles in mind. Some of these stories were adapted or translated into English, not always with an acknowledgement of their origin. A popular writer of the story of sentiment and poor children was the prolific Gustav Nieritz of Dresden (1795–1876). He produced over two hundred volumes. Typical among them is *Der Blinde Knabe* (*The Blind Boy*) (1837), which came out in an English version in 1869. It tells of the poor child Magda and her little brother who is blind, and their goodness and cheerfulness in adversity. The reader can at last dry his eyes, for all ends happily. Little Raphael recovers his sight, and the virtue and industry of the fatherless family receive their reward in the last chapter. Its English title, *Busy Hands and Patient Hearts*, very well discloses its nature.

The mediocrity and superficiality of much writing for youth at the end of the nineteenth century were sharply criticised by Heinrich Wolgast (1860–1920) in an epoch-making book, *Das Elend unserer Jugendliteratur* (1896) (Bibl. 328). He was by no means the first to evaluate contemporary literature for youth in Germany, and an excellent account of critical writings from the end of the eighteenth century to the 1920s is given by H. L. Koster in the last chapter of his *Geschichte der Deutschen Jugendliteratur* (Bibl. 325). Wolgast believed in education through art, and that literature for children should have a higher aim than any utilitarian, religious, patriotic or other subservient purpose. '*Die Jugendschrift muss ein Kunstwerk sein*' (writing for children must be a work of art) was his watchword. Through a Commission of teachers and others in Hamburg he did much to improve the selection of books and to encourage the reading of good literature by young readers. With his co-workers he rendered a valuable service by producing a cheap series of worthwhile books, including the great classics of German literature.

SWITZERLAND

A small country of mountains and four separate tongues, Switzerland has many regional differences which have affected her literature and culture. Rather more than two-thirds of her population belong to the German-speaking cantons, so books in German have formed the main contribution she has made to children's literature at home and abroad. Much interchange took place between Germany and German-speaking Switzerland, and some books by Swiss writers were first published in Germany, for example the stories by Johanna Spyri were issued in Gotha, and the picture-books by Ernst Kreidolf in Cologne.

According to Irene Dyrenfurth-Graebsch in a chapter in her history of German children's books (Bibl. 324), Swiss books for children followed a similar pattern of development to those in Germany. But the Swiss developed in books for youth a national and historical approach quite early, and this was firmly established in the mid-eighteenth century largely through the efforts of J. J. Bodmer, a professor of history at Zurich. Bettina Hürlimann also includes a chapter on the history of Swiss books for children (Bibl. 307) and this is a most useful summary now available in an English translation. She begins with an account of that special feature in the early publication of material for children in Switzerland – the issue of *Neujahrsstücke* or *Neujahrsblätter* (New Year sheets) which began in Zurich in 1645. These illustrated annuals continued until the middle of the nineteenth century, and the engravings were often of high quality. At first serious matters predominated, Biblical excerpts, moral advice, table-manners, for example, but later subjects became more diverse and recreational, including history and national themes, biography, travels, music and plays.

The first book from Switzerland for children to make a real impression abroad was the popular *Swiss Family Robinson*, by J. D. Wyss, first published 1812–1813 (p. 158). This earnest and compelling tale about a shipwrecked family reflects the Swiss passion for education, and famous Swiss educationalists including Pestalozzi have had much influence on writing for children. Much less known than the Crusoe tale, but equally important for young Swiss readers, was a heroic, saga-like yet 'warm-hearted family story' by Jeremias Gotthelf (1797–1854), inspired by the famous national hero, William Tell. *Der Knabe des Tells* (*Tell's Son*) (1846) narrates the life of the boy who experienced the ordeal of the shot at the apple. It is highly praised by Mrs. Hürlimann as enshrining Swiss aspirations and as a breakaway from the prison of didacticism.

Towards the end of the nineteenth century Switzerland was to become known in many lands through the transmigration of *Heidi*. First published in 1881 as *Heidi's Lehr und Wanderjahre*, it came out in England in 1884 in two volumes, *Heidi's Early Experiences* and *Heidi's Further Experiences*, apparently translated by Louise Brookes, whose version came out in America the same year. The author, Johanna Spyri (1829–1901), was the daughter of a doctor. She was married to a lawyer and lived near Zurich. *Heidi*, one of her earliest books, proved overwhelmingly the most popular. Love of children and love of her native land are expressed in the author's many stories, but they are also much affected by the contemporary emphasis on sentiment and pathos. Homeless, orphan, or otherwise unfortunate children predominate. Sorrows and trials are overcome by goodness, and happiness usually prevails at the end. In some ways *Heidi* is typical of its time, but the little heroine's story is unfolded with so much true feeling and vivid description that it transcends its limitations. How clearly the Alpine scenes are depicted, where Heidi lives at first a simple and happy existence with her grandfather! Sent away to the city the child becomes lonely, sad, and ill, but she does not complain. At last all comes right. Heidi goes back to her beloved Alps, with new friends she has made, and radiates love and friendship to make everyone happy. Religious faith and sincere emotion animate this charming story, which has the sharp contrasts that young readers love. Most of Johanna Spyri's books are now forgotten but Heidi lives on, endearing herself and her mountain home to new generations of children everywhere.

Other developments took place in Switzerland in the making of children's books of an entertaining rather than a moralistic nature during the nineteenth century. Swiss fairy tales go back in print at least to 1873, according to Mrs. Hürlimann, when the *Kinder-und Hausmärchen der Schweiz (Household and Children's Fairy Tales from Switzerland)*, by Otto Sutermeister, was published.

Good illustration and picture-books in embryo for children date back to some of the better examples of the *Neujahrsblätter*. At the close of the nineteenth century illustrated children's books reached a new standard in the work of Ernst Kreidolf (1863–1956), a distinguished Swiss artist, who made some fine picture-books, beginning with *Blumenmärchen (Flower Fairy Tales)* in 1898. These personified floral fancies recall the style of Walter Crane, but both pictures and text (written by the artist) have a delicate individuality. Kreidolf's picture-books display much artistic skill as well as a poetic gift. Too little-known outside the German-language countries, he is an author-artist to be ranked with the leading practitioners of the age in the making of fine illustrated books for the young.

THE NETHERLANDS

Centre of printing and home of toleration, the Netherlands have surprisingly produced no lasting work of international importance for youth up to the early twentieth century, although much was published for children and much has been written on the subject of children's books and their history.

An excellent critical history of Dutch children's books has been written by Dirk L. Daalder, *Wormcruyt med Suycker* (Bibl. 329), but it is unfortunately only available in Dutch. The student ignorant of the language, however, can glean a little information from the excellent illustrations, title-pages, and other reproductions from old Dutch children's books displayed in a compilation by Leonard de Vries, *Bloempjes der Vreugd'*

(Bibl. 330). This covers a period from 1712 to 1898, and indicates a wealth of material, seemingly not dissimilar in nature from its English or German counterparts. It also makes plain how much the printing and publishing of children's books were spread throughout the provinces, and by no means confined to Amsterdam. One interesting item included by Mr. de Vries is a Dutch version of John Newbery's *Renowned History of Giles Ginger-bread* (1764) issued in Amsterdam in 1781. One wonders if there was also a Dutch *Goody Two-Shoes*. Mr. de Vries also includes some attractive hand-coloured examples of ABC and other nursery books from about 1800 onwards. A useful summary in English on the history of children's books in the Netherlands has been made from his writings (Bibl. 331).

In the first centuries after printing Dutch children had the usual fables, *Aesop* and *Reynard the Fox*, little works of piety and instruction including *Haneboeken* – ABC books or little primers so-called because of the crowing cockerel imprinted on their covers. This symbol of the cock was a feature on such little works in Northern Europe. A little later came picture-sheets and chapbooks versions of romances and famous tales. Developments followed the usual European pattern, and in the eighteenth century the moral tale arrived in prose and verse, and also the first newspapers or journals for youth. There was a *Vriend der Kinderen* (*Children's Friend*) issued at Haarlem from 1780–1785.

It is generally agreed that the true beginning of a special literature for children, combining pleasing entertainment with good advice, was the work of Hieronymus van Alphen (1746–1803). Still intent on admonition he had the wit to address boys and girls in a new style of simple verse they could enjoy. He sought to please, but also to teach the truths of morality and religion, doing this in a mild and gentle fashion, avoiding any harsh ideas about sin or punishment. Two volumes of *Proeve van kleine Gedigten voor Kinderen* (*Specimens of little Verses for Children*) came out in Utrecht in 1778, and another followed in 1782. Their success was immediate and lasting, but the verses did not make their way abroad until the nineteenth century. The first German edition was published in 1831, a French edition in 1838, but no English translation appeared until 1856, when Partridge and Co. brought out '*Poetry for Children* by H. v. Alphen'. It was put into English verse by F. J. Millard, a teacher in Amsterdam. There were sixty-six poems in this edition. They stress the innocence and play of children, love and affection in their lives, sympathy with affliction, happy feelings about simple things. But the translation fails to convey the literary appeal of the original, perhaps being too literal in its aim. Van Alphen's verses were to be criticised later in the nineteenth century for their didactic tone and circum-scribed outlook, but for their period they are outstanding.

A Dutch writer of moral tales was Maria Geertrude de Cambon, who freely adapted the novels of Samuel Richardson for young readers, probably the best-known being *De kleine Grandisson* (ca. 1788–1789). In 1790 this came out in England as *The Young*

Grandison, somewhat adapted and abridged by its translator. There is in the story an exchange of visits between William from Holland and Charles of England, and this allows an opportunity for some comments on the Dutch nation. Charles finds them a 'mild people, polite and honest, and free from those dreadful vices which prevail so much in England'. Arnaud Berquin also made '*un traduction libre*' – *Le petit Grandison* – from the same work.

In the nineteenth century children's literature developed steadily, and many works from abroad were translated into Dutch. The reverse was much less common, and few works by popular Dutch writers seem to have been translated into English. J. J. A. Goeverneur (1809–1889) brought many foreign and classic works to Dutch children, and wrote for them rhymes and other compositions. Romance and historical fiction was supplied by P. J. Andriessen (1815-1877). Popular in their day, these writers and others contributed little that has endured in Dutch books for children.

The first Dutch writer to give young readers stories of real quality was Ninke van Hichtum (1860–1939). This was the pseudonym of M. D. Bokma de Boer S. Troelstra. She began to write children's books at the end of the nineteenth century, and the most outstanding of her tales is *Afke's Tiental* (*Afke's Ten*), published in 1903, but not translated into English until 1936, when it appeared in America and the year afterwards in England. It is a heartfelt story about a poor family in Friesland in former times, and their daily life is pictured with much vitality and tenderness. Each member, from Sipke 'the dolly' to Mother Afke herself, is made the centre of an episode within a continuous narrative.

The format and illustration of Dutch books for children has been criticised as unworthy of the achievement of the national art of printing in other fields. But at least three artists who made picture-books at the close of the century and in the next decade have a claim to excellence. Nelly Bodenheim (1874–1951) is notable for a pretty style of silhouette pictures from about 1896 onwards. Theo van Hoytema (1863–1917) made some large picture-books in colour lithography, with pictures and text designed as a unit, often within a frame. The illustrations he did for some of the Andersen fairy tales – though pictures dwarf the text – are among his best. H. Willebeek Le Mair (b. 1889) is better known abroad than either of these artists, as her work came out in England and America, not in Holland. Her pale pastel colours and naïve style are reminiscent of the work of Boutet de Monvel with whom she studied. *Our Old Nursery Rhymes* came out in 1911, the first of a series of song books which included *Old Dutch Nursery Rhymes* (text by Rosie Helen Elkin) in 1917. But these decorative volumes, though by a Rotterdam-born artist, are not picture-books made for Dutch children.

'Northerness' has an allure for the Briton for there is cultural and racial affinity between his country and the lands of the Norsemen going far back into the past. In children's literature this ancient common heritage lingers on in the sagas and the myths of the Norse gods. For over a century this lore has been a living part of English children's books.

The kinship between the nations of Scandinavia is naturally very much closer. 'Noteworthy is the fact', writes P. M. Mitchell in the preface to his *History of Danish Literature* (Bibl. 332), 'that since the beginning of the historical era Denmark, Sweden and Norway have spoken mutually intelligible dialects or languages'. This has had its effect upon literature for grown and growing.

DENMARK

Denmark stands high in the realm of children's books, for Denmark is synonymous with the name of Hans Christian Andersen, the great pioneer of a new kind of imaginative story for boys and girls, and author of some of the best-loved fairy stories in the world (p. 108). Maybe the lustre of his fame has tended to obscure, even to discourage, other developments in Danish children's literature.

From the beginning Denmark tended to rely on importations and influences from abroad for her children's books, especially from Germany. But when the age of reason encouraged the introduction of amusement into works of serious purpose for youth, the model to find favour was French – *Le Magasin des Enfans*, by Madame Le Prince de Beaumont (p. 213). The Danish imitation was *Den danske Skoelmester* (*The Danish Schoolmaster*) (1766–1767). According to Vibeke Stybe (Bibl. 334) this lacked the *esprit* shown by the French governess, being pedantic and didactic, unrelieved by fairy tales even of a moral purpose. It was followed by translations and adaptations from other French and German moral tales. Little books of knowledge, with hand-coloured pictures, notably from Germany, were another feature of Danish publishing for children as the eighteenth century elapsed.

Among the most popular translations in the first half of the nineteenth century was *Den Store Bastian* (1847), a Danish version of *Struwwelpeter* by Heinrich Hoffmann, containing three additional episodes in similar vein by an unknown writer. This introduced an element of nonsense into children's picture-books in Denmark. The German influence continued to affect books for children of many kinds, and the Romantic movement had its impact on Andersen, who admired the work of the Grimm brothers.

Picture fables were inspired by the popular fables by Hey, illustrated by Speckter. These were translated into Danish in 1834 and 1838. In 1844 H. V. Kaalund (1818–1885) produced some animal fables in verse in a similar style for a fine picture-book illustrated by J. T. Lundbye – *Fabler for Børn* (*Fables for Children*). The Hey fables were translated by Christian Winther (1796–1876), a romantic poet who contributed much to Danish literature. His narrative poem *Hjortens Flugt* (*The Flight of the Hart*) (1855) reflected Scott's influence and appealed to young people in their teens. Winther also translated and adapted some of the classic fairy tales for children, including Perrault, and he wrote for them original verses and fables. A famous picture-book, with pictures by Alfred Schmidt, was published in 1900, made from Winther's poem written about seventy years earlier – *Flugten til Amerika* (*The Flight to America*). It describes how two small boys plan to run away to this land of marvels full of huge sweetmeats and other delights, but their mother calls them away from their dream before they can put it into effect.

Picture-books and illustrated books increased in number and variety in the second half of the nineteenth century. Two gifted artists were Lorenz Frölich (1820–1908) and Louis Moe (1859–1945). Frölich was born in Denmark, but worked mainly in Germany and then in France, where many of his picture-books were first issued. Louis Moe, born in Norway, lived and worked in Denmark. Some of his picture-books became known in England in the 1920s. His first Danish picture-book came out in 1894.

A popular and enduring work of the mid-century is *Peters Jul* (*Peter's Christmas*), written in verse by Johan Krohn, and first published with undistinguished illustrations in 1866. Another edition with attractive pictures by Pietro Krohn came out in 1870. The pleasant wood-engravings in colour are exactly in harmony with these happy verses about a family Christmas and its delights. It has been little known outside Denmark, but an English version by Hugh F. Pooley was published in Copenhagen in 1968 with the original illustrations by Krohn.

The rich store of Danish ballads, folk-tales, and nursery rhymes became increasingly valued. Something has been given about the work of Svend Grundtvig in collecting Danish folk-tales and fairy tales (p. 122). Nursery rhymes were first printed for children in 1843, and ever since have had their place in books for young children in Denmark, inspiring poets to make verses for them in the same spirit.

About the middle of the nineteenth century English books began to rival those from Germany, especially realistic and adventure stories. Adaptations of English classic works, including Dickens and Marryat, and the American Fenimore Cooper, were published, and much preparation of Danish versions was done by Danish teachers and educationalists. There was also a flowering of home talent in writing for youth, although few Danish books became known abroad.

One writer of merit whose work had some vogue internationally early in the twentieth century was Carl Ewald (1856–1908). Some of his naturalistic *Eventyr*, published from

1882 onwards, were put into attractive English versions for children from 1907. Like Andersen he personified all kinds of creatures, but he was more influenced by the facts of natural history, and he sought to present an accurate picture of the natural world in an appealing yet profitable way to children. But today his tales are nearly forgotten, and Carl Ewald never captured the children's allegiance like his great predecessor. Hans Christian Andersen, perhaps honoured even more abroad than in his own land, has had no rival yet to take from him the appellation given by Paul Hazard to him as 'the very prince of all story writers for children'.

NORWAY

Norway was part of the kingdom of Denmark until 1814 and her literary language was Danish until the national awakening fostered a more Norwegian form of language in writing. A truly Norwegian literature for youth emerges therefore in the nineteenth century. The opening of a new epoch was marked by the publication of the *Norske Folkeeventyr* – the Norse folk tales – collected and adapted by Peter Christen Asbjørnsen and Jørgen Moe from 1841–1844 (p. 113). Told in the language of the Norwegian people these traditional tales contain more humour and fewer gruesome elements than in the Grimm collection. They form the great legacy to children's literature from this land of fjords and fjelds.

Both Asbjørnsen and Moe contributed much else to the development of children's books in Norway, writing original tales and adapting others, some still enduring. The need to educate and improve, however, long dominated the scene. 'Apart from folk tales, practically all Norwegian juvenile literature before 1850 is coloured by religion', writes Sonja Hagemann in the English summary appended to her history of Norwegian books for children up to that date (Bibl. 337). Evangelistic trends led to more solemn and pietistic attitudes in writing for youth in the first half of the nineteenth century. The effects of the Enlightenment also lingered in Norway longer than elsewhere. But there were gleams of morning. A great lyric poet, Henrik Wergeland (1808–1845), used his gifts to give children verses for their delight. He went to traditional rhymes and *Des Knaben Wunderhorn* for inspiration and material, but he could also reflect the conventions of the time. His *Vinterblommer i Barnekammeret* (*Winter Flowers in the Nursery*) (1840) is the foundation of children's verse in Norway.

The growing belief throughout Europe that children's reading should offer genuine entertainment and an outlet for the imagination made headway by the middle of the century. The first original work of literary merit to express this new attitude was by Jørgen Moe – *I Brønnen og i Tjernet* (*In the Well and the Tarn*) (1850). It appeared in an English translation by Jessie Young in 1883. The stories in it are centred on the experiences of five-year-old Beata and her elder brother Viggo. More about children's fancies than a fantasy, there is at least one magical element, a floating island that comes and goes and can grant a wish. Moral lessons are disguised within the narrative, so that the children find goodness themselves without any precepts from adults.

In the Well and the Tarn is now little-known outside Norway. Few Norwegian children's books seem to have made their way outside Scandinavia although a thriving literature developed at the close of the nineteenth century to supplement many translations and importations. One writer who became known in England and America was Hans Aanrud (1863–1953). His most famous story for youth is *Sidsel Sidserk* (1903), published in England as *Little Sidsel Longskirt* (1932). This is an idyllic tale of peasant life, about a little orphan herdsgirl and the two boys she meets on the summer mountain pastures. It reveals a love of animals and the countryside and sympathy with simple folk. *Sölve Solfeng (Solve Suntrap)* (1910) is in similar vein and came out in English in 1926. Both stories were to be illustrated in charming fashion by the D'Aulaires (Ingri Mortensen D'Aulaire being Norwegian born) in America in 1935.

The art of illustration was slow to reach distinction in Norway, and the first really notable picture-book came out in 1888. This is *Norsk Billedbok for Barn* (*Norwegian Picture-book for Children*) and according to Astrid Feydt (Bibl. 336) it is still a favourite. Elling Holst (1849–1915), a folklorist and scientist, provided for it a medley of songs, jingles and entertaining scraps dear to young children, and the pictures were by Eivend Nielsen.

SWEDEN

Swedish literature for children from the sixteenth century to the 1950s has been fully recorded, with much scholarship by Göte Klingberg up to the year 1839 (Bibl. 339), and in a copiously illustrated and more popular survey by Eva von Zweigbergk for the period 1750–1950 (Bibl. 342). Both authors treat their subject from the wider viewpoint covering European developments and translations, and append useful summaries in English. No European literature for children has been better chronicled.

As in other smaller countries in Western Europe children's books in Sweden relied to a large extent on foreign works in the earlier centuries, particularly from Germany and France. Before the eighteenth century religious and courtesy books predominated, but there were fables of course. From 1603 young Swedes had their version of the Chytraeus-Luther fables from Aesop – *Hundrade Esopi Fabler* – taken from the German. Later the French fabulists became influential, especially Fénelon and La Fontaine, and Swedish writers began to imitate these models. Original fables were written by Olof von Dalin and Carl Gustaf Tessin (1695–1770) for their royal pupil, the young crown prince Gustaf, born in 1746. Tessin included stories and prose fables in the letters he addressed to the little prince from 1751 to 1753. These were published as *Utkast af en Gammal Mans Dageliga Bref . . . til en Späd Prints*. The letters are a most interesting work, reflecting the more liberal ideas about education advocated by Fénelon and other pioneers, and it is important as the first Swedish book for children to make its way abroad. Two English versions soon appeared after its first publication in 1751–1753. The first in 1755 was apparently founded on a German translation. The second was a translation from the Swedish by J. Bercken-hout, and dedicated to the Prince of Wales. It came out in two volumes in 1756 as *Letters from an old Man to a Young Prince*. A few letters at the end from the young prince to his 'dear Tess' reveal the depth of affection between master and pupil.

Not many English books seem to have reached Sweden before the nineteenth century, but there was a Swedish edition of Sarah Fielding's *The Governess* in 1790. Other trends in Europe made their mark in the second half of the eighteenth century, especially the works by the German eductionalists, Weisse and Campe, and the French writers of moral tales, Arnaud Berquin and Madame de Genlis.

Literature to stimulate feeling and imagination rather than to instruct and improve began to emerge in the 1820s, including myths and fairy tales. But the moral or sentimental story about daily life, often with a religious aim, also flourished. Christian ideals permeated the work of Fredrika Bremer (1801–1865), who wrote novels as well as tales for younger readers. She travelled in England and America and became friendly with Mary Howitt, who translated some of her works into English. At least one book by Mary Howitt was put into Swedish by Miss Bremer – *The Children's Year* (1847) – published in 1848 as *Barnens År*. Fredrika Bremer was also a pioneer of women's rights and active in the provision of suitable books in cheap editions for poor children.

The outstanding landmark in the development of Swedish books for children in the nineteenth century is centred on Finland. Zachris Topelius (1818–1898), writer, professional historian, and patriot, lived in the Swedish-speaking region of Finland, then under Russian suzerainty. He is the first author to write Swedish stories, poems and plays of true imaginative quality and powerful appeal for children. His first volume of six stories came out in 1847, soon to be followed by others, and a collected edition of *Läsning for Barn* (*Reading for Children*) was issued in Stockholm from 1865 to 1896. Topelius's many tales and verses and little dramas were also published in Finnish. They are still treasured in his homeland, for they express a heartfelt love of Finland, her lakes and forests and traditions.

Topelius has a reverence for the wonder of life, a feeling for nature, and an understanding of the child mind, reminiscent of Andersen, his direct inspiration. But there are many differences between the two writers. Andersen's story-telling power is greater, more concise, more ironic, but the tales of Topelius have their own compelling and tender charm. 'I grew up in an atmosphere saturated with fairy tales, all things in nature lived, felt, and spoke . . .', he records of his boyhood.[1] There was a quickening interest at that time in Finnish history and traditions. The great collection of legends, forming the national epic, *The Kalevala*, had been published by Elias Lönnrot in 1835, and with other folklore then being explored, it was to be important in the development of a literature for children in Finland. But Finnish literature really began with the first translation of Topelius into Finnish in 1848.

The first English translations of children's tales by Topelius appeared in America in 1873, when six of his stories were included in a volume of translations by Selma Borg and Marie A. Brown, entitled *Northern Lights*. The distinction of introducing Topelius to English readers belongs to H. K. F. Gatty and Mrs. Ewing, the editors of *Aunt Judy's Magazine*. Towards the end of 1874 there appeared a tale about a proud birch tree putting out its tiny leaves or 'mouse-ears' in the spring, and how it learned a lesson in humility – *The Birch's great Plans during Mouse-ear Time*. Typical of Topelius is the happy ending, for at last the birch tree's dream of glory comes true. From its seed springs a little tree destined for the garden of a princess. More Topelius stories were printed in *Aunt Judy* in 1875 and 1876, including one of the best-known, *Sampo Lappelil*. Topelius identified the trolls, elves and goblins with the powers of darkness and evil, and the threat of these powers makes an exciting part of this tale about a boy who defies the wicked Fjeld King, and makes a thrilling escape.

In 1881 two volumes of stories appeared, translated by Albert Alberg, *Snowdrops* and *Whisperings in the Wood*. In 1910 Andrew Lang included several tales in the *Lilac Fairy Book*, and there was a selection, *Canute Whistlewinks and other stories*, published in America in 1927. A few Topelius stories may still linger in collections, but they have proved too altruistic and romantic in tone to appeal to the more materialistic outlook of today.

The finest edition of *Läsning för Barn* is undoubtedly the splendid two-volume edition published by Albert Bonnier in Stockholm in 1902–1903. A copy is in the British Museum and it enables the enquirer to appreciate something of the variety and excellence of Swedish book illustration for children, for the work is profusely illustrated by leading artists of the period, including Ottilia Adelborg and Carl Larsson. The Swedish picture-book for children had reached maturity, and soon a newcomer, Elsa Beskow (1874–1953), was to achieve fame with a series of attractive books for young children, better-known abroad in America than in England.

An interesting story of social import to make an impression abroad early this century

[1] *Zachris Topelius.* Chapter 4. Zweigbergk. (Bibl. 342). MS trans. by Ann Fowler.

was the last book to be written by Laura Fitinghoff (1848–1908). *Barnen ifrån Frostmof-jället* (*The Children of Frostmo Fell*) (1907) depicts a realistic aspect of Swedish life in the late 1860s. It came out in England as *The Children of the Frostmoor* in 1914, and it tells the story of seven children in the great famine of 1867, their journey south to find food, and their efforts to keep together.

Children in many lands know Sweden best in their books from the marvellous flight of Nils with the wild geese over the length and breadth of the land. *Nils Holgerssons underbara Resa genom Sverige* – published in English as *The Wonderful Adventures of Nils* and *The Further Adventures of Nils* – came out in two parts in 1906 and 1907. They were translated into English by Velma Swanston Howard, and first issued in America, the first part in 1907, the second in 1911. The author, Selma Lagerlöf (1858–1940), had been asked by the National Teachers' Association to write a geographical reader on Sweden, and after spending three years studying the folklore and natural history of the Swedish provinces, she produced this work of genius.

The land of Sweden, its climate, its landscape, its wild creatures, its people, its traditions, are seen through this magical device of story. Young Nils, a farmer's son, is not a pleasant child when his adventures begin, for he is bad-tempered and unkind to animals. Turned into a tiny elf he rides on the back of a wild goose and begins to find enlightenment, understanding the speech of animals. The narrative presents a unique blend of fantasy, natural history, folklore and description in a series of episodes, one of the most memorable being the great crane dance on Killaberg, a long low mountain near the sea in Skåne. Towards the end of his journey Nils meets at Mårbacka in Värmland his creator – and Selma Lagerlöf recalls in a brief interlude what this old manor where she spent her childhood meant to her. As living today as when it was written this saga of Swedish life is one of the great contributions from the north to have enriched children's literature.

Appendix 1

Chronological List, 1479 - 1798

Some significant or important works in children's literature from Caxton to the end of the eighteenth century.

A reference is added to those items written or partly intended for children from which the location of copies of first or earliest extant editions can be traced, or the actual location of a copy is given. This location of copies is neither systematic nor complete, merely a guide to those items which have come to the knowledge of the compiler. A fuller bibliography of important items in children's literature with location of editions is much needed.

Reference is also made to numbers in Appendix II if a work appears in this bibliography.

The place of publication is London unless otherwise stated.

Abbreviations

B.M.	Department of Printed Books, The British Museum
Bodl.	The Bodleian Library, Oxford
V. & A.	The Library of the Victoria and Albert Museum, South Kensington
Renier	The Library of Anne and Fernand Renier now gradually being transferred to the Library of the Victoria and Albert Museum
Arber	*The Term Catalogues, 1668–1709.* Edited by Edward Arber. 1903–1906. 3 vols.
Wing	Wing, Donald. *Short-title catalogue of books printed in England, Scotland, Ireland, Wales and British America, and of English books printed in other countries, 1641–1700.* Printed for the Index Society by Columbia University Press. New York. 1945–1951. 3 vols.

For details of the following see Appendix II under numbers given:

Evans	292	STC	49
Higson	39	Toronto	46
Roscoe	104	Welch	298
Sloane	74		

Year	Description	References in Appendix II
1479	*Stans puer ad mensam* (The Boy is standing at the table). A courtesy book ascribed to John Lydgate, based on the Latin of Sulpitius. Printed by Caxton. STC 17030	55, 57
1481	*The historye of Reynart the foxe* Translated from the Flemish and printed by Caxton. STC 20919	61, 62
1484	*The book of the subtyl historyes and fables of Esope . . .* Translated out of the French and printed by Caxton. STC 175	59, 60
1485	*Le Morte D'Arthur . . .* by Sir Thomas Malory. Printed by Caxton. STC 801	67, 68
1500 (ca.)	*A Lytell Geste of Robyn Hode . . .* Printed by Wynken de Worde. STC 13687 & 13689	72, 73

Year	Description	References in Appendix II

1500 (ca.) *Guy of Warwick* (popular medieval romance)
Printed by Richard Pynson. STC 12450
Printed by Wynken de Worde. STC 12541
Printed by Wm. Copland. ca. 1560. STC 12542 — 65

1517 *Gesta Romanorum* (Tales of the Romans)
English translation printed by Wynken de Worde. Bennett (II, 47), pp. 251, 264, 313 — 63

1532 Erasmus, Desiderius
De civilitate morum puerilium
Translated into English as *A Lytell booke of good manners for chyldren*, by Robert Whittington. Printed by Wynken de Worde. STC 10467. The original was printed abroad in 1526.

1537 *The Bible*
First licensed edition in English issued by James Nycolson of Southwark, text by Miles Coverdale, first printed abroad in 1535. STC 2064, 2065.
Another licensed edition, 'Matthew's Bible', edited by John Rogers, printed abroad, was issued by R. Grafton and E. Whitchurch the same year. STC 2066

1538 *The BAC* (*sic*) *bothe in Latyn and in Englysshe.* (The earliest extant reading book for children)
Printed (without authority) by Thomas Petyt. STC 19. Emmanuel College Lib., Cambridge. — 52

1550– Straparola, Gian Francesco
1553 *Le piacevoli notti* (Pleasant nights)
(A collection containing traditional tales). Venice. 2 pts. B.M.

1563 Foxe, John
Actes and monuments . . . (Foxe's Book of Martyrs)
Printed by John Day. STC 11222

1563 Newbery, Thomas
A Booke in Englysh metre of the great Marchaunt man called Dives Pragmaticus . . .
Printed for Alexander Lacy. STC 18491. John Rylands Lib. — 81

1579 Plutarch
The lives of the noble Grecians and Romans . . .
Translated out of the French into English by Thomas North. T. Vautroullier. STC 20065 — 64

1595 *The Children in the Wood* (traditional ballad)
Entered by Thomas Millington, Register of the Stationers' Company, 15th Oct., 1595. No. 174, *Oxford Book of Ballads* (II, 72)

1605 Cervantes Saavedra, Miguel de
El ingenioso Hidalgo Don Quijote de la Mancha
Madrid. B.M.
English translation 1612, by Thomas Skelton, *The History of the valorous and witty knight-errant, Don Quixote of the Mancha.* B.M. — 323

1605 *The vertuous Life and memorable Death of Sir Richard Whittington . . . a ballad*
Entered by John Wright, Register of the Stationers' Company, 16th July 1605.

1611 *The Bible*
The King James I authorised version.

Year	Description	References in Appendix II

1634–
1636 Basile, Giambattista
Lo cunto de li cunti (*The 'Pentamerone'*) (traditional tales)
Naples. 2 vols.
First English translation *The Tale of Tales* (1674)   313

1658 Comenius, John Amos
Orbis sensualium pictus (The visible world)
Nuremberg. Michael Endter. Translated into English by Charles Hoole. Printed for
J. Kirton. 1659. Wing 5523, B.M., Dr. Williams' Lib.   79, 80

1668 La Fontaine, Jean de
Fables choisis, mises en vers
Paris. Claude Barbin. Other fables followed in 1678–9 and 1694. B.M.

1671–
1672 Janeway, James
A Token for children . . .
Printed for Dorman Newman, 2 pts. Arber, I, 72, 122. Sloane 102. Wing J. 478–480.
The earliest copy extant is dated 1676, including a 1673 edition of Pt. 2. Bodl.

1674 Jole, William
The Father's blessing, penn'd for the instruction of his Children . . .
Printed for G. Conyers. Sloane 117. B.M.

1678 Bunyan, John
The Pilgrim's Progress, from this World to the next . . . (second part issued 1684)
Printed for N. Ponder. B.M.

1685 Crouch, Nathaniel ('R.B.' or 'Richard Burton')
England's Monarchs (an early example of secular history for youth)
Printed for N. Crouch. Wing 7314. B.M., Bodl.

1686 Bunyan, John
A Book for Boys and Girls . . . (later *Divine Emblems*)
Printed for N. Ponder. Wing B 5489. B.M., Harvard Univ. Lib.   78

1687–
1700 *The New England Primer*
Fragment of a printing by Bradford, New York. Sloane 163

1692 L'Estrange, Roger
The Fables of Aesop and other eminent mythologists
Printed for R. Sare, T. Sawbridge and others. B.M., Manchester City Lib.

1693 Locke, John
Some thoughts concerning education.   83, 84

1697 Perrault, Charles
Histoires ou contes du temps passé, avec des moralitez
Paris, Claude Barbin. First English translation by R. Samber issued in 1729 by
J. Pote and J. Montague. For text of original French edition in the Bibliothèque
Nationale, Paris, see II, 91. For facsimile of first English edition from photostat copy
in Harvard Univ. Lib. see II, 87.   87–92

1697–8 Aulnoy, Marie Catherine de Berneville, *Comtesse d'*
Contes de fées. Paris. 1697. 4 vols.
Nouvelles contes de fées. 1698. 4 vols. Storer, II, 93.
The first selection translated into English was *Tales of the Fairys.* T. Cockerill. 1699.
Arber. III, 123. The first comprehensive English edition was printed for J. Nicholson
and others in 1707. B.M.   86

1699   Fénelon, François de Salignac de la Mothe
Les Aventures de Télémaque, fils d'Ulysse
Paris. La veuve de Claude Barbin (first four and a half books only). Complete editions were issued in Brussels and The Hague the same year. A copy of The Hague edition B.M.

       The first part was issued in an English translation by Isaac Littlebury, *The Adventures of Telemachus*, by A. & J. Churchill, 1699. Other parts followed 1700–1701. B.M.

1700   Janeway, James (and Cotton Mather)
A Token for children . . . to which is added A Token for children of New England (by Cotton Mather).
Boston. Printed for Nicholas Boone. Welch 607.1. Sloane 102, 250. American Antiquarian Soc.

1702   W., T.
A Little book for little children . . . . (an early book of amusement for children)
Printed for Geo. Conyers. Sloane 257. B.M.

1704–   *Mille et une nuits* (The Arabian Nights' Entertainments)
1717   Translated from the Arabic by Antoine Galland. Paris. 12 vols. The first English version was issued by A. Bell, 1706–1708, in 7 vols. Seven vols. were recorded for a third edition in Arber, Easter 1711.

       B.M. has an incomplete set of 6 vols. dated 1712–1715   95

1715   Watts, Isaac
Divine songs, attempted in easy language for the use of children
Printed for M. Lawrence. Dr. Williams Lib.   111a

1719   Defoe, Daniel
The Life and strange surprising adventures of Robinson Crusoe, Mariner . . .
For W. Taylor. B.M.   232

1722   *Fables of Aesop, and others, newly done into English . . .* (by Samuel Croxall)
For J. Tonson & J. Watts. B.M.

1726   Swift, Jonathan
Travels into several remote nations of the world, in four parts, by Lemuel Gulliver
For Benj. Motte. B.M.

1727   Gay, John
Fables
For J. Tonson & J. Watts, Second vol. 1738. B.M.

1727   *The New England Primer*
Boston. Printed by S. Kneeland and T. Green. See also 1687–1700 above. Evans 2927. Sloane 163. New York Public Lib.   299

1730   *A Description of three hundred animals; viz. beasts, birds, fishes, serpents, and insects*
For Richard Ware, Tho. Boreman, and Tho. Game. B.M. (ascribed to Thomas Boreman and also to a Mr. McQuin. See note p. 201)

1740   *The Gigantick history of the two famous giants, and other curiosities in Guildhall, London*
For Thomas Boreman. 2 vols. Guildhall Lib.   101

Year	Description	References in Appendix II

1740– Richardson, Samuel

1741 *Pamela; or, virtue rewarded*
For E. Rivington & J. Osborne. A second volume followed in 1741, and two more in 1742. B.M.

An abridgement for youth of Richardson's novels came out in 1756 as *The Paths of Virtue delineated*, published by R. Baldwin. B.M.

1742 *The Child's new plaything; or, best amusement . . .*
For T. Cooper. Alston (II, 33). No. 551, Plate LIV, shows an advertisement for the first edition. Second edition 1743. B.M.

1744 *A Little Pretty Pocket-book.*
J. Newbery. Roscoe 225. For facsimile of earliest extant complete copy of 1767 (B.M.) see II, 102 — 102

1744 *Tommy Thumb's Pretty Song Book . . .* by Nurse Lovechild (the first nursery rhyme book for children)
For M. Cooper. B.M. (vol. 2 only). Issued by Isaiah Thomas in Worcester, Mass., 1788. — 107

1749 Fielding, Sarah
The Governess; or, little female academy
Printed for the author and sold by A. Millar. For facsimile of privately-owned first edition see II, 218. Second edition 1749. B.M., Bodl. — 218

1751 *The Lilliputian Magazine* (the first periodical for children)
Published by T. Carnan at Mr. Newbery's. Advertised in monthly numbers early in 1751. Roscoe 219. Earliest extant copy a collected volume ca. 1752. B.M. — 286

1751 Tessin, Carl Gustav
Utkast af en gammal mans dageliga bref . . . til en späd prints (An old man's daily letters to a young prince).
Stockholm. Lars Salvius. A further series came out in 1753.

English translations: *Letters to a young prince from his governor.* For A. Linde and S. Crowder, etc. 1755. B.M.

Letters from an old man to a young prince, translated by J. Berckenhout. For R. Griffith. 1756. 2 vols. B.M. — 340, 341

1756 Le Prince de Beaumont, Jeanne Marie
Le Magasin des enfans (includes the fairy tale, *Beauty and the Beast*)
J. Haberkorn. 4 vols. B.M. (wanting vol. 3). An English version was issued by J. Nourse in 1757, 4 vols. in 2, as *The Young Misses Magazine*. Second edition 1767. B.M.

1756(ca.) *A New Gift for children*
Boston. D. Fowle. 'The earliest known non-Biblical child's book in America'. Welch 848a, 848.1 Henry E. Huntington Lib., San Marino

1761 *The Newtonian system of philosophy* (*The Philosophy of tops and balls*) . . . .by Tom Telescope, A.M.
J. Newbery. Roscoe 348. B.M.

1762 Rousseau, Jean-Jacques
Émile; ou, de l'éducation — 124, 125

Year	Description	References in Appendix II

1782–
1787

Musaeus, J. K. A.

Volksmärchen der Deutschen (an early collection of German traditional tales) Gotha. B.M. (new ed. 1787–1788). English edition, *Popular tales of the Germans*, translated by W. Beckford, issued by J. Murray, 2 vols., 1791. B.M.

1782–
1783

Berquin, Arnaud

L'Ami des enfans

Paris. *chez* Pissot & Theophile Barrois, later Au Bureau de *L'Ami des enfans*. 24 pts. Jan. 1782–Dec. 1783. N.B.L. 454, B.M. (8 vols.). Also issued in London by Elmsley, 1782–1783. 24 pts. in 12 vols. Hockliffe, II, 40, incomplete. B.M. (1783). Toronto (1783)

First English translation, *The Children's Friend*, T. Cadell & P. Elmsley. 1783–1786. 6 vols. B.M. (wanting vol. 4). Another translation by Mark Anthony Meilan issued by J. Stockdale in 24 vols., 1786. B.M., Higson B 106

1783

A Curious hieroglyphic Bible . . . represented with near five hundred emblematical figures for the amusement of youth

T. Hodgson. V. & A. (Renier)

1783–
1789

Day, Thomas

The History of Sandford and Merton

J. Stockdale. 3 vols. B.M. Higson B 279

1783

Kilner, Dorothy ('M.P.')

The Village school

J. Marshall. 2 vols. N.B.L., 470 (II, 41). Bodl. (early undated copy, vol. 1 only)   32

1783–
1784

Kilner, Dorothy

The Life and perambulation of a mouse

J. Marshall. 2 vols. B.M., Toronto, N.B.L., 471 (II, 41)., Manchester City Lib. (ca. 1790)

1784

Genlis, Stéphanie Félicité du Crest de Saint Aubin, *Comtesse de*

Les Veillées du château; ou, cours de morale à l'usage des enfans

Paris. Les Libraires Associés. 4 vols. B.M. (vols. 1 & 3), Herts. County Lib. (vol. 2). English edition *Tales of the Castle*, translated by Thomas Holcroft. G. Robinson. 1785. 5 vols. Bodl., Toronto.

1785

The Beauty and the monster

A comedy from the French of Madame de Genlis. Worcester, Mass. Isaiah Thomas. The first children's book to be issued by the pioneer publisher of American books for children. Evans 19021, Welch 399. American Antiquarian Soc.

1785–
1789

Le Cabinet des fées

(Edited by C. J. Mayer). Amsterdam & Geneva. 41 vols. A collection of fairy tales chiefly those issued in France from the end of the 17th century. B.M., John Rylands Lib.

1786

Trimmer, Sarah

Fabulous histories: designed for the instruction of children respecting their treatment of animals (later *The History of the Robins*)

For T. Longman and others. B.M., V. & A., Toronto.

Year	Description	References in Appendix II

1789   Blake, William
Songs of innocence
Author & printer, W. Blake. A set of the original prints is in the Print Room at the
B.M.   143

1792–   Aikin, John and Barbauld, Anna L.
1796   *Evenings at home; or, the juvenile budget opened*
J. Johnson. 6 vols. B.M., Higson B 18, Toronto

1795   More, Hannah
The Shepherd of Salisbury Plain (one of the most famous of the 'Cheap Repository
Tracts')
Bath. Samuel Hazard. London. J. Marshall. Many original issues of the tracts are in
the B.M. and in collections at the Bath and Bristol City Libs.
    A volume of 18 original tracts, including *The Shepherd* is in the John Rylands Lib.   118, 119

1795   Ritson, Joseph, *editor*
Robin Hood. A collection of all the ancient poems, songs, and ballads now extant
Illus. by Thos. Bewick. T. Egerton & J. Johnson. 2 vols. B.M., Toronto   73

1795   Edgeworth, Maria
The Parent's assistant
J. Johnson. No copy of a 1795 edition has been traced. Second edition 1796. 2 pts. in
4 vols. Bodl. (wanting pt. 2, vol. 1), B.M. (pt. 1, vol. 1), Toronto, (pt. 2, 2 vols.).
Earliest complete edition the third edition 1800, 6 vols. B.M.

1798   Kendall, Edward Augustus
Keeper's travels in search of his master
E. Newbery. Roscoe 206. B.M., Renier, Toronto

Appendix II

Bibliography

This bibliography contains only a majority of the books consulted, and it can be supplemented from the lists given by Darton (5), Muir (17), Elva Smith (18) and Crouch (35). Among works not listed is one of the most important, the British Museum Catalogue of Printed Books.

Apart from the unequalled and vast resources of the British Museum Library, two other national libraries are important for their stock of children's books – the Bodleian Library, Oxford, and the Library of the Victoria and Albert Museum. The existence of a separate card catalogue for all children's books now held by the Victoria and Albert Museum Library is most useful. The extensive collection there is now being enlarged by a most valuable acquisition, the private library of old children's books owned by Anne and Fernand Renier.

Special collections of children's books in other libraries have also been valuable. No attempt is made to list them as it is understood a guide to these collections is now just published by the London and Home Counties Branch of the Youth Libraries Group of the Library Association.

The bibliography does not include editions of children's books or texts, except in cases where an introduction has been useful or a facsimile reproduction has been made.

Unless stated otherwise the place of publication is London.

A   General Sources

1   ANDREAE, Gesiena   *The Dawn of juvenile literature in England.*
    Amsterdam. H. J. Paris. 1925
    Deals with theories of education, and the child in literature and poetry, as well as the evolution of children's books in the eighteenth century. Superseded bibliographically but interesting for its analysis of the background.

2   AVERY, Gillian   *Nineteenth century children; heroes and heroines in English children's stories, 1780–1900*
    With the assistance of Angela Bull. Hodder & Stoughton. 1965
    In three parts: The child improved; The child amused; Adult attitudes.

3   BARRY, Florence V.   *A century of children's books*
    Methuen. 1923
    Chiefly the eighteenth century. Contains useful information about romances and chapbooks, but there is no index.

4   COVENEY, Peter   *The image of childhood.* With an intro. by F. R. Leavis, Rev. ed.
    Penguin Books. 1967

First published as *Poor Monkey* in 1957. 'The individual and society: a study of the theme in English literature'.

5　Darton, F. J. Harvey　*Children's books in England: five centuries of social life.* 2nd. ed.
　Cambridge University Press. 1958
　　The standard history of the subject. It contains detailed bibliographies brought up to date by Kathleen Lines. There is also a shorter and simpler outline by Darton (largely superseded by this history) in the *Cambridge History of English Literature*, vol. xi, chapter xvi, *Children's Books* (first published 1914).

6　Dictionary of National Biography　Edited by Leslie Stephen and Sir Sidney Lea
　1908–1909. 21 vols. Also Supplements, 1909–1912, etc.
　　The source for valuable information about most writers and other persons concerned in the history of books for children.

7　Doyle, Brian, *editor*　*The Who's who of children's literature*
　Evelyn. 1968
　　Selective, but useful for information about lesser writers not easily found elsewhere.

8　Egoff, Sheila, Stubbs, G. T., and Ashley, L. F., *editors*　*Only connect: readings in children's literature*
　Toronto. Oxford University Press, 1969
　　Includes some articles on writers of the past, notably: Janeway, Elizabeth. *Meg, Jo, Beth, Amy and Louisa* (L. M. Alcott): Eliot, T. S. *Huckleberry Finn*: Williams, Alan M. *Hans Christian Andersen*: Laws, Frederick. *Randolph Caldecott*: White, Alison. *With birds in his beard* (Lear). Also Tolkien, J. R. R. *Children and fairy stories*.

9　Ellis, Alec　*A History of children's reading and literature*
　Pergamon Press. 1968
　　Covers the period from the end of the eighteenth century to recent times, chiefly relating children's books to the history of education and school libraries.

10　Field, Louise Frances (Mrs. E. M. Field)　*The Child and his book*
　Wells Gardner. 2nd ed. 1892. Reprinted Detroit, Singing Tree Press, 1968.
　　Out of date but useful for its early chapters on the period from Saxon to Tudor times, and for educational books.

11　Green, Roger Lancelyn　*Tellers of tales: children's books and their authors from 1800 to 1964.* Rev. ed.
　Edmund Ward. 1965
　　First published 1946. Includes a chronological table of famous children's books to the present day, and lists of titles by each author.

12　Hazard, Paul　*Books, children and men.* Trans. (from *Les Livres, les enfants, et les hommes,* Flammarion, 1932) by Marguerite Mitchell. 3rd. ed.
　Boston. The Horn Book Inc. 1947
　　A French professor's critical and stimulating survey analysing the classics in children's literature. He also examines national traits in children's books, and looks at the subject from a comparative and historical viewpoint, with few bibliographical details. An excellent introduction.

13　James, Philip　*Children's books of yesterday.* Special autumn number of 'The Studio', edited by C. G. Holme. 1933
　　Chiefly reproductions of title-pages and illustrations, with brief notes, and an introduction. Covers the period from Comenius to Kipling.

14　Mahony, Bertha E., *and others*　*Illustrators of children's books, 1744–1945*
　Boston. The Horn Book Inc. 1947
　　Includes a bibliography of works illustrated by English, American and foreign artists, and chapters on the history of children's book illustration in America and in England.

15   MEIGS, Cornelia, *editor*   *A Critical history of children's literature: a survey of children's books in English prepared in four parts . . . Rev. ed.*

New York & London. The Macmillan Co. 1969

     First issued 1953. Pt. 1, *Roots in the past up to 1840*, by Cornelia Meigs: Pt. 2, *Widening horizons, 1840–1890*, by Anne Thaxter Eaton: Pt. 3, *A Rightful heritage, 1890–1920*, by Elizabeth Nesbitt: Pt. 4, *Golden years and time of tumult, 1920–1967*, by Ruth Hill Viguers. Especially useful for American books.

16   MORRIS, Charles H.   *The Illustration of children's books*

The Library Association. Pamphlet No. 16. 1957

     An introduction of 18 pages.

17   MUIR, Percy H.   *English children's books, 1600–1900*

Batsford. 1954. Reprinted 1969

     Excellent for bibliographical information not to be found elsewhere and for its illustrations. Not a book for the beginner, but valuable for its lists of sources, and as a work of reference.

18   SMITH, Elva S.   *The History of children's literature: a syllabus with selected bibliographies*

Chicago. American Library Association. 1937

     Covers the period from Anglo-Saxon times to the end of the nineteenth century. An outline for study with lists of sources, rather than a history. Founded on the lecture courses for children's librarians at the Carnegie Library School, Pittsburgh.

19   SMITH, Janet Adam   *Children's illustrated books*

Collins. 1948

     A general introduction in the 'Britain in Pictures' series.

20   TARG, William, *editor*   *Bibliophile in the nursery: a bookman's treasury of collector's lore on old and rare children's books, edited and with an intro. and notes*

Cleveland & New York. World Publ. Co. 1957

     Includes a selection from the Exhibition Catalogue of the Pierpont Morgan Library (43), chapters on London cries, the work of the brothers Grimm etc., and extracts from various works on children's literature.

21   TOWNSEND, John Rowe   *Written for children*

Garnet Miller. 1965

     'An outline of English children's literature'. An introduction to the main features of the subject.

22   WHITE, Gleeson   *Children's books and their illustrators.*

Special Winter number of 'The Studio', 1897–1898

     Interesting as a survey of seventy years ago assessing children's books and their development, especially in the late Victorian period.

COLLECTIONS AND ANTHOLOGIES

23   AVERY, Gillian, *editor*   *The Hole in the wall, and other stories.* Illustrated by Doreen Roberts

Oxford University Press. 1968

     Contents: *The Hole in the wall*, by Annie Keary: *The old story of Mrs. Howard*, and *The stolen child*, by Mrs. Sherwood: *A Puzzle for a curious girl* (anon.): *Waste not, want not*, by Maria Edgeworth: *The Grandmother's shoe*, by Jean Ingelow: *The Little rick-burners*, by Charlotte Yonge: *Snap-dragons*, by J. H. Ewing.

24   AVERY, Gillian, *editor*   *In the window-seat: a selection of Victorian stories.* Illustrated by Susan Einzig

Oxford University Press. 1960

     Contents: *Through the fire*, by Mary de Morgan: *The Hundredth birthday*, by Mrs. Gatty: *A Bad habit*, by J. H. Ewing: *Johnny and Nayum*, by Annie Keary: *The Travels of two Kits*, by Charlotte

Yonge: *The Yew-Lane ghosts*, by J. H. Ewing: *The Apple-pie*, by Ann Fraser Tytler: *The Nurnberg stove*, by Ouida.

25   Lucas, E. V., *editor Forgotten tales of long ago*. With illustrations by F. D. Bedford
Wells Gardner. 1906
      Twenty tales, some slightly abridged, nearly all within 1780–1830. Includes *Jemima Placid*, by Mary Kilner.

26   Lucas, E. V., *editor Old-fashioned tales*. With illustrations by F. D. Bedford
Wells Gardner. 1905
      Contains nineteen stories of the same period as 25, including *The History of little Jack*, by Thomas Day.

27   Tuer, A. W., *editor Pages and pictures from forgotten children's books*. With 400 illustrations
Leadenhall Press. 1898–1899
      Reproductions from about 100 children's books published between 1780 and 1830.

28   Tuer, A. W., *editor Stories from old-fashioned children's books*. With 250 cuts
Leadenhall Press, 1899–1900 Reprinted Evelyn, Adams and Mackay, 1969
      Extracts, title-pages, and some complete tales from about 200 books, 1780–1830.

29   Not used.

30   Vries, Leonard de *Flowers of delight, culled by Leonard de Vries from the Osborne collection of early children's books*. Embellished with some 750 woodcuts and engravings . . . of which upwards of 125 are neatly coloured.
Dennis Dobson. 1965
      Items selected from the collection housed at the Toronto Library, covering the period 1765 to 1830.

31   Vries, Leonard de *Little Wideawake*. An anthology from Victorian children's books and periodicals in the collection of Anne and Fernand Renier
Arthur Barker. 1967
      Mainly from the lesser-known and more typical products of the period.

32   Yonge, Charlotte M., *editor A Storehouse of stories*
Macmillan. 1872. 2 vols.
      vol. 1: *The History of Philip Quarll: Goody Two-shoes: The Governess: Jemima Placid: The Perambulations of a mouse: The Village school: The Little Queen: History of Little Jack*.
      vol. 2: *Family stories: Elements of morality: A Puzzle for a curious girl: The Blossoms of morality* (selections).

CATALOGUES AND BIBLIOGRAPHIES

33   Alston, R. C. *Bibliography of the English language, vol. 4, Spelling books*
Bradford. Printed for the author by Ernest Cummins. 1967
      No. 551 is an advertisement for *The Child's New Plaything* (1742). Most items are educational or scholastic.

34   Cambridge Bibliography of English Literature. Edited by F. W. Bateson
Cambridge University Press. 1940. 4 vols. also supplement 1957
      There are lists of children's books (excluding school books, traditional fairy tales, annexed books, romances, fables, nursery rhymes and chapbooks) as follows:
vol. 2 pp. 553–560
vol. 3 pp. 564–579
      There are also other helpful sections in this bibliography.

35   CROUCH, Marcus, *editor*   *Books about children's literature*
Library Association. 1963
    Includes the books in the Woodfield collection now housed at the Manchester School of Librarianship.

36   FLORIDA STATE UNIVERSITY   *Shaw Childhood in Poetry Collection*
Shaw, John Mackay. A Catalogue of the Shaw Childhood in Poetry Collection, with biographical and critical annotations of the books of English and American poets, with lists of poems that relate to childhood, notes and index
Detroit. Michigan. Gale Research Co. 1967. 5 vols.
    Covers the contents of many old children's books. There is a comprehensive subject index of poems.

37   GUMUCHIAN et Cie   *Les Livres de l'enfance du xve au xixe siècle*
Paris. 1930. 2 vols.
    A French bookseller's catalogue of over 6000 items, with an introduction in French and English. It covers English, French, German and American books, with annotations in the language of the original. Vol. 1 comprises the catalogue, vol. 2 the plates.

38   HAVILAND, Virginia, *editor*   *Children's literature: a guide to reference sources*
Washington. Library of Congress. 1966
    An annotated list which covers historical aspects as well as many others.

39   HIGSON, C. W. J., *editor*   *Sources for the history of education*
Library Association. 1967
    'A list of material (including school books) contained in the libraries of the Institutes and Schools of Education, together with works from the libraries of the Universities of Nottingham and Reading'. Includes old children's books in these libraries from the 15th century.

40   HOCKLIFFE collection. Boggis, Doreen H., *compiler*   *Catalogue of the Hockliffe collection of early children's books*
Bedford College of Education. 1969

41   NATIONAL BOOK LEAGUE   *Children's books of yesterday*. Catalogue of an exhibition compiled by Percy H. Muir
National Book League. 1946
    A catalogue of 1001 items, with notes, including school-books, games, puzzles, etc. There is no index.

42   NATIONAL BOOK LEAGUE   *Festival of Britain*   Exhibition of books at the Victoria and Albert Museum, 1951
Cambridge University Press, 1951
    Pages 22–39 are devoted to the 'Children's Corner' of 80 items, fully annotated, from the sixteenth to the twentieth century.

43   NEW YORK   Pierpont Morgan Library   *Children's literature: books and manuscripts*. Catalogue of an exhibition, November 19th, 1954 – 28th February, 1955, compiled by Herbert Cahoun
New York. The Pierpont Morgan Library. 1954

44   PELLOWSKI, Anne   *The World of children's literature*
New York and London. R. R. Bowker Co. 1968
    A comprehensive bibliography of 4496 entries, with useful annotations and introductory comments about children's books in 80 countries. History is one of many aspects covered.

45   PRESTON   Harris Public Library Spencer Collection   *A Catalogue of the Spencer collection of early children's books and chapbooks*, presented to the Harris Public Library by Mr. J. H. Spencer, 1947. Compiled by David Good. With an introduction by Percy H. Muir.
Preston. Harris Public Library. 1967

Arranged under types of literature. Includes adult chapbooks. There are indexes of artists and engravers as well as authors and titles.

46   TORONTO PUBLIC LIBRARY   *The Osborne collection of early children's books, 1566–1910.* A catalogue prepared by Judith St. John at Boys' and Girls' House. With an introduction by Edgar Osborne Toronto Public Library. 1958. Revised with minor corrections 1966

A fully-annotated catalogue of about 3000 books, under headings which group them in the same way as the modern books at Boys' and Girls' House. There are useful appendices, including an annotated list of engravers and illustrators, and one of publishers, printers, and booksellers. Its excellent index enhances its value as a reference book.

A short supplement was issued in 1964 'A Chronicle of Boys' and Girls' House and A selected list of additions to the Osborne collection'.

B   Chapter Bibliographies

1   (i) PRINTING: ITS HERITAGE AND PROMISE

47   BENNETT, H. S.   *English books and readers, 1475–1557.* 2nd ed.
Cambridge University Press. 1969
Also his *English books and readers, 1558–1603* (C.U.P. 1965). The first volume has a chapter on literacy and a handlist of publications printed by Wynken de Worde.

48   DUFF, E. G.   *The Introduction of printing in England and the early work of the press.* Chapter xiii, vol. 2 Cambridge History of English Literature, edited by Sir A. W. Ward and A. R. Waller
Cambridge University Press. First publ. 1908

49   POLLARD, A. W. and REDGRAVE, G. R. (and others)   *A Short title catalogue of books printed in England, Scotland and Ireland, and of English books printed abroad, 1475–1640*
Oxford. The Bibliographical Society. 1926. Reprinted 1946

ABCS, PRIMERS AND HORNBOOKS

50   BUTTERWORTH, C. C.   *Early primers for the use of children*
New York. Papers of the Bibliographical Society of America. vol. 43. 4th quarter. 1949

51   FOLMSBEE, BEULAH   *A Little history of the hornbook*
Boston. The Horn Book Inc. 1942

52   SHUCKBURGH, E. S.   Introduction to facsimile edition of *The BAC both in Latyn and Englysshe* (the earliest extant English reading book)
Elliott Stock. 1889

53   TUER, A. W.   *The history of the hornbook*
Leadenhall Press. 1897. 2 vols.

CAXTON

54   BLADES, WILLIAM   *The Biography and typography of William Caxton.* 2nd ed.
Trubner & Co. 1882. Reprinted, Murray 1971.

55   FURNIVALL, F. J.   *Manners and meals of olden time.* (*The Babees Book*, etc.)
       Early English Text Society, 1868. reprinted 1904
         Includes texts of some fifteenth and sixteenth century courtesy books, with explanatory prefaces, including 'Stans puer ad mensam', 'Urbanitatis', Russell's 'Book of Nurture', Seager's 'School of Virtue' etc.

56   MASON, JOHN E.   *Gentlefolk in the making:* studies in the history of English courtesy literature and related topics from 1531–1774
       Philadelphia. 1935
         A dissertation presented to the Faculty of the Graduate School of Pennyslvania. An exhaustive treatise not confined to children's literature.

57   RICKERT, Edith, *editor* *The Babees book*
       Chatto. 1908
         Some medieval and sixteenth century courtesy books modernised from the texts of Dr. Furnivall.

FABLES

58   QUINNAM, Barbara, *editor*   *Fables from incunabula to modern picture books: a selective bibliography*
       Washington. Library of Congress. 1966

59   AESOP   *Caxton's Aesop.* Edited with an introduction and notes, by R. T. Lenaghan
       Cambridge, Mass. Harvard University Press. 1967
         The woodcuts are not taken from Caxton's Aesop, but from the Augsburg *Esopus* of 1477.

60   AESOP   *Fables of Aesop as first printed by Caxton in 1484* ... edited by Joseph Jacobs
       Nutt. 1889. 2 vols.
         Jacobs also edited a children's edition from Caxton in one volume containing 82 fables, with pictures by Richard Heighway (*Fables of Aesop*. Macmillan. 1894).

61   *Reynard the Fox, and other mediaeval Netherlands secular literature.* Edited and introduced by E. Colledge. Trans. by Adriaan J. Barnouw and E. Colledge
       Heinemann. 1967

62   *The Most delectable history of Reynard the Fox.* Edited with an introduction and notes by Joseph Jacobs. Done into pictures by W. Frank Calderon
       Macmillan. 1895
         A text for children founded on Caxton's version. A retelling was made from this by Roy Brown in 1969, published by Abelard-Schuman.

63   GESTA ROMANORUM   Entertaining and moral stories invented by the monks. Trans. by Charles Swan, with a preface by E. A. Baker
       Routledge. 1905. (Library of Early English Novelists)
         First translated by Swan in 1824.

64   PLUTARCH's   *Lives of the noble Grecians and Romans.* Englished by Sir Thomas North, anno 1579. With an introduction by George Wyndham
       Nutt, 1895. 6 vols.

1 (ii) ROMANCE AND TRADITIONAL LITERATURE

65   ASHTON, John   *Romances of chivalry.* Told and described in facsimile
       Unwin. 1887
         Guy of Warwick, Melusine, Valentine and Orson, Sir Bevis of Hampton, and eight other romances, mostly as first printed in English.

66 CAMBRIDGE HISTORY OF ENGLISH LITERATURE, vol. 1, Chapters xii, xiii, and xiv (see 48)

67 MALORY, Sir Thomas *Works*. Edited by Eugene Vinaver. 2nd ed.
Oxford University Press. 1967. 3 vols.
    Also shorter one volume edition published 1954.

68 MALORY, Sir Thomas *Le Morte d'Arthur*. Edited by Janet Cowen, with an introduction by John Lawlor. Penguin Books. 1969. 2 vols.
    A modernised version chiefly founded on Caxton's text.

69 The MABINOGION Translated by Gwyn Jones and Thomas Jones
Dent. 1949. (Everyman's Library)
    The former volume in the series was the translation by Lady Charlotte Guest, who first translated these Welsh bardic tales into English in 1838–1849.

BALLADS

70 GUMMERE, F. B. *Ballads*. Vol. 2., chapter vii. Cambridge History of English Literature. (see 48)

71 CHILD, F. J. *English and Scottish ballads*. New edition.
Oxford University Press. 1957. 5 vols.
    First published 1882–1898. A useful shorter edition, giving fewer variants, is that edited by Helen Sargent and George Lyman Kittredge (Houghton & Mifflin Co., 1904).

72 COUCH, Sir Arthur Quiller-, *editor* *The Oxford book of ballads*
Oxford University Press. 1910. Reprinted 1963
    No. 115 is 'A Lytell geste of Robin Hood and his meiny'.

73 RITSON, Joseph, *editor* *Robin Hood*. A collection of songs and ballads. Routledge. 1884
    First published 1795.

1 (iii) DEVELOPMENTS IN THE SIXTEENTH AND SEVENTEENTH CENTURIES

74 SLOANE, William *Children's books in England and America in the 17th century*: a history and a checklist, together with 'The Young Christian's Library', the first printed catalogue of books for children. New York. King's Crown Press. Columbia University. 1955
    A full and scholarly account with many references to sources for the period 1557–1710.

75 WATSON, Foster *The English grammar schools to 1660: their curriculum and practice*
Cambridge University Press. 1908

76 FREEMAN, Rosemary *English emblem books*.
Chatto & Windus. 1948. Reprinted 1967

77 ASCHAM, Roger *The Schoolmaster* (1570). Edited by Lawrence V. Ryan
Oxford University Press (Cornell University Press). 1968
    The text is also in Ascham's *English works*, edited by W. A. Wright
Cambridge University Press, 1904

78 BUNYAN, John *A Book for boys and girls* (1686). Facsimile of the first edition, with an introduction by John Brown
Elliott Stock. 1890

79 COMENIUS, John Amos *Orbis sensualium pictus*. Facsimile of the third London edition (from the copy in the Bodleian Library). With an introduction by James Bowen
Australia. Sydney University Press. 1967

80 COMENIUS, John Amos *Orbis pictus*. A facsimile of the first English edition of 1659 (British Museum copy), introduced by John E. Sadler
Oxford University Press. 1968. (The Juvenile Library)

81 NEWBERY, Thomas *A Booke in Englysh metre of the great marchaunt man called Dives Pragmaticus . . .* (1563). Reproduced in facsimile from the copy in the John Rylands Library, Manchester, together with an introduction by Percy Newbery
Manchester University Press. 1910

82 SIDNEY, Sir Philip *A Defence of poetry* (*Apologie for poetrie*, first published 1591). Edited with an introduction and notes by J. A. Van Dorsten
Oxford University Press. 1966

2 (i) REASON VERSUS FAIRY LORE

LOCKE, JOHN

83 LOCKE, John *The Educational writings of John Locke.* Critical edition, with introduction by James A. Axtell
Cambridge University Press. 1968

84 LOCKE, John *Some thoughts concerning education* (*1693*). With an introduction and notes by R. H. Quick. 2nd ed.
Cambridge University Press. 1899
The text is also included in 83 above.

85 WILLEY, Basil *The Seventeenth century background. Chapter xi, John Locke*
Chatto & Windus. 1942. Penguin Books. 1962

PERRAULT AND THE FRENCH FAIRY TALE

86 AULNOY, Marie Catherine le Mothe, *Comtesse* d' *Fairy tales.* Translated by J. R. Planché, with an introduction
Routledge. (1855) 1858

87 BARCHILON, Jacques and PETTIT, Henry, *editors The Authentic Mother Goose: fairy tales and nursery rhymes*
Denver, Colorado. Alan Swallow. 1960
Includes a facsimile of the first English translation of Perrault's *Histories or Tales of past times* (1729) made from a photo-stat in the Houghton Library, Harvard University. Besides the eight prose tales by Perrault, this edition includes *The Discreet Princess*, by Jeanne l'Heritier. The second part is a facsimile of *Mother Goose's Melody* (1791 edition). See 108, Roscoe 250.

88 PERRAULT, Charles *The Fairy Tales of Charles Perrault.* Translated with an introduction by Geoffrey Brereton
Penguin Books. 1957

89 PERRAULT, Charles *The Fairy Tales of Charles Perrault.* Translated by Norman Denny
Bodley Head. 1951

90 PERRAULT, Charles *Histories or Tales of past times, told by Mother Goose; with morals . . .* Englished by G. M. *Gent.* newly edited by J. Saxon Childers
Nonesuch Press. 1925
Reproduces the text of an eleventh edition dated 1719, now believed to be a misprint for 1799. There was also a facsimile of the 12th edition of 1802 issued in 1928 by the Fortune Press.

91 PERRAULT, Charles *Popular tales.* Edited from the original edition, with an introduction by Andrew Lang
Oxford. Clarendon Press. 1888
Reproduces the French text of 1697.

92 SORIANO, Marc *Les Contes de Perrault: culture savante et traditions populaires*
Paris. Gallimard. 1968
   A thorough analysis going into the evidence for Perrault's authorship, derivation and the place of the tales in letters and folklore.

93 STORER, Mary Elizabeth *La Mode des contes de fées (1685–1700)*
Paris. Champion. 1928

ARABIAN NIGHTS' AND EASTERN TALES

94 CONANT, Martha Pike *The Oriental tale in England in the eighteenth century*
New York. Columbia University Press. 1908

95 THE THOUSAND AND ONE NIGHTS: The Hunchback, Sinbad, and other tales. Trans. with an introduction by N. J. Dawood
Penguin Books. 1954. (Penguin Classics)
   Another volume translated by Dawood, *Aladdin and other tales*, appeared in the Penguin Classics series in 1957

CHAPBOOKS

96 ASHTON, John *Chapbooks of the eighteenth century.*
Chatto. 1882. Reprinted Seven Dials Press. 1969
   Mainly reproductions of illustrations, texts, extracts from a variety of chapbooks 1700–1800.

97 HINDLEY, Charles *The History of the Catnach Press, at Berwick-upon-Tweed, Alnwick, Newcastle-upon-Tyne, and Seven Dials, London.* With the original illustrations
London. Charles Hindley (the younger). 1887

98 NEUBURG, Victor E. *Chapbooks.* A bibliography of references to English and American chapbook literature of the eighteenth and nineteenth centuries
The Vine Press. 1964

99 NEUBURG, Victor E. *The Penny histories.* A study of chapbooks for young readers over two centuries. Illustrated with facsimiles of seven chapbooks
Oxford University Press. 1968. (The Juvenile Library)
   Contains much information about chapbook publishing here and in America. The items reproduced are: *Guy of Warwick* (also in 96), *Fairy stories* (two shortened d'Aulnoy stories), *The Children in the wood, Cock Robin, Toads and diamonds* (a Catnach press version), a religious tract, *The Rod*, and an American chapbook, *A Peep at various nations.*

JOHNSON, RICHARD

100 WEEDON, M. J. P. *Richard Johnson and the successors to John Newbery.* Bibliographical Society. *The Library.* Fifth series. vol. 5. June 1949

2 (ii) JOHN NEWBERY AND THE BEGINNINGS OF A PUBLISHING TRADE FOR BOYS AND GIRLS

BOREMAN

101 STONE, Wilbur Macey *The Gigantick histories of Thomas Boreman*
Portland, Maine. The Southworth Press. 1933

NEWBERY, JOHN

102 A LITTLE PRETTY POCKET-BOOK A facsimile with an introductory essay and bibliography by M. F. Thwaite
  Oxford University Press. 1966 (The Juvenile Library)
    A facsimile of the 1767 copy in the British Museum. A facsimile of the first Worcester edition of 1787 by Isaiah Thomas in Massachusetts was issued in New York by F. G. Melcher in 1944.

103 The HISTORY OF LITTLE GOODY TWO-SHOES. Facsimile reprint of the third edition of 1766, with an introduction by Charles Welsh
  Griffith Farran etc. 1881
    For details of the unique copy of the first edition of 1765 now in the British Museum see article by Julian Roberts in the *British Museum Quarterly*, vol. xxix, 3–4, 1965.

104 ROSCOE, Sydney, *editor Newbery-Carnan-Power*. A provisional check-list of books for the entertainment, instruction and education of children and young people, issued under the imprints of John Newbery and his family in the period 1742–1802
  William Dawson & Sons. 1966
    A revised bibliography is now being printed.

105 WELSH, Charles *A Bookseller of the last century*. Griffith Farran etc. 1884
    The list of Newbery publications in the appendix has now been revised by S. Roscoe (104).

For Christopher Smart see 112–114.

NURSERY RHYMES

106 OPIE, Iona and Peter *The Oxford Dictionary of nursery rhymes*
  Oxford University Press. 1951

107 TOMMY THUMB'S SONG BOOK for all little Masters and Misses. A facsimile of the first American edition published by Isaiah Thomas, Worcester, Mass. in 1788
  New York. F. G. Melcher. 1946
    This American edition was closely based on the 1744 English edition published by M. Cooper.

108 MOTHER GOOSE'S MELODY; or, Sonnets for the cradle. Facsimile of the earliest extant edition of 1791, printed for F. Power. With an introduction and notes by W. F. Prideaux
  Bullen. 1904

109 MOTHER GOOSE'S MELODY; or, Sonnets for the cradle. Facsimile of the second Worcester edition published by Isaiah Thomas in 1794 (first issued in 1786)
  New York. F. G. Melcher. 1945
  See also note by M. J. P. Weedon on *Mother Goose's Melody*, in *The Library*, 5th ser., vol. 4. Dec. 1951. Also 87.

2 (iii) THE CHRISTIAN TRADITION: FROM ISAAC WATTS TO THE SUNDAY SCHOOLS

110 JONES, M. G. *The Charity School movement: a study of eighteenth century Puritanism in action*
  Frank Cass. 1964
    First published 1938. Contains a valuable chapter on the establishment of Sunday Schools.

WATTS, ISAAC

111 DAVIS, A. P. *Isaac Watts*. Independent Press. 1948

111a WATTS, Isaac *Divine songs* . . . Facsimile reproductions of the first edition of 1715 and an illustrated edition of ca. 1840, with an introduction and bibliography by J. H. P. Pafford
  Oxford University Press. 1971 (The Juvenile Library)

SMART, CHRISTOPHER

112   BRITTAIN, Robert E.   *Christopher Smart's Hymns for the amusement of children*. New York. Papers of the Bibliographical Society of America. vol. 35. 1941. pp. 61–5

113   DEVLIN, Christopher   *Poor Kit Smart*
Hart-Davis. 1961

114   SMART, Christopher   *Hymns for the amusement of children*. A facsimile of the third edition of 1775, with an introduction by Edmund Blunden. Oxford. Printed for the Luttrell Society
Basil Blackwell. 1947

SUNDAY SCHOOLS

115   KENDALL, Guy   *Robert Raikes: a critical study*
Nicholson & Watson. 1939
      Based on an earlier authoritative biography, *Robert Raikes, the man and his work*, by J. H. Harris (Arrowsmith, 1899).

116   RICE, Edwin Wilbur   *The Sunday-school movement and the American Sunday School Union*. 2nd ed. Philadelphia. Published by the Union. 1927
      Traces the history of English as well as American Sunday Schools. See also 288.

TRACTS

117   GREEN, Samuel G.   *The Story of the Religious Tract Society for one hundred years*
Religious Tract Society. 1899

118   JONES, M. G.   *Hannah More*. Cambridge University Press. 1952

119   SPINNEY, G. H.   *Cheap Repository Tracts. The Library*. ser. 4. xx. 1939. pp. 295–340
For American tracts see 297.

SHERWOOD, MRS. M. M.

120   SHERWOOD, Martha M.   *The Life and times of Mrs. Sherwood, 1775–1851*. Edited from the diaries of Captain and Mrs. Sherwood by F. C. Harvey Darton
Wells Gardner. 1910

121   SMITH, Naomi Royde   *The State of mind of Mrs. Sherwood*
Macmillan. 1946

TRIMMER, MRS.

122   TRIMMER, Sarah   *Some account of the life and writings of Mrs. Trimmer, with original letters and meditations and prayers, selected from her journal*
Rivington. 1814. 2 vols.

2   (iv) ROUSSEAU AND THE MORAL SCHOOL

FÉNELON

123   FÉNELON, Francois de Salignac de la Mothe   *Fénelon on education*. A translation of the '*Traité de l'éducation des filles*', and other documents illustrating Fénelon's educational theories and practices, together with an introduction and notes, by H. C. Barnard
Cambridge University Press. 1966

124 ROLLAND, Romain   *Rousseau*. In *French thought in the eighteenth century*, with an introduction by Geoffrey Brereton
Cassell. 1953

125 ROUSSEAU, Jean-Jacques   *Emile; or, education* (trans. from *Émile; ou de l'éducation*, 1762)
Dent. 1911. (Everyman's Library).

GENLIS, LA COMTESSE DE
126 DOBSON, Austin   *Madame La Comtesse de Genlis*. In his *Four Frenchwomen*
Chatto. 1893

BERQUIN, ARNAUD
127 BERQUIN, Arnaud   *The Looking-glass for the mind; or, intellectual mirror*, chiefly translated from . . . *L'Ami des enfants*, and adapted by the Rev. W. D. Cooper (i.e. Richard Johnson). A facsimile reprint of the 1792 edition with Bewick cuts, and an introduction by Charles Welsh
Griffith Farran etc. 1885

For Richard Johnson see 100 above.

BARBAULD, MRS. A. L.
128 RODGERS, Betsy   *Georgian chronicle: Mrs. Barbauld and her circle*
Methuen. 1958

DAY, THOMAS
129 SCOTT, Sir S. H.   *The exemplary Mr. Day, 1745–1789*
Faber. 1935

EDGEWORTH, MARIA
130 EDGEWORTH, Maria   *The Life and letters of Maria Edgeworth*. Edited by A. J. C. Hare
Arnold. 1894. 2 vols.

131 SLADE, Bertha Coolidge   *Maria Edgeworth, 1767–1849*. A bibliographical tribute
Constable. 1937

ELLIOTT, MARY (BELSON)
132 JORDAN, Philip D.   *The Juvenilia of Mary Belson Elliott*
New York Public Library Bulletin, Nov. 1935
Revised and published separately 1936.

TURNER, ELIZABETH
133 TURNER, Elizabeth   *The Daisy; or, cautionary stories in verse* . . . with 30 engravings by Samuel Williams. Facsimile of 'a new edition' published by Cornish Brothers, Birmingham, 1899. It was first published in 1807

WOLLSTONECRAFT, MARY
134 WOLLSTONECRAFT, Mary   *Original stories from real life*. Facsimile of the 1791 edition, with five illustrations by William Blake, and an introduction by E. V. Lucas
Frowde. 1906

For the Taylor sisters see 203, 204.

3 THE DAWN OF IMAGINATION: FROM SONGS OF INNOCENCE TO GRIMM'S FAIRY TALES

135   BOWRA, Sir Maurice   *The Romantic imagination*
Oxford University Press. 1950
    Especially chapters I, II (Songs of Innocence and Experience), and IV (Ode on Intimations of Immortality).

BEWICK

136   ANDERTON, B.   *The Bewicks and their books for children. Junior Bookshelf*, vol. 2. no. 3. May 1938

137   BEWICK, Thomas   *A Memoir of Thomas Bewick, written by himself.* Edited and with an introduction by Montague Weekley. With wood engravings by Thomas Bewick
The Cresset Press. 1961

138   ROSCOE, Sydney   *Thomas Bewick.* A bibliography *raisonné* of editions of the *General history of Quadrupeds, The History of British Birds*, and the *Fables of Aesop*, issued in his lifetime
Oxford University Press. 1953

139   WEEKLEY, Montague   *Thomas Bewick*
Oxford University Press. 1953

BLAKE, WILLIAM

140   BLAKE, William   *Poetry and prose of William Blake (complete writings).* Edited by Geoffrey Keynes. 4th ed.
Nonesuch Press. 1967
    First published 1927. The pages of *The Gates of Paradise* are reproduced.

141   BLAKE, William   *William Blake's engravings.* Edited with an introduction by Geoffrey Keynes
Faber. 1950

142   BLAKE, William   *The Gates of Paradise. For children. For the sexes.* A facsimile with notes and an introductory volume by Geoffrey Keynes.
The Trianon Press for the William Blake Trust. 1968

143   BLAKE, William   *Songs of innocence and experience* . . . (1789–1794). Reproduced with an introduction and commentary by Sir Geoffrey Keynes
Rupert Hart-Davis in association with the Trianon Press. 1967
    Also paperback edition by the Oxford University Press 1970.

GRIMM, J. L. AND W. K.

144   GRIMM's *Household stories.* With the author's notes, translated from the German, and edited by Margaret Hunt. With an introduction by Andrew Lang
Bell. 1884. 2 vols.
    This text was used for a complete English edition of the tales published by Routledge in 1948, revised by James Stern.

145   GRIMM's *Popular stories.* Translated by Edgar Taylor, and illustrated by George Cruikshank. A reprint of the first English edition of 1823–6
Clowes. 1913

LAMB, CHARLES AND MARY

146   LAMB, Charles   *The King and Queen of Hearts.* An 1805 book for children . . . illustrated by William Mulready. Now re-issued in facsimile with an introduction by E. V. Lucas
Methuen. 1902

147   LAMB, Charles   *Prince Dorus*. With nine coloured illustrations in facsimile. Introduction by A. W. Tuer. (a facsimile of the 1811 edition)
       The Leadenhall Press. 1890–1891
148   LAMB, Charles   *The Letters of Charles Lamb*. Edited by E. V. Lucas
       Methuen. 1935. 3 vols.
149   LUCAS, E. V.   *The Life of Charles Lamb*.
       G. P. Putnam's Sons. 1905. 2 vols.
150   ANTHONY, Katherine   *The Lambs: a study of pre-Victorian England*
       Hammond. 1948

ROSCOE, WILLIAM

151   ROSCOE, William   *The Butterfly's Ball and the Grasshopper's Feast*. Facsimile reproduction of the issue of 1808, with an introduction by Charles Welsh
       Griffith & Farran etc. 1883
       There were two other reproductions in this series with introductions by Welsh, *The Peacock at Home*, by Mrs. Dorset, and *The Elephant's Ball*, by W. B., both published soon after *The Butterfly's Ball*.

4 (i) DEVELOPMENTS IN THE NINETEENTH CENTURY

152   ALTICK, Richard D.   *The English common reader*. A social history of the mass reading public 1800–1900
       Phoenix Books (Univ. of Chicago Press). 1963
153   BARNARD, H. C.   *A Short history of English education from 1760–1944*. 2nd ed.
       University of London Press. 1961
154   CRUSE, Amy   *The Englishman and his books in the early nineteenth century*
       Harrap. 1930
155   CRUSE, Amy   *The Victorians and their books*
       Allen & Unwin. 1935
156   MACLEAN, Ruari   *Victorian book design and colour printing*
       Faber. 1963
       Especially useful for its chapters on 'Children's books up to 1850', 'Joseph Cundall', and 'Colour printing'.
157   SMILES, Samuel   *Self-help* (1859). Centenary edition with an introduction by Asa Briggs
       Murray. 1958
158   TREVELYAN, G. M.   *English social history*. Chapters xv-xviii
       Longmans Green. 1944

COLE, SIR HENRY ('FELIX SUMMERLY')

159   COLE, Sir Henry   *Fifty years of public work of Sir Henry Cole, K.C.B., accounted for in his deeds, speeches, and writings*
       Bell. 1884. 2 vols.

GOODRICH, S. G. ('PETER PARLEY')

160   GOODRICH, S. G.   *Recollections of a lifetime*
       New York. Miller, Orton & Mulligan. 1856. 2 vols.
161   JORDAN, Alice M.   *Peter Parley*
       Boston. *The Hornbook*. vol. 10. no. 2. March 1934
       Also in her *From Rollo to Tom Sawyer* (293).

SMITH, SARAH ('HESBA STRETTON')

162   SALWAY, Lance   *Pathetic simplicity*. An introduction to Hesba Stretton and her books for children
Stroud. *Signal*. No. 1. Jan. 1970

REVIEWING AND CRITICISM

163   THE GUARDIAN OF EDUCATION Edited Mrs. Sarah Trimmer
J. Hatchard. 1802–1806. 5 vols.

164   [RIGBY, Elizabeth]   *Children's books* (a critical essay and booklist)
Quarterly Review. June 1844

165   AUNT JUDY'S MAGAZINE. Bell & Daldy, etc. 1866–1885

166   YONGE, Charlotte M.   *What books to lend and what to give*
National Society's Depository. 1887
Lists over 950 books 'suitable for parish work and village children' with comments.

167   SALMON, Edward   *Juvenile literature as it is*
H. J. Drane. 1888

168   DARLING, Richard L.   *The Rise of children's book reviewing in America, 1865–1881*
New York & London. R. R. Bowker Co. 1968

4 (ii) FAIRY LORE AND FANTASY

169   BRIGGS, K. M.   *The Fairies in tradition and literature*
Routledge and Kegan Paul. 1967

170   COOK, Elizabeth   *The Ordinary and the fabulous*. An introduction to myths, legends and fairy tales
for teachers and storytellers
Cambridge University Press. 1969
An appendix gives comparative versions from standard editions, and a useful bibliography.

171   SMITH, Lillian H.   *The Unreluctant years: a critical approach to children's literature*. Chapter iv. The art
of the fairy tale. Chapter v. Gods and men
Chicago. American Library Association. 1953

172   TOLKIEN, J. R. R.   *On fairy stories*.
In *Tree and leaf*. Allen & Unwin. 1964
Also in *Essays presented to Charles Williams* (1947) and in Egoff(8).

ANDERSEN, HANS C.

173   HANS CHRISTIAN ANDERSEN 1805 – 2nd April – 1955. Catalogue of a Jubilee Exhibition held at the
National Book League. Arranged in association with the Danish Government in co-operation with
the Royal Library, Copenhagen, and Dr. R. Klein. London. Copenhagen. 1955
There is an introduction by Elias Bredsdorff 'Hans Andersen as seen through British eyes'.

174   ANDERSEN, Hans Christian   *Fairy tales*. Edited and introduced by Svend Larsen, and translated by
R. P. Keigwin
Edward Ward. 1951–1960. 4 vols.
A standard edition of 84 tales produced in Odense. Illustrated by Vilhelm Pedersen. All 168 stories
by Andersen, translated into English by Jean Hersholt, can be found in *The Complete Andersen*.
New York. The Heritage Press. 1942–1948.

175   BAIN, R. N.   *Hans Christian Andersen*
Lawrence and Bullen. 1893
Includes an assessment of early translations. A list of translations from 1846–1950 is given by
Bredsdorff in his *Danish literature in English translation*. (Copenhagen, 1950).

DODGSON, C. L. ('LEWIS CARROLL')

176 CARROLL, Lewis *Alice's adventures underground*, being a facsimile of the original MS book, afterwards developed into *Alice's Adventures in Wonderland*. Illustrated by the author
Macmillan. 1886. Edited with a new introduction by Martin Gardner. New York, Dover Publs. 1965

177 CARROLL, Lewis *The Complete works of Lewis Carroll*. With an introduction by Alexander Woolcot, and the illustrations by John Tenniel
The Nonesuch Press. 1939

178 CARROLL, Lewis *The Diaries of Lewis Carroll*. Edited and supplemented by Roger Lancelyn Green
Cassell. 1953. 2 vols.

179 DE LA MARE, Walter *Lewis Carroll*
Faber. 1932

180 GREEN, Roger Lancelyn *Lewis Carroll*
Bodley Head Monograph. 1960

181 WILLIAMS, Sidney Herbert and MADAN, Falconer *The Lewis Carroll handbook*. A new version of 'A Handbook of the literature of the Rev. C. L. Dodgson', first published in 1931, now revised, augmented and brought up to 1960, by Roger Lancelyn Green
Oxford University Press. 1962

GRAHAME, KENNETH

182 GRAHAM, Eleanor *Kenneth Grahame*
Bodley Head Monograph. 1963

183 GRAHAME, Kenneth *First whisper of 'The Wind in the Willows'*. Edited with an introduction by Elspeth Grahame. 3rd ed.
Methuen. 1946

184 GREEN, Peter *Kenneth Grahame: a biography*
Murray. 1959

KINGSLEY, CHARLES

185 HENNESSY, Una Pope- *Canon Charles Kingsley*
Chatto. 1948

LANG, ANDREW

186 GREEN, Roger Lancelyn *Andrew Lang*.
Bodley Head Monograph. 1962

187 GREEN, Roger Lancelyn *Andrew Lang: a critical biography*
Edward Ward. 1946

MACDONALD, GEORGE

188 MACDONALD, Greville *George Macdonald and his wife*. With an introduction by G. K. Chesterton
Allen & Unwin. 1924

189 WOLFF, Robert Lee *The Golden key*. A study of the fiction of George Macdonald.
New Haven. Yale University Press. 1961
Chapter three deals with his fairy tales and fantasies for children.

MOLESWORTH, M. L.

190 GREEN, Roger Lancelyn *Mrs. Molesworth*.
Bodley Head Monograph. 1961
Mentions a full-length biography in preparation by Ruth Robertson. See also 214.

MORGAN, MARY DE

191   MORGAN, Mary de   *The Necklace of Princess Fiorimonde and other stories.* Being the complete fairy tales of Mary de Morgan, with original illustrations . . . Introduction by Roger Lancelyn Green
Gollancz. 1967

NESBIT, E.

192   BELL, Anthea   *E. Nesbit*
Bodley Head Monograph. 1960

193   MOORE, Doris Langley   *E. Nesbit.* A biography revised with new material
Ernest Benn. 1967

194   NESBIT, E.   *Long ago when I was young.* Illustrated by Edward Ardizzone
Ronald Whiting & Wheaton. 1966
       First published in the *Girl's Own Paper* as 'My School-days', 1896–1897.

4 (iii) NONSENSE, VERSE AND DRAMA

NONSENSE

195   CAMMAERTS, Emile   *The Poetry of nonsense.* A series of five articles
Junior Bookshelf, vol. 15. 1951

196   DAVIDSON, Angus   *Edward Lear: landscape painter and nonsense poet, 1812–1888*
1938. Penguin Books 1950

197   LEAR, Edward   *Complete book of nonsense.* With an introduction by Holbrooke Jackson
Faber. 1947

For Lewis Carroll see 176–181.

VERSE

198   DE LA MARE, Walter, *compiler*   *Come hither.* A collection of rhymes and poems for the young of all ages made by Walter de la Mare
Constable. 1960 (First published 1923)
       An anthology of many kinds of poetry for the young, covering some examples described in the present history. There are copious and illuminating notes.

199   LUCAS, E. V. *compiler*   *A Book of verses for children*
Chatto. 1897
       This and its companion volume, *Another book of verses for children* (Wells Gardner, 1907) contain some old-fashioned and forgotten rhymes as well as others more famous.

200   ORIGINAL DITTIES *for the nursery, so wonderfully contrived they may be said or sung by Nurse or Baby*
J. Harris, ca. 1805. Facsimile edition edited by Iona Opie. Oxford University Press. 1954

DE LA MARE, WALTER

201   CLARK, Leonard   *Walter de la Mare*
Bodley Head Monograph. 1960

ROSSETTI, CHRISTINA

       see 135 BOWRA. Chapter xi. Christina Rossetti
202   ROSSETTI, Christina   *Poetical works.* With a memoir and notes by William Michael Rossetti
Macmillan. 1904

FARRAR, F. W.

217   FARRAR, F. W.   *Eric; or, little by little*. Introduction by John Rowe Townsend
      Hamish Hamilton. 1971

FIELDING, SARAH

218   FIELDING, Sarah   *The Governess; or, little Female Academy*. A facsimile reproduction of the first edition
      of 1749, with an introduction and bibliography by Jill E. Grey
      Oxford University Press. 1968 (The Juvenile Library)

HOWITT, MARY

219   HOWITT, Mary   *An autobiography*. Edited by her daughter, Margaret Howitt
      Isbister. 1889. 2 vols.

HUGHES, THOMAS

220   HUGHES, Thomas   *Tom Brown's schooldays*. With a preface by Lord Kilbracken, and an introduction
      notes and illustrations, edited by F. Sidgwick
      Sidgwick & Jackson. 1913

221   MACK, Edward C. and ARMITAGE, W. H. G.   *Thomas Hughes: the life of the author of Tom Brown's
      Schooldays*
      Ernest Benn. 1952

MARTINEAU, HARRIET

222   WHEATLEY, Vera   *The Life and work of Harriet Martineau*
      Secker & Warburg. 1957

REED, TALBOT BAINES

223   REED, Talbot Baines   *The Fifth form at St. Dominics*. Introduction by Brian Alderson
      Hamish Hamilton. 1971

WARNER, SUSAN ('Elizabeth Wetherell')

224   JORDAN, Alice M.   *Susan Warner and her wide, wide world*
      Boston. *The Hornbook*. vol. 10. no. 5. September 1934
          Also in *From Rollo to Tom Sawyer* (293).

225   WARNER, Anna B.   *Susan Warner*
      G. P. Putnam's Sons. 1909

YONGE, CHARLOTTE M.

226   BATTISCOMBE, Georgina and LASKI, Marghanita, *editors*.   *A Chaplet for Charlotte Yonge* . . . Papers
      edited for the Charlotte Yonge Society
      Cresset Press. 1965

227   MARE, Margaret and PERCEVAL, Alicia C.   *Victorian best-seller*. The world of Charlotte M. Yonge
      Harrap. 1947

For Kipling see 257–259.

For Mrs. Molesworth see 190, 214.

4 (v) THE TALE OF ADVENTURE

BALLANTYNE, R. M.

228 OSBORNE, Edgar *Ballantyne the pioneer*
Junior Bookshelf. vol. 8. No. 1. March 1944

229 QUAYLE, Eric *Ballantyne the brave: a Victorian writer and his family*
Rupert Hart-Davis. 1967

BUCHAN, JOHN

230 SMITH, Janet Adam *John Buchan: a biography*
Rupert Hart-Davis. 1965
Especially chapter 10: Storyteller.

COOPER, J. FENIMORE

231 GROSSMAN, James *James Fenimore Cooper*
Methuen. 1950. (American Men of Letters)

DEFOE, DANIEL

232 DEFOE, Daniel *The life and adventures of Robinson Crusoe.* Now first correctly reprinted from the original edition of 1719 with an introduction by William Lee. Illustrated by Ernest Griset
Frederick Warne. 1869
There is a modern unabridged edition, with an introduction by Guy Pocock, published by Dent, 1945, in Everyman's Library.

233 ULLRICH, Hermann *Robinson und Robinsonaden: Bibliographie, Geschichte, Kritik*
Weimar. 1898
A source book for the history of the 'Robinsonade'.

DOYLE, SIR ARTHUR CONAN

234 NORDEN, Pierre *Conan Doyle.* Trans. from the French by Frances Partridge
John Murray. 1966
Part II 'The Writer' deals extensively with the Sherlock Holmes series and other novels.

HAGGARD, SIR H. R.

235 COHEN, Morten N. *Rider Haggard: his life and work.* 2nd. ed.
Macmillan. 1968

JEFFERIES, RICHARD

236 JEFFERIES, Richard *The Jefferies companion.* Selected and arranged with an introduction by Samuel L. Locker
Phoenix House. 1948

KINGSTON, W. H. G.

237 KINGSTON, Maurice Rooke *The Life, work and influence of William Henry Giles Kingston*
Toronto. Ryerson Press. 1947

MARRYAT, FREDERICK

238 WARNER, Oliver *Captain Marryat: a rediscovery*
Constable. 1953
Also article in the *Junior Bookshelf* vol. 17. No. 3. July 1953.

STEVENSON, R. L.

239 BALFOUR, Graham   *The Life of Robert Louis Stevenson*
Methuen. 1901. 2 vols.

240 BUTTS, Dennis   *R. L. Stevenson*
Bodley Head monograph. 1966
Also article in the *Junior Bookshelf*, vol. 29. No. 6. Dec. 1965 'The Child's voice'.

241 FURNAS, J. C.   *Voyage to windward: life of Stevenson*
Faber. 1952

242 STEVENSON, R. L.   *A Gossip on romance.* Chapter xv in *Memories and portraits* (first published 1887)
The writer's analysis and defence of his approach to incident in fiction and the art of story-writing.

TWAIN, MARK (S. L. Clemens)

243 ELIOT, T. S.   *Huckleberry Finn.* Essay reprinted in Egoff (8)

244 SMITH, Henry Nash, *editor   Mark Twain: a collection of critical essays*
New Jersey. Prentice-Hall Inc. 1963
Includes an appreciation by Maurice Le Breton, and various other excerpts and essays, among them
Tom Sawyer by Walter Blair, from his *Mark Twain and Huck Finn, 1960.*

245 TWAIN, Mark   *The Adventures of Huckleberry Finn.* Edited with an introduction by Peter Coveney.
Penguin Books. 1966. (Penguin English Library)

VERNE, JULES

246 ALLOTT, Kenneth   *Jules Verne*
Cresset Press. 1940

247 EVANS, I. O.   *Jules Verne and his work*
Arco Publications. 1965
See also Trigon (319). Chapter vii, Jules Verne.

4 (vi) THE RECREATION OF THE PAST

248 BUTTERFIELD, Herbert   *The historical novel*
Cambridge University Press. 1924
See also SMITH (171) Chapter xi, Historical fiction.

HENTY, G. A.

249 FENN, George Manville   *George Alfred Henty*
Blackie. 1907

250 KENNEDY, R. S. and FARMER, B. J. *editors   Bibliography of G. A. Henty and Hentyana.* Mimeographed
Published by B. J. Farmer, London, N. 2. 1956

251 TREASE, Geoffrey   *G. A. Henty: fifty years after*
Junior Bookshelf vol. 16, No. 2. Oct. 1952

MASEFIELD, JOHN

252 FISHER, Margery   *John Masefield*
Bodley Head monograph. 1963

SCOTT, SIR WALTER

253   CECIL, Lord David   *Sir Walter Scott*
      Constable. 1933

254   DEVLIN, D. D. *editor*   *Walter Scott: modern judgments*
      Macmillan. 1968

For John Buchan see 230.

For Kipling see 257–259

For Harriet Martineau see 222.

4 (vii) THE ANIMAL STORY

255   OSBORNE, Edgar   *Animals in books* (for children)
      Junior Bookshelf. vol. 9 Nos. 1 & 2. March & July 1945

GATTY, MARGARET

256   MAXWELL, Christabel   *Mrs. Gatty and Mrs. Ewing*
      Constable. 1949

KIPLING, RUDYARD

257   CARRINGTON, Charles   *Rudyard Kipling: his life and work*
      Macmillan. 1955

258   GREEN, Roger Lancelyn   *Kipling and the children*
      Elek. 1965

259   KIPLING, Rudyard   *Something of myself*
      Macmillan. 1937

SETON, ERNEST THOMPSON

260   SETON, Ernest Thompson   *Trail of an artist naturalist*
      Hodder & Stoughton. 1951 (New York. Scribners. 1940)
         There is also a short appreciation in the *Junior Bookshelf* vol. 10. no. 3. October 1946, and an introduction by Roger Lancelyn Green in the Dent C.I.C. edition (1966), *The Trail of the Sandhill Stag*.

SEWELL, ANNA

261   BAKER, Margaret J.   *Anna Sewell and Black Beauty*
      Harrap. 1956

For Newbery see 102–105.

4 (viii) PICTURE-BOOKS AND BOOKS FOR YOUNG CHILDREN

262   BLAND, David   *A History of book illustration*
      Faber. 1958
         Covers many European developments. For other books about foreign artists see entries under 5 (iii) below.

263   BLAND, David   *The Illustration of books*. 3rd ed.
      Faber. 1962

264   HARDIE, Martin   *English coloured books*
      Methuen. 1906

265   LEACH, Eileen M.   *Walter Crane and after:* a century of changing fashions in the illustration of children's books, 1865–1965
      Unpublished F.L.A. thesis accepted 1966. Available at the Library Association

266   REID, Forrest   *Illustrators of the sixties*
      Faber and Gwyer. 1928
      See also Mahony (14), Maclean (156), Morris (16) and Tuer (27 and 28) and other general sources.

BROOKE, L. LESLIE

267   MOORE, Anne Carroll   *Leslie Brooke: pied piper of English picture-books.* Boston. *The Hornbook.* Vol. 1. No. 3. March 1925. (also further article, Vol. 17. No. 3, May 1941).

CALDECOTT, RANDOLPH

268   GRAHAM, Eleanor   *Randolph Caldecott. Junior Bookshelf.* vol 10. No. 1. March 1946
      See also article by Laws in 8 and 275.

CRANE, WALTER

269   CRANE, Walter   *An artist's reminiscences*
      Methuen. 1907

270   VAUGHAN, J. E.   *Walter Crane – first, second or third?*
      Junior Bookshelf, vol. 32, no. 2. April 1968

EVANS, EDMUND

271   EVANS, Edmund   *The reminiscences of Edmund Evans.* Edited and introduced by Ruari Maclean
      Oxford University Press. 1967

272   WOODFIELD, H. J. B.   *Edmund Evans: colour printer. Junior Bookshelf.* vol. 10. no. 1. March 1946

GREENAWAY, KATE

273   CUNDALL, H. M.   *Kate Greenaway.*
      Junior Bookshelf. vol. 10. no. 1 March 1946

274   GREENAWAY, Kate   *The Kate Greenaway treasury.* Introduction by Ruth Hill Viguers. An anthology of the illustrations and writings of Kate Greenaway. Edited and selected by Edward Ernest, assisted by Patricia Tracy Lowe
      Collins. 1968 (World Publ. Co. 1967)
        Includes an abridgement of her biography (276).

275   JORDAN, Alice M.   *Kate Greenaway and Randolph Caldecott.* An American tribute
      Junior Booksehelf. vol. 10. no. 1. March 1946

276   SPIELMANN, M. H. and LAYARD, G. S.   *Kate Greenaway*
      Black. 1905

POTTER, BEATRIX

277   CROUCH, Marcus   *Beatrix Potter*
      Bodley Head monograph. 1960

278   LANE, Margaret   *The Tale of Beatrix Potter: a biography.* 2nd ed.
      Warne. 1968. (first published 1946)

279   POTTER, Beatrix   *The Art of Beatrix Potter.* With an appreciation by Anne Carroll Moore
      Warne. 1955
        'Direct reproductions of Beatrix Potter's preliminary studies and finished drawings, also examples of her original MS, selected and arranged by L. Linder and W. A. Herring'.

RACKHAM, ARTHUR

280 CROUCH, Marcus *Arthur Rackham, 1867–1939*
   Junior Bookshelf. vol. 31. no. 5. Oct. 1967
281 HUDSON, Derek *Arthur Rackham: his life and work*
   Heinemann. 1960

UPTON, BERTHA AND FLORENCE

282 OSBORNE, Edgar *The Birth of 'Golliwogg'*
   Junior Bookshelf. vol. 12, no. 4. Dec. 1948

4 (ix) BOOKS OF KNOWLEDGE

Very little appears to have been published on this aspect of children's books, so that the chief sources used have been the general histories, bibliographies and catalogues. The classified sections in the Toronto Catalogue (46) have been very useful, and so have various parts of the National Book League Exhibition Catalogue (41), especially pp. 27–58 'special subjects', and pp. 133–137, 'Books of trades' etc.

For Boreman see 101

For Newbery see 102–105

For Plutarch see 64

FARADAY, MICHAEL

283 KENDALL, James *Michael Faraday*
   Faber. 1955

4 (x) PERIODICALS

284 COX, Jack *The Story of the B.O.P.*
   Boy's Own Paper. 1954
      A leaflet giving a short history by a former editor.
285 EGOFF, Sheila A. *Children's periodicals in the nineteenth century: a survey and bibliography*
   Library Association. Pamphlet no. 8. 1951
286 GREY, Jill E. *The Lilliputian Magazine – a pioneering periodical?*
   Journal of Librarianship. vol. 2, no. 2. April 1970
287 TURNER, E. S. *Boys will be boys.* New edition
   Michael Joseph. 1957
      A history of 'penny dreadfuls' and other cheap and sensational literature for boys.

5 CHILDREN'S BOOKS ABROAD
(i) NORTH AMERICA

THE UNITED STATES

The history of children's books in North America is dealt with incidentally in several general histories of children's literature. but it is an important part of the history edited by Cornelia Meigs (15). Many chapters in this four-part survey deal with American writers and developments, notably I (11) *The New England Primer,* (12) Hugh Gaine, Isaiah Thomas, (13) Samuel Goodrich, Jacob Abbott, 2 (6) the American family story, (10) magazines in the nineteenth century, 3 (1) Howard Pyle, etc. On American illustrators there is much information in Mahony (14).

For the early period up to 1821 the most valuable source is the bibliography by Dr. Welch (298). Sloane (74) describes only a few seventeenth century American books for children. For the American Sunday School movement see 116 and 288.

Much new information about the publishing of books for children in the nineteenth century in America, as well as their reception and criticism, is given by Dr. Darling in his *Rise of children's book reviewing in America, 1865–1881* (168).

For authors already covered in earlier chapters see:

288   ANDREWS, Siri, *editor   The Hewins lectures, 1947–1962.* Introduction by Frederic G. Melcher
Boston. The Horn Book. 1963

Among the lectures are Haviland. The travelogue storybook of the 19th century: Lysta I. Abbott. Jacob Abbott: Cushman on the American Sunday School movement: Boutwell on Kate Douglas Wiggin. Also Jordan's outline From Rollo to Tom Sawyer, the first of the lectures.

289   BLANCK, Jacob   *Peter Parley to Penrod:* a bibliographical description of the best-loved American juvenile books
New York. R. R. Bowker. 1956. (First publ. 1938)

290   CUNLIFFE, Marcus   *The Literature of the United States.* Rev. ed.
Penguin Books. 1967
Contains useful information on Washington Irving, James Fenimore Cooper, Mark Twain and others.

291   DICTIONARY of American biography. Edited by Allen Johnson, later by Dumas Malone. 1928–1936
New York. Scribners. London. Oxford University Press. 21 vols. Supplements, 1946. 1958

292   EVANS, Charles   *American bibliography: a chronological dictionary* ...
Chicago. 1903–1934. 12 vols.
Covers the period 1639–1799. Also vol. 13, 1799–1800, completed by Clifford K. Shipton, vol. 14, index

293   JORDAN, Alice M.   *From Rollo to Tom Sawyer, and other papers*
Boston. The Horn Book. 1948
Contains essays on 'The Juvenile Miscellany' etc., Peter Parley, The Children of Jacob Abbott, The dawn of imagination in American books for children, Elijah Kellogg, Horace E. Scudder, 'Our Young Folks', 'St. Nicholas', The golden age (the 1880s). See also 288.

294   KIEFER, Monica   *American children through their books, 1700–1835*
Philadelphia. University of Philadelphia Press. (London Univ. Press). 1948

295   MEIGS, Cornelia   *Louisa M. Alcott and the American family story*
Bodley Head (Walck) monograph.   1970
Pt. 2 describes the work of Susan Coolidge, Laura E. Richards, Kate Douglas Wiggin and other writers of domestic tales.

296   ROSENBACH, A. W.   *Early American children's books.* With bibliographical descriptions of the books in his private collection
Portland, Maine. The Southworth Press. 1933
Covers the period 1682–1836. The collection is now at the Philadelphia Public Library.

297   THOMPSON, Lawrence   *The Printing and publishing of the American Tract Society from 1825–1850*
New York. Bibliographical Society of America. Proceedings. vol. 35. 1941

298   WELCH, d'Alté A.   *A Bibliography of American children's books printed prior to 1821*. Printed in Proceedings of the American Antiquarian Society
      Worcester. Mass. 1963–1967
      An introduction outlines the history of American books for children for the period. Copious
information is given about editions, including the English originals from which American copies
were adapted. The bibliography is now being reprinted by the American Antiquarian Society. The
volumes of the Proceedings concerned are 73 (April and Oct. 1963), 74 (Oct. 1964), 75 (Oct. 1965),
77 (April and Oct. 1967).

ABBOTT, JACOB
      See 288, 293.

NEW ENGLAND PRIMER
299   FORD, Paul L. *editor*   *The New England Primer*. A history of its origin and development with a reprint
of the unique copy of the earliest known edition and many facsimile illustrations and reproductions.
      New York. Dodd Mead & Co. 1897
      Reprinted 1962. The facsimile is of the 1727 copy now in the New York Public Library. Other
facsimiles include *The New English Tutor* (ascribed to Benjamin Harris, ca. 1702–1714) and *Spiritual
Milk for Babes*, by John Cotton. Gives variations in the different editions of the *Primer*.

PYLE, HOWARD
300   NESBITT, Elizabeth   *Howard Pyle*
      Bodley Head (Walck) monograph. 1966

THOMAS, ISAIAH
301   SHIPTON, Clifford K.   *Isaiah Thomas, printer, patriot and philanthropist, 1749–1831*
      Rochester, N.Y. Leo Hart. 1948
      For facsimiles of Isaiah Thomas publications see 102, 107 and 109.

CANADA
302   EGOFF, Sheila   *The Republic of childhood*. A critical guide to Canadian children's literature in English
      Toronto. Oxford University Press. 1967
      Chapter 8 deals with early Canadian children's books. For Thompson Seton see 260.

(ii) AUSTRALIA

303   LIBRARY COUNCIL of Victoria. Children's Libraries Services Division. *Australian literature for children,
1830–1966*. A select bibliography
      Melbourne. 1967
      A stencilled list useful for its chronological arrangement.

304   MUIR, Marcie, *compiler*   *A Bibliography of Australian children's books*
      André Deutsch. 1970
      A comprehensive alphabetical record under authors of children's books relating to Australia, as
well as by Australian authors.

305   WIGHTON, Rosemary   *Early Australian children's literature*
      Melbourne, Lansdowne Press. 1963

306   Geneva. International Bureau of Education. *Children's books and international goodwill*. Booklist and report of an enquiry. 2nd ed.

    The Bureau. 1932

        The first report was issued in 1929. A survey of children's books submitted by 37 countries, with a list of books on children's reading and literature in many languages.

307   Hürlimann, Bettina   *Three centuries of children's books in Europe*. Translated and edited by Brian W. Alderson from *Europäische Kinderbücher in drei Jahrunderten*. 2nd ed., and slightly amended, Zurich, Atlantis Verlag, 1963. Oxford University Press. 1967

        Surveys some aspects of literature for children from Comenius up to the present time, grouped under types rather than countries. There is a chapter on Heinrich Hoffmann, and on the history of Swiss children's books.

308   Jan, Isabelle   *Essai sur la littérature enfantine*

    Paris. Les Éditions Ouvriéres. 1969

        A short outline of children's literature, not confined to France.

309   Munich. International Youth Library. *History and theory of youth literature*. (Catalogue of an exhibition at the library 21st July – 4th Sept. 1964). Stencilled. Munich I.Y.L. (1964).

        There is now available from G. K. Hall & Co., Boston, Mass. (in association with Unesco) a series of five catalogues on cards representing the library's holdings from 1957–1968.

For comparative literature and outstanding classics see Hazard (12).

For bibliographical references and brief introductions to the literature for children of most countries in the world see Pellowski (44).

ITALY

310   Hawkes, Louise Restieaux   *Before and after Pinocchio*. A study of Italian children's books.

    Paris. The Puppet Press. 1933

311   Hazard. Paul   *La Littérature enfantine en Italie. Revue des deux mondes*

    Paris. 84e année. 6 période. Tome 19. Feb. 15, 1914

312   Melegari, V.   *Children's books in Italy before Pinocchio. Pinocchio, Cuore, and other Italian books Junior Bookshelf*. vol. 18. no. 3. Oct. 1946 and vol. 19. no. 2. March 1955

BASILE, GIAMBATTISTA

313   Basile, Giambattista   *The Pentamerone*. Translated from the Italian of Benedetto Croce (1925). Edited by N. M. Penzer

    John Lane. 1932. 2 vols.

FRANCE

314   Averill, Esther   *The History of French children's books, 1750–1900*. Preface to the catalogue of the collection of J.-G. Deschamps exhibit and sale, January 1934

    Boston. The Bookshop for Boys and Girls. 1934

315   Bishop, Claire Huchet   *Seven centuries of children's books in France*

    Boston. *The Hornbook*. vol. 18, no. 3. May 1942

        Describes an Exhibition in New York in 1942.

316   Jan, Isabelle   *La littérature enfantine*. In the vol. Littératures of *Encyclopédie Clarté*

    Paris. 1965

        Not seen by the compiler, but recommended by a French librarian.

317 Latzarus, Marie-Thérèse *La Littérature enfantine en France dans la seconde moitié du xixe siècle*
Paris. Les Presses Universitaires de France. 1924

318 Mistler, Jean and others *Épinal et l'imagérie populaire*
Paris. Hachette. 1961

319 Trigon, Jean de *Histoire de la littérature enfantine de ma mère L'Oye au Roi Babar*
Paris. Hachette. 1950

For Perrault and the French fairy tale see 86–93.

Berquin see 127.
Fénelon see 123.
Genlis see 126.
Rousseau see 124, 125.
Verne see 246, 247.

SPAIN

320 Bravo-Villasante, Carmen *Antologia de la literatura infantil en lengua española*. 2nd ed.
Madrid. Doncel. 1966. 2 vols.

321 Bravo-Villasante, Carmen *Historia de la literatura infantil española*. 2nd ed.
Madrid. Doncel. 1963

322 Fromkes, Eva Maurice *Spain and the books her children read*
Boston. The Hornbook. vol. 4. no. 4. July 1934

323 Cervantes Saavedra, Miguel de *The Adventures of Don Quixote*. Translated with an introduction by J. M. Cohen
Penguin Books. 1950 (Penguin Classics).
A modern version of the complete text.

GERMANY

324 Dyrenfurth-Graebsch, Irene *Geschichte des deutschen Jugendbuches*. 3rd ed.
Zurich. Atlantis Verlag. 1967
First published 1942. Revised by the author, with a chapter on developments since 1945 by Margarete Dierks.

325 Koster, Herman L. *Geschichte der deutschen Jugendliteratur*. 4th ed.
Braunsweig, Berlin, Hamburg. Georg. Westermann. 1927
Reprinted 1968 by Verlag Dokumentation, München-Pullach etc., with notes and bibliography by Walter Scherf.

326 Kunze, Horst *Schatzbehalter vom besten aus der älteren deutschen Kinderliteratur*
East Berlin. Der Kinderbuchverlag. 1964
Extracts with excellent illustrations from 'the best of old German children's literature', prefaced by a study of previous histories and critical works, and an outline of the aim of the book which reflects the author's social outlook.

327 Langfeldt, Johannes *Children's books in Germany*
Junior Bookshelf. vol. 12, no. 2. July 1948

328 Wolgast, Heinrich *Das Elend unserer Jugendliteratur*. 7th ed.
Worms. Ernst Wunderlich. 1950
'The misery of our children's literature'. First published 1896. It pleads for an aesthetic approach and high artistic values in the selection of books for children.

For the Grimm brothers see 144, 145.

SWITZERLAND

see 307   *Towards a history of children's books in Switzerland.* Chapter 17 in Hürlimann's *Three centuries of children's books in Europe.*

see 324   *Deutschsprachiges Jugendschriftum der Schweiz.* pp. 265–297. In Dyrenfurth-Graebsch. *Geschichte . . .*

THE NETHERLANDS

329   DAALDER, Dirk L.   *Wormcruyt met suycker*
       Amsterdam. De Arbeiderspers. 1950
       'A critical-historical survey of children's literature in the Netherlands with illustrations'.

330   VRIES, Leonard de   *Bloempjes der vreugd' voor de lieve jeugd*
       Amsterdam. De Bezige Bij. 1958
       Extracts and illustrations from old Dutch children's books 1712–1898.

331   VRIES, Leonard de   *A Short history of children's books in the Netherlands*
       The Hague. 1964
       A four page mimeographed pamphlet, issued by the Ministry of Foreign Affairs.

SCANDINAVIA

DENMARK

332   MITCHELL, P. M.   *A History of Danish literature*
       Copenhagen. Gyldendal. 1957
       Includes a chapter on Andersen considered from a wider aspect than as a writer for children.

333   MOLLERUP, Helga   *Danish children's books before 1900*
       Junior Bookshelf. vol. 15. no. 2. March 1951

334   STYBE, Vibeke   *Fra Askepot til Anders And (From Cinderella to Donald Duck)*
       Copenhagen. Munksgaard. 1962
       A critical history of children's literature with emphasis on developments in Denmark and Scandinavia. There is no English summary, but a six page stencilled pamphlet was issued separately by the writer, *Survey of the history of books for children in Denmark.*

335   STYBE, Vibeke   *Børnespejl: uddrag af aeldre børne-litteratur på dansk*
       Copenhagen. Gyldendal. 1969
       Extracts with comments covering Danish children's books from 1556–1850.

For Andersen see 173–175.

NORWAY

336   FEYDT, Astrid   *Norwegian books for children. Pt. 1*
       Junior Bookshelf. vol. 18. no. 5. Nov. 1954

337   HAGEMANN, Sonja   *Barnelitteratur i Norge inntil 1850*
       Oslo. H. Ascheboug & Co. (W. Nygaard). 1965
       A history of children's books in Norway up to 1850. Includes a four page summary in English.

338   TENFJORD, Jo   *Children's books in Norway*
       Junior Bookshelf. vol. 10. no. 3. Oct. 1946. also vol. 26. no. 1. Jan. 1962

SWEDEN

339   KLINGBERG, Göte   *Svensk barn-och ungdomslitteratur, 1591–1839*
       Stockholm. Natur och Kultur. 1964
       'An educational, historical and bibliographical survey'. Contains a summary in English 'Swedish literature for children and adolescents, 1591–1839'.

340 KLINGBERG, Göte *Kronologisk bibliografi over Barn-och ungdomslitteratur utgiven i Sverige, 1591–1839*
Stockholm. Årsböcker i Svensk undervisningshistoria, 118. 1967
Full bibliographical entries for Swedish children's books from 1591–1839. An explanation of the method of editing etc. is given in English.

341 TESSIN, Carl Gustaf *Utkast af en gammal Mans dagelica bref . . .* (1751). I urval samt med inledning och kommentar av Göte Klingberg.
Stockholm. Natur och Kultur. 1964
Tessin's *Letters from an old man to a young prince* reprinted with an introduction and notes by Göte Klingberg.

342 ZWEIGBERGK, Eva von *Barnboken i Sverige, 1750–1950*
Stockholm. Rabén & Sjögren. 1965
A well-illustrated and comprehensive survey, with an English summary.

Index

All books are given a reference under the name of the author, including those listed in Appendix II. References to items listed in Appendix II relate to the numbered entries, not to pages, and are printed in italics.

Children's books are also given an entry under their title, often in a shortened or familiar form (e.g. *Goody Two-shoes, Robinson Crusoe*). Foreign children's books are usually only given a title entry in English, in the form known in an English translation.

Boutet de Monvel, M., *illus.* 198, 251, 254–5, 267

Bowman, James F. 164

Bowra, Sir M. *The Romantic imagination* II 135

Boy hunters of the Mississippi (Reid) 162

Boy's adventures in the wilds of Australia (Howitt) 143, 162, 244

Boy's country book (Howitt) 134, 143

Boys of England 98, 140, 217–8

Boy's Own Magazine 176, 211, 219

Boy's Own Paper 155, 167n., 219–221, *illus.* 220, 223, 224, II 284

Boy's school (Sandham) 152

Brabourne, Lord *see* Hugessen, E. H. Knatchbull

Bradburn, Eliza W. 137

Bradford, William, *American printer* 277

Braun & Schneider, *German publs.* 262

Bravo-Villasante, Carmen: books on Spanish children's literature 255, II 320, 321

Brazil, Angela 156

Bredsdorff, Elias *Danish literature in English translation* II 175: intro. to Andersen Exhibition Catalogue II 173

Bremer, Fredrika 272

Bremer, Lady J. J. Gordon 243

Brentano, Clemens 260

Brethren of the White Cross (De Mille) 242

Brett, Edwin J. 217–8

Briggs, K. M. *The Fairies in tradition and literature* II 169

British Critic 102–3

Brittain, R. E. *Christopher Smart's Hymns* II 112

Broderip, Frances 193

Bronte, C., *Jane Eyre* 84, 156, 215

Brooke, Henry 70

Brooke, L. Leslie, *illus.* 105, 198, II 267

Brookes, Louise, *trans.* 264

Browne, Frances 114

Browne, Gordon, *illus.* 198

Brownies, The (Ewing) 118–9

Browning, Robert 136

Bryant, W. C. 222

Bruce, Mary Grant: Billabong series 244

Buchan, John 170, 179, II 230

Buckley, Arabella B. 212

Buffon's *Histoire naturelle* 205

Bunyan, John *Book for boys and girls* (later *Divine Emblems*) 22, 28–9, 277, II 78: *Pilgrim's Progress* 28, 30, 95, 277

Burnett, Frances H. 140, 150, 222, 237, II 213–4

Burton, Richard, *pseud. see* Crouch, N.

Busch, Wilhelm 262

Bush boys (Reid) 162

Busy hands and patient hearts (Nieritz) 263

Butterfield, H. *The Historical novel* II 248

Butterfly's ball (Roscoe) 85–6, 101, 102–3, 129, 130, 191, II 151

Butterworth, C. C. *Early primers* II 50

Butts, D. *R. L. Stevenson* II 240

Cabellero, Fernán 256

Cabinet des fées 36, 38, 68, 281

Cabinet of Lilliput 86

Cadell, T., *publ.* 280, 281

Caldecott, Randolph 136, 193, 197–8, II 8, 268, 275: illus. of Ewing 148, *illus.* 149

Caldecott Medal Award 197

Calendar of nature (Aikin) 205

Callcott, Lady 210–1

Cambon, Maria G. de 266

Cambridge Bibliography of English Literature II 34

Cambridge History of English Literature II 48, 66, 70

Cameos of history (Yonge) 211

Cameron, Lucy 62, 65

Cammaerts, Emile *The Poetry of nonsense* II 195

Campbell, J. F. *Popular tales of the western Highlands* 107

Campe, J. H. 158, 258, 272, 280: travel and exploration 206

Canadian children's books 242–3, II 302

Canadian Crusoes (Traill) 242

Canton, William 212

Canute Whistlewinks (Topelius) 273

Careful parent's gift 230

Carnan, Thomas, *publ.* 57, 71, 279, 280, II 104

Caroline Mordaunt (Sherwood) 192

Carrington, Charles. *Rudyard Kipling* II 257

Carroll, Lewis (C. L. Dodgson) II 176–181: *Alice* books 56, 104, 114–7, 127–8, 136, 140, 198, 199, 238: *Aunt Judy's Mag.* 104, 116, 222: *Easter greeting* 116: nonsense verses 127–8: *Sylvie and Bruno* 116–7

Carrots (Molesworth) 119, 148

Carved lions (Molesworth) 149–150

Cassell, *publs.* 221, 222

317

Greenaway, Kate: picture-books 195–7, *illus.* 196: other refs. 7, 126, 136, 223, *II 273–6*

Greenaway Medal Award 197

Green's Nursery Annual 217

Grey, Jill E. *Lilliputian Magazine* 213, *II 286:* editor of *The Governess* *II 218*

Griffith & Farran, *publs.* 193

Griffith, R., *publ.* 279

Grimm, J. L. and W. K.: fairy tales (various titles) 90–1, 106–7, 110, 195, 258, 259, *II 144–5: illus. Grimm's Goblins* 91: minor refs. 103, 120, 198

Griselidis 250

Grossman, James *James Fenimore Cooper II 231*

Grundtvig, S. *Danish folktales* 122, 269

Guardian of Education (ed. Trimmer) 60, 85, 103, 183, 184, 206, *II 163*

Gulliver's Travels (Swift) 43–4, 278: chapbooks 41: minor refs. 102, 120, 252, 254

Gummere, F. B. *Ballads II 70*

Gumuchian & Cie *Catalogue II 37*

Guy of Warwick (Sir) 12, 13, 40, 46, 100, 276, *II 65, 99*

Gypsy Breynton series (Ward) 237

Haberkorn, J., *publ.* 213, 279

Hachette, *French publ.* 166, 253

Hadfield, A. M. *King Arthur* 15

Hagemann, Sonja *Children's literature in Norway* 270, *II 337*

Haggard, Sir H. R. 169, 187, 224, *II 235*

Hakluyt's *Voyages* 206

Hale, Lucretia P. 222

Halfpenny Marvel: Halfpenny Wonder 219

Hall, Anna M. (Mrs. S. C. Hall) 216, 217

Halliwell, J. O.: works on folk-lore and nursery rhymes 121

Hamilton, C. H. St. J. ('Frank Richards') 219

Hamilton, Gail 239

Hans Brinker (Dodge) 162

Happy Prince (Wilde) 123

Hardie, M. *English coloured books II 264*

Hare, The (anon.) 184

Hare and many friends (Gay) 10, 184

Harmsworth, Alfred, *publ.* 218–9

Harper, *publs.* 122

Harper's Young People 242

Harris, Benjamin, *publ.* 22, 40, 228

Harris, J. H. *Robert Raikes II 115*

Harris, Joel, C. *Uncle Remus* tales 122

Harris, John, *publ.* 71, 79, 85–6, 101, 106, 126, 136, 191, 207–8: successors 193

Harry and Lucy see Early Lessons (Edgeworth)

Hart, John *A Method or comfortable beginning . . .* 6, *illus.* 6, 189

Harte, Bret 197, 222

Hauff, Wilhelm: fairy tales 259–260

Haviland, Virginia: ed. *Children's literature (reference sources) II 38: Travelogue story book II, 288*

Hawkes, Louise, R. *Before and after Pinocchio II 310*

Hawthorne, Nathaniel: retelling of Greek myths 112, 238

Hazard, Paul *Books, children and men II 12:* article on Italian children's literature *II 311:* on national and international characteristics in children's books 225, 246–7: French childrens' books 255: Italian 249: Spanish 255

Hazard, S., *Bath publ.* 61, 63, 282

Heart (Cuore) (Amicis) 249, 250

Heidi (Spyri) 264–5

Heir of Redclyffe (Yonge) 144, 145

Hemans, F. 133–4

Hemyng, Bracebridge 218

Henderson, James, *editor* 222

Hennessy, Una Pope- *Canon Charles Kingsley II 185*

Henty, G. A. 165, 176–7, 221, *II 249–251*

Hereward the Wake (Kingsley) 175–6

Hermit, The (Philip Quarll) 157–8

Heroes, The (Kingsley) 112, 114

Heroes of Asgard (Keary) 113

Heroes of England (Edgar) 211

Hester Wilmot (tract) 62

Hetzel, J., *French publ.* 166, 253

Hewins, C. *Books for the young* 103

Hey, Wilhelm *Picture fables* illus. 261, 262, 268–9

Hey diddle and *Baby Bunting* (Caldecott) 197

Hiawatha (Longfellow) 235

Hichtum, Ninke van 267

Hieroglyphic Bible see Curious Hieroglyphic Bible

Higson, C. W. J., *editor* *Sources for the history of education II 39*

337

338

Acknowledgements

Grateful acknowledgement is made to publishers and other holders of copyright material for permission to quote short extracts from works as listed below, and also to the various institutions and individuals for the reproduction of photographs as set out on pp. ix–x.

Messrs.

Allen & Unwin Ltd. (*On Fairy Stories*, from *Tree and Leaf*, by J. R. R. Tolkien).

Arco Publs. (*Jules Verne*, by I. O. Evans).

Aschehoug & Co., Oslo (*Barnelitteratur i Norge inntil 1850*, by Sonja Hagemann).

Bookshop for Boys and Girls, Boston (U.S.A.). (*Catalogue of the J.-G. Deschamps exhibit of French children's books*).

The Syndics of the Cambridge University Press. (*Children's Books in England*, by F. C. Harvey Darton).

Chatto & Windus, and the literary executrix for Edith Rickert. (*The Babees Book*, by Edith Rickert).

Constable & Co. Ltd. (*Sir Walter Scott*, by Lord David Cecil), (*Come Hither*, by Walter de la Mare, for which permission has been given by the Society of Authors, representing the author's literary Trustees).

Gerald Duckworth & Co. Ltd. (*The Bad Child's Book of Beasts*, by Hilaire Belloc).

J. M. Dent & Sons Ltd. (*Notes on Life and Letters*, by Joseph Conrad).

Gyldendal, Copenhagen. (*A History of Danish Literature*, by P. M. Mitchell).

Hart, Leo, Rochester, N.Y. (*Isaiah Thomas*, by Clifford K. Shipton).

William Heinemann. (*Rudyard Kipling*, by Charles Carrington).

The Horn Book Inc., Boston (U.S.A.). (*Books, Children and Men*, by Paul Hazard), (*From Rollo to Tom Sawyer*, by Alice M. Jordan), (*Illustrators of Children's Books*, by Bertha E. Mahony and others).

The Editor of *The Junior Bookshelf*. (Article on G. A. Henty by Geoffrey Trease).

Lansdowne Press, Melbourne. (*Early Australian Children's Literature*, by Rosemary Wighton).

Librairie Hachette, Paris. (*Histoire de la Littérature Enfantine*, by Jean de Trigon).

Macmillan Co., N.Y. (Collier-Macmillan, London), (Introduction to *The Parent's Assistant*, by Anne Thackeray Ritchie), (*Something of myself*, *The Jungle Book*, *Puck of Pook's Hill*, all by Rudyard Kipling, for which permission has been given by Mrs. Geo. Bambridge, the author's daughter), (*The Story of a Red Deer*, by Sir John Fortescue), (*Critical History of Children's Literature*, edited by Cornelia Meigs).

Methuen & Co. Ltd. (*A Century of Children's Books*, by F. V. Barry), (*A Life of Robert Louis Stevenson*, by Graham Balfour), (*Letters of Charles Lamb*, introduction to vol. 2, by E. V. Lucas).

Oxford University Press, Toronto. (*The Republic of Childhood*, by Sheila Egoff).

Penguin Books, Ltd. (*A Thousand and One Nights*, introduction by N. J. Dawood).

Rabén & Sjögren, Stockholm. (*Barnboken i Sverige*, by Eva v. Zweigbergk).

Edmund Ward, Ltd. (*Tellers of Tales*, by R. L. Green).

Ward, Lock & Co. (*The Gentle Heritage*, by Frances E. Crompton).

Frederick Warne and Co. Ltd. (*The Tale of Beatrix Potter*, by Margaret Lane.).

ROYAL BATTLEDORE; being the first Introductory Part of the *Circle of the*
Sciences, &c.   Publish'd by the King's Authority.

Printed by Newbery & Carnan, in St. Paul's Church-yard, and B. Collins, in Sarum. Price

the Royal Primer, or Second Book for Children, Price 3d. Bound, adorn'd with Cuts.

a b c d e f g h i j k l m n o p
r ſ s t u v w x y z.

A B C D E F G H I J K L M
O P Q R S T U V W X Y Z

ſt ſi fi ſſ ff ſl fl ſſi ffi ffl ſt &.

Douce   a   e   i   o   u   y.   *Adl: St*

ab	eb	ib	ob	ub	ba	be	bi	bo	bu
ac	ec	ic	oc	uc	ca	ce	ci	co	cu
ad	ed	id	od	ud	da	de	di	do	du

IN the Name of the Fa-ther, and of the
Son, and of the Ho-ly Ghoſt. *A-men*

I Pray God to bleſs my Fa-ther and Mother, Bro-thers and Siſ-ters, and all my
good Friends, and my E-ne-mies. *A-men*

OUR Fa-ther, which art in Hea-ven,
hal-low-ed be thy Name; thy Kingdom come; thy Will be done on Earth as
it is in Hea-ven.   Give us this Day our
dai-ly Bread; and for-give us our Treſ-paſ-
ſes, as we for-give them that treſ-paſs
a-gainſt us; and lead us not in-to Temp-
ta-tion, but de-li-ver us from E-vil; for
thine is the King-dom, the Pow-er and
the Glo-ry, for e-ver and e-ver. *A-men*